Contents

Contents cont.

THE ROUGH GUIDE TO
Bob Dylan

by
Nigel Williamson

ROUGH
GUIDES

www.roughguides.com

Credits

The Rough Guide to Bob Dylan

Layout: Link Hall & Diana Jarvis
Proofreading: Diane Margolis
Production: Katherine Owers
Editing: Duncan Clark & Matthew Milton

Rough Guides Reference

Series editor: Mark Ellingham
Director: Andrew Lockett
Editors: Peter Buckley, Duncan Clark, Tracy Hopkins
Matthew Milton, Joe Staines, Ruth Tidball

Picture credits

Corbis: pp. 7, 31, 41, 43, 53, 58, 77, 82, 90, 100, 129, 148, 153, 161, 214, 263, 270, 277, 279, 293, 297
Redferns: pp. 3, 10, 17, 20, 26, 32, 36, 51, 52, 65, 71, 74, 87, 93, 102, 108, 117, 122, 134, 137, 143, 165, 221, 227, 242, 249, 286

Publishing Information

This second edition published August 2006 by
Rough Guides Ltd, 80 Strand, London WC2R 0RL
345 Hudson St, 4th Floor, New York 10014, USA
Email: mail@roughguides.com

Distributed by the Penguin Group:
Penguin Books Ltd, 80 Strand, London WC2R 0RL
Penguin Putnam, Inc., 375 Hudson Street, NY 10014, USA
Penguin Group (Australia), 250 Camberwell Road, Camberwell, Victoria 3124, Australia
Penguin Books Canada Ltd, 90 Eglinton Avenue East, Suite 700, Toronto, Ontario M4P 2Y3, Canada
Penguin Group (New Zealand), 67 Apollo Drive, Mairongi Bay, Auckland 1310, New Zealand

Printed in Italy by LegoPrint S.p.A

A catalogue record for this book is available from the British Library

ISBN 13: 978-1-84353-718-2
ISBN 10: 1-84353-718-4

1 3 5 7 9 8 6 4 2

Introduction

Like most Bob Dylan fans, I've never actually met the man whose songs have changed my life. I'm not even sure that I want to, in case the shock of discovering he's as fallibly human as the rest of us proves too much. But like most Bob Dylan fans, I feel like I've known him all my adult life.

This, of course, is precisely the kind of attitude that would highly irritate Dylan, who has fiercely guarded his privacy over the years. "You don't know me at all", he would surely counter. "You know my songs. But that's not the same as knowing me." And therein lies our endless fascination with every facet of Dylan's life and art. Where does one end and the other begin? Despite his songs being analysed and dissected as if they were holy scripture, and countless biographies poking into every nook and cranny of his existence, we still don't really know him at all. He remains an enigma.

And yet his influence on modern popular culture is all-pervasive. When asked how he had been influenced by Dylan, Pete Townshend of The Who replied that it was like asking how he had been affected by being born. Bob Dylan changed the world. There is not a songwriter on the planet who has not been influenced by him. Even those who have never listened to a Dylan record will find they were affected by others who did fall under his dancing spell. Emmylou Harris tells a lovely story of being given a bracelet by the country singer/songwriter Gillian Welch, engraved with the initials "WWDD". When she asked what they meant, she was told they stood for "What Would Dylan Do?". "When you're writing a song, just ask yourself that question", she says.

And the story is far from over. In October 2004, Dylan published *Chronicles Volume One*, the spectacular first part of his autobiography. Almost a year later came Martin Scorsese's magnificent documentary film, *No Direction Home*. These two events created a level of media interest in Dylan and a volume of column inches unseen since the 1960s.

So this fully updated and revised edition of the *Rough Guide to Bob Dylan* takes into account the many fresh insights and additions to our knowledge provided by both book and film. It also brings the story up-to-date with the inclusion of the various other books and CDs that have appeared since the first edition and covers recent legs of Bob's 'Never Ending Tour'.

For Dylan is, of course, still up there doing it night after night, reinventing the songs that changed the world and making them new again before our very eyes. It's not dark yet. Not, we hope, by a long way.

Nigel Williamson, 2006

Acknowledgements

Many thanks to Allan Jones, editor of *Uncut* magazine, who has continued to indulge me by offering generous space to write about all things Dylan in the pages of his magazine.

Then there are the authors of previous Dylan books whose work inspired and informed this volume. Principal among them were Anthony Scaduto, Bob Shelton, Clinton Heylin, Howard Sounes, Cameron Crowe, C.P. Lee, Paul Williams, Andy Gill, Patrick Humphries, Michael Gray and now Dylan himself, who has given us arguably the best book on music ever written.

Thanks also to Jeff Rosen, chief aide-de-camp on Dylan's staff, who proved to be a true gentleman as well as a staunch defender of Bob's legacy. Thanks to all at Rough Guides, especially Mark Ellingham, Andrew Lockett and, above all, Duncan Clark, an editor with the unerring habit of asking all the right questions. My two adult sons Adam Williamson and Piers Williamson helped an unreconstructed old Luddite with computer back-up. Finally, a very special thank you to Magali Williamson. Despite not even liking the music, she has now lived with me and Bob in a ménage à trois for over 30 years with only the mildest of complaints. One day she'll get it.

The Rough Guide to

Bob Dylan

by Nigel Williamson

Part 1:
The Life

> "*My mind got mixed with ramblin',*
> *When I was all so young*"
>
> Bob Dylan, "Long Time Gone"

The Early Years
1941–59

"I have no respect for factual knowledge," Bob Dylan once declared. "I don't care what anybody knows. I don't care if somebody's a walking encyclopaedia." And, over the years, he has often attempted to confuse and mislead those seeking factual knowledge about his life with a stream of misinformation and even downright lies. "My childhood is so far away," he told one interviewer with typically diversionary tactics. "It's like I don't even remember being a child. I'm not even sure what happened to me yesterday was true." Yet Dylan's persistent evasions and the fierceness of his desire to protect his privacy have only served to enhance the myth and to fuel our curiosity yet further – as he knows only too well.

1941–55: North Country Blues

The bald facts of Dylan's early existence are well-enough known. **Robert Allen Zimmerman** – who was also given the Hebrew name **Shabtai Zisel ben Avraham** – was born at 9.05pm on May 24, 1941. The twenty-and-a-half-inch baby boy, weighing 8lb 13oz and reportedly with a disproportionately large head, was the first born of **Abraham and Beatrice Zimmerman** of Duluth, Minnesota, a small mining town near the Canadian border. For those who think these factors are significant, Dylan's birth date makes him a Gemini – though as late as 1991 he was still laying smokescreens of confusion by reproducing his driving licence in the booklet accompanying a career-retrospective CD with his date of birth mischievously altered to May 11. Thus,

with a dash of Tipp-Ex, he transformed himself into a fake Taurus and sent Dylan-watching astrologists into star-chart meltdown.

In Europe, the German forces were in the throes of completing the invasion of the Greek islands. But the United States was still officially at peace and the attack on Pearl Harbor on December 7, 1941 – which would trigger the US's entry into World War II – was still more than six months away. Still, the Zimmermans must have wondered about the war several thousands of miles away, for Dylan's paternal grandparents **Zigman and Anna Zimmerman** had fled the Tsarist pogroms, sailing from the Black Sea port of Odessa in 1907 to seek a new life in the Land of the Free.

The Zimmermans believed in the virtues of hard work and the sanctity of the family and had done tolerably well for themselves in the New World. Beatrice's family, the Stones, were also Jewish immigrants from Eastern Europe and her father owned a small chain of regional theatres. By 1946, however, they had fallen on harder times. A second son, David, had arrived, and Abe had lost his job and been stricken with polio, which left him with a permanent limp. The following year the family moved 75 miles up country from Duluth to **Hibbing** (see box opposite), built on the rocky western shore of Lake Superior. Hibbing was also Beatrice's hometown and the Zimmermans moved in with her widowed mother. But Abe was soon back on his feet and joined his brothers Paul and Maurice in a new business venture, selling furniture and electrical goods. With the war over and a mass-market consumer boom in full swing, the Zimmermans' circumstances swiftly improved. By 1948, the family had moved into a two-storey detached home at 2425 Seventh Avenue.

In such respectable and relatively comfortable middle-class circumstances, Dylan grew up a quiet and introspective child and a well-behaved and dutiful son. As Patrick Humphries has written, "With every crumb picked up from the detritus of Dylan's early years and adolescence, you try to detect the extraordinary, sifting for signs of that remarkable future. But in truth, and without the benefit of hindsight, you would have been hard-pressed to distinguish the young Robert Zimmerman from his contemporaries." In *Chronicles Volume One*, Dylan himself describes an existence that was ordinary to the point of dullness. Even the regular air-raid drills which forced him and his fellow school pupils to take cover under their desks in simulation of a Russian bomb attack, became part of the routine. "Mostly what I did growing up was bide my time," he concludes.

At **Nettleton** elementary school, the young Dylan was not a bad student. And he showed an early love for **poetry**, spending hours in his room scribbling and drawing, and writing poems for his parents on Mother's Day and Father's Day. Yet his relationship with his father was characterized by an Old Testament–style sternness. When he received a lifetime achievement award in a televised ceremony in 1991, he stood silently for a long half-minute. Then he made a rare and extraordinary comment on his childhood: "My daddy once said to me, he said, 'Son, it is possible for you to become so defiled in this world that your own mother and father will abandon you. If that happens, God will believe in your own ability to mend your own ways.'"

Yet amid such solemn pronouncements, there were youthful diversions: reading Classics Illustrated comic books, watching cowboy films at Hibbing's Lybba Theater (owned by relatives and named after Dylan's Lithuanian maternal great-grandmother), and hours spent in front of the television purchased by the family in 1952, one of the first sets to appear in Hibbing. Dylan was **bar mitzvahed** in May 1954 and for a while he appears to have taken his Jewish background seriously. Years later he described the rabbi he used to meet. "He was an old man from Brooklyn who wore a white

Hibbing, Minnesota

"There was really nothing there" Bob Dylan

The town of **Hibbing** provided an unremarkable backdrop to Bob Dylan's largely unremarkable existence from the age of six until eighteen, when he moved to Minnesota to enrol as a university student.

In the 1920s, the area's rich **iron-ore** deposits had brought a mini-boom to the town and huge open-cast mines scarred the local countryside. The demand for iron in World War II had also brought prosperity. But by the time Dylan was growing up, the best deposits had been exhausted and employment was in short supply. He later revisited this depressingly unglamorous environment in **North Country Blues** in 1964, a song in which he painted an evocative picture of a town where the red iron pits had once "ran plenty" but where "the cardboard-filled windows and old men on the benches tell you know that the whole town is empty".

"There was really nothing there," he later claimed. "The only thing you could do there was be a miner and even that kind of thing was getting less and less." Yet he still maintained a certain sentimental fondness for the place: "The people that lived there, they're nice people. I've been all over the world since

I left there and they still stand out as being the least hung-up. The mines were dying, that's all, but that's not their fault. I didn't run away from it. I just turned my back on it."

In the 1990s, he was to paint a more idealised portrait of Hibbing. "Knife sharpeners would come down the street," he claimed. "Every once in a while a wagon would come through town with a gorilla in a cage or, I remember, a mummy under glass. It was a very itinerant place, just country roads everywhere. There was an innocence about it all and I don't remember anything bad ever happening. That was the '50s, the last period I remember as being idyllic."

A contemporary map of the district more than forty years after Dylan left it for good is revealing. The Hull-Rust Mahoning Mine is still marked, a gash in the earth three miles wide and 500 feet deep. But other, newer landmarks, such as The Iron Range Tour, The Minnesota Museum of Mining and Ironworld USA indicate a mining industry not only rusted, but decayed, destroyed and eventually, decades later, turned into a heritage attraction.

beard and wore a black hat and black clothes. They put him upstairs above the café where I used to hang out. I used to go there every day to learn this stuff, after school or after dinner. After studying with him for an hour or so, I'd come down and boogie."

A 1955 photo from the **Hibbing High School** yearbook shows a bright-eyed, clean-cut, smart Jewish boy with slightly chubby cheeks, known as "**Zimbo**" to his classmates. But, as with mil-

lions of other teenagers of the time, the spirit of rebellion was beginning to stir in him – and its main instigator was **James Dean** (see box, over), whose death in September 1955 gave the nascent rock'n'roll era its first martyr. His film *Rebel Without A Cause* reached Hibbing that winter. The young Dylan saw it several times, trading lines from the film with his closest friend John Bucklen and covering his bedroom walls with pictures of the dead actor.

The Life

The Rebel Who Gave Dylan a Cause

James Dean puts his feet up in *Giant*, which the young Dylan watched time and time again

When **Rebel Without A Cause** reached Hibbing's picture houses in the winter of 1955, James Dean was already dead, killed in an automobile accident near Paso Robles at the age of 24. The young Robert Zimmerman saw the film and bought in to the Dean myth, like a million other American teenagers of the time. But Dylan's fixation appears to have been peculiarly strong.

It was almost as if he thought he was **Jim Stark**, the character Dean had played in the film. He bought a red biker-jacket like the one worn by Stark, mouthed the lines and scoured movie magazines for pictures of his hero, which he pasted on his bedroom walls. He also devoured Dean's two other movies, **East Of Eden** and **Giant**, watching them over and over again at every opportunity. One night, Dylan was caught by

his parents sneaking home past his curfew after seeing *Giant*. His father followed him to his room. "James Dean! James Dean!", Abe Zimmerman repeated as his son tried to explain. He ripped one of the dead actor's pictures off the wall. "Don't do that!", Dylan yelled as his father tore it into pieces and threw them on the floor.

Elvis Presley would soon supersede Dean as Dylan's pre-eminent teenage inspiration. "When I first heard Elvis's voice I just knew I wasn't going to work for anybody and nobody was gonna be my boss," he later said. "Hearing him for the first time was like busting out of jail." But Dean was there first to turn the key in the cell door. "I liked him for the same reasons you like anybody, I guess," Dylan recalled in 1987. "You see something of yourself in them."

1956–59: Busting Out of Jail

"I ran away from home when I was 10, 12, 13, 15, 15 and a half, 17 an' 18. I been caught and brought back all but once." Bob Dylan

Dylan had shown some musical ability at an early age, amusing the Zimmermans' relatives by singing "Accentuate The Positive" at family parties when he was five. By the age of eleven he'd learned the rudiments of **piano** playing from his cousin, Harriet Rutstein, though he soon dispensed with her services, opting to teach himself instead. He also tried other instruments, including the saxophone and trumpet, before settling on a cheap **acoustic guitar**.

Before long, he was listening to scratchy versions of tunes by the "King of Country Music", **Hank Williams**. Also known as "the Hillbilly Shakespeare", Williams was already dead by the time Dylan discovered him, having expired on New Year's Day 1953 when his heart, overtaxed by booze and pills, gave out in the back of a Cadillac. But he has remained one of Dylan's musical heroes for half a century. "In time," he wrote in *Chronicles*, "I became aware that in Hank's recorded songs were the archetypal rules of poetic songwriting." Then there were the "race" records he heard on stations out of Little Rock and Chicago, by the likes of **John Lee Hooker, Howlin' Wolf** and **Jimmy Reed**. Dylan not only loved the music – he soon adopted the hipster jive he heard the DJs talking between the records.

He also heard rock'n'rollers. Indeed, long before Dylan discovered folk music and mod-elled himself on Woody Guthrie, his musical role models were the likes of **Elvis Presley** and **Chuck Berry**. **Little Richard** was a particular inspiration and Dylan spent hours copying his pounding piano riffs, played standing up at the Zimmerman family's baby-grand piano. Such was the impact on the youthful Dylan that, as the writer John Harris put it, "Abe's hopes that his elder son might eventually join him in the family business probably went belly-up the moment "Tutti Frutti"'s fearsome 'Awopbopal oobopawopbamboom' first came howling over the Minnesota airwaves."

By 1956, Dylan was playing in a group called **The Jokers**, formed at a Jewish summer camp. They went on to perform at high-school dances and even appeared on a local television show in Minneapolis, 190 miles south of Hibbing, where that summer Dylan and friends Howard Rutman and Larry Keegan paid five dollars to cut a 78rpm record. Dylan played piano while they all harmonised on a rock'n'roll medley that included Gene Vincent's "Be-Bop-A-Lula" and The Penguins' "Earth Angel". Had his early musical leanings been better known, then perhaps there would not have been quite such controversy when almost a decade later in 1965 he abandoned his acoustic guitar and "went electric".

Dylan continued with The Jokers for a year or more, playing in matching hand-knitted red-and-grey sleeveless cardigans on weekend visits to the twin cities of Minneapolis and St Paul. His first hometown band, **The Shadow Blasters,** was formed with school friends in 1957, when they played a Jacket Jamboree talent show in the high-school auditorium and Zimbo massacred two Little Richard numbers at the piano. "African shrieking", one teacher called his singing style. The Shadow Blasters only ever played one further gig, but Dylan was on the way. Soon he had graduated to an **electric guitar,** first a cheap model from a Sears Roebuck catalogue and then a solid-body Surpo with a gold sunburst.

He was growing fast, and Hibbing would soon no longer be able to hold him. For his sixteenth birthday in 1957 he got his first car, a pink Ford convertible. A Harley-Davidson motorcycle followed. He was a terrible driver whether on two or four wheels and there were various scrapes and accidents.

Soon after, he met **Echo Helstrom.** Echo's family had come from Finland and lived in the woods, three miles out of Hibbing at Maple Hill. Dylan was attracted to her blonde hair and the leather jacket and jeans she sported on a weekend. She first set eyes on Dylan playing his guitar and singing on a street corner in the snow. They met later that night in the L&B Café and discovered a shared love of a late-night radio music show called *No-Name Jive.* Dylan wanted to show off his limited piano skills and they went next door to the Moose Lodge. Echo prised the locked piano lid open with her pen-knife for Bob to play and he was hooked. For the next year or so they became inseparable.

Dylan's next band was **The Golden Chords,** a trio that included **Leroy Hoikkola** on drums, **Monte Edwardson** on guitar and Bobby Zimmerman, as he was now billed, on piano. When they appeared at a high-school show in early 1958, Dylan adapted the words of a Little Richard number to sing, "Gotta get a girl

Little Richard, whose pounding piano riffs took the young Dylan by storm

How Robert Zimmerman became Bob Dylan

Broadway star Ethel Merman once remarked, "Can you imagine the name Zimmerman in lights? It would burn you to death." Her solution was simply to lop off the first syllable of the ungainly Jewish name. As far as we know, it wasn't a solution considered by the young Robert Allen Zimmerman, who officially changed his name to **Bob Dylan** at New York's Supreme Court building in August 1962. At various times, before then and since, he has offered confusing and contradictory accounts of the new name's origin.

On the surface, the most straightforward answer is the one he gave several times in the early 1960s – that it came from an uncle on his mother's side of the family, whose name was Dillon. The only problem with this version of events is that there was no Dillon in the family. However, there was a Hibbing family called Dillion that traced its origins back to the days of the original pioneers, something that may have impressed the youthful Robert Zimmerman. A more likely inspiration was the character **Matt Dillon** from the television show *Gunsmoke*, which the future Bob Dylan must have watched as a teenager after it premiered on CBS in 1955.

The popular notion that he borrowed his name from the Welsh poet is one that for many years he sought to refute. "Straighten out in your book that I did not take my name from Dylan Thomas," he told Robert Shelton, who among all of Dylan's many biographers is the one who came closest to enjoying official status. Friends from the early Greenwich Village days, such as Dave Van Ronk, confirm that, though Dylan devoured poetry, they recall a taste for the French symbolists such as Rimbaud rather than the author of *Under Milk Wood*. Yet Larry Kegan, an early friend from Hibbing, does remember him walking around with a book of Dylan Thomas's poetry. And another Hibbing friend, John Bucklen, reckons Dylan specifically told him in 1959 that the name came from the Welsh poet.

In 1968, Dylan himself claimed, "I haven't read that much of Dylan Thomas. It wasn't that I was inspired by reading his poetry and going 'Aha!' and changing my name to Dylan. If I thought he was that great, I would have sung his poems and could just as easily have changed my name to Thomas." On another occasion, he observed, "I've done more for Dylan Thomas than he's ever done for me. Look how many kids are probably reading his poetry now." He finally came clean in *Chronicles* and admitted that he'd been thinking of calling himself Robert Allyn after a sax player called David Allyn, but rejected it because the abbreviated Bob Allyn "sounded like a used-car salesman". Around the same time he had "seen some poems" by Dylan Thomas and "Dylan and Allyn sounded similar". For once, this account has the ring of truth.

and her name is Echo". But he was beginning to feel restricted by the limitations of white rock'n'roll, and The Golden Chords didn't last long. "Tutti Frutti and Blue Suede Shoes were great catchphrases and driving pulse rhythms and you could get high on the energy," he said in the liner notes to 1985's Biograph compilation. "But they weren't serious or didn't reflect life in a serious way."

One day in 1958, according to Echo, Bob drove up to her house in his pink Ford convertible and told her that he had changed his

Ten tall tales in the self-mythology of Bob

1 **ONLY A HOBO** "I was raised in Gallup, New Mexico. Got a lot of cowboy songs there. Indian songs. Carnival songs. Vaudeville kinda stuff," Dylan claimed in his first-ever radio interview on WNYC in autumn 1961. He also claimed to have lived in Cheyenne and Sioux Falls, South Dakota; Phillipsburg, Kansas; Hibbing, Minnesota; and Minneapolis. At least the last two were true.

2 **THE CIRCUS BOY** "Oh yeah, I spent about six years in the carnivals. Clean-up boy; worked on the ferris wheel … went all the way around the Midwest," Dylan told a radio interviewer in 1961. "Didn't that interfere with your schooling?", he was asked. "Oh, I skipped a bunch of school," he blithely replied.

3 **THE NAME GAME** "That's just a rumor made up by people who like to simplify things," Dylan said when asked if he'd taken his name from Dylan Thomas. "It's the name of my family … on my mother's side. It's spelt D-I-L-L-O-N and I changed it from there." In fact, his mother's family name was Stone.

4 **THE INDIAN CONNECTION** When he arrived in Greenwich Village, Dylan reinvented several new lives for himself. But of all his tall tales, none was more preposterous than his claim that he was descended from the Sioux Nation. "I remember he solemnly gave us a demonstration of Indian sign language, which he was obviously making up as he went along," recalls Dave Van Ronk.

5 **THE GIGOLO FANTASY** Dylan told Robert Shelton in 1966 that, on his arrival in New York five years earlier, he had made his money as a male prostitute in Times Square, "Hustling with this cat, you dig? Sometimes we'd make 150 or 250 dollars a night. Cats would pick us up and chicks would pick us up. We would do anything you wanted, as long as it paid."

6 **THE ORPHAN BOY** "I don't know my parents," Dylan told *Newsweek* in New York in November 1963. It was one of his many claims to orphanhood. But at that precise moment, Abe and Beattie Zimmerman were just a

name to **Dylan**. If true, it's the earliest of the many conflicting stories about the adoption of his new name (see box, p.11). Soon there were less-serious names floating around, too. In January 1959, Dylan and friends appeared as **Elston Gunn and His Rock Boppers** at a Hibbing High School jamboree. By now, he'd split up with Echo (they discussed marriage but he told her he couldn't commit himself because he had to think of his "career") and was spend-

ing more time in Duluth, where he formed a band called **The Satin Tones**.

It was also in Duluth – on January 31, 1959 – that Dylan saw the 22-year-old **Buddy Holly** play at the National Guard Armory with Ritchie Valens, The Big Bopper and Link Wray. Five days later, Holly died in a plane crash. Dylan, who had been at the very front of the stage (and told friends that Holly had made eye contact with him during the concert) was badly few blocks away proudly waiting to watch their son's debut performance at New York's Carnegie Hall. Dylan's parents were deeply hurt by his repeated denials of their existence, and blamed Dylan's manager, Albert Grossman.

7 DREAMING OF WOODY "I used to see Woody whenever I had enough money," Dylan told Izzy Young in October 1961. "Met him in California before I was really playing. I think Jack Elliott was with him." Dylan would have been just 13 at the time for the story to be true. He didn't make his first trip to California until 1963.

8 LIVING THE BLUES In an early interview with Robert Shelton of *The New York Times*, Dylan claimed he had learned to play bottleneck blues guitar "from an old guy named Wigglefoot in Gallup, New Mexico. He was a beaten-down old bluesman who wore a patch on his eye. I do a lot of material I learned from Mance Lipscomb. I met him in Navasota, Texas, five years ago." At that time, Dylan would still have been a fifteen-year-old schoolboy in Hibbing, Minnesota. But that didn't prevent him adding, "I'm giving it to you straight. I wouldn't tell you anything that isn't true."

9 COWBOY RACER DREAMS "I like to ride motorcycles … was a racer in North and South Dakota and Minnesota … There was a farm hand in Sioux Falls, South Dakota, who played the autoharp. Picked up Wilbur's way of singing. Never remember his last name … Cowboy styles I learned from real cowboys. Can't remember their names. Met some in Cheyenne … I played with Gene Vincent in Nashville." Another interview, another self-reinvention, from October 1961.

10 BORN UNDER A BAD SIGN "My being a Gemini explains a lot," Dylan once said. "It forces me to extremes. I'm never really balanced in the middle. I go from one side to the other without staying in either place very long." Three decades later in the booklet that accompanied the official *Bootleg Series Volumes I–III*, Dylan reproduced his driving licence, altering his birth date from May 24 to May 11, and thus becoming a Taurus.

shaken by his death. **The Everly Brothers** were also added to Bob's list of heroes, after hits such as "Bye Bye Love" and "Wake Up Little Susie". But even Elvis by now took second place to Little Richard in Dylan's pantheon. When he graduated in May 1959, Bob declared under his picture in the school yearbook that his ambition was "to join Little Richard".

At the graduation party his parents threw for him, an uncle gave him a pile of 78rpm records by Huddie Ledbetter (better known as **Leadbelly**). The songs, such as "Rock Island Line" and "Midnight Special", were a revelation to the young Dylan, and prompted the beginning of his passion for **folk music**. A rare and fascinating insight into what the schoolboy Dylan sounded like emerged some 46 years later on the soundtrack of the film *No Direction Home*, where he can be heard hesitantly singing "When I Got Troubles", recorded in 1959

The Life

by school friend Ric Kangas. But there was to be another throw of the rock'n'roll dice before he was to pursue his new musical interest as an acoustic minstrel.

Straight after graduation, the 18-year-old Dylan caught a Greyhound to Fargo in North Dakota and got a job as a busboy at the Red Apple Cafe. It was the only time in his life, according to biographer Howard Sounes, that he tried to make a living at anything other than music. The top group locally was **Bobby Vee and The Shadows**, who went on to have several big hits, notably "Take Good Care Of My Baby". Dylan talked himself into an audition by lying that he had played piano with Conway Twitty. He played a couple of local gigs with the band but was not taken on as a permanent member – largely, it seems, because he could only really play in the key of C. "A spacey little guy, just sort of worming his way around," was how Vee later recalled him. That

didn't prevent Dylan from telling everyone back in Hibbing that he'd played piano on Vee's hit record, "Suzie Baby". Few believed him: Bob's ability to conflate truth and fiction was already infamous among those who knew him.

But Dylan's Hibbing days were rapidly drawing to an end. He claimed in the prose poem **My Life In A Stolen Moment** that he'd run away from home half a dozen times. It was another piece of his notorious self-mythologizing, and when he did finally make his escape, it was at the bidding of his parents. Beattie Zimmerman admitted to Robert Shelton that she had told the son who would one day be considered a serious contender for the Nobel Prize for Literature, "Don't keep writing poetry, please don't. Go to school and do something constructive. Get a degree." In the autumn of 1959, Dylan enrolled at the **University of Minnesota** in the Twin Cities and moved into the Jewish fraternity house, Sigma Alpha Mu.

1959–60 The University of Dinkytown

"I suppose what I was looking for was what I read about in On The Road – looking for the great city, looking for the speed, the sound of it, looking for what Allen Ginsberg had called the 'hydrogen jukebox world'." Bob Dylan, *Chronicles*

Minneapolis and St Paul – the Twin Cities – face each other across the Mississippi River, which runs all the way down to the Delta, and the land of the blues musicians Dylan had come so much to admire. He was uninterested in studying and life on campus. Instead, he gravitated immediately towards Dinkytown,

the bohemian neighbourhood adjacent to the campus, but which offered an education of a rather different kind.

Despite the Leadbelly records he was given on his graduation, Dylan arrived in the Twin Cities with his head still full of rock'n'roll. In Dinkytown, and particularly at the Ten

O'Clock Scholar coffeehouse he began to frequent, he heard a very different kind of music. Regulars at the Scholar included Spider John Koerner and Dave Ray, both accomplished, young, white acoustic blues players who would go on to record for Elektra, and Frank Morton, who played folk songs such as "Gypsy Davey". Morton also added his own words about contemporary events to ancient folk tunes, a technique borrowed from Woody Guthrie, which Dylan, too, would soon copy.

By the winter of 1959, Dylan had been asked to leave the fraternity house and spent his time crashing on the floors of friend's apartments. He traded in his electric guitar for a double-O Martin acoustic and earned a few dollars playing at the Scholar with Koerner, who also taught him about the blues and introduced him to the records of Blind Lemon Jefferson, Charlie Patton and others. Later he got a regular gig at the Purple Onion, a pizza joint in St Paul, where he began to play his own early compositions, "One Eyed Jack" and "Greyhound Blues", alongside songs such as "A Man Of Constant Sorrow" and "House Of The Rising Sun". Support came from a new girlfriend, Bonnie Beecher, who smuggled food out of her sorority house for him and became the second significant woman in his life, after Echo Helstrom. The identity of the true love he would later immortalise in "Girl From The North Country" has long been debated. The likelihood is that it was a composite of both Bonnie and Echo and possibly one or two other early girlfriends who "brought out the poet" in him, as he put it on Martin Scorsese's documentary film, *No Direction Home*.

He first heard Woody Guthrie's records in Minneapolis, via a drama student called Flo Castner, and recalled the moment in *Chronicles Volume One* as "an epiphany, like some heavy anchor had just plunged into the waters of the harbour".

Another significant Dinkytown influence was Dave Whittaker, a bohemian character involved in radical political movements, who knew Beat writers such as Allen Ginsberg and Lawrence Ferlinghetti and had got drunk with Jack Kerouac. It was at Whitaker's apartment that Dylan first smoked cheap Mexican weed at a time when marijuana was still rare on university campuses. Then there was Jon Pankake, a student who played banjo, ran a folk-music fanzine called *The Little Sandy Review* and – more importantly – owned a rare copy of Harry Smith's six-disc *Anthology Of American Folk Music*.

Bob was a regular visitor to his apartment and on one occasion, when Pankake was away and finding his door unlocked, he borrowed without permission around 20 LPs, including a set of albums by Ramblin' Jack Elliott and, Pankake believes, the Harry Smith anthology which was to become a source of inspiration for the rest of his career.

When Pankake found the records were missing, he confronted Dylan, who denied everything. When threatened with a beating, he confessed and returned some of the records, although not the Harry Smith set. As his biographer Howard Sounes put it, it seems Dylan did not regard it as stealing at all. Rather he was hungry for the music and, not for the last time, he simply bypassed the usual courtesies of asking permission. He talks at length about Pankake in his autobiography, describing him as "part of the folk police, if not the chief commissioner", but omitting to mention the story of the "borrowed" records.

With his head now full of folk music and inspired by reading Kerouac's *On The Road*, in the summer of 1960, the 19-year-old Dylan hitchhiked 900 miles west to Denver, Colorado. Among those he met there were Judy Collins, then an aspiring young 21-year-old folk singer, and the 64-year-old Jesse Fuller, the bluesman who had written "San Francisco Bay Blues" and who was playing at a local club called The Exodus. It was all part of his rapidly expanding musical education. But there was more trouble over records he once again borrowed from the apartment of friends in Denver, without asking their permission first. This time the police were called. Charges were not pressed against Dylan, although he reportedly got so upset he burst into tears. By the time he got back to Dinkytown, the incident had provided more grist for the burgeoning self-mythology he was building. "I was run out of Denver for robbing a cat's house," he boasted to friends.

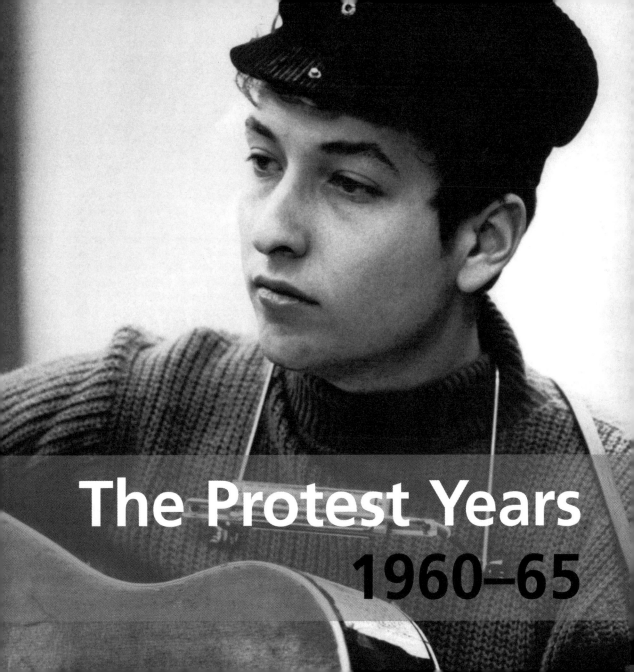

The Protest Years
1960–65

"The truth rang out so loud in his words. Not just for me, but for an entire generation."

Arlo Guthrie

The Protest Years
1960–65

1960: Bound for Glory

"I'm a-leavin' tomorrow but I could leave today,
Somewhere down the road someday" Bob Dylan, "Song To Woody"

One of the most significant events in Dylan's education at the "University of Dinkytown" was not musical but literary, when David Whittaker gave him a copy of **Woody Guthrie's** autobiography *Bound For Glory* (see box, overleaf). In its pages, Dylan found a hero on whom he could model himself. He soon adopted the language of Guthrie's hobos and wove the mythology of riding the rails and jumping trains into his own self-fantasy. According to Bonnie Beecher – his girlfriend at the time – he grew so fixated that for a while he even insisted on being called Woody and wouldn't answer to any other name. In *Chronicles* he admitted Guthrie was "an influence on every move I made, what I ate and how I dressed".

Of course, Dylan learned all of Guthrie's best-known songs – **Tom Joad, This Land Is Your Land, Pastures Of Plenty, Deportees**. And when he discovered that Guthrie was dying in a New Jersey hospital, he telephoned and announced he was coming to see him. Before he did, Dylan took the trouble to learn to play rudimentary harmonica from **Tony Glover** (a friend of Spider John Koerner and Dave Ray, with whom he later formed an influential folk–blues trio and made a series of mid-60s albums for Elektra). Then Bonnie Beecher used a reel-to-reel Webcor tape machine to record two tapes of Dylan singing in his new Guthrie-influenced style. One of the tapes has survived and has circulated for years among collectors as the earliest known Dylan boot-leg, so we know exactly what he sounded like at this formative stage of his career (see pp.252–253).

His search for Woody was deferred for a while by a bout of **bronchitis** which, according to some theories, altered his voice forever and lent it the slightly nasal whine that would soon become so familiar. Then, while he was still dreaming of his escape, **Odetta**, already one of the biggest stars of the burgeoning folk revival scene and once described by Dylan as "the first thing that turned me on to folk singing", came to town.

Hey, hey, Woody Guthrie, I wrote you a song...

When Dylan read Woody Guthrie's autobiography **Bound For Glory**, he was captivated by the sheer romance of the story. His family decimated by tragedy, Guthrie hit the road at sixteen, lived the live of a hobo, rode freight trains and box cars and busked his songs which championed the downtrodden and dispossessed. If it seemed like another world from the dullness of his own background, there was nevertheless a vital point of connection, for in the book Guthrie described jumping trains in Duluth, the town of Dylan's birth. "Woody Guthrie had never seen nor heard me," he wrote in *Chronicles*. "But it felt like he was saying, 'I'll be going away but I'm leaving this job in your hands'."

A prolific songwriter, Woody's compositions included **Pastures Of Plenty**, **Vigilante Man**, **Grand Coolie Dam**, **Ramblin' Round**, **Jesse James**, **Hard Travelin'**

Woody Guthrie, "the greatest holiest godliest one in the world" according to Dylan in 1961

She heard him perform and when asked if she thought he could make it professionally, replied that she believed it was possible.

With Odetta's words of encouragement ringing in his ears, Dylan finally resolved that the Twin Cities were no longer big enough to hold him. "When I arrived in Minneapolis, it had seemed like a big city. When I left it was like some rural outpost you see once from a passing train," he later said. He briefly returned to Hibbing to tell his parents he was leaving college and had then hoped to spend Christmas with Bonnie at her family's home. When her disapproving parents vetoed this plan, he hit the road on December 21, 1960, in search of Woody, Greenwich Village and fame.

and **This Land Is Your Land** (widely regarded as America's "alternative" national anthem). But by the autumn of 1960, Guthrie – still only 48 – was lying in Greystone Park Hospital, New Jersey, with the hereditary nervous-system disease that had previously killed his mother, Huntington's chorea.

Dylan got the records and learned the songs and became even more fixated with Woody than he had been with James Dean five years earlier. Guthrie played a harmonica, which hung around his neck on what looked like a bent coat-hanger so his hands were left free to play the guitar. Dylan had Bonnie Beecher make him a similar contraption. Then he asked Dinkytown blues musician Tony Glover to teach him to play.

Finally, Dylan rang the hospital and asked to speak to Woody. He was too sick to get out of bed and come to the phone, but a nurse told Dylan he liked visitors. "I'm coming out there. Tell Woody I'm coming to see him," Dylan yelled excitedly. He arrived in New York on January 24, 1961, and visited Woody for the first time a few days later. He wrote to friends back in Minneapolis, "I know Woody. I know him and met him and saw him and sung to him. Goddam … he's the greatest holiest godliest one in the world." Within weeks he'd written **Song To Woody**, "the first song I ever wrote that I performed in public". A

friendship ensued that went on to transcend mere hero worship on the younger man's part. "The most important thing I know I learned from Woody Guthrie is I'm my own person," he said in the liner note of his second album, *The Freewheelin' Bob Dylan*.

At his first major-league concert at the New York Town Hall, in April 1963, Dylan marked the occasion by reading a seven-minute poem entitled **Last Thoughts On Woody**. Despite the apparent valediction in the title, his passion for Guthrie's music has remained with him all his adult life. After 1966's motorcycle crash and his "retirement" from touring, the only event that could persuade him to return to the stage was a Guthrie memorial concert at New York's Carnegie Hall, January 1968 (Woody had eventually died in 1967). Dylan performed "Grand Coulee Dam", **Mrs Roosevelt** and **I Ain't Got No Home**. He was even considered for the part of Guthrie in the 1970s biopic *Bound For Glory*, but the role eventually went to David Carradine.

In the booklet accompanying the 1985 box-set *Biograph*, Dylan was still offering aspiring singers and songwriters this advice: "Disregard all the current stuff. Forget it. You're better off if you read John Keats, Melville, and listen to Robert Johnson and Woody Guthrie."

Dylan, like his hero, was finally doing some hard travellin', hitchhiking through the snow first to Chicago, where he spent Christmas with friends, and then to Madison, Wisconsin. There he saw **Pete Seeger** perform a set that included several Guthrie songs and his resolve to visit the dying man was reinforced. When

he found University of Wisconsin students Fred Underhill and David Berger were looking for a co-driver to share the long trip to New York, he eagerly asked to join them. He drove them to distraction by singing Woody Guthrie songs incessantly throughout the thousand-mile journey.

1961: **Talking New York**

"I swung on my old guitar, Grabbed hold of a subway car, And after a rocking, reeling, rolling ride I landed up on the downtown side – Greenwich Village."

Bob Dylan, "Talking New York"

Bob Dylan arrived in New York on January 24, 1961. Or rather two versions of him did. One was the baby-faced, romantic, idealistic folk-singer in the corduroy cap and sheep-skin jacket, singing out against injustice and prejudice. The other was the cunning and cal-culating young man his biographer Howard Sounes described as pursuing his ambition with an undeniable "briskness", using friends and dropping them when they were of no further use, mimicking artists he admired, borrowing and stealing tunes and lyrics at will and fabricating improbable stories about his past.

It was Woody Guthrie who had drawn him to New York, but **Greenwich Village** – with its cheap rents and large student population – was also a powerful lure. The coffeehouses and clubs in the streets around Washington Square had reverberated to the sound of bebop jazz during the beatnik years, and it was the epicentre of the burgeoning folk revival.

By the time Dylan arrived, the coffeehouses such as the **Gaslight** and the **Café Wha?** on MacDougal Street (where he headed on his first night in town) were full of earnest folk-singers and holding regular "hootenannies": open-mic nights when any young hopeful could get up and sing. On his first night Dylan performed a couple of Guthrie songs and told the crowd, "I

been travelin' round the country, followin' in Woody's footsteps."

Contrary to popular mythology, Dylan did not head out to the hospital to sit at Guthrie's bedside the next morning, but got to meet his hero for the first time the following Sunday, January 29. Guthrie was confined to his bed in **Greystone Park Hospital,** New Jersey. But every Sunday, his friends the Gleasons took him out to spend the day at their home in nearby East Orange. There Guthrie's friends and family gathered, as did young musicians such as **Phil Ochs, Peter La Farge** and Dylan.

Guthrie basked in the attention and could not have failed to be delighted in the young man who knew all his songs and clearly held him in awe. Dylan made Woody "laugh and twinkle", according to Norah Guthrie. On their first meeting, Woody wrote the words "I ain't dead" on a card and gave it to Dylan, who flashed and flourished it at everyone he met, as if it were the Holy Grail. Woody also encouraged Dylan to visit again and the two struck up a genuinely warm relation-ship. He also told Dylan about a box of songs and poems he'd had written which had never been set to melodies and instructed him where to find them in the basement of his family home on Coney Island. Dylan made the trip out there but Guthrie's wife Margie wasn't in and he soon forgot about it. Some 35 years later, the material was finally put to music by Billy Bragg and Wilco on their two *Mermaid Avenue* albums.

Back in Greenwich Village, Dylan was busily using his official endorsement to establish himself as the nouveau Woody Guthrie. He wrote **Song To Woody**, his first serious composition, and was soon performing around the Village anywhere they would give him a stage. Monday night was hootenanny night and Dylan avidly shuttled his way from club to club, singing his new song and those of Guthrie. At the Gaslight one night, he was introduced as "a legend in

his own lifetime", at which point the presenter Hugh Romney, later known as "Wavy Gravy", turned to Dylan and asked, "What's your name, kid?"

He slept on friends' couches, hung out at Izzy Young's Folklore Center and insinuated himself into the community of Village musicians, something which his mixture of charm and cunning made easy. Among those whose friendship he cultivated was **Robert Shelton**, a journalist at *The New York Times* who became his first champion in the press.

In April 1961, Dylan was given a two-week slot supporting **John Lee Hooker** at **Gerde's**

Bob's first write-up

Robert Shelton was the all-powerful folk-music critic of **The New York Times** and a familiar face in Greenwich Village, where he trawled the clubs and coffeehouses looking for promising new artists to write about. He first heard Dylan in early 1961, probably at an open-mic night, and recommended him to Mike Porco, the owner of Gerde's Folk City. By April, Porco had given Dylan a slot supporting John Lee Hooker; Shelton reviewed the bluesman's show but, to Dylan's dismay, he did not turn up in time for Dylan's set.

In September, Dylan was back at Gerde's doing a two-week stint supporting The Greenbriar Boys. Shelton caught the first night and was astonished at how quickly he had progressed. He interviewed Dylan backstage and his review appeared in *The New York Times*, under the headline "Bob Dylan: A Distinctive Folk-Song Stylist", on September 29.

"A bright new face in folk music is appearing at Gerde's Folk City. Although only 20 years old, Bob

Dylan is one of the most distinctive stylists to play in a Manhattan cabaret in months," he wrote. "Mr Dylan's voice is anything but pretty. He is consciously trying to recapture the rude beauty of a southern field-hand musing in melody on his porch. All the husk and bark are left on his notes and a searing intensity pervades his songs." The piece praised his growing songwriting talent and in particular Dylan's facility for "droll musical monologues", singling out for mention **Talking Bear Mountain**, **Talking New York** and **Talkin' Hava Nagilah**.

Sensibly, Shelton glossed over some of the tall tales Dylan had told him about working as a carnival hand and hitching around the South learning tunes from blues musicians. "Mr Dylan is vague about his antecedents and birthplace, but it matters less where he has been than where he is going – and that would seem to be straight up." A few weeks later, Shelton wrote the sleeve notes of Dylan's debut album under the pen name Stacey Williams.

The Life

Friends and rivals in Greenwich Village

Mark Spoelstra (born Kansas City, 1940) had only been in the Village a couple of months when Dylan arrived. They became inseparable friends, hustling together, playing chess and backing each other on stage at the Café Wha?, where a version of **Muleskinner Blues** was the highlight of their double act. Dylan was performing with Spoelstra when Suze Rotolo first heard him. They even had a record-company audition as a duo, but were rejected. Spoelstra went on to record for Folkways and Elektra, both labels which had turned Dylan down.

Phil Ochs (born El Paso, Texas, 1940) had much in common with Dylan. Both were born into Jewish families, only months apart; both worshipped James Dean in their teens; and both gravitated to New York, drawn by the legend of Woody Guthrie, who they both visited at the Gleasons' home in New Jersey. For a time, Ochs was Dylan's greatest rival as a topical songwriter. The two fell out when Dylan played him his new single, **Can You Please Crawl Out Your Window?**, in the back of his limo one day in late 1965. When he was less than enthusiastic, Dylan threw him out of the car, shouting "You're not a folk singer, Ochs. You're a journalist!" Yet Ochs was not one of those who condemned Dylan going electric; in a way he attempted to ape him, dressing in a gold lamé suit and claiming he wanted to "wed Elvis Presley to the politics of Ché Guevara". The two men patched up their friendship in the 1970s when Dylan played at an Ochs-organised benefit for democracy in Chile. Dylan wanted to invite him to join the Rolling Thunder Tour in 1975–76, but by then he was in no fit state. Schizophrenia had taken hold and he believed much of the time that he was a character called John Train. He hung himself at his sister's house in Queens, New York, on April 7, 1976, while Dylan was rehearsing for a Rolling Thunder gig in Florida.

Dave Van Ronk (born New York, 1936) was only 25 when Dylan landed in Greenwich Village, but he'd already released four albums and was something of a mentor to many of the young singers on the scene. In his first months in New York, Dylan often slept on the sofa in the Van Ronks' apartment on 15th Street. Terri, Dave's wife, briefly acted as Dylan's first booking agent and in June 1961, Dylan and Van Ronk shared a week's residency at the Gaslight. Dylan's arrangement of **The House Of The Rising Sun** on his debut album was cribbed from Van Ronk, who was more than a little peeved, as he had intended to record it on his next album himself.

Folk City by owner Mike Porco, who had to pay Bob's Musicians Union subscription before he could take the engagement. As Dylan was under 21, Porco also had to sign as his guardian, after Bob had persuaded him that he was an orphan. In *Chronicles*, Dylan described him as "the Sicilian father I never had."

Yet by May, Dylan was back in Minneapolis and claiming he didn't intend to return to New York. He recorded a tape of 25 songs at the apartment of former girlfriend Bonnie Beecher (see pp.254–255), but when Dylan came on to her, she told him she had found someone else. The rejection appears to have spurred his return to New York and when he later wrote about a "kneeing in the guts" in the early prose poem **My Life In A Stolen Moment**, it was Bonnie he had in mind.

Tom Paxton (born Chicago, 1937) arrived in Greenwich Village in 1960 after serving in the army, and his military bearing led some to suspect he was an undercover cop. But he was already an experienced performer when he met Dylan at Gerde's Folk City on one of his first open-mic-night appearances. Paxton and Dylan once extemporised a song together called **Talkin' Central Park Mugger Blues**, but Paxton was not a fan of **Blowin' In The Wind**, which he described as "a grocery list song". The two men renewed their friendship years later when Dylan bought a house on Long Island, near Paxton's East Hampton home. Paxton, whose best-known compositions include **The Last Thing On My Mind**, **Goin' To The Zoo** and **Talkin' Vietnam Pot Luck Blues**, continues to record.

Fred Neil (born St Petersburg, Florida, 1937) gave Dylan occasional employment as a backing harmonica player when he first arrived in New York. The two weren't particularly close, but the fact that Neil was writing his own songs when most were singing traditional material must have influenced Dylan. Neil's best-known songs include **The Other Side Of This Life** (covered by Jefferson Airplane, Lovin' Spoonful and The Youngbloods) and **Dolphins** (made famous by Tim Buckley and also recorded by

Eddi Reader, Beth Orton and others). He also wrote **Everybody's Talkin'**, which became the theme for John Schlesinger's film *Midnight Cowboy* after Dylan failed to deliver **Lay Lady Lay** in time. Neil suffered problems with heroin addiction and returned to Florida in the late 1960s. In the 1990s, Dylan sometimes played his **I've Got A Secret (Didn't We Shake Sugaree)** in concert.

Ramblin' Jack Elliott (born New York, 1931) was a decade older than Dylan and had lived the kind of life the youthful Dylan fantasized about, joining the rodeo as a teenager and putting in some hard travellin' with Woody Guthrie. He spent the late 1950s in Europe, but was back in the Village by 1960, when he released an album of Woody Guthrie songs. With Guthrie hospitalized, Dylan never saw his hero perform and many of the stage mannerisms that it was assumed were Woody-isms were, in fact, modelled on Elliott. Under the pseudonym Tedham Porterhouse, Dylan part repaid the debt when he played harmonica on Elliott's eponymous 1964 album on Prestige. When Dylan put together the Rolling Thunder Review in 1975, Elliott was one of the first to sign on. He nostalgically recalled their Greenwich Village days together in the song **Bleeker Street Blues**, written in 1997 after Dylan fell seriously ill.

However, Bonnie was soon forgotten when, some time in the early summer of 1961, Dylan met **Suze Rotolo** (see pp.30–31). Although she was only 17, she was to play a key role in his political education and become his muse for the next three years. Her sister Carla – who Dylan would later viciously put down in "Ballad In Plain D" –

worked for the legendary musicologist **Alan Lomax**, whose field recordings of Leadbelly, Mississippi Fred McDowell and others hold a unique and vital place in American folk music. It was another useful contact and Dylan took to hanging around Lomax's West Third Street apartment as a way of expanding his musical scope.

Columbia guru John Hammond enjoying a moment with his "folly"

"Hammond's Folly"

By the autumn of 1961, Dylan was ensconced in an $60-a-month apartment at **161 West fourth Street** (an address later celebrated in the song "Positively Fourth Street") and making sufficient waves in Greenwich Village to entertain serious hopes of a recording contract. But just as Decca Records a year later would famously pass on The Beatles, several respected specialist labels made the wrong call on Dylan. **Folkways Records** weren't interested. And neither was **Elektra**'s Jac Holzman, who signed such Village troubadours as Tom Paxton and Fred Neil as well as Dylan's old Minneapolis colleagues, Koerner, Ray and Glover. Manny Solomon at **Vanguard** – the label which already had Joan Baez – might have signed him but didn't. Dylan must have been dispirited to be rejected by all of the specialist folk labels that might have appeared to offer him a natural home. But his despondency would not last long.

> *"Everyone thought I was crazy. Dylan had been turned down by Folkways and every other label there was at the time. But I thought he had something."* John Hammond

A legendary figure in the recording industry, **John Hammond** was head of A&R at Columbia. He had signed Billie Holiday and Count Basie, and by the beginning of the 1960s, he was on the hunt for folk revivalists. Hammond first encountered Dylan in early September 1961, when he played harmonica on three songs on the debut album by Carolyn Hester, a sweet-voiced Texan folk-singer who at the time was the wife of Richard Farina (who later married Joan Baez's younger sister Mimi). Hammond was producing Hester's album and was intrigued by the scruffy, Guthrie-obsessed folk singer, particularly when Dylan told him he was now writing his own songs. He was probably further swayed by Dylan's first-ever review, a highly enthusiastic *New York Times* write-up of the first night of a two-week residency supporting The Greenbriar Boys at Gerde's Folk City (see p.23). Hammond arranged an audition and Dylan formally signed with Columbia at the end of October. The debut album *Bob Dylan* (see p.167) was recorded – with Hammond producing – over two days in November 1961, for a total cost of $402.

By this point, Dylan had also met his soon-to-be manager, **Albert Grossman** (see p.29), a larger-than-life figure who already handled Odetta and Peter, Paul and Mary, and was perfectly positioned to oversee Dylan's promotion to the major league. But success was hardly instant. *Bob Dylan* was eventually released in March 1962 and sold a mere 5000 copies in its first year. There seemed a strong possibility that Dylan would be dropped. Around the Columbia building on Sixth Avenue, known as "the Black Rock", Dylan was openly referred to as **"Hammond's Folly"**, and it was whispered that the veteran producer had lost his grip. But Hammond had faith in his protégé, and at Columbia his word was law.

The Life

1962: Firing the First Broadsides

"The songs are there. They exist by themselves, just waiting for someone to write them down. If I don't do it, someone else would." Bob Dylan

In the five months between the recording of his first album and its release in March 1962, Dylan had dramatically moved on. *Bob Dylan* contained eleven covers and just two original compositions – "Talkin' New York" and "Song To Woody", neither of which was remotely political. But in early 1962, under the influence of **Suze Rotolo** (see p.30), a committed left-wing activist who worked at the Congress of Racial Equality, Dylan became a very active and highly politicised songwriter. "America was changing. I had a feeling of destiny and I was riding the changes," he recalled in his autobiography more than four decades later.

Dylan wrote his first "protest" song – **The Death Of Emmett Till** – some time in early 1962. It's a modest enough composition, commemorating an event that had happened some seven years earlier. Till had been the victim of a notorious race killing in Mississippi, and the sentiments of the song were noble. But it concluded lamely with an exhortation to unite to "make this great land of ours a greater place to live".

Still, Rotolo, who was by now living in Dylan's apartment on West Fourth Street, encouraged him to come up with more songs in a similar vein – "Suze was into this equality/freedom thing long before I was," he later admitted. And, in less than a month, he had

followed "The Death Of Emmett Till" with **The Ballad Of Donald White**, the satirical **Talking John Birch Society Blues** and the anti–nuclear war song, **Let Me Die In My Footsteps**. All were published in *Broadside*, a magazine started by Pete Seeger and others as a vehicle for topical contemporary songs.

By April 1962, however, Dylan had eclipsed all of these early expressions of social conscience with **Blowin' In The Wind**. The song was allegedly written in a matter of minutes in a café on MacDougal Street in the Village, with a melody hastily borrowed from an old slave song, **No More Auction Block**. Few, including Dylan, were immediately aware of the significance the song would come to assume. But within days of it being published in the May issue of *Broadside*, every folkie in the Village was singing it and the song swiftly took its place alongside **We Shall Overcome** as the ultimate protest anthem.

From the outset, Dylan exhibited mixed feelings about the world of protest and political activism. When he performed "Blowin' In The Wind" for the first time at Gerde's Folk City, he introduced it with a preamble that was soon to become a familiar refrain. "This here ain't a protest song or anything like that, 'cause I don't write protest songs," he insisted. Yet at the same time that he was vainly attempting to deny protest status, he was telling the folk magazine *Sing Out!* that songwriters had a duty to tackle social and political issues. "There's other things in the world besides love and sex that're important, too. People shouldn't turn their back on 'em just because they ain't pretty to look at. How is the world ever gonna get any better if we're afraid to look at these things?"

A brief sabbatical from writing protest songs occurred over the summer of 1962, for Dylan had other things on his mind. With Suze on a six-month vacation in Europe, he pined and wrote her love songs, among which were the beautiful **Tomorrow Is A Long Time** and the much-covered **Don't Think Twice, It's All Right.** Dylan grew increasingly despondent at her continued absence and it took the near outbreak of World War III fully to engage him with the world again.

Trembling on the Brink

The trigger for one of Dylan's greatest protest songs was the **Cuban missile crisis,** in which America and the Soviet Union went eyeball-to-eyeball over the USSR's deployment of nuclear weapons in Uncle Sam's Caribbean backyard. For a while, it appeared that confrontation between the two superpowers was inevitable

Albert Grossman

You've only got to watch **Don't Look Back**, the film of Dylan's 1965 British tour, to see that Albert Grossman was the first of rock's rottweiler managers. In one scene, a hapless hotel employee is sent up to Dylan's suite to ask him to keep the noise down. Grossman chases him out into the corridor and tells him, "There's been no noise in this room. And you're one of the dumbest assholes I've ever spoken to in my life. If we were someplace else, I'd punch you in your goddam nose, you stupid nut."

When he took on managing Dylan in May 1962, he already had **Odetta** and **Peter, Paul and Mary** on his books – which at the time was about as big as it got in folk music. And he would go on to add not only Dylan but **Janis Joplin**, **The Band**, **Gordon Lightfoot** and **Todd Rundgren** to his roster of clients.

Grossman's hard bargaining style was based around a belief that artists should be masters of their own product – a revolutionary attitude in the record business at the time. Yet he was an astute manipulator of

the press. When Dylan complained about the burden of being tagged the spokesman for his generation, did he know that Grossman had bullied many a critic into using just that very phrase?

Grossman was also very astute at looking after himself, of course. When he took Dylan on, for 25 per cent of not very much, with his vast experience and extensive book of contacts it looked as if he was doing the singer a favour. By the end of the 60s, he was a very rich man indeed and when the contract came up for renewal in August 1969 – on the very weekend of the Woodstock festival – it was no surprise that Dylan declined to renew it.

Grossman went on to sue Dylan for unpaid commissions and the suit was not settled until 1987. The manager won, but it didn't do him any good: by then he had been dead almost two years, having suffered a fatal heart attack on a flight to London, aged 59. Dylan attended neither the funeral nor the memorial service.

and that the Cold War was about to turn very hot indeed.

As the storm clouds gathered and the world trembled on the brink of catastrophe, Dylan unveiled the apocalyptic **A Hard Rain's A-Gonna Fall**, his most remarkable lyric to date, set to the tune of the traditional folk ballad **Lord Randall**. He performed it first in September 1962 at Greenwich Village's Gaslight Café, and it was immediately evident to everyone who heard it that he'd written a masterpiece that brilliantly and terrifyingly encapsulated the most dangerous moment in world history up until that time.

"I wrote that when I didn't figure I'd have enough time left in life, didn't know how many other songs I could write, during the Cuban thing," Dylan said of the song. "I wanted to get the most down that I knew about in one song, the most that I possibly could. Every line in that is actually a complete song."

Suze Rotolo

"I once loved a girl, her skin it was bronze,
With the innocence of a lamb, she was gentle like a fawn"

Bob Dylan, "Ballad In Plain D"

Would Dylan ever have written his protest songs without Suze Rotolo? Certainly she was a seminal figure in his political education and it was not until after they had become lovers in the summer of 1961 that his writing began to address issues such as **civil rights** and the threat of **nuclear war**. Fittingly, Suze is pictured arm in arm with Dylan on the cover of *The Freewheelin' Bob Dylan*, the album that made his reputation as a protest singer and social commentator. But, just as significantly, she was also the object of several of his greatest love songs.

The Rotolos were an Italian-American family, reduced to an all-female clan after Suze's father died when she was fourteen. Her mother, Mary, brought up Suze and her older sister Carla to be left-wing activists. When Dylan met her in the summer of 1961, Suze was working for **CORE** (the Congress of Racial Equality) and the anti-nuclear group **SANE**, and picketing Woolworth stores around New York because their lunch counters were segregated in the South.

Suze was only seventeen, and Mary and Carla were not enthusiastic about her relationship with Bob, particularly after she moved in with him in January 1962. Suze's mother referred to Dylan as "the twerp" and cast aspersions on his personal hygiene. An even stronger animosity developed between Bob and **Carla**, who he dismissed as a "parasite" in "Ballad in Plain D". But Suze and Bob adored each other. She called him 'Pig' or 'Raz' (a nickname based on his initials). He called her his "fawn in the forest" in his poem **11 Outlined Epitaphs** and talked of marriage.

In June 1962, partly in a bid to get her away from Dylan, Mary Rotolo took her youngest daughter to Italy for a summer study course at the University of Perugia. Dylan was distraught, particularly when Suze found an Italian boyfriend called Enzo Bartoccioli. Consumed with jealousy and longing, Dylan wrote her two of the most beautiful love songs he was ever to pen – **Don't Think Twice, It's All Right** and **Tomorrow Is A Long Time**.

"A Hard Rain" was swiftly followed up with **Oxford Town,** a song about the violent stand-off over the registration of the first black student at the University of Mississippi, which became an emblematic event in the civil rights struggle. By now, Dylan's songwriting was developing so fast that when, in December 1962, he resumed sessions for the album that was to become **Freewheelin',** the earlier protest numbers, such as "Emmett Till", "Donald White", "Talking John Birch Society Blues" and "Let Me Die In My Footsteps" – which had been recorded back in April – were all dropped in favour of the newer songs. At the new session, "A Hard Rain" and "Oxford Town" were dispatched in single takes. Within weeks, they were joined by the coruscating **Masters Of War,** which was followed swiftly by the satirical **Talkin' World War Three Blues.**

Suze had been due to return in September but delayed until December, by which time Dylan had wearied of waiting and had taken his own trip to London and Rome. They were reunited when he returned to New York in mid-January 1963, but by August that year Suze had moved out of Dylan's Fourth Street apartment, increasingly distressed by Dylan's flagrant affair with **Joan Baez**.

To make matters worse, she moved in with sister Carla, who made no effort to hide her belief that Dylan was manipulative, selfish and emotionally immature. Suze became pregnant and had an abortion, and the relationship deteriorated further. They eventually split up in March 1964 after a horrible screaming and shouting match in which Carla got embroiled and which is detailed in distressingly graphic detail in **Ballad In Plain D**. It is one of Dylan's least attractive songs and he belatedly apologized to Carla and Suze in the liner notes of the 1985 *Biograph* compilation, admitting, "I must have been a real schmuck to write that … it was a mistake to record it and I regret it."

Suze went on to marry Enzo Bartoccioli, the boyfriend she had met in Italy.

Suze and 'Raz' hanging out, November 1963

Bob at work just before Christmas 1962, during his first trip to London

London Calling

Dylan made his first visit to London at the end of 1962 at the invitation of the BBC director **Philip Saville**, who had seen him perform in Greenwich Village and who had cast him for the role of "Bobby The Hobo" in Evan Jones' TV play, *Madhouse On Castle Street*. He arrived in London on December 17 and booked into the Cumberland Hotel, near Marble Arch.

Pre-Christmas rehearsals were disastrous. According to his fellow star David Warner, Dylan was almost incapable of reading his lines and when the play was eventually filmed on December 30, his speaking part was reduced to a single sentence – "Well I don't know, I'll have to go home and think about it," But it did include Dylan singing **Ballad Of A Gliding Swan** and the first-ever recorded version of **Blowin' In The Wind**, which played out over the credits. Sadly, after the play was transmitted in January 1963, the BBC did not keep the recording and no copy has ever turned up. However, a recording of "Ballad Of A Gliding Swan" did come to light when in 2005 the BBC commissioned the documentary film *Dylan In The Madhouse*, to tell the story of Dylan's first visit to London. After issuing an appeal for a recording of the song, at least two fans came forward with tapes made by holding a microphone in front of the TV. The programme, including the first broadcast of the song in 43 years, was screened in October 2005 as part of a BBC "Dylan season" that included the premiere of *Don't Look Back*. The song itself turned out to be a stunning update of the old Border ballad with such startling new lines as "The doctor gave Sally a sad surprise,/ a Thalidomide baby with no eyes", and "My father has cancer/ My mother's insane/ The girl I'm in love with takes cocaine."

Far more profitable was the time Dylan spent immersing himself in the London folk scene. The night after he arrived, he turned up at the **Troubadour** club, where he sang "The Ballad Of Hollis Brown" and met the English folk singer **Martin Carthy**, who invited him to stay at his flat in Hampstead. The weather was freezing and Carthy recalls Dylan helping him chop up an old wardrobe to fuel the fire.

During his stay in London, Dylan also sang at a number of other folk venues, including Bunjies, the King and Queen pub, Les Cousins and the Pindar of Wakefield in Gray's Inn Road; the often-told story that he sang at Surbiton Folk Club in Surrey appears to be untrue.

From other singers on the circuit, Dylan learned several traditional songs, which were swiftly recycled into his own repertoire. Carthy taught him **Scarborough Fair**, parts of which fed into the tune of "Boots Of Spanish Leather" (more famously, Carthy would later teach the song to Paul Simon). From **Bob Davenport**, Dylan picked up "Nottamun Town", the tune of which he adapted to become "Masters Of War", and from **Dominic Behan** he learned "The Patriot Game", which gave him the melody for "With God On Our Side".

Immediately before he flew back to New York on January 16, Dylan contributed backing vocals to half a dozen tracks for an album being recorded by Dick Farina and Eric Von Schmidt in the basement of Dobell's jazz shop in Charing Cross Road. When the LP appeared, Dylan was credited as Blind Boy Grunt.

The Life

1963: Pointing the Finger

"I don't think what comes out of my music is a call to action." Bob Dylan

Dylan returned from Europe in mid-January 1963 with new songs and new tunes, several of which were not protest songs at all. But, reunited with Suze, he threw himself back into the Greenwich Village scene and began furiously writing more political songs.

By the time *The Freewheelin' Bob Dylan* appeared in May 1963, he was playing the part of the protest singer with conviction. **Joan Baez** had adopted him as her personal cause célèbre and took him out on tour with her (see pp.40–41). Soon he was unveiling new and increasingly sophisticated protest songs to her captive folk audience.

Among them was **Only A Pawn In Their Game**, written in response to the murder of civil-rights leader Medgar Evers in June 1963. It's instructive to compare Dylan's composition with the song written by Phil Ochs on the same subject. In the **Ballad of Medgar Evers**, Ochs delivers a didactic, literal and ultimately sterile account of how "the country gained a killer and the country lost a man". Dylan's song is on an altogether different level. He tells the story of the race murder with the precision of a news bulletin in the first verse. Then he explores why it happened and comes up with a staggeringly mature conclusion that belies his extreme youth. The killer is "a poor white man", who can't really be blamed because "he's

only a pawn in their game". The real villains are the Southern politicians and the sheriffs, soldiers, governors, marshals and cops who uphold segregation.

The final verse is even more stunning. In a symbolic act, both President Kennedy and his brother Robert attended Evers' funeral. Dylan describes the graveyard scene and how they "lowered him down like a king". Then, in a stroke of pure genius, he contrasts the dignified burial of Evers with the fate of "the one that fired the gun", whose unremarkable headstone will bear the epitaph, "only a pawn in the game". It's arguably the most profound of all Dylan's finger-pointing songs, if only because he doesn't point the finger, as Ochs does, at the obvious and easy target, but at the shadowy figures of authority and the system that sustain racism and bigotry.

"Only A Pawn In Their Game" was premiered in July, when Dylan flew down to **Greenwood**, Mississippi, to join the likes of Pete Seeger at a black-voter-registration rally. It was his first visit to the South, so he had never before seen segregation first-hand. At the rally, on a farm at the edge of a cotton patch, Dylan's searing performance of the new song was captured on film. Later, he joined hands with his fellow campaigners to sing **We Shall Overcome** and put his money

Ten causes that raised Dylan's voice in protest

1. EMMETT TILL in **The Death Of Emmett Till**. Dylan's first-ever protest song concerned a race killing in Mississippi in 1955. After boasting that he had a white girlfriend, Emmett Till was shot in the head and thrown in the Tallahassee River.

2. WITCH-HUNTERS in **Talkin' John Birch Society Blues**. The John Birch Society was a thoroughly nasty outfit dedicated to witch-hunting alleged "reds" and "commies" in America. When Dylan was banned from performing his song parodying the witch-hunters on the *Ed Sullivan Show*, he walked off the programme in protest.

3. NUCLEAR WEAPONS in **A Hard Rain's A-Gonna Fall**. The hard rain of one of Dylan's best-known protest songs was not, in fact, nuclear fall-out. "I mean all the lies that are told on the radio and in the newspapers," Dylan explained. But the song was inspired by the Cuban missile crisis when the world trembled on the brink of nuclear war.

4. MILITARISM in **With God On Our Side**. Dylan surveys his country's military history, from the massacre of the native Indians, then the Mexicans, through two world wars to the stand-off with the Russians, and mocks the notion of politicians manipulating God to justify their killing.

5. CIVIL RIGHTS in **The Times They Are A-Changin'**. The genius of many of Dylan's protest songs is their universality. "The Times They Are A-Changin'" had a specific meaning in the context of the civil-rights struggle in early 1960s America, but it also serves as an anthem for the downtrodden and dispossessed throughout time.

6. HATTIE CARROLL in **The Lonesome Death Of Hattie Carroll**. A black mother of eleven children, Hattie Carroll was struck on the head with a cane when serving a drink to William Zantzinger in a Baltimore hotel. "When I order a drink, I want it now, you black bitch," he told her. She died of a brain haemorrhage; he received six months for manslaughter.

7. MEDGAR EVERS in **Only A Pawn In Their Game**. Black civil-rights organizer Medgar Evers was killed by a white, working-class racist in Mississippi in June 1963. Dylan doesn't excuse his action, but goes on to point the finger of true blame at the entire official infrastructure that supported segregation in the South.

8. THE ARMS INDUSTRY in **Masters Of War**. Dylan kept perhaps his most vicious attack for those who profit from war – the military-industrial complex which dictates American foreign policy. "Even Jesus would never forgive what you do," he rails.

9. GEORGE JACKSON in **George Jackson**. After years away from "the cause", Dylan returned to his protest vein with an elegy on the death of the incarcerated black activist George Jackson. Some dismissed it as a cynical ploy. But he not only released it as a single: he put it on both sides to ensure radio stations could not flip it over.

10. RUBIN CARTER in **Hurricane**. Dylan wrote "Hurricane" in 1975 after reading the autobiography of boxer Rubin Carter, incarcerated for a murder he claimed he had not committed. Dylan even visited him in jail and his campaign helped Carter secure a retrial – at which he was again found guilty.

Heading South: Dylan in Mississippi, 1963

where his mouth was with a financial donation to the cause.

In August, Dylan sang "With God On Our Side" in duet with Baez at the **Newport Folk Festival**. Later that same month – in August 28, 1963 – he joined her on the civil-rights march in Washington, DC, where **Dr Martin Luther King** made his most famous speech. Sitting on the steps of the Lincoln Memorial, Dylan and Baez were just a few feet away from King as his sonorous voice exclaimed "I have a dream" to a crowd of some 200,000 protesters. Dylan was apparently visibly moved, though he raised a grin when noted prankster and activist Wavy Gravy leaned over and whispered, "I hope he's over quick. Mahalia Jackson is on next." Later, Dylan himself sung **Only A Pawn In Their Game** and **Blowin' In The Wind**. And, by the time the march had dispersed, he had officially become "the voice of a generation" – at least for the white protesters and middle-class activists, if not the more militant contingent of African-American youth.

In the few short weeks between the Mississippi rally and the Washington march, Dylan poured out further "finger-pointing" songs, among them **When The Ship Comes In, The Lonesome Death Of Hattie Carroll** and that unforgettable battle-hymn of the new generation, **The Times They Are A-Changin'**. All three were due to appear on his next album, which by October he had already completed.

On November 22, 1963, **President Kennedy** was assassinated. Dylan, as we have seen, had long been vehemently insisting that he wasn't a protest singer, despite all appearances to the contrary. But, paradoxically, events in Dallas, Texas, put a further wedge between him and the protest cause. For Kennedy's assassination not only shocked Dylan to the core: it terrified him. If they could gun down the President in broad daylight, what might they do to the Voice of a Generation as he stepped out of the stage door into some dark alley after a gig one night?

If Dylan had been martyred, his message would surely have been amplified rather than silenced. But such considerations were unlikely to hold much sway with far-right extremists who might believe that with the principle articulator of generational disaffection out of the way, American youth could return to its former meek compliance. The danger of Elvis Presley had been neutered by packing him off first to the army and then to Hollywood. Neither tactic was going to work with Dylan, so perhaps sterner measures were needed.

Dylan spent the 48 hours following Kennedy's assassination watching TV with Suze in their apartment in Greenwich Village. It's almost impossible to imagine the mounting levels of paranoia that must have been going on in his head, but he gave several hints of what he was feeling. "If somebody really had something to say to help somebody out, well, obviously they're gonna be done away with. What it means is that they are trying to tell you, 'don't ever hope to change things'," he told friends. "Being noticed can be a burden," he told others. "Jesus got himself crucified because he got himself noticed. So I disappear a lot."

From this point on, Dylan becomes deliberately more elusive. **The Times They Are A-Changin'** was about to be released and he was acutely concerned that putting out an album of such potent and subversive protest at such a time of heightened tension made him a prime target. The stress and resulting confusion was evident when, just 21 days after Kennedy's death, Dylan received the **Tom Paine award** at the annual Bill of Rights dinner organized by the Emergency Civil Liberties Commission. It was a prestigious honour, which the year before had gone to the philosopher Bertrand Russell. But Dylan was discomfited by the occasion and got drunk. By the time he came to make his acceptance speech, he had lost the plot and offended his audience. He even told them that he saw something of himself in Lee Harvey Oswald, the man who had allegedly killed Kennedy. In the light of "Only A Pawn In Their Game", a song which had attempted to understand how we are all shaped for good or ill by the forces around us, it was perhaps not as extreme a comment as it at first appears. But it was hardly the occasion for such subtle psychological nuances and Dylan was understandably booed and hissed.

He swiftly apologized in the form of a lengthy prose poem to the ECLC. But he later admitted his dislike of the middle-class, middle-aged "radicals" in the audience. "I looked down from the platform and saw a bunch of people who had nothing to do with my kind of politics. They were supposed to be on my side but I didn't feel any connection with them," he complained.

Dylan wasn't quite done with protest, even if he was sick to death of the protest movement. But in future his "finger pointing" would be done in far less direct a manner.

1964: No Direction Home

"If they can't understand my songs, they're missing something.
If they can't understand green clocks, wet chairs, purple lamps
or hostile statues they're missing something, too." Bob Dylan

At the beginning of 1964, Bob Dylan undertook a trip that in its way was as significant as his momentous journey from Minnesota to Greenwich Village three years earlier. This trip was different in that it lacked the single-minded purpose of that earlier pilgrimage to find Woody Guthrie. This journey, which he embarked on February 3, 1964, was more of a Jack Kerouac experience, an on-the-road odyssey in which the real destination is within.

Dylan and his party – friends **Victor Maimudes**, **Pete Karman** and **Paul Clayton** – began by driving south to New Orleans, where they took in Mardi Gras. They took a detour to Dallas, to see the site where Kennedy was assassinated, only to be told by a local, after asking directions to Dealey Plaza, "You mean where they shot that sonofabitch Kennedy?" Then they headed west for San Francisco and Los Angeles.

The trip marked important changes, both personal and musical. While in California, Dylan had called on **Joan Baez** and the pair's increasingly brazen relationship proved too much for **Suze Rotolo**. Soon after Dylan returned to New York in mid-March, the couple split for good (after a traumatic row that he would unwisely choose to chronicle in "Ballad In Plain D"). On the musical level, meanwhile, Dylan was moving away from the overt protest song and finding a new, more personal style. By the time he arrived back in New York, it had already born fruit in the form of **Mr Tambourine Man** and **The Chimes Of Freedom**. On stage, however, Dylan was still singing his protest songs and, when he flew to London to begin a British tour in May, few were aware of the turn his career was about to take.

On his way home from the UK, Dylan stopped off for a working holiday in **Greece** and wrote most of the songs for his next album, **Another Side Of Bob Dylan** (see p.170). Recorded on his return to New York in early June, many of the songs were intensely personal, rather than political, and dealt with his break-up with Suze. For those ready to read the runes, Dylan signalled his intention to leave his protest persona behind in **My Back Pages**, with the refrain "Ah, but I was so much older then, I'm younger than that now". And the album's title appeared to negate the ideals of the past.

In fact, Dylan was relatively upfront about the change. "There ain't no finger-pointing songs in here," he said. "I don't want to write for people any more. You know, be a spokesman. From now on I want to write from inside of me." As Dylan's producer Tom Wilson put it, "He's not a singer of protest so much as he's a singer of concern about people." To many, this appeared to be a cop-out. Dylan's unfocused concern for the countless confused, accused, misused, strung-out ones an' worse was all well and good. But it was no substitute for active political campaigning.

To their fans, Dylan and Baez were still the king and queen of the acoustic folk movement and the couple headlined the Newport festival that July. But when *Another Side Of Bob Dylan* was released the following month, many of his old supporters on the Greenwich Village scene were disappointed by the lack of protest. In a stern rebuke, **Irwin Silber**, the editor of *Sing Out!*, wrote an open letter to Dylan in which he complained that the new songs were "all inner-directed now, inner-probing, self-conscious".

In retrospect, the album was hugely significant and can be seen as having launched an entire school of confessional singer-songwriting that would reach its peak in the early 1970s in the work of artists such as James Taylor and Joni Mitchell. But Dylan would soon move on once again. On August 28, John Lennon, who was on tour with **The Beatles** on their second US visit, asked journalist Al Aronowitz, a close friend of Dylan, if he could arrange a meeting. They duly got together in The Beatles' suite in the Hotel

The Life

Dylan and Baez: The King and Queen

For a brief period in the mid-1960s, Dylan and **Joan Baez** were the king and queen of folk music. By the time Dylan arrived in Greenwich Village in 1961, Baez (although only six months older) was already an established star. Her first impressions when she saw him at Gerde's Folk City were unfavourable. "Absurd" and "grubby beyond words", she later recalled.

But she was intrigued and their paths continued to cross as she observed with growing interest the rapid development of his songwriting. By spring 1963, she was besotted by both the songs and the man. After they had appeared together at the **Monterey Folk Festival** in May 1963, Dylan went to stay at Baez's house in Carmel – and the first rumours of their affair soon filtered back to Suze Rotolo in New York.

In July, the pair stormed the **Newport Folk Festival** together and the following month Baez took Dylan on tour with her, introducing him as her "very special guest". She tried to smarten up his image, buying him tailored jackets and even cuff links, and gave him access to far bigger audiences than he would ever have played on his own. "There's a boy wandering around New York City and his name is Bob Dylan," she told an audience of 15,000 at Forest Hills, Queens. "It just so happens that Bob Dylan is here with me tonight." He received an ecstatic ovation. The names of Baez and Dylan would became inextricably linked forever in the public's mind but, even by this stage, Dylan was probably already thinking about moving on.

At some point during 1964, the pair discussed marriage and even names they might give their kids. Yet many had felt all along that Dylan was cynically using Baez to promote his own career. And, as she herself had feared, once he became as big a star as she was, his passion for her and her virginal voice appeared to cool rapidly. "I'm scared," she told him at one point. "You will be the rock'n'roll king and I'll be the peace queen."

The final break came when she accompanied him on his explosive 1965 tour of Britain, captured in the film **Don't Look Back**. According to D.A. Pennebaker, who directed the film, it was pretty obvious Dylan was "trying to get out from under being her partner". Baez, in turn, although still bedazzled by him, was unhappy that he was leaving behind the protest songs that had first attracted her to him.

The most outward sign of their growing estrangement was that at no point during the tour did Dylan invite Baez on stage with him, even though he had no band and was performing solo. Then, when Dylan took advantage of a break in the touring schedule to fly to Portugal for a brief vacation, he did not invite Baez to accompany him and instead flew in **Sara Lowndes** from America. It was the first Baez knew of the existence of the woman who would soon become Dylan's wife, and it marked the end of their relationship. Baez quit the tour and she and Dylan did not sing together again in public until the Rolling Thunder road show in the mid-1970s.

But, even after their relationship ended, Baez remained a presence in his songs – many critics have perceived references to her in **She Belongs To Me** on *Bringing It All Back Home* and **Queen Jane Approximately** on *Highway 61 Revisited*. There has also been much speculation that she was also the inspiration for **Visions Of Johanna**, one of Dylan's greatest songs of all. Certainly Baez herself thought so. Yet, as with most Dylan songs, the truth is almost certainly that "Johanna" was a composite of different characters.

Perhaps wanting to atone for any past wrongs, Dylan was extraordinarily generous about Baez in his autobiography. "That she was the same age as me almost made me feel useless," he wrote. "The sight of her made me high. All that and then her voice. A voice that drove out bad spirits. It was like she'd come down from another planet."

Folk's king and queen take a break from royal duties in London's Embankment Gardens, 1965

It Ain't Me Babe

"Songs aren't going to save the world." Bob Dylan, Los Angeles, 1965

How sincere were Dylan's protest songs? The controversy, anger, resentment and misunderstanding still rage some 40 years on. "What you have to remember is that Bobby was never a marcher," Joan Baez told this author. "He gave us the music for the marches. But he didn't go on them. I don't think I ever saw him on a march." Oddly, she seemed to have forgotten his presence in Washington in August 1963 on perhaps the most famous march in the history of the civil-rights struggle. But Baez was essentially right in her recollection. Unlike, say, Phil Ochs or Pete Seeger, Dylan was not by temperament a marcher.

Yet despite his subsequent assertions that he only became a protest singer in order to jump into a scene that was about to happen, there was surely no way given the racial and social climate of America in the early 1960s that someone of Dylan's sensibility could *not* have become deeply politicized. Not only did he revere and, indeed, copy the music of oppressed Southern blacks, but his great hero Woody Guthrie had adorned his guitar with a sticker that bore the legend, "This machine kills fascists." To that list of enemies, Dylan added racists, bigots, cold-war warriors, gung-ho generals, the Ku Klux

Klan, corrupt politicians, complicit clergy and all those who stood in the way of the change that was surely gonna come.

It's impossible to believe anybody – least of all Dylan himself – who claims that he didn't mean it. *The Freewheelin' Bob Dylan* and *The Times They Are A-Changin'* are the greatest protest albums ever recorded. It's inconceivable that Dylan could have faked the righteous anger and laser-beam intensity that informs songs such as "A Hard Rain's A-Gonna Fall", "Masters Of War" and "The Lonesome Death Of Hattie Carroll". Yet when Baez asked him why he had written protest songs in the first place, he responded cruelly, "Hey, news can sell, right? You know me. I knew people would buy this kind of shit, right? I was never into that stuff."

In 2003, while researching this book, I asked Baez if she had been hurt by Dylan's disowning of the cause. "No, because I didn't believe him," she answered. "That was a pile of shit. Actually I'll give you a good old English word. It was codswallop and I told him. Nobody could have written those songs and not meant it. Whether he likes it or not, he goes down in the history books as a leader of dissent and social change."

Delmonico (see p.45) and the impact on both parties was profound. As Dylan biographer Howard Sounes put it, after their historic meeting Bob "integrated a Beatles-like use of rock'n'roll into his music and The Beatles began to write lyrics that had the depth and seriousness of Dylan songs". Pop music would never be the same again.

A liaison of an altogether different kind but of equal significance took place around the same time, when Dylan met his future wife, the model Sara Lowndes. By the end of 1964, he had quit his Fourth Street apartment and moved in with her and her 3-year-old daughter, Maria, to the **Chelsea Hotel** on West 23rd Street.

The Chelsea is one of the great institutions

Dylan and Baez on stage at Newport, 1964

The Life

of bohemian New York. With rooms rented cheaply on flexible leases, it has been a haunt for artists, musicians and writers almost since it was built in 1884. Aaron Copland composed there. Willem de Kooning painted there. Arthur C. Clarke wrote *2001: A Space Odyssey* there. Leonard Cohen wrote a song about making love to Janis Joplin in one of the hotel's rooms. And, in the 1970s, Sid Vicious's girlfriend Nancy Spungen died there. Dylan, Sara and Maria moved into Room 211, although few of even his closest friends knew they were there. Certainly Joan Baez did not – it would be another six months before she was even aware of Sara's existence.

Dylan also moved a piano into the room and began composing the songs that would constitute **Bringing It All Back Home**, the album on which he was to fuse folk and rock music in an extraordinary sonic crucible that was utterly new and, in some quarters, deeply shocking. Few, of course, had seen Dylan in his teenage years, pounding the piano with such high-school bands as The Shadow Blasters and Elston Gunn and His Rock Boppers, astonishing classmates and appalling teachers with his Little Richard impersonations. If they had, the shock might not have been quite so great.

But regardless of what anyone else thought, Dylan's rock'n'roll heart had been reawakened by The Beatles, whose influence led him to grow increasingly dissatisfied with his own sound. "I ask myself, 'Would you come to see me tonight?' And I'd have to truthfully say, 'No, I wouldn't come. I'd rather be doin' something else'," he told a friend some time in late 1964. "That something else is rock. That's where it's at for me."

1965: From Folk Hero to Electric Messiah

"My words are pictures, and the rock's gonna help me flesh out the colors of the pictures." Bob Dylan, May 1965

The session musicians who assembled at Columbia's New York studio on January 14, 1965, to add the bright and brave new hues Dylan had described included **John Sebastian** (soon to be leader of The Lovin' Spoonful), drummer **Bobby Gregg**, bassists **Joseph Macho Jr** and **William E. Lee**, guitarists **Bruce Langhorne**, **Kenny Rankin** and **Al Gorgoni**, and pianist **Paul Griffin**. The entire album – *Bringing It All Back Home* – was recorded in two days, with Dylan teaching the arrangements one by one to the different instrumentalists. The photographer Daniel Kramer, who was employed to document the sessions, also picked up on Dylan's analogy between music and painting. "He worked like a painter, covering a huge canvas with the colours that the different musicians could supply him, adding depth and dimension to the total work," he said.

The songs were unlike anything Dylan had written before, packed with anti-authoritarian

Dylan and The Beatles

Early in 1964, *Melody Maker* ran an article with the headline, "The Beatles Dig Dylan". It was probably the first time the two names had appeared alongside each other in print. But was the feeling mutual? Not at first, it seems. Back in Greenwich Village in 1963, Dylan had told friends they were "just bubblegum". Yet by the time he met them for the first time in a New York hotel on August 28, 1964, he was not only a serious fan but claiming he had been a secret admirer all along. "I just kept it to myself that I really dug them," he said. "Everybody else thought that they were for teenyboppers, that they were gonna pass right away. But it was obvious to me that they had staying power. In my head, the Beatles were it. It seemed to me a definite line had been drawn."

On that first meeting, Dylan allegedly introduced them to marijuana. He was amazed that they had not tried it before, having misheard the line "I can't hide", in **I Want To Hold Your Hand**, as "I get high" (a strange error on the part of someone who described similar misinterpretations of his own songs as "vulgar"). It was an important event in the lives of the Fab Four: "Till then we'd been hard Scotch and coke men," Paul McCartney said. "It sort of changed that evening." It has subsequently been claimed that Lennon and Harrison had both smoked before, but Ringo had not. When handed his first joint by Dylan, he is said to have smoked the lot as if it were an ordinary cigarette, oblivious to the dope-smokers' etiquette of spliff-passing.

The Dylan influence in The Beatles' work was already evident, with Lennon admitting it had been very much present when he wrote **A Hard Day's Night**. **You've Got To Hide Your Love Away** also bore an obvious mark. The Beatles' influence took a little longer to percolate through in Dylan's work, but was a key element in his decision to go electric.

Dylan met The Beatles again on his tour of Britain in 1965. He was suspicious of **McCartney**, whose songs such as "Yesterday" he dismissed as "muzak". But he developed a closer relationship with **John**, who he visited at his home. The two reportedly played each other songs and worked together on a now-lost musical doodle.

In May 1966, in an act of solidarity, all of The Beatles were present to support Dylan at the **Albert Hall** when he was getting heckled by the folkniks. During the same tour, Dylan and Lennon were filmed riding around London in the back of a limousine. The film depicts a very stoned Lennon. But whatever Dylan has taken has made him positively ill. A snippet of the encounter can be seen in D.A. Pennebaker's film **Eat The Document**.

Dylan was not a fan of The Beatles' 1967 summer-of-love manifesto *Sgt Pepper's Lonely Hearts Club Band*, which he viewed as self-indulgent. But Lennon, Harrison and Starr attended Dylan's comeback gig at the Isle of Wight festival in 1969, and jammed together at Dylan's rented farmhouse. Dylan was also taken by helicopter to Lennon's Tittenhurst mansion, near Ascot, where the two reportedly recorded an unreleased version of Lennon's **Cold Turkey**.

After that, Lennon and Dylan drifted apart. "Don't believe in Zimmerman," the ex-Beatle declared in the song **God** on his 1970 album, *John Lennon And The Plastic Ono Band* (though in the same song he also claimed not to believe in his own former group). Lennon was enraged when in 1979 Dylan became a born-again Christian, recording a satire of his "You Gotta Serve Somebody" called **Serve Yourself**, which was eventually released on 1998's *John Lennon Anthology*.

In the end, it was Dylan and Harrison who became close friends. George visited Woodstock in November 1968, when the pair co-wrote **I'd Have You Any Time**, and they got together again in 1970, recording a joint version of **If Not For You**. The following year Harrison coaxed Dylan on stage at Madison Square Garden for his **Concert For Bangladesh**, and in 1985 he covered an unrecorded Dylan song called "I Don't Want To Do It" (which he had originally demoed for 1971's *All Things Must Pass*). Four years later, the two of them teamed up in the Traveling Wilburys.

Dylan and The Byrds

It's easy to see The Byrds as talented imitators who did little more than take Dylan's songs and turn them into cute, radio-friendly pop hits. But such a view would be unfair. Their cover of **Mr Tambourine Man**, which topped the charts in June 1965, did far more than merely ape Dylan's version. It helped to invent folk-rock. It wasn't just the added jingle-jangle of the twelve-string electric Rickenbacker guitar which cleverly echoed the lyric. As Roger McGuinn explained, "The time signature, changed from two-four to four-four, is the most important difference. It rocks."

Formed in Los Angeles in 1964 with a line-up that included McGuinn, David Crosby, Chris Hillman, Michael Clarke and Gene Clark, The Byrds took the pop harmonies of The Beatles and fused them to the lyrics of Dylan with wonderful and immediate results. In addition to "Mr Tambourine Man", their debut album also included versions of **Spanish Harlem Incident**, **Chimes of Freedom** and **All I Really Want To Do**.

The group continued to plunder Dylan's songbook and when in 2001 Sony hit on the bright idea of compiling an album of their covers as *The Byrds Play The Songs Of Bob Dylan*, the CD contained sixteen of his compositions, recorded between 1965 and 1971. And that didn't include **The Ballad Of Easy Rider**, which Dylan co-wrote with McGuinn – Dylan famously refused to take a credit for the song, because he didn't like the ending of the film for which it was written.

McGuinn later played on Dylan's soundtrack to **Pat Garrett & Billy The Kid** and joined him on 1975's **Rolling Thunder** Tour.

---

cynicism and biting satire, offering up what the critic Andy Gill has described as "a surreal distorting-mirror to modern life and American history". There were stories in some of the songs. But they took absurd twists and turns that mocked the very concept of narrative continuity. Side one was all electric. Side two was essentially acoustic, apart from a few subtle but iridescent electric-guitar embellishments. But despite the fact that Dylan still had an acoustic guitar in his hands and a harmonica brace around his neck, even these songs were imbued with the rock'n'roll spirit.

By April, the half-electric and half-acoustic album was in the shops. It went to number six in America and the following month to number one in Britain, where something approaching Dylan-mania was happening, fuelled by the extraordinary tour, so brilliantly captured on film by D.A. Pennebaker in ***Don't Look Back*** (see pp.265–267). From the moment his plane touched down in London on April 26, Dylan conducted himself like the ringmaster of a surreal rock'n'roll circus. Asked what his message was at his first press conference on landing at Heathrow airport, he answered, "Keep a good head and always carry a light bulb."

His shows were still all-acoustic. But backstage Dylan was courted by the rock aristocracy, with members of **The Beatles** and **The Rolling**

Stones prominent among them. There was a drunken recording session with **John Mayall's Bluesbreakers**, who included **Eric Clapton**, and **Alan Price** of The Animals attached himself to the Dylan entourage for much of the trip. Dylan was a particular fan of the group's electric version of **The House Of The Rising Sun**, and their recording was a considerable influence on his own new direction.

Poor Joan Baez found herself totally frozen out in such company. She was not once invited on stage for the duets Dylan's folk-oriented audiences undoubtedly wanted to see. And she was subjected to some merciless banter from Dylan and his cruel sidekick Bob Neuwirth, some of which is captured in *Don't Look Back*. When Sara arrived halfway through the tour, it was the last straw for Baez. It was the first she even knew of her rival's existence and she immediately quit the tour. But the presence of Baez and the arrival of Sara still did not prevent Dylan from making a pass at **Marianne Faithfull** and having a fling with the 16-year-old **Dana Gillespie**.

Dylan arrived home in early June, to find he had his first number-one single with **Mr Tambourine Man** – albeit in a jangling folk-rock cover version by **The Byrds**. But Dylan already had something even more potent up his sleeve that was to take his transformation from folk hero to electric messiah a dramatic step further.

On June 15 and 16, 1965, he went into the Columbia studios in New York with a bunch of musicians including **Mike Bloomfield** on guitar and **Al Kooper** on organ, and cut the song that was to become his signature tune. "The Times They Are A-Changin'" had come to define the protest era, but with **Like A Rolling Stone**, Dylan created a milestone in pop history. Six minutes of rippling waves of organ, piano and guitar, it's as dense and portentous as anything ever dreamed up by Phil Spector, with Dylan's vocal delivering a magisterial put-down in a sour, offhand monotone that curled and twisted from the corner of his mouth with withering disdain.

The next step was to translate the dynamic electric studio sound to his stage act. And, as if to maximize the impact of his new rock'n'roll image, Dylan plugged in for the first time in front of a live audience at the most provocative place possible: the Newport Folk Festival.

The Newport Affair

On July 25, Dylan arrived on stage at the Newport Folk Festival looking more like a pop star dressed from a Carnaby Street boutique than a folk hero and, with an amplified blues band in tow, he was famously greeted by a quite extraordinary barrage of vituperation and hostility. Backed by Mike Bloomfield on guitar, Sam Ley on drums and Jerome Arnold on bass, plus Al Kooper on organ and Barry Goldberg on piano, the now legendary set consisted of just three songs: **Maggie's Farm, Like A Rolling Stone** (released that very week as a single) and **Phantom Engineer** (later to become "It Takes A Lot To Laugh, It Takes A Train To Cry").

However, the accepted view of what happened at Newport doesn't give the whole picture. For one thing, not everyone who was there claims that the reception was as universally negative as myth has it (see p.48). Furthermore, contrary to popular belief, Dylan did not arrive at Newport hellbent on confrontation with the folk purists. His electric performance was unscripted and unplanned until the night before, when he put together a pick-up band mostly assembled from the **Paul Butterfield Blues Band,** who were there to play their own set. It was undeniably intended to get up the noses of a certain section of the crowd. But it was a spontaneous gesture rather

What really happened at Newport?

Almost everybody who was there seems to have a different memory of what exactly happened at the Newport Folk Festival on July 25, 1965. The commonly accepted version is that Bob Dylan, the leader of the folk revival, the prince of protest and champion of real music against the commercial banalities of Tin Pan Alley, took the stage with a hot electric blues band and played three amplified songs of off-kilter white noise. He was greeted by howls of ferocious outrage from a large section of the audience who took it as a personal affront that their Woody Guthrie-inspired hobo should desert them for rock'n'roll Babylon. A shell-shocked Dylan was then forced to return to the stage and attempt to placate the crowd with acoustic versions of **It's All Over Now, Baby Blue** and **Mr Tambourine Man**.

Yet **Al Kooper**, who was playing organ in Dylan's band, has a different recollection. "The reason they booed is because he only played for fifteen minutes when everybody else played for 45 minutes to an hour and he was the headliner of the festival," Kooper insists. "They were feeling ripped off. Wouldn't you? They didn't give a shit about us being electric. They just wanted more." It's an interesting theory – but not one that explains why they booed Dylan throughout his brief set as well as at the end.

The truth is that both versions are probably right. According to **Paul Rothschild**, who was on the sound desk, the crowd was split down the middle: "It seemed everybody on my left wanted Dylan to get off the stage, everybody on my right wanted him to turn it up. And I did. I turned it up." Festival production manager **Joe Boyd** also felt there were two opposing camps: "You know, more and boo sound very similar if you have a whole crowd going more and boo. I think it was evenly divided between approbation and condemnation," he recalls.

How did Dylan take his hostile reception? Once again, it depends who you ask. His roadie **Jonathan Taplin** said, "I saw Dylan backstage from a little bit of a distance and he seemed to be crying." The footage of when he reappeared to sing "It's All Over Now Baby Blue", also seen in *No Direction Home*, would appear to confirm this, although it could conceivably be perspiration running down his cheeks. But Al Kooper claims he "was standing right next to Bob backstage and not only was he not crying, he was feeling good about having played electric". The likelihood is that he went through a gamut of different emotions. But, if he was upset, Dylan at least seemed to get over it pretty quickly. According to the late Mike Bloomfield: "The next night he was at this party and he's sitting next to this girl and her husband and he's got his hand right up her pussy and she's letting him do this and her husband's going crazy. So Dylan seemed quite untouched by it the next day."

In the footage of "Maggie's Farm" and "Like A Rolling Stone" included in the film *No Direction Home*, the boos from the audience are clearly audible. Maria Muldaur recalls in the film that about a third of the crowd were booing, while Dylan himself says he thought they were shouting out, "Are you with us?"

than a premeditated one. Indeed, it wasn't so much the boos that forced them off the stage after just fifteen minutes, nor was it the threats of veteran folkie and festival committee-member **Pete Seeger** to cut the power cable. The simple truth is that, having got together for the first time the night before, the band had only rehearsed three songs.

Whatever the reasons, it's odd that many in the Newport audience were so shocked. Had they not listened to *Bringing It All Back Home* and registered the fact that Dylan had already gone electric? Perhaps they had been sufficiently mollified by side two, with its acoustic versions of "Gates Of Eden", "It's Alright Ma (I'm Only Bleeding)" and "It's All Over Now, Baby Blue" to overlook the raucous rock'n'roll indiscretions of "Subterranean Homesick Blues", "Maggie's Farm" and "On The Road Again". Or perhaps they had simply not expected him so brazenly to flaunt his electric side at a folk festival.

Backstage Dylan was visibly shaken, according to most eye witnesses. After a lengthy pause, he was persuaded to return for a solo spot, and when the crowd saw him carrying not an electric guitar but an acoustic Gibson borrowed from Johnny Cash, many of those who had only a few minutes earlier shouted abuse cheered loudly in the belief that they had somehow won. They hadn't, of course. Dylan was the true victor and the experience put a steel in his soul and fed the vengeful streak that was undoubtedly part of his character at that time. Was he turning on the folkies who had booed him when four days later he recorded **Positively Fourth Street** with its opening line, "You've got a lot of nerve, to say you are my friend"? Of course he was.

Forming The Band

"Positively Fourth Street" was just one product of a week of furious writing and recording that followed Newport and, by August 4, with "Like A Rolling Stone" already at number two in the Billboard charts, *Highway 61 Revisited* had been completed. With **Bob Johnston** (a Nashville producer whose main claim to fame was working with Patti Page) behind the desk and Bloomfield and Kooper prominent on guitar and organ, respectively, the songs surged with a raw blues power that perfectly complemented the sardonic and surrealistic lyrics. "Half the people involved were studio musicians, and half weren't, so it's got that rough thing which Dylan loves," Al Kooper later recalled.

Meanwhile, Dylan was determined to build on what he had started at Newport and as soon as the recording of the album was complete he began rehearsing a new road band. Several of its members, including bassist Harvey Brooks and Al Kooper, came from his recent studio ensemble. But others came from **Ronnie Hawkins'** former backing band, who had greatly impressed Dylan when he saw them perform in a New Jersey club. They were called **Levon and The Hawks**, soon to become The Hawks and then **The Band** (see pp.50–51). Drummer **Levon Helm** and guitarist **Robbie Robertson** were immediately invited to join Dylan's new band, which made its debut at Forest Hills stadium at the end of August 1965, the same week that *Highway 61 Revisited* was released. Previewing six of the songs from the

Dylan and The Band

Dylan has played with literally hundreds of musicians over the past 40 years. But the alchemy that he and **The Band** conjured up was truly unique. The dream teaming was not the brainwave of some highly paid A&R man, but of **Mary Martin**, a young secretary who worked for Dylan's manager, Albert Grossman. She knew Dylan was looking for an electric band and she reckoned her fellow Canadians, **Levon and The Hawks**, were just the ticket. "Mary was a rather persevering soul as she hurried around the office on her job," Dylan told *Rolling Stone* in 1969. "She knew all the bands and singers from Canada and she kept pushing these guys The Hawks to me."

The Hawks had a history backing **Ronnie Hawkins**, a rabble-rousing rock'n'roller from Arkansas. With drummer **Levon Helm** as his henchman, Hawkins had moved up to Canada, where they then recruited **Robbie Robertson** on guitar, **Rick Danko** on bass, **Garth Hudson** on keyboards and the multi-talented **Richard Manuel**. But the group had split from Hawkins in 1964 and was playing a season at a Toronto place called Tony Marts in the summer of 1965 when Mary Martin called Helm between sets and asked if he and Robertson would be interested in backing Dylan, who had just done his first controversial electric set at Newport.

Robertson and Helm played with Dylan at his next two shows, one in New York and the second at the Hollywood Bowl, and he was impressed enough to fly to Toronto in mid-September to check out the rest of the band. He liked what he heard and, after a couple of all-night rehearsals, Dylan and The Hawks made their live debut ten days later in Austin, Texas. Over the next nine months, they made some of the fiercest and most exciting rock'n'roll ever played, but everywhere they went the pattern was the same: a solo acoustic set was ecstatically greeted; then Dylan brought on The Hawks and large sections of the audience booed.

Dylan appeared to enjoy the confrontation, but The Hawks were less convinced. Helm for one couldn't stand it. Although he would later rejoin, he quit in November 1965 to be replaced by **Mickey Jones**. The rest were kept going by the inner knowledge that the music they were making may not have been appreciated but nevertheless it had value. "We would listen to the tapes sometimes after the show, just to see what they were booing at, and we thought, God, it's not that bad," recalls Robertson, who grew so close to Dylan that the rest of the band dubbed him Barnacle Man. "It's not terrible. And nobody else sounds this way. It's got something. That was the only thing that enabled us to go on."

Following the motorcycle crash in July 1966 (see p.62), Dylan took eight years off from gigging. But **The Band** – as they soon became known – played an equally significant part in the next phase of his musical development. Throughout the summer of 1967, they worked with Dylan in a house they dubbed **Big Pink** in West Saugerties, upstate New York. The music they recorded there – known as *The Basement Tapes* – laid the groundwork for the musical roots movement that subsequently came to be known as Americana.

With Helm back in the fold, it was The Band that Dylan called on to back him on his occasional and exceedingly rare returns to the live stage, including a Woody Guthrie tribute concert in New York in autumn 1968 and the **Isle of Wight** festival in August 1969. But it was 1974 before they next toured together, by which time The Band had become a mighty name in their own right, with a series of seminal albums that included *Music From Big Pink* (1968), *The Band*

(1969), **Stage Fright** (1970), **Cahoots** (1971), the live set **Rock of Ages** (1972) and the covers collection **Moondog Matinee** (1973).

They reconvened with Dylan in Los Angeles in November 1973, backing him on his Planet Waves album and rehearsing for his first tour since 1966, which finally opened in Chicago in January 1974. The tour was captured on the live album **Before The Flood**, which also featured several of The Band's own songs.

Despite the success of the tour, The Band were never to work with Dylan again. The group released two further albums: 1975's **Northern Lights Southern Cross** and 1977's **Islands**. The latter appeared posthumously following The Band's farewell show, **The Last Waltz**, in November 1976. Dylan was among a glittering cast in attendance to pay tribute, fittingly providing the climax to both the show and the career of perhaps the world's most famous backing group.

Dylan with The Band's Richard Manuel

new album, there were boos for the electric set. But Robert Shelton gave the show a rave notice in *The New York Times*, while another reviewer memorably wrote: "Dylan used to sound like a lung cancer victim singing Woody Guthrie. Now he sounds like a Rolling Stone singing Immanuel Kant."

Anyhow, even if live audiences were still sceptical of Dylan's electric side, the release of

Visions of (the) Johanna:
Dylan at work recording *Highway 61 Revisited*

Highway 61 Revisited confirmed his position as the second-hottest property in pop music. Only The Beatles had ever bettered his achievement of eight songs (half of them covers by other artists) in the American Top 40 in the same week. And, as Dylan was embraced by a new pop audience, not all of his old Greenwich Village acquaintances deserted or denounced him. "With Highway 61 Revisited I knew he'd produced the most important and revolutionary album ever made," Phil Ochs said. "He's done something that's left the whole field ridiculously in back of him."

By September Dylan had a new backing band. Kooper had decided he didn't want to tour and so Dylan opted to hire not just Helm and Robertson from Levon and The Hawks but the entire band. After rehearsals in Toronto, they played their first historic gig in Austin on September 24 and entered a studio two weeks later to cut Dylan's next single, the non-album track **Won't You Please Crawl Out Your Window**.

He had made two albums that changed the face of rock music in less than six months and even Dylan, often his own sternest critic, admitted to some satisfaction: "I'm not gonna be able to make a record better than that one," he claimed. "Highway 61 is just too good. There's a lot of stuff on there that I would listen to." Yet there was arguably an even better album to come. Dylan married Sara in a secret ceremony attended only by Albert Grossman on November 22, but there was no time for a honeymoon as he had new songs to record. By the end of November he was back in the studio with The Band, cutting a song called "Freeze Out", soon to be renamed **Visions of Johanna**.

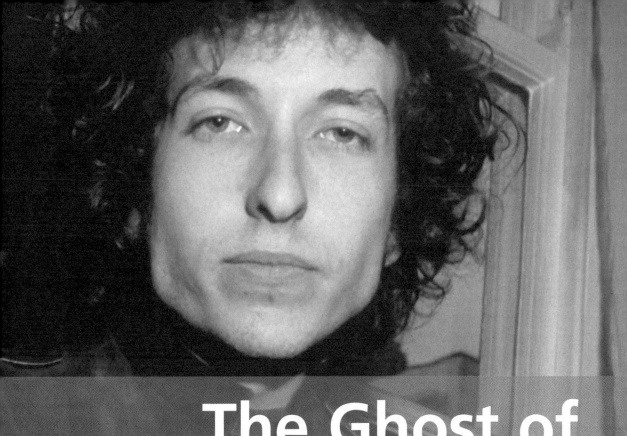

The Ghost of
Electricity
1966–69

"It's just development. We're always changing. You use new imagination and you get a new look."

Bob Dylan, New York City, January 1968

The Ghost of Electricity
1966–69

1966: That Thin, Wild Mercury Sound

"The closest I ever got to the sound I hear in my mind was on the Blonde on Blonde album. It's that thin, wild mercury sound. It's metallic and bright gold, with whatever that conjures up." Bob Dylan

Dylan and The Hawks went back into the studio in January 1966 to begin recording a new album. Yet, for some reason, something wasn't right. On stage, they were beginning to gel wonderfully as a unit, with a strong sense of common purpose generated by the boos and catcalls that greeted them most nights. Yet in the studio progress was slow and Dylan was dissatisfied with the sound. Al Kooper was drafted back in on organ and they managed one useable cut that would prove to be a highlight of *Blonde on Blonde*: the melodramatic and magnificent "(Sooner Or Later) One Of Us Most Know". But Dylan was still unhappy.

On Bob Johnston's suggestion, during a week's break from touring in the middle of February, he turned up in **Nashville** at Columbia's **Music Row studios**. From the earlier sessions, only

Robbie Robertson and Al Kooper were retained. Johnson put his Nashville contacts to good use and recruited an A-list of the best country session musicians money could buy, including guitarists **Wayne Moss** and **Jerry Kennedy**, multi-instrumentalist **Charlie McCoy**, **Joe South** on bass, **Kenny Buttrey** on drums and the blind pianist **Hargus Pig Robbins**. It was an extraordinary thing to do. By early 1966, Dylan was just about the hippest human being on planet rock. Nashville, by contrast, was anything *but* cool, a music factory where the musicians punched the clock and churned out formulaic country-and-western hits with a paint-by-numbers predictability.

To the musicians Johnson employed, Dylan was like a creature from another planet. As Kenny Buttrey told biographer Bob Spitz, "I

The Life

Dylan and drugs

Dylan first smoked **marijuana** in Minneapolis in 1960. He took his first **LSD** trip in April 1964. He famously turned The Beatles on. And he took industrial quantities of **amphetamines** simply to keep going. In 1969 he was asked if drugs had influenced his songs. "No, not the writing of them, but it did keep me up there to pump 'em out," he admitted.

Yet the debate about Dylan's drug use is ultimately pointless. Of course he was an enthusiastic user. It was the 1960s, it was in his temperament to experiment, and anything that pushed open the doors of perception was always going to be eagerly embraced. "Opium, hash and pot – now those things aren't drugs, they just bend your mind a little," he told *Playboy* in 1966. "I think everybody's mind should be bent once in a while."

But how heavily into drugs did he get? Certainly, by his 1965 tour of Britain, pills and pot were no longer doing it for Dylan. According to eyewitness Marianne Faithfull, **methedrine** had become the drug of choice, although he was almost certainly snorting rather than shooting it. The singer Nico, who knew a thing or two about hard drugs, also described Dylan at the time as completely drugged up.

By the time of the 1966 world tour, Dylan's drug consumption was huge. He was taking them for recreation and he was also taking them on prescription. "It takes a lot of medicine to keep up this pace," he told Robert Shelton. "A concert tour like this has almost killed me." Bootleg tapes of his acoustic set on the Australian leg of the tour make it pretty obvious that he was "narcoticised up to the eyeballs", as biographer Clinton Heylin put it. And, after a short intermission, he would emerge for the electric set pumped up and howling at the moon.

Heylin believes that before the show he was taking heroin, probably snorted, which accounted for his mesmerised self-absorption in the first half of the concert. Then a speedball of heroin and cocaine ingested in the break explained his up-beat second-half transformation. D.A. Pennebaker, who filmed the British dates in May 1966, recalls Dylan scratching all the time (a classic junkie trait) and staying up for days on end without any sleep. Somewhat naively, he did not at the time comprehend the reason. Much later he was forced to admit, "I may have made a movie about drugs without realising it."

The chemical intake temporarily allowed Dylan to transcend the pressures, vacillating wildly between a kind of narcotic sleep-walk and bursts of manic energy. He knew he couldn't keep it up and the retreat to Woodstock from July 1966 onwards was an essential part of a healing process that had to address both the physical and psychic imbalances his drug use had created.

Dylan continued to use drugs in later years. Cocaine, for example, was in plentiful supply both on the 1974 tour with The Band and on the Rolling Thunder cross-country jaunt in 1975–76. But the theory that he has sustained a junkie habit for the last thirty years – which still holds currency on the wilder fringes of Dylanology – is well wide of the mark.

"I never got hooked on any kind of drug," Dylan emphatically told *Rolling Stone* in 1984. On the road, in the white-hot crucible of 1965–66, he had come dangerously close. But he cleaned up of his own volition and – in his mind and by his own loose definition – the 1984 statement is probably more or less true. And, at the end of the day, it is frankly nobody's business but his own.

have to admit, I thought the guy had blown a gasket, and we were basically humouring him." Charlie McCoy conceded that he also won-

dered "what in the hell this guy was trying to pull". And they were astonished to find that Dylan thought nothing of keeping them waiting

*"We were playing so out of this world,
we didn't even know what the fuck we were doing."* Robbie Robertson

around in the studio for hours while he worked on songs. "They would be sitting there for maybe ten hours while he went into the studio and wrote," Kooper said. However, "nobody bitched or complained or rolled their eyes. That was the tempo of the sessions in Nashville, that anything could happen, and these guys were fine with that. Their temperaments were fabulous – they were the most calm, at-ease guys I'd ever worked with." But then why would they complain? They were being paid by the hour, whether they were working or sitting around drinking and playing cards. Still, when they were called upon, they certainly worked for their money, cutting lengthy and complex epics such as **Visions Of Johanna** and **Sad Eyed Lady Of The Lowlands** in single takes. Further sessions were fitted in between tour dates in February and March, as Dylan and his improbable Nashville crew refined what he called "that thin, wild, mercury sound".

Dylan relied heavily on Robertson and Kooper as his go-betweens with the other musicians. "Bob had a piano put in his hotel room, and during the day he would write," Kooper recalls. "And as there were no cassette machines in those days, I would sit and play the piano for him, over and over, while he sat and wrote. For the sessions at night, I would go in and teach the first song to the band, then he would arrive an hour later, and the band would be ready to play. These were guys that knew how to play

together, and were incredibly versatile. I'd never seen anything like that."

Against all the odds, the results were amazing – "like taking two cultures and smashing them together with a huge explosion," as Kooper put it. Released in May 1966 as the first-ever rock'n'roll double album, *Blonde On Blonde* (see p.174) had a sophistication, controlled power and sheer lyricism that took Dylan's art to new heights. It reached number nine in the American charts and number three in Britain, where by the time of the album's release Dylan was already embarking on what would prove to be one of the most tumultuous tours in the history of rock music.

The 66 World Tour: "Play fucking loud!"

With *Blonde On Blonde* completed and Mickey Jones deputising for the still-absent Levon Helm on drums, Dylan and The Band headed off on a world tour, starting in Australia, where they played their opening concert on April 13. A remarkable bootleg of a wasted but inspired Dylan a week later in Melbourne (where he announced that "Visions of Johanna" had been re-titled "Mother Revisited") captures the first indications of what Cameron Crowe has called "the otherworldly quality" which the tour rapidly assumed. By the time they arrived in Europe three weeks later for the opening concert in Copenhagen, Dylan sounded like he was delicately poised somewhere between incandescent genius and psychic meltdown.

It was partly the drugs (see p.56). He was restless and manically creative, eating and sleeping little. "It takes a lot of medicine to keep up this pace," he admitted to Robert Shelton in March 1966. But his heightened state of mind was equally due to the adrenaline generated by the polarized reactions his music was creating, and the energy he was drawing from the confrontation. There had been boos in America but no mass walkouts, as had happened during the electric half of his concerts in Australia. And the hostility gathered pace when Dylan arrived in Europe. In Dublin on May 5 the audience slow-handclapped the electric set from the start and there were shouts of "traitor" and "throw out the backing group". A censorious *Melody Maker* critic joined in the disapproval. "It was unbelievable to see a hip-swinging Dylan trying to look and sound like Mick Jagger," he complained. "For most it was the night of the big let down."

The attacks grew even more vituperative when Dylan hit **London**. He gave his by now usual enigmatic and evasive press conference, and the British press worked itself up into one of its hypocritically self-righteous lathers. Jonathan King attacked Dylan for his "downright bad manners" while *Disc* and *Music Echo* complained that he was "rude and uncooperative". The first British concert, on May 10 at Bristol's **Colston Hall**, was savaged by reviewers and the electric set was greeted by the walkouts that were becoming characteristic. One newspaper critic accused Dylan of "sacrificing

A break between the jeers: Dylan strolls round Elsinore, Denmark, on the European leg of the 1966 world tour

lyric and melody to the god of big beat", while a letter in another paper denounced the concert as "a funeral", in which Dylan had been buried in "a grave of deafening drums".

Cardiff, the next night, proved more receptive but the **Birmingham Odeon** show on May 12 was another debacle. Dylan and The Hawks by all accounts played magnificently, yet there were more walkouts amid cries of "traitor", "phoney" and "Yank, go home". Two nights later in Liverpool, Dylan hit back in classic fashion. When someone seated on the balcony shouted, "Where's the poet in you?" and "What's happened to your conscience?", he acidly responded: "There's a guy up there looking for a saint."

The adverse reaction continued in **Leicester** the following night. The first acoustic half of the show was cheered but when Dylan reappeared with The Hawks there were whistles and the by now obligatory walkout. On May 16, at the **Sheffield Gaumont,** the fire brigade and police searched the building for two hours after a hoax bomb warning (whether courtesy of a crank or an outraged folk purist we shall never know). Then it was on to **Manchester** for a much-bootlegged gig – for years erroneously credited to the Royal Albert Hall – that was eventually released officially in 1998 and became infamous for the Judas incident (see box below). By now, the press and sections of the audience were behaving as "a conformist, Neanderthal mob", as Robert Shelton put it. They were out to crucify Dylan and each

The man who shouted "Judas!"

It is one of the most electrifying moments in the annals of rock'n'roll. "Judas!" yells a voice to cheers from the audience before a laconic and wired-sounding Bob Dylan retorts, "I don't believe you." He strums the first chord of the next song and, with perfect timing, adds "You're a liar!" As he tells the band to "play fuckin' loud", they launch into a blistering version of **Like A Rolling Stone**. The recording of the incident, which took place at **Manchester Free Trade Hall** on May 17, 1966, for years enjoyed legendary status among bootleg collectors, although it was for a long time erroneously attributed to a concert at London's Albert Hall ten days later.

All these years on, its sheer, edgy intensity still makes the hairs on the back of the neck stand on end. But the perpetrator of the Judas slur had no idea of his notoriety until 32 years later when the live recording was officially released. As he read a review of the **Live 1966** album in the *Toronto Sun* in October 1998, something stirred in the memory of Keith Butler, a Keel University student back in 1966, who had emigrated to Canada in 1975. As he read on, he suddenly realised that an event he had barely even thought about in more than three decades had earned him an infamous place in rock'n'roll history.

He came forward and his identity was confirmed by his youthful presence in the film of the 1966 tour, **Eat The Document**. Interviewed outside the hall after he had walked out in disgust, a 20-year-old Butler can be seen declaring, "Any pop group could produce better rubbish than that. It was a bloody disgrace. He's a traitor." In 1999 Butler participated in a BBC Radio documentary about the concert and was asked what he now thought of his behaviour. "I kind of think, you silly young bugger," he replied.

Tarantula

In some of his earliest interviews, Dylan talked vaguely about unspecified novels and plays he was writing. Most likely it was more myth-spinning, like his claims that he had worked in a circus and run away when he was ten. But ever since he had read and been captivated by Woody Guthrie's autobiography **Bound For Glory**, he had dreamed of writing his own book, and in late 1964 he signed a lucrative publishing deal with Macmillan.

For some six months or so from autumn 1964 into spring 1965, Dylan worked flat out on the project, producing far more material than he needed in a stream-of-consciousness style. He wrote at Joan Baez's house in Carmel, leaving dozens of pages of typewritten manuscript behind that he never bothered to reclaim. And he worked on the book at Albert Grossman's house in Woodstock. Early extracts even appeared in the magazines *Sing Out!* and *Pageant*, although neither published sample made the final manuscript.

In January 1965, he told *Sing Out!* the book was called **Walk Down Crooked Highway**. In March that year, he informed a reporter it was now called **Bob Dylan Off The Record** (a title that sounds as if it was inspired by the recently published *John Lennon*

In His Own Write). By April when he began his British tour, the book was almost finished and he had come up with the title **Tarantula**.

The cover of a pirated copy of *Tarantula* from 1970

concert on the tour was becoming another station of the cross.

But Dylan hit back. "Oh come on, these are all protest songs" and "It's the same stuff as always, can't you hear?", he told the hecklers. Then, in a long monologue that seemed to sum up his feelings about the entire tour, he rounded upon his critics: "We've been playing this music since we were ten years old. Folk

music was just an interruption, which was very useful. If you don't like it that's fine. This is not English music you are listening to. You really haven't heard American music before... You can take it or leave it. If there's something you disagree with that's great. I'm sick of people asking what does it mean? It means nothing." In Liverpool he even challenged one heckler to "Come up here and say that!" The bouncers

The problem was that much as Dylan's intellectual vanity was drawn to the *idea* of writing a book, in reality he had little to say that he was not saying better in his songs. What poured forth was unstructured speed-freak jive, which owed something to the beats and perhaps a little to the French symbolists, but ultimately constituted little more than a series of in-jokes in unpunctuated free verse, comprehensible only to the author and a tiny inner circle of friends. By late 1965 he himself was already doubting the value of what he had written. He told Nat Hentoff that he had asked himself, "Is this gonna be *the* novel? *The* statement? Is this my message?" Then he answered his own self-doubts: "No matter how many pages – I had about 500 pages of it – I said no, of course not. That's bullshit. This is nothing."

When asked by others about the book he took to increasingly vague descriptions – "it's about spiders, it's an insect book … a book of confusions, tiny little sayings, a splash on the wall … I don't really know what it's about." Years later after its publication, Howard Sounes came up with perhaps the most accurate description of all, describing *Tarantula* as "137 pages of liner notes for a Dylan album that did not exist".

Yet as Dylan turned against the idea of publishing the book, he found he was trapped both by the expectations of his public and the contract he had signed with his publisher. Despite his misgivings, which he does not appear to have shared with Macmillan, they printed up his manuscript into galley proofs and pressed ahead with preparations for publication. Dylan took receipt of the galleys and promised to make final changes within two weeks – and did nothing. He later admitted that when he read the text he was simply "embarrassed" at the nonsense he had written. But Macmillan had already geared up its publicity machine and had even manufactured promotional *Tarantula* button badges and shopping bags.

The **motorcycle crash** on July 29, 1966 (see p.62) was Dylan's let-out. *Tarantula* went unpublished for the next five years, although copies pirated from the galleys were soon in widespread circulation. They revealed a work of trifling account and when Dylan eventually consented to *Tarantula*'s **official publication** in 1971, nobody any longer cared. By then even Dylan's most die-hard fans had wised up to the fact that being the greatest songwriter in the world doesn't make you an author, any more than being the planet's top soccer player means you will be any good at tennis.

prevented the angry fan from taking up the offer.

Scotland was marginally better – or at least Glasgow was, where the traitor-yellers were drowned out by Dylan supporters. But the next night in Edinburgh a section of the audience, in a prearranged protest, produced their own harmonicas in an attempt to drown out the band. And on May 24, his 25th birthday,

Dylan played L'Olympia in **Paris,** where the French even jeered his acoustic set. At one point he told the audience to "Go to the bowling hall until I'm finished." Later, during the electric set, he announced, "Don't worry, I'm just as eager to finish and leave as you are." *Le Figaro*'s review echoed the British press with the headline "The Fall Of An Idol". The concert was recorded for French radio but never broadcast. Reportedly it was vetoed by Dylan in a fit of pique over his reception.

Then it was back to Britain for two final cathartic nights at the **Royal Albert Hall** on May 26 and 27, and the biggest organized walkouts of the tour. Hundreds streamed for the exits when The Hawks appeared, but The Beatles were there in the audience offering support and could be heard cheering from their box, and telling the hecklers to shut up. George

This Wheel's On Fire: the motorcycle crash

When news filtered out to the world of Dylan's motorcycle accident at the end of July 1966, press reports variously claimed that he had been rendered unconscious, broken his neck and almost been killed. Fans feared the worst. At the other extreme, conspiracy theorists have postulated that there was never any accident at all and that it was all a ruse to get Dylan out of contractual obligations over his book, the *Eat The Document* film and further touring commitments being lined up by Albert Grossman. The truth appears to lie somewhere in between: the available evidence suggests that there was an *incident*, but that it was nowhere near as serious as has often been claimed.

This much we now know: on the morning of Friday July 29, 1966, Dylan left the home of the Grossmans in Bearsville, Woodstock, on his motorcycle, with Sara following in a car. A short time later, Sara returned with Bob in the car. As he lay on the floor of the front porch, Sara explained that he had slipped off the bike. Sally Grossman (the woman on the cover of *Bringing It All Back Home*) was back at the house. She spoke for the first time about the incident to Howard Sounes for his 2001 biography, *Down The Highway*, reporting that Dylan was "moaning and groaning but that there were no visible signs of injury".

Sally believes the accident happened on Glasco Turnpike, the road from Bearsville to Dylan's house at Byrdcliffe. Other friends claim it happened on Striebel Road, right outside the Grossmans' property. Certainly,

it can't have been far from the house: Sally was on the phone to her husband Albert when the Dylans left and was still on the same conversation when they returned.

No ambulance was called and there is no police report of an accident. Sara did not even take Dylan to hospital. Instead, she drove him to the house of Dr Ed Thaler in Middletown, some fifty miles away. Dylan stayed with Thaler for six weeks, fuelling theories that he was actually being treated for drug addiction and was undergoing detoxification. Thaler has since denied this suggestion.

Dylan himself has given various versions of what occurred. Somewhat melodramatically, he told journalist and friend Al Aronowitz that as he hurtled through the air he was certain he was going to be killed and his whole life had flashed in front of him. In 1987, he talked of being blinded by the morning sun and stomping on the brake pedal too hard with the result that the rear wheel had locked. What is undeniable is that the crash – whether principally physical or psychological in nature – afforded Dylan a much-needed opportunity to slow down and reassess his life. "I was pretty wound up before that accident happened," he said later. "I probably would have died if I had kept on going the way I had been."

In *Chronicles* he devotes barely two lines to the crash: "I had been in a motorcycle accident and I'd been hurt. But I recovered. Truth was that I wanted to get out of the rat race."

Harrison denounced those who walked out as "idiots" who didn't understand the real Dylan. But Ray Coleman in *Melody Maker* thought the performance was "a shamble of noise" and *The Daily Telegraph* reported that whole rows sat with scarcely a sign of applause and described Dylan as "a performer who does not care whether he communicates or not".

Many years later Robbie Robertson described the tour to this author. "I think that experience toughened my skin. They booed us everywhere we went. My memory is that they were so angry, so upset, saying this is horrible and throwing junk and garbage at us. We had to stand there and let the stuff bounce off us. We kept on playing and we'd go on to the next place and they would do the same thing again. And that happened all over the world." Robertson painted a picture of a besieged Dylan and entourage virtually living in a bunker. "After those shows we were lonely guys. Nobody wanted to hang out with us. We made tapes for our own sanity. We recorded the shows and then we would play them back and we'd say this isn't that bad. It doesn't sound

that terrible. We had to tell ourselves they were wrong and we were right. We stood up against the whole world. Now everybody says they knew it was great all along."

Angry and exhausted, The Hawks returned home to America while Dylan and Sara recuperated with a brief Spanish holiday. Back in New York, Bob spent several days looking at the rushes of the film shot on tour by D.A. Pennebaker, who had also made *Don't Look Back* a year earlier. Sadly the resulting hour-long colour documentary, *Eat The Document*, has rarely been screened in public (see p.327), although extracts from it can be seen in *No Direction Home*.

Then on July 29, he crashed his Triumph 650 Bonneville motorcycle on a back road in Woodstock. How seriously he was injured is the subject of some controversy (see opposite). But, with the benefit of hindsight, he was living his life at such an unsustainable pace that far from almost costing him his life as was reported at the time, the accident and the opportunity it presented to get off the merry-go-round may have been the only thing that saved him from an early grave.

1967–68: The Woodstock Years

"Have a bunch of kids who call me pa, That must be what its all about" Sign On The Window, Bob Dylan, 1971

On the surface, the significance attached to Dylan's motorcycle crash in July 1966 may seem disproportionate. "Man Falls Off Motorbike, Not Badly Hurt" is hardly a world-changing headline. Yet it was a symbolic

moment in Dylan's career. When he re-emerged after the accident, he looked different, his voice sounded different and the music he made was also dramatically different.

It was the late spring of 1967 before the

outside world got another glimpse of Dylan. Today, of course, journalists, TV crews and paparazzi would have been camped outside Hi Lo Ha, his Byrdcliffe home in Woodstock. Yet, in those gentler times, the media appeared to respect his desire for privacy and nobody made any real attempt to check out the rumours that continued to circulate that he had been horribly injured in the crash. *The New York Daily News* even hinted that he would never perform again, so badly had he been disfigured – yet still didn't send anyone to snoop around and check out the claim. When journalist Michaël Iachetta turned up in Woodstock, in May 1967, he was the first journalist to see Dylan in ten months. "It's great to see you're up and around and the rumours aren't true," he blurted out.

Considering what Dylan had been through, it's impossible not to think of his motorcycle crash as falling off a roller coaster. With his mind seemingly racing at a thousand miles an hour, in little more than a year he had recorded three albums that constitute probably the greatest trilogy in the history of rock'n'roll. He had spent much of the time zonked to the eyeballs, both on lawfully prescribed stimulants to stave off fatigue and drugs of his own, less conventional prescription. He had dragged himself round the world making some of the greatest music ever heard to audiences who often jeered in his face. It was a traumatic time and it's small wonder that by late 1966 he had decided a complete volte face was in order.

He came closest to admitting the kind of psychic meltdown that had been going on a dozen years later during a round of interviews to promote the film *Renaldo & Clara*. "I was straining pretty hard and couldn't have gone on living that way much longer," he said. "The fact that I made it through what I did is pretty miracu-

Painter Man

Dylan met his neighbour Bruce Dorfman every morning when the pair walked their daughters to the school bus. Dorfman was a painter and soon they got to discussing art. When Sara Dylan bought Bob a box of oil paints for his 27th birthday, he asked Dorfman to give him informal lessons.

At the first lesson Dylan arrived with a book of Vermeer reproductions and announced he wanted to paint in a similar style. He was disappointed with the results and the next day returned with a book of Monet reproductions. The results were, in Dorfman's words, a mess.

Next he turned up with a book of Vincent Van Gogh paintings and managed a reasonable landscape in the style, but still wasn't satisfied. After skipping a day, he returned, this time with a Marc Chagall book.

This is the one that worked. Dorfman later told Dylan biographer Howard Sounes, "It was perfect, because you had all these multi-layered images – things flying, things walking, clocks flying, rabbits with green faces. It was all there. Chagall was it. He made the connection."

And so the extraordinary style of painting that was soon to grace the covers of The Band's *Music From Big Pink* and his own *Self Portrait* album was born.

lous. But you know, sometimes you get too close to something and you got to get away from it to be able to see it. And something like that happened to me at the time." The pre-crash period had seen him pursuing knowledge through what Rimbaud had called "the derangement of the senses". After such deliberate psychic bombardment, Dylan subsequently came to call his period of retreat "the amnesia".

Immediately after the accident, Dylan was receiving only the closest friends and key business associates. The filmmaker D.A. Pennebaker called on him only days after the accident, and found him walking around but in a brace. "He didn't appear very knocked out," he reported. "But he was very pissed off at everybody." Three weeks after the accident, Allen Ginsberg arrived with a box of books, including volumes of poetry by Sir Thomas Wyatt, Campion, Emily Dickinson, Rimbaud, Lorca, Apollinaire, Blake and Whitman. In addition to reading widely, Dylan also took up painting (see opposite).

When **Michael Iachetta** turned up to interview him almost ten months after the motorcycle accident, Dylan described a process that today sounds very like therapy, although it appears to have been of the self-help variety. "What I've been doin' mostly is seeing only a few close friends, reading little

Dylan the family man: with Jesse, 1968

The Life

> *"We were all up there sort of drying out, making music and watchin' time go by. So in the meantime, we made this record. Actually it wasn't a record, it was just songs which we'd come to this basement and recorded."* Bob Dylan, 1975

'bout the outside world, porin' over books by people you've never heard of, thinking about where I'm goin' and why I'm runnin' and am I mixed up too much and what I am knowin' and what am I givin' and what am I takin'," he said.

Dylan was seeking stability in his life for the first time since he had been a child, and, seeking refuge from the world in his marriage to **Sara**, he threw himself wholeheartedly into the role of contented family man. By 1967, in addition to **Maria** – Sara's 5-year-old daughter from her first marriage – the couple had a 1-year-old-son, **Jesse**, and another child on the way. Significantly, Bob also sought a rapprochement with his parents. He took Sara to see his old boyhood home and in 1969 even attended a high-school reunion, the first time he had done so in the decade since he had left Minnesota. "What I was fantasizing about was a 9-to-5 existence. A house on a tree-lined block with a white picket fence, pink roses in the backyard," he claimed in *Chronicles*. "That would have been nice. That was my deepest dream." Late in the book he added: "My family was my light and I was going to protect that light at all costs."

But the chaos of his life in the mid-1960s had generated an astonishing burst of creativity. The question he now faced as an artist was

would his new-found domesticity and stability blunt that creativity? Ironically, according to the number of copyrights taken out by his publisher, 1967 turned out to be his most prolific year as a songwriter, but they were songs of a very different nature from what had gone before. And it was to be some time before we were aware of the 100-plus songs he recorded with The Band during the summer and fall of 1967.

Music from Big Pink

It was a visit in the summer of 1967 from writer and old friend Al Aronowitz that first alerted the world to what Dylan was up to in Woodstock. After Dylan allowed him to sit in on a jam session with The Band, Aronowitz wrote an article in *Cheetah* magazine in which he revealed that, in a renewed burst of prolific creativity, Dylan was not only writing again but turning out "up to ten songs a week". It was the first published reference to what were to become known as *The Basement Tapes*.

Rick Danko, Robbie Robertson and **Richard Manuel** from The Band – as they were about to become known – had arrived in Woodstock in February 1967. Still on Dylan's payroll, their presence was initially to shoot further scenes for the movie *Eat The Document*, to supplement the scenes they had already shot on the 1966 world tour.

But inevitably their attention soon switched to music.

Every morning Dylan would walk Maria to the school bus stop. Then sometime around noon he would drive the short distance over to **Big Pink**, the house (so named because it was painted the colour of a strawberry milkshake) that The Band had rented in the nearby hamlet of West Saugerties from a local restaurant-owner. Danko, Manuel and **Garth Hudson** had moved into the house and set up a rehearsal and recording room in the basement with equipment borrowed from Peter, Paul and Mary. Robertson and his girlfriend, in search of a little more privacy, took a place down the road. Dylan would turn up most days for the next seven or eight months, with short breaks during the summer when Sara gave birth to their daughter **Anna Lea** and for a visit by Dylan's parents (almost certainly the last occasion he saw his father alive).

Down in the Big Pink basement, Garth Hudson set up a two-track reel-to-reel recorder with four mics mixed down to a stereo pair, with the sound leaking from one mic to another. It was basic, to say the least. But, recording with the windows open to let in the spring air, and with a dog called Hamlet either roaming the studio or asleep on the floor, they began working on a vast collection of songs. In addition to Dylan's own new compositions, there were dozens of old folk ballads plus covers of songs by the Stanley Brothers, Johnny Cash, John Lee Hooker and others. The Band were astonished at just how many songs Dyl knew, and they added a few of their

gestions. The sessions were relaxed, convivial and pleasantly stoned on "reefer run amok", as Robertson put it.

What emerged was utterly different from the awesome racket that had so offended hardcore folk fans on the 1965–66 tours. Many of the songs had a mysterious, musty, olde-worlde flavour, drawing together strands of folk, country, blues and gospel music that was totally out of step with the spirit of the times. In its way, it was as revolutionary as Dylan's electric heresy. "Psychedelic rock was taking over the universe and we were singing these homespun ballads," as Dylan himself later observed.

"It was just a routine," recalls Robertson. "We would play music every single day. There was no particular reason for it. We weren't making a record. We were just fooling around. The purpose was whatever comes into anybody's mind, we'll put it down on this shitty little tape recorder. The idea was for The Band just to have our little clubhouse, where everybody could go every day, hang around, play a little music, work on some songs, without disturbing anybody."

Garth Hudson paints a similarly informal picture: "We were doing seven, eight sometimes 15 songs a day. So ballads and traditional so would make up as h melody, he'd e then m typewriter. But some of the best songs were more or less improvised on the spot.

Some number were recorded away from Big Pink, either in the "red room" at Dylan's home in Byrdcliffe or at the home of Clarence Schmidt, the "Man Of The Mountain" (an eccentric stone mason and would-be architect who they befriended). Eventually, Dylan ended up with more than a hundred recordings, perhaps a third of which were his own compositions. He lodged them with his publisher, Dwarf Music, and even before the end of 1967, the songs were appearing in cover versions by other artists. **Peter, Paul and Mary** were first out of the blocks, covering "Too Much Of Nothing" in November 1967. **Manfred Mann** recorded "Quinn The Eskimo (The Mighty Quinn)". **The Byrds** covered "You Ain't Goin' Nowhere". And **Julie Driscoll, Brian Auger and The Trinity** had a hit with "This Wheel's On Fire".

Even though the sessions were recorded in primitive fashion, with no thought of making an album, the songs possess a warmth and intimacy that is unique in Dylan's work. A selection of them was belatedly released as *The Basement Tapes* in 1975, although it represented only a fraction of what they had recorded. But, long before then, a batch of the songs had been circulating illicitly on *Great White Wonder* (see p.248), the world's first bootleg album, which hit the streets in 1969. The unauthorized album was boosted by a campaign in *Rolling Stone*, which had run a cover story on "the missing Bob Dylan

Tapes Should Be Released". More of the Big Pink recordings made it on to bootleg in 1986 and a third, larger batch appeared in 1990.

There were two outcomes of the Big Pink recordings. The first was the process of what Robertson called Dylan "educating us a little": this vast treasure-trove of non-rock'n'roll led The Band to discover a rich vein of roots-tinged American music, something which came to fruition on their own hugely influential 1968 debut album, *Music From Big Pink*.

The second outcome was that – after the long creative limbering-up of *The Basement Tapes* – Dylan felt ready to make a "proper" record again. However, there was also a more mercenary reason for waiting 18 months between *Blonde On Blonde* and its follow-up. Dylan's contract with Columbia was up for renewal, and he and Albert Grossman were anxious for it to be renegotiated on more favourable terms. There was a million-dollar deal from MGM on the table, but Dylan eventually re-signed with Columbia at a dramatically enhanced 10 percent royalty on July 1, 1967. The way was now clear for the next album.

Drifters, Hobos, Immigrants and Saints

Dylan began work on *John Wesley Harding* in Nashville, on October 17, 1967. He was still recording simultaneously with The Band up at Big Pink. But the idea of returning to the scene of his *Blonde On Blonde* triumphs appears to have come once again from producer Bob Johnston, who visited Dylan in Woodstock in September. He found him uncommunicative but ascertained that Dylan was ready to make another record. This time the words were mostly written before he arrived in Nashville and drummer Kenny Buttrey and bassist Charlie McCoy, the only musicians retained from the *Blonde On Blonde* sessions, found a very different and considerably calmer Dylan than the fright-wigged hipster from another planet who had so baffled them less than two years earlier.

With **Pete Drake**'s pedal steel on two tracks supporting Dylan's own guitar, piano and harmonica, the album was finished by mid-November. The dozen songs took only three days to record, in sessions totalling little more than nine hours. "We went in and knocked them out like demos. It seemed to be the rougher the better," Buttrey recalls. At the beginning of December, Dylan played the tapes to Robertson and asked him and Garth Hudson to embellish the sparse tracks. To his credit, Robertson declined, telling Dylan the album didn't need to be "hot-rodded" and its straightforward honesty sounded fine the way it was. Dylan was convinced and the unadorned *John Wesley Harding* arrived in the shops in the commercially dead period between Christmas and New Year.

Even the timing of its release seemed to reflect its wilfully uncommercial nature. "I asked Columbia to release it with no publicity and no hype because this was the season of hype," Dylan later said. But his absence from the public stage had only served to heighten his mystique and the album, with all its shuffling modesty, went to number two in the American album charts and had two spells totalling 13 weeks at number one in Britain.

There is a common thread between *The Basement Tapes* and *John Wesley Harding* (a transition that has been likened by Clinton Heylin to that between Shakespeare's *The Winter's Tale* and *The Tempest*). But, although they share a similar distance from the modern world, the two records are very different in mood. While the Big Pink recordings are characterised by jovial wit and informal humour, *John Wesley Harding* is far more austere. And while several of the songs on *The Basement Tapes* contained references to holy salvation – including "I Shall Be Released" and "Sign On The Cross" – the religious themes on *John Wesley Harding* are far more explicit, with a host of biblical images drawn from both Old and New Testaments in a series of terse and even spooky parables.

Some have seen the record as Dylan's countermanifesto to the Baroque ornamentations of *Sgt. Pepper's Lonely Hearts Club Band*, others as a pointed rejection of his own recent "wild mercury sound" and a return to his folk roots. In reality, it is neither: *John Wesley Harding* is not a reaction against anything, but a reflection of Dylan's growth and his changing preoccupations and concerns.

The album's mood of austerity can only have been heightened by the news, two weeks before Dylan began recording, that **Woody Guthrie** had died of Huntington's chorea. Although

The Dylan–Cash Sessions

Bob Dylan had been a **Johnny Cash** fan since his teens, when he first heard the records the country star cut at Sam Phillips' Sun studios in Memphis. They first met at the Newport Folk Festival in 1964, when both men were so excited by the encounter that in his autobiography Cash reported they had jumped up and down on the bed in his motel room like kids. The following year, Cash was again on hand backstage at Newport to support Dylan when he was booed for going electric. It was Cash's guitar Dylan borrowed when he was pushed back out on stage to placate the crowd with a couple of acoustic numbers. And the country singer also wrote to the folk magazine *Broadside*, demanding that the critics should "Shut up… and let him sing!"

By 1969, they were old friends and when, in Nashville, it turned out that Cash was in the adjoining studio to the one in which Dylan was making **Nashville Skyline**, it was the most logical thing in the world for them to record together. They laid down eighteen songs, with producer Bob Johnson calling out requests. There was talk of a Dylan/Cash album as both shared the same record company. But in the end,

only **Girl From The North Country**, which appeared on *Nashville Skyline*, and **One Too Many Mornings**, which appeared in an NBC documentary on Cash, were ever released.

A few months later, Dylan made one of his very rare TV appearances on Cash's ABC show, recorded at Nashville's Ryman Auditorium. Again they performed "Girl From The North Country" together. And Cash also penned a liner-note-in-verse for *Nashville Skyline*, in which he revealed himself to be a somewhat less accomplished poet than Dylan: "This man can rhyme the tick of time, The edge of pain, the what of sane."

Although the quality of the duets album was deemed too unpolished to release, Dylan retained a huge respect for The Man In Black, complaining after his own 1989 induction into the Rock 'n' Roll Hall of Fame that "If Johnny Cash isn't in it, there shouldn't even be a Hall of Fame." Cash was eventually inducted in 1992.

When his old friend died in 2003, Dylan appeared genuinely overcome with emotion.

his death had long been expected, it must have felt like the end of an era to Dylan. He did not attend the funeral, but he rang Guthrie's manager Harold Leventhal to offer his services at any memorial concert that was being planned. And, true to his word, he appeared alongside the likes of Arlo Guthrie, Judy Collins, Odetta (in magnificent voice) and Ramblin' Jack Elliott at New York's **Carnegie Hall** on January 20, 1968. It was his first concert appearance since May 27, 1966, at London's

Albert Hall and, as he had been then, he was backed by The Band. They played three songs: "Grand Coulee Dam", "Dear Mrs Roosevelt" and "I Ain't Got No Home". But afterwards, at a celebratory party, Dylan made clear it was a one-off and that with Sara pregnant again with his third child (**Samuel,** who would be born in June 1968), his family was now more important to him than touring. "I won't be giving any concerts for a while. I'm not compelled to do it now," he was quoted as saying in *Newsweek*. "I went around the world a couple of times. But I didn't have anything else to do then."

It would be 1974 before Dylan took to the road again. Nor was he in any hurry to make the next record, keeping the world waiting more than another year until *Nashville Skyline* appeared in April 1969.

Bob and Johnny play to TV cameras at the Ryman Auditorium, Nashville

The Life

The Life

1969: Are You Ready for the Country?

"Sometime in the past I had written and performed songs that were most original and most influential, and I didn't know if I ever would again and I didn't care."

Bob Dylan, *Chronicles*

If fans had been surprised by the stripped-down arrangements and biblical imagery of *John Wesley Harding*, they were shocked rigid by the follow-up, the cover of which depicted an almost unrecognisable Dylan grinning like a country bumpkin. True, he had already made two albums with Nashville session men and *John Wesley Harding* had betrayed a country tinge, particularly on songs such as "I'll Be Your Baby Tonight". But it was lyrically rich with allusion and allegory and certainly hadn't prepared anybody for this. With a liner note and guest appearance by Johnny Cash, and such lyrics as "Love is all there is, it makes the world go round", *Nashville Skyline* followed a standard country-and-western pattern, not merely in sound but also in attitude.

It was as if Dylan was deliberately courting the kind of howls of protest he faced after going electric, since the counterculture at the time regarded country music not just as supremely un-hip, but as little more than drinking music for rednecks. To compound matters, *Nashville Skyline* didn't even inhabit the raw, grittier end of the genre that had given Hank Williams credibility. And it had only a tangential connection to the recent experimental country-rock fusions of the International Submarine Band and The Byrds. This was country music of the most mainstream and conservative kind, which gave off the clear message that Dylan wanted no part of the leadership of the new youth movement that was busy burning its draft cards and opposing the Vietnam war. His main preoccupation was "staying out of people's hair", he told *Rolling Stone* on the album's release.

To many he had chosen the worst possible moment to abdicate. The social and political unrest that had been building through the 1960s and which Dylan had mirrored and chronicled had, as Andy Gill put it, reached "critical mass" by 1968. **Robert Kennedy** and **Dr Martin Luther King** had been assassinated, and violent protests were taking place on the streets of Paris, London and Chicago. The apocalyptic vision of the collapse of civilization that Dylan had painted in songs such as "Desolation Row" and "Gates Of Eden" appeared to be becoming a reality – and, instead of rallying the troops, he was nowhere to be seen. Just as the die-hard folkies had felt betrayed at Newport in 1965, it was now the turn of the hippies and long-haired counterculturalists to feel their prophet and messiah had deserted them in their hour of need.

Dylan returned to Nashville in February 1969, with Bob Johnston again behind the controls. This time the band was slightly larger, with the rhythm section of Buttrey and McCoy supplemented by **Pete Drake** on pedal steel, **Bob Wilson** on piano and **Norman Blake** and **Charlie Daniels** on guitars. Again, they rattled through the songs in double-quick time – three tracks that made the album were completed on the first day, four more on the second and two more (including **Tonight I'll Be Staying Here With You,** written overnight in the Ramada Inn) at a third session later the same week. That left just one more song that was to make the album: a duet with Cash on **Girl From The North Country,** a number that had first appeared on *The Freewheelin' Bob Dylan* six years earlier. But it was just one of a huge raft of songs Dylan recorded with Cash at the time (see p.70).

Domestic bliss informed the lyrics of just about every song on the album, sung in a smooth croon that was barely recognisable as Dylan – apparently the consequence of having given up smoking. There's an effortless craftsmanship to it all, and songs such as **Lay Lady Lay** and the tender **Tonight I'll Be Staying Here With You**

of routine country arrangements," concluded Andy Gill in 1998. "A slight work, largely made up of scraps, doodles and glorified jams," wrote a dismissive Sean Egan five years later.

Dylan's own attitude towards the record has grown lukewarm over the years. In 1969 he improbably claimed, "These are the type of songs that I always felt like writing when I've been alone to do so. They reflect more of the inner me than the songs of the past... The smallest line in this new album means more to me than some of the songs on my previous albums." Which left fans wondering what internal profundities we were all missing in, "Oh me oh my, love that country pie" and "Peggy Day stole my poor heart away, by golly what more can I say... "

By 1978, he'd abandoned such preposterous claims. "I was trying to grasp something that would lead me on to where I thought I should be and it didn't go nowhere," he admitted. "It just went down, down, down. I couldn't be

"They make too much of singers over there. Singers are front page news."

Bob Dylan, returning from the Isle of Wight Festival, August 1969

might have sounded masterpieces if they'd been sung by Merle Haggard or Charley Pride. But it wasn't what Dylan's fans wanted or expected and the critics were mostly hostile. In a devastating review, *Billboard* noted: "The satisfied man speaks in clichés and blushes as if every day were Valentines' Day." More than three decades on, attitudes have remained largely negative. "At best efficient and mostly perfunctory; a series

anybody but myself and at that point I didn't know it or want to know it."

Regardless of the controversy, *Nashville Skyline* topped the charts on both sides of the Atlantic, produced one of his biggest-ever hit singles in "Lay Lady Lay", helped country music to cross over to a rock audience for the first time, and paved the way for **The Eagles** to become the biggest band of the 1970s.

The Life

A disappointing comeback: Dylan on stage at the Isle of Wight Festival, 1969

From Woodstock to the Isle of Wight

In August 1969, as Dylan continued to snub those who wanted his leadership, half a million of them decided to come and camp on his doorstep for "three days of peace, love and music". It has been suggested that the location of the Woodstock Festival had been specifically chosen by its promoters to try to tempt Dylan back on stage. It had the desired effect – but it was not their stage that he decided to appear on.

Dylan's desire for privacy had not always been respected by his fans, who had increasingly begun to turn up at his door. On one occasion they even broke into the house. By mid-1969, he no longer felt safe, and in May he moved from the Hi Lo Ha house to a twelve-room Arts and Crafts mansion set in 39 acres of land high up on Ohayo Mountain Road. And, to extend his privacy further, he purchased another 83 acres of surrounding woodland.

Partly in order to escape half a million stoned hippies running half-naked around his bailiwick (even though the festival site was actually 60 miles away), Dylan accepted an invitation to appear at the **Isle of Wight Festival**, booking a passage to depart for Europe on the QEII the day before the Woodstock Festival was due to start. Later he complained, "It seemed to have something to do with me, this Woodstock nation and everything it represented. So we couldn't breathe. I couldn't get any space for me and my family."

In the end, Dylan and family didn't make the sea voyage and flew to Britain instead.

When he took to the stage at the Isle of Wight Festival shortly after 11pm on August 31, he was dressed in a white suit and looked more like a door-to-door Bible salesman than a rock messiah. Backed by The Band, he played for just an hour, which, given that he was paid £50,000 – ten times the amount paid to The Who, the band who had headlined the festival on the previous night – worked out as not a bad rate. The press had been speculating about a three-hour show with an all-star jam session as its finale, and so many departed feeling that they had been short-changed. Worse, the performance – what there was of it – was also distinctly lacklustre.

Dylan himself also seems to have been dissatisfied. Although in an interview before the festival he referred to the appearance as his "comeback", the outcome was so disappointing that he abandoned tentative plans to go back on the road that autumn. He retreated back to the cocoon of his family and it would be another two years before he appeared on a stage (at George Harrison's benefit gig, Concert for Bangladesh) and another five before his own next paid appearance. Unsurprisingly, plans for a live album of the less-than-glorious "comeback" were also scrapped.

Dylan's "Woodstock years" officially ended soon after his return from the Isle of Wight. In autumn 1969 he moved his family into a New York townhouse on **Greenwich Village**'s MacDougal Street without even first viewing his new piece of real estate. It was as if the festival had tainted the very name Woodstock in his eyes and he had to escape.

Though he was occasionally spotted out in New York at concerts by the likes of Janis Joplin, Dr John and John Mayall, Dylan's return to his old hunting ground did not signal a change in his family-oriented lifestyle, and **Jakob Luke,** his fourth child (five counting Maria), was born in December 1969. However, some elements of Dylan's lifestyle did change. Naively, he appeared to believe that he could continue his semi-reclusive, private existence right in the heart of Greenwich Village. He couldn't, of course, and A.J. Weberman, who made a habit of going through Dylan's dustbins looking for clues about his life (see pp.281–282), was only the most extreme of the intrusive fans who plagued him. Some 15 years later, Dylan was forced to admit that moving back to New York had been a "stupid" mistake. "The Woodstock Nation had overtaken MacDougal Street also," he complained. "There'd be crowds outside my house."

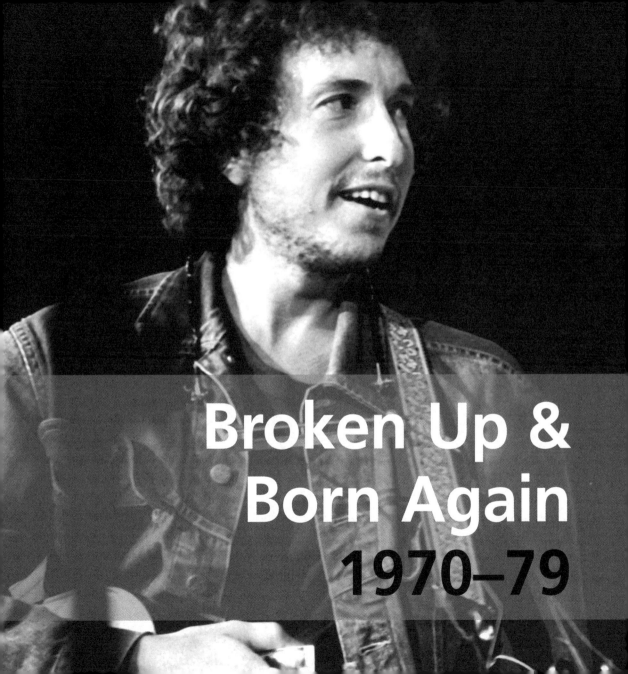

**Broken Up &
Born Again
1970–79**

"*I said 'well fuck it, I wish these people would just forget about me'*"

Bob Dylan, 1984, looking back on the early 1970s

Broken Up & Born Again
1970–79

1970–72: The Amnesia

"What is this shit?" Greil Marcus reviewing *Self Portrait* in *Rolling Stone*

"What kind of alchemy, I wondered, could create a perfume that would make reaction to a person lukewarm, indifferent and apathetic? I wanted to get some." Bob Dylan, *Chronicles*

By 1970, Dylan was growing not merely irritated by his own celebrity but increasingly resentful of his public. So he hit upon a plan to get his fans off his back. He would make an album that was so awful, so lacking in any of the imagination and craft and innovation that had made him such a figurehead that none of his fans could possibly like it.

The result was ***Self Portrait***, an ill-assembled double album of bizarre interpretations of traditional songs, substandard and incongruous covers of material by other singer-songwriters, a handful of weak originals and slapdash live versions of a couple of his own classics. Then several of the songs were overdubbed with syrupy strings, horns and backing vocals. Dylan put a piss-poor painting he'd done of an unrec-

ognisable face on the cover and called it *Self Portrait* in apparent mockery of the fact that the record revealed precisely nothing about the artist whatsoever. The whole product could not have been more deliberately designed to insult his fans, many of whom felt that "Self Parody" would have been a better title.

Dylan for one agreed. "I said 'well fuck it, I wish these people would just forget about me. I wanna do something they can't possibly like, they can't relate to'," he confessed in 1984. "I mean there was no title … and I said, 'well I'm gonna call this album Self Portrait.' To me it was a joke." On another occasion, he admitted, "We released that album to get people off my back. They would not like me any more. That's the reason that album was put out, so people

Dylan and Elvis

Elvis was one of Dylan's early heroes and he was thrilled when Presley recorded his **Tomorrow Is A Long Time** in 1966. "That's the one recording I treasure the most," he told *Rolling Stone* three years later. Presley also recorded **Don't Think Twice It's All Right** in 1971.

Some time in between, Dylan wrote another song he thought was suitable for Presley and asked his producer Bob Johnston, who had worked with both men, to arrange a meeting. "I tried to get them to record together. I think Dylan would have done it in a second," Johnston says. However, Presley's manager Colonel Tom Parker blocked the suggestion and the idea may never even have been put to Elvis. The identity of the song is unknown, although some believe it was the Elvis-sounding **Tell Me That It Isn't True**, which appeared on *Nashville Skyline*.

Whether they ever met at all is the subject of some debate. Dylan's **Went To See The Gypsy**, on his 1970 album *New Morning*, describes a meeting with Elvis in a dark and crowded room in a big hotel. If, when, or where the meeting took place has never been proved, and beyond that lyric Dylan has never publicly spoken of it. Michael Gray, in his magisterial study *Song and Dance Man*, attempted to narrow down the occasions when they might have met but failed to find any conclusive proof that they did. It is known that Dylan attended a Presley concert at Madison Square Garden in June 1972 at least two years after the song was written. But once again there's no evidence of a backstage meeting.

What is in no doubt, however, is how strongly Dylan felt about Elvis. When he heard of Presley's death in August, 1977, Dylan broke down. "One of the very few times in my whole life. I went over my whole childhood, I didn't talk to anyone for a week after Elvis died. If it wasn't for Elvis and Hank Williams I couldn't be doing what I do."

would just at that time stop buying my records. And they did."

Released in June 1970, *Self Portrait* sparked the most famous review in the history of rock music when **Greil Marcus** opened his assessment of the album in *Rolling Stone* with the immortal words: "What is this shit?" Elsewhere, the album was greeted with a mixture of derision, bafflement and sheer disbelief. Yet people didn't stop buying Dylan's records to quite the extent he later claimed: *Self Portrait* still managed to top the British charts and went to number four in America. Not that people necessarily liked what they heard when they got

the record home. Copies were soon clogging the secondhand bins.

While there was something patently ludicrous about hearing Dylan warble **Blue Moon**, there has to be some debate about whether this was genuinely a case of him trying to debunk his own mythology. He had begun recording the album in April 1969 when Bob Johnston recalls him turning up in Nashville with an armful of songbooks and saying, "What do you think about doing an album of other people's songs?" He'd talked about doing something similar at the time of *John Wesley Harding*, so the project had been on his mind for at least three years. And if he was trying to make a deliberately piss-poor self-parody of a record intended to insult his fans, why go to the trouble of stretching the sessions over eleven months when he could presumably have made something equally shoddy in a day?

In addition, there is a revisionist theory, subscribed to among others by Ryan Adams, that *Self Portrait* is actually a far more interesting record than it has ever been given credit for. Yet even if we take at face value his insistence that the mockery that greeted *Self Portrait* was exactly what he had wished, the sheer ferocity of the backlash appears to have shaken him. In an apparent loss of nerve, his next album, *New Morning*, hit the shops just four months later in October 1970. It was hailed as a return to form, if only because the songs all came from his own pen. But after the hotchpotch that was *Self Portrait*, almost anything short of an album of nursery rhymes would have seemed like a triumph.

Most of the songs on *New Morning* had been written and worked on before *Self Portrait*. In 1975 Dylan insisted, "I didn't say 'oh my God, they don't like this, let me do another one'. It wasn't like that. It just happened coincidentally." But the fact that he went back into the studio to finish the *New Morning* songs the very month that *Self Portrait* was released to such a critical mauling – and with **Al Kooper** augmenting Bob Johnston's production – clearly suggests he was desperate to claw back some of his lost reputation.

What we didn't know at the time was that, concurrently with *New Morning*, Dylan had recorded another album of covers in the style of *Self Portrait*, including mediocre versions of **Mr Bojangles**, Joni Mitchell's **Big Yellow Taxi** and two songs associated with Elvis Presley: **A Fool Such As I** and **Can't Help Falling In Love**. The tracks were released on the album *Dylan* in 1973 by Columbia, who were in a fit of pique because Dylan had signed for David Geffen's Asylum label. The album's one saving grace was a superb version of **Spanish Is The Loving Tongue**, a passionate, naked solo performance at the piano, which was also released as the B-side of the 1971 single, "Watching The River Flow".

Had these sessions rather than *New Morning* been released as the follow-up to *Self Portrait*, the effect on Dylan's career might well have been terminal. The original running order for *New Morning* had been a hybrid of new songs and covers. By changing his mind and filling the album with entirely new material, Dylan was clearly making a statement that his songwriting skills had not deserted him. The hymns to domestic bliss hardly constituted a generational manifesto of rebellion. But it bought Dylan time and an excited *Rolling Stone* headline that proclaimed, "We've Got Dylan Back Again".

Today, *New Morning* stands up as a fine album. But it cannot match the heights of, say, *Highway 61 Revisited* or *Blonde On Blonde*. Reviewing the record at the time, Richard Williams, a longtime champion, conceded that Dylan had been left behind by changing times and that "a newer generation finds it hard to understand what the fuss is about". Many years later, Sean Egan astutely summed up the change that had taken place in Dylan's art: "His music was no longer an elemental thing. He was now a jobbing musician, not somebody who lived merely to express his world view through his art. In any case, his world view was limited to the end of the driveway of the home that his wife baked in and his children caroused through." Dylan himself admits as much, writing in *Chronicles* that the songs "weren't the kind where you hear an awful roaring in your head. I knew what those kinds of songs were

like and these weren't them... the album itself had no specific resonance to the shackles and bolts that were strapping the country down, nothing to threaten the status quo."

Despite the enthusiasm that greeted *New Morning*, it turned out to be more of a false dawn. Dylan did not release a new studio album in 1971 and there was no return to the road. But there were a couple of straws in the wind in the course of the year that suggested he was trying to prove that he had not

The Concert for Bangladesh: Dylan's first live appearance in two years

totally abandoned The Cause. He hung out and recorded with **Allen Ginsberg** (see pp.86–87) and his two main musical interventions that year had a sociopolitical impetus. First he appeared at George Harrison's benefit gig, **Concert for Bangladesh** at Madison Square Garden on August 1. With all profits going to UNICEF, he took no fee and, unlike the uneasy performance at the Isle of Wight two years earlier, he seemed at ease with the experience of being on stage again.

Then, a few weeks later, he released the single **George Jackson**. A moving elegy for the black civil-rights activist who had been killed in a Californian prison, it was his first topical song in years and was a spontaneous outpouring. He had read a newspaper report of Jackson's death on November 3, written the song on the spot and asked Columbia to book a recording studio for the following day. The single was in the shops eight days later with an acoustic version on one side and a band version on the other.

A gaggle of previously unavailable songs also filtered out on the compilation *Bob Dylan's Greatest Hits Volume 2*. They included three songs from *The Basement Tapes* re-recorded with "Happy Traum" and "When I Paint My Masterpiece", a sublime composition which had already appeared on The Band's *Cahoots* album and which he performed with them to considerable excitement during their New Year's Eve show at New York's Academy Of Music.

As 1972 dawned, Dylan's fans clutched at these straws and prayed that the "amnesia" was coming to an end. Dylan, it seemed, was finally on his way back. But, instead, he confounded us all over again. The year 1972 turned out to be the most inactive of his career to date. He tried to maintain interest in what was happening and attended concerts by Elvis Presley, Jackson Browne, Link Wray, the Grateful Dead and Loudon Wainwright. He also turned up in disguise in the audience at the Mariposa Folk Festival and as himself at Mick Jagger's 29th birthday party. He got on stage for three songs with **John Prine** at the Bitter End and sang backing vocals on albums by **Doug Sahm** and **Steve Goodman**. And that was it.

In his absence, 1972 became the year when the search for a replacement leader – "the new Bob" – turned frantic. Every fresh young singer-songwriter on the block with an acoustic guitar and something to say found himself hailed as the inheritor of Dylan's mantle, including Prine, Goodman and Wainwright (see pp.296–299). Dylan dutifully checked them all out – and concluded that, though the pretenders all had their merits, none of them was about to steal his crown, regardless of whether he still cared to wear it or not. In any case, by the end of the year, he was down in Durango, Mexico, with **Sam Peckinpah**, reliving his boyhood James Dean fantasy and dreaming of a new career in movies.

1973: A Man Called Alias

"I'm not a movie star. But I've got a vision to put up on the screen."

Bob Dylan, January 1974

Ever since his early teens, when he first saw James Dean in *Rebel Without A Cause*, Dylan had entertained dreams of being a film star. So when he was approached in 1972 to write music for Sam Peckinpah's *Pat Garrett & Billy The Kid*, he was delighted. Dylan admired Peckinpah's work and *The Wild Bunch* was a particular favourite. So he was all the more thrilled when a small part playing a character called **Alias** was written into the screenplay for him.

In late November 1972, Dylan and Sara and three of their children moved to **Durango, Mexico**, where shooting was due to begin. But the experience didn't turn out to be an entirely happy one. Peckinpah proved almost impossible to work with – drunk, irascible, unpredictable, and given to throwing knives and firing off live rounds of ammunition when he grew frustrated (which was a daily occurrence). On one famous occasion, when Dylan and **Kris Kristofferson** were in the screening room reviewing the results of that day's shooting, Peckinpah stood up and urinated all over the screen because he thought the picture was out of focus. "I remember Bob turning and looking at me with the most perfect reaction, you know, what the hell have we gotten ourselves into?", Kristofferson recalled.

Filming continued all through Thanksgiving, Christmas and the New Year, but Dylan's part was minimal and he had little to do. Sara grew thoroughly depressed and the children fell ill. By early January, Dylan had also had enough and he and Sara took a trip to London, where they hung out with **George and Patti Harrison**.

The soundtrack – which Dylan hadn't even begun recording – was to prove even more problematic than the filming. Recording eventually began at the CBS studios in **Mexico City**. Dylan had written one song, **Billy**, after reading the screenplay before he travelled to Durango. For the rest, he had hoped to find inspiration on the set. But it was slow in coming and the disciplined process of creating an entire soundtrack turned out to be far more taxing than he had anticipated. Four versions of "Billy" were recorded and another song called **Goodbye Holly**, which was later dropped.

By the end of January it was obvious that Dylan was struggling and Jerry Fielding, an experienced Hollywood composer, was brought in to assist. Fielding immediately insisted that they needed another major song and Dylan, relieved to have some professional support, came up with **Knockin' On Heaven's Door**. In February, they transferred to Los Angeles, Dylan and family renting a house in Malibu while the soundtrack was recorded in two sessions at Burbank Studios. Despite having little idea how to assemble a conventional soundtrack and match his music to the film's scenes, Dylan's stumbling approach in the end produced some fine incidental music that perfectly captured the spirit of the film and reflected its evocative image of the Old West. For more on the movie itself, see p.268.

label (see box, p.88).

The ruthless Geffen was already an exceedingly rich man when he began courting Dylan's signature, having sold his Asylum label for seven million dollars. A year later he had resumed control of the merged **Elektra-Asylum**, making him one of the most powerful players

"All of a sudden it seemed to really make sense. It was a good idea, a kind of step into the past... The other guys in The Band came out and we went right to work." Robbie Robertson

Making Waves: The Return of The Band

By now, Dylan had sacked **Albert Grossman** as his manager. The contract between them had expired in 1970 and Dylan had himself taken charge of the books with a team of advisers. He felt that Grossman had grown rich at his expense and refused to have any further dealings with him, although the ex-manager still received an income from his share of Dylan's publishing, said to average $250,000 a year. Legal action between them did not finally end until 1987 when, almost two years after Grossman's death, Dylan paid his widow Sally two million dollars in full and final settlement.

After Grossman, Dylan never again placed his affairs in the hands of a single all-powerful manager. When his contract with Columbia came up for renewal in 1973, he took the lead hand himself in the negotiations that resulted in him signing with **David Geffen**'s Asylum

in the music industry. His desire to sign Dylan had more to do with ego than with money, and he set about landing his prey with single-minded determination.

He began by befriending **Robbie Robertson**, taking him and his wife Dominique on an all-expenses-paid holiday to Paris. He also took Joni Mitchell on the trip, who then wrote the song "Free Man In Paris" about Geffen. By now, Dylan and his family had moved to California, where he had bought a house on the **Point Dume** peninsula, ten miles north of Malibu Beach and a short walk from Zuma Beach. Geffen found the Robertsons a house in Malibu nearby to advance the next part of his plan. Once Robertson was installed, he suggested that it was time **The Band** and Dylan should tour together again. It was seven years since they had last done so and when Geffen convinced the guitarist it would be the most lucrative tour in the history of rock'n'roll and outsell Elton John, Led Zeppelin and the

The Life

Two poets in a pod: Dylan and Ginsberg

Allen Ginsberg's *Howl*, published in 1956, made him the foremost American poet of the Beat generation, and you only have to read its opening apocalyptic couplet to discern the obvious influence on Dylan's lyrics: "I saw the best minds of my generation, destroyed by madness, starving hysterical naked, dragging themselves through the negro streets at dawn looking for an angry fix…"

Dylan later said he had discovered Ginsberg's verse in Minneapolis when he was eighteen. They met for the first time in New York in late 1963, when the openly homosexual Ginsberg made little secret of the fact that he fancied Dylan. The two got on well, but the poet declined Dylan's offer to accompany him the next day to Chicago, where he was playing a concert. Ginsberg later admitted he didn't want to become a groupie and was "afraid I might become his slave or something … his mascot".

Nevertheless, they became close friends and Ginsberg subsequently joined Dylan on the road several times, including in Britain in 1965. He also introduced other literary figures to the singer, including *One Flew Over The Cuckoo's Nest* author Ken Kesey, playwright Michael McClure and poet Gary Snyder. And, after Dylan's motorcycle accident, Ginsberg was one of the first to visit him in Woodstock, bringing with him a box of books.

They grew closer after Dylan moved back to Greenwich Village, and they recorded together on October 31, 1971, when Dylan turned up at Ginsberg's Lower East Side apartment. The poet thrust a guitar into Dylan's hands and, with himself playing the harmonium and improvising around various poems and Indian mantras, he turned on a tape recorder.

Nine days later, they went into the Record Plant studios in New York with a group of friends and an informal plan to produce a joint album of poetry set to music. Among the tracks they recorded were a major new Ginsberg poem, **September On Jessore Road**, a version of William Blake's **Nurses Song** and an entirely improvised number called **Gimme My Money Back**, on which Dylan sang the first verse. A week later they were back in the studio again and there were further collaborations into early 1972. Eventually two Ginsberg albums were compiled from the sessions.

Ginsberg later joined Dylan on tour for the Rolling Thunder Revue tour, writing the liner notes for **Desire** and assisting and appearing in the film **Renaldo & Clara**. Ginsberg was also on hand during Dylan's divorce from Sara, going trick-or-treating with him and his children on Halloween, 1977. And the same year the pair of them added raucous, drunken vocals to a song called **Don't Go Home With Your Hard-On**, on Leonard Cohen's Phil Spector–produced album, *Death Of A Ladies' Man*. When Ginsberg died of cancer on April 5, 1997, Dylan was on the road in Canada and, at that night's concert, he dedicated **Desolation Row** to his memory.

Rolling Stones, Robertson approached Dylan, who agreed to meet Geffen.

The record-company mogul played his hand brilliantly. Business meetings were conducted informally, walking along the beach at Malibu. Dylan felt relaxed in Geffen's company. When he mentioned in passing that he wanted to learn to speak French, Geffen said that he also wanted to learn and arranged a course for them to take together. When he outlined his plans for a tour with The Band that would hit every major city in America and told Dylan he

Thinking outside the box: Dylan and Ginsberg at Byrdcliffe, July 1964

didn't even want a fee, the deal was clinched. Although he didn't mention it at the time, Geffen was, of course, playing a much bigger game in which the ultimate prize would be signing Dylan to Asylum. The tour was just a bold and brilliant opening gambit.

Not only was Dylan's contract with Columbia up for renewal. The company was in turmoil following the sacking – for alleged improper use of funds – of label boss **Clive Davis**, who had recently offered Dylan a new contract involving a $400,000 advance on each new

The Life

David Geffen

Born in 1943, **David Geffen** was the only man to ever woo Dylan away from CBS/Columbia, and also the one who, in 1973, managed to persuade him to tour again for the first time in eight years. He achieved this feat using the mixture of manipulation, abrasiveness, flattery and charm that he had honed while working his way to the top of the music industry. A mover and shaker if ever there was one, Geffen founded three successful record labels – **Asylum, Geffen and Dreamworks** – and the first new Hollywood movie studio in almost sixty years.

In the early 1970s, with Elliott Roberts, Geffen managed **Joni Mitchell**, **Crosby, Stills and Nash**, **Jackson Browne** and **Linda Ronstadt** through what he claimed with typical braggadocio was "the largest music management firm in the world". He launched Asylum in 1972 with **The Eagles**, who he helped to become the most successful group of the decade in America. Within two years he had sold the label to Warners but stayed on as chairman to take over the combined **Asylum-Elektra Records**. In typically ruthless style, his first move was to fire 25 of the label's 35 acts.

Geffen triumphed by signing Dylan in late 1973, but the following period proved to be a career low-point. In 1975, he only lasted a year as vice-chairman of the Warners movie studio and was kept under contract to prevent him starting rival new ventures. He also lost Dylan, of course, and for a while he resented it. However, the two remained acquaintances, if not friends, and it was on Geffen's recommendation that Dylan brought in **Chuck Plotkin** to produce his 1981 album, *Shot Of Love*.

Geffen returned to the music business in 1980, when he set up **Geffen Records**. During the ensuing decade, he signed **John Lennon** (it was Geffen who accompanied Yoko Ono back home from the hospital where John was pronounced dead), **Neil Young** (who he later sued for making "wilfully uncommercial" records) and **Elton John**. In 1990 he sold the label to MCA for 550 million dollars' worth of shares – which soon leaped in value, making him "the richest man in Hollywood" – and in 1994 he teamed up with Steven Spielberg and Jeffrey Katzenberg to launch Dreamworks SKG as an independent Hollywood studio with separate television and record divisions.

album. Dylan was shocked by Davis's dismissal and later appeared for him in court as a character witness against Columbia. It was increasingly apparent to rival labels that, for the first time in a dozen years, there was a real prospect of tempting Dylan away from the label he had been with since the start of his career.

Atlantic was also discreetly courting Dylan. But Geffen had the whip hand. With the tour in place to start in January 1974, he pointed

out that there needed to be a new album in the stores for fans to purchase – otherwise it would be merely a "60s nostalgia show", the very thing Dylan wanted to get away from. And if there was to be a new album, what could make more sense than to release it on Asylum? In a typically grandiose gesture, Geffen also told Dylan he could sell more records than Columbia had ever managed, promising one million units per album. Dylan cautiously signed a one-record deal for a new studio album and, on a handshake, agreed to allow Geffen to release an album of the tour, the first official live recording of his career and something that was now essential to defeat the bootleggers, who would inevitably be out in force. Geffen had got his man.

Boxed in by the imminent tour dates, Dylan hastily set about writing a new album. He had a couple of songs, **Never Say Goodbye** and **Forever Young**, which he had demoed in June. But in October 1973, he relocated to New York for two weeks with the intention of writing enough songs to fill the record. He returned with half a dozen new compositions and went in to **Village Recorders studio** in Los Angeles with The Band on November 2. Within three days they had more or less finished *Planet Waves* although, typically, Dylan could not resist tinkering and added a final, newly written track, **Wedding Song**, a week later.

The album was meant to be in the shops at the beginning of January to coincide with the start of the tour. But Dylan didn't finish writing a poem he intended for the sleeve notes until New Year's Eve, just three days before the opening date. The album eventually reached stores in mid-January, two weeks after the tour had started. Ironically, Dylan later decided to drop the poem from the CD reissue.

Like *New Morning*, the album was inspired by Dylan's domestic contentment, particularly on the hymn-like "Forever Young" and "Wedding Song". The latter was added at the very end of the sessions and was a tribute to Sara, the loyal wife who had given him "babies one, two, three". There was actually a fourth, Jakob, but the arithmetic messed with the scansion. In any case, Jakob had his own song: he is widely held to have been the inspiration for "Forever Young", which appeared in two versions.

Overall, the album was honest and personal but largely devoid of the layers of meaning that characterized Dylan's songwriting in the 1960s. Among the most perceptive reviews was one by **Ellen Willis** in *The New Yorker*. "I think the subject of Planet Waves is what it appears to be", she wrote, "Dylan's aesthetic and practical dilemma and his immense emotional debt to Sara." Yet it was to be the finalé of that phase of his life, for his next album would deal harrowingly with his estrangement from Sara, their relationship unable to stand the strains of the road and its various temptations.

Under the circumstances, *Planet Waves* was an impressive-enough piece of work and – *The Basement Tapes* apart – is the only studio album Dylan ever made with The Band. "It was as good as we could make it in the situation," Robbie Robertson said. "He didn't have a bag of songs, so it was just a last-minute thing." Nevertheless, boosted by positive reviews and with Geffen hyping the tour for all it was worth, *Planet Waves* became Dylan's first American number one album, topping the chart for four weeks. In Britain, where he would not play live again until 1978, the record appeared on **Island** and reached number seven.

1974: On the Road Again

"Well it wasn't planned. I saw daylight. I took off …
the songs I'm singing mean as much to the people as to me,
so it's just up to me to perform the best I can." Bob Dylan, Montreal, 1974

The statistics of Dylan's first tour since 1966 make impressive reading. Travelling on a private jet named **Starship One** and starting on January 3, 1974, he played 40 dates in 21 cities over

a 42-day period. Excitement was heightened when Geffen hit on the then-unique idea of making tickets available only through mail order. Crowds materialized at post offices all over America at midnight on December 2, the earliest postmark accepted on ticket applications.

The response was even greater than Geffen had predicted, with an estimated five and a half million applications received for the 651,000 tickets – sent in, Geffen proudly boasted, by nearly four percent of the entire US population. With a top ticket price of $9.50, some $92 million was received, and, with such over-subscription, scalpers were able to charge upwards of $100 per ticket. The demand raised a burden of expectation that Dylan found daunting. In the years away from the stage, he had grown shy and diffident. In his occasional appearances, such as the Isle Of Wight Festival, he had appeared awkward in the spotlight. As Clinton Heylin puts it, "The confidence of youth had been replaced by a self-consciousness that he now needed to overcome."

When Bob and The Band arrived in Chicago for the first date, Levon Helm admits they were "very unready". Yet Dylan rose to the occasion and received what *Rolling Stone* described as "a hero's welcome". Where they had booed in 1965–66, they now cheered. Robertson found

The Life

"You gotta keep changing … shirts, old ladies, whatever."
Neil Young, *Rolling Stone*, 1975

"something kind of hypocritical in it". But eight years is a long time in rock'n'roll and many in the audience had been too young to see him the last time he had toured. "The people that came out to see us came mostly to see what they'd missed first time around," Dylan said.

Dylan himself sounded strong and exhilarated. "The voice was reminiscent of Highway 61, the transitional rock voice, with less of the harshness, more of the confidence," Ben Fong-Torres wrote of the opening night in *Rolling Stone*. As the tour went on, some of the harshness returned to his voice along with a raucous theatricality that was perhaps an inevitable consequence of playing large stadia every night. Dylan later said he felt they had sacrificed sensitivity for "full-out power".

The shows also grew more nostalgic in tone. As Dylan admitted, "It's a very fine line you have to walk to stay in touch with something once you've created it." Many of the songs from *Planet Waves* were dropped in favour of older material and by the end of the tour in Los Angeles on February 14, only **Forever Young** remained. One of the nightly highlights was **It's Alright Ma (I'm Only Bleeding)**, during the acoustic segment, with its prophetic line "even the president of the United States sometimes must have to stand naked" given new meaning by Nixon's embroilment in the Watergate scandal.

It was greeted by thousands holding matches and cigarette lighters aloft, a gesture that was to become a familiar ritual at rock concerts.

Dylan's 1974 tour is the first recorded instance of it, and a photograph of the flickering flames adorned the cover of the subsequent live album, **Before The Flood.** Another highlight came in the electric set, when **All Along The Watchtower** was turned into a tribute to **Jimi Hendrix**'s explosive version.

Off stage, groupies were in abundance. The Band's **Richard Manuel** made the road crew take Polaroid photos of the available women and then selected the best looking. Dylan fell for **Ellen Bernstein**, a 24-year-old Columbia executive working in the label's San Francisco office. Sara clearly feared the worst and turned up unannounced halfway through the tour in Houston to reclaim her husband, attending the final end-of-tour party on his arm. Dylan seemed relieved simply to have got through it. "From the first moment I walked onstage at the opening concert, I knew that going through with the tour would be the hardest thing I had ever done," he said. "The problem was that everyone had his own idea of what the tour was about. Everybody had a piece of the action. I had no control over what was going on."

Yet he felt they had delivered. "We were expected to produce a show that lived up to everybody's expectations. And we did."

After the Flood

Something changed in Dylan when he went back on the road in early 1974. His cosy domesticity with Sara had satisfied him for a

The Life

while, as his own creativity went into abeyance and he was seemingly content to live in the shadow of past glories. He had cut himself off from the rock'n'roll mainstream while he crooned hymns to the joys of family life. He seems to have been genuinely happy and it was probably the most harmonious period of his entire career. But the Before the Flood tour threw him back into the maelstrom, rekindling both his creative spark and his bohemian spirit in a way that put his nine-year marriage in imminent peril.

The fallout was almost instant once the tour was over. While the tapes were being picked over and mixed for the forthcoming live album, Dylan wasted little time in getting back in touch with Ellen Bernstein – about a week, according to her account. Soon, Dylan was travelling up the coast to visit her in San Francisco, or having her to stay in his Malibu house. Sara moved out of the family home and the first press reports that the Dylans' marriage was breaking up appeared in July. The story was true in outline but the gossip columnists got the wrong woman, citing **Lorey Sebastian**, former wife of The Lovin' Spoonful's John Sebastian. The incident was to inspire the opening line of the song **Idiot Wind**: "Someone's got in for me, They're planting stories in the press."

By late April, Dylan was back in **Greenwich Village**. He renewed his acquaintance with **Phil Ochs,** who persuaded him to appear in a **Friends of Chile** benefit, organised in the wake of the CIA-backed coup that had overthrown Salvador Allende's democratically elected Marxist government the previous autumn.

Unfortunately Dylan sampled rather too much of a particularly fine Chilean wine backstage and by the time the show started, he could hardly stand up.

When I Paint my Masterpiece

While in New York in the early summer of 1974, Dylan signed on for painting classes with the artist **Norman Raeben**. Throughout his life, he has sought out guru-like figures, and in Raeben he found one. At 73, Raeben had no idea who Dylan was. He even thought his scruffy student was homeless and offered to let him sleep on the couch in his studio, in return for cleaning duties. Dylan was highly amused by the misunderstanding and was delighted to be able to conduct a relationship without the burden of his fame getting in the way.

According to other students, the acerbic Raeben would frequently tell Dylan he was "an idiot" and, after spending so much of his adult life surrounded by fawning sycophants, he apparently found these insults endearing. And Raeben taught him far more than how to daub a canvas. As Dylan later put it, the painter was "more powerful than any magician" and equipped him with an entirely new way of looking at the world that affected both his songwriting and his personal life. "That's when our marriage started breaking up," he said. "She never knew what I was talking about, what I was thinking about. And I couldn't possibly explain it."

Dylan turned up at Raeben's five days a week for two months. "He didn't teach you how to paint so much. He didn't teach you

"I went home after that and my wife never did understand me ever since that day." Bob Dylan

how to draw. He didn't teach you any of those things. He taught you putting your head and your mind and your eye together," Dylan said in 1978. "He looked into you and told you what you were. He taught me how to see in a way that allowed me to do consciously what I unconsciously felt."

By July 1974, he had left New York and was on the eighty-acre farm he had bought in **Minnesota** on the banks of the Crow River. His children joined him, but Sara did not. In between visits to family and old friends in Hibbing, he worked on applying Raeben's techniques to a new bunch of songs he was writing. They would

A relationship running on empty: Bob and Sara looking frosty in the mid-1970s

prove to be his finest compositions in years. Many of the songs were clearly about his disintegrating marriage. But one of them, **You're Going To Make Me Lonesome When You Go**, was about Ellen Bernstein, who was staying with him on the farm. The song even mentioned Ashtabula, the town where she was born.

While Sara Dylan has never publicly discussed her marriage, Bernstein has spoken at length about her year-long relationship with Dylan. "I would cook and we would run around. He was at his best there, at his most comfortable, with his brother's house down the road," she said of their time on the farm. "He had a painting studio out in the field and the house was far from fancy, out in the middle of nowhere. He was very relaxed and that's where and when he was writing Blood On The Tracks." According to Bernstein, Dylan would write in the morning and appear around noon and play her the songs and ask her opinion. But although many of them were clearly about Sara, she says they never discussed his collapsing marriage. "I never thought to ask, 'What's going on with your wife?'," she insists. "I didn't want to get married and I wasn't being asked to leave."

On August 2, Dylan resigned with **Columbia** at the Century Plaza Hotel during the company's annual convention in Los Angeles. He had grown disenchanted with Geffen, who not for the first or last time in his career was caught out by his overinflated promises. He had told Dylan he could sell one million copies of *Planet Waves*. The album had stalled at 600,000, a thoroughly respectable figure at the time. But given the far larger demand for tour tickets,

Dylan felt the record should have sold more. He even threatened to renege on his handshake agreement to allow Geffen to have the live album, although he relented when Asylum came up with more money. The huge numbers who had seen the shows and wanted a souvenir guaranteed healthy sales and *Before The Flood* made number three in America – an almost unprecedented showing for a live album. Even in Britain, where Dylan hadn't played since 1969, the album made number eight.

The success of the tour had made Columbia keen to win Dylan back and they came up with a much-improved offer. They also had a certain amount of coercion at their disposal: Dylan had been deeply unhappy about the *Dylan* album of three-year-old outtakes that Columbia had put out when he left the label in 1973. Only by returning to the fold could he prevent them flooding the market with further unauthorized archive releases.

Although she has denied any part, it's impossible to believe that Dylan's relationship with Bernstein did not play some role in luring him back – particularly as she then assumed the role of liaison officer between Dylan and her employers, Columbia, while he made his next album. When he went into **A&R Studios** in New York on September 16 to begin recording *Blood On The Tracks*, Bernstein was at his side throughout.

Like a Corkscrew to My Heart

Initially, Dylan appears to have toyed with the idea of recording *Blood On The Tracks* with a full-on electric band. In August, while staying at

Ellen Bernstein's home in Oakland, he looked up San Francisco resident **Mike Bloomfield**, who had played electric guitar with him at Newport in 1965. But the meeting did not go well. Dylan played the songs so fast, one after another, that Bloomfield, a highly accomplished musician, could not keep up. "He just kept on playing. He just did one after another and I got lost," Bloomfield recalled. "They all began to

was ditched, swiftly and unceremoniously. **Eric Weissberg** and his band **Deliverance** were initially employed as session musicians and sacked after two days, as perplexed as Bloomfield had been. Dylan continued working with bassist **Tony Brown** from the first line-up, adding keyboardist **Paul Griffin**, who had played on some of his greatest mid-1960s recordings, and pedal steel player **Buddy Cage**.

"A lot of people tell me they enjoy that album. It's hard for me to relate to that. I mean, people enjoying that type of pain?" Bob Dylan

sound the same to me, they were all in the same key, they were all long. It was one of the strangest experiences of my life. He was sort of pissed off that I didn't pick it up."

Discouraged by this experience, Dylan decided on a more acoustic approach when he entered A&R Studios, actually the old **Columbia Studio A** where he had recorded his first six albums between 1961 and 1965. As ever, his way of working was eccentric. "Never turning off the tape machine was part of the way you recorded Dylan," noted **Phil Ramone** who engineered the sessions. "He would go from one song to another like a medley. Sometimes he will have several bars and, in the next version, he will change his mind about how many bars there should be in between a verse. Or eliminate a verse. Or add a chorus when you don't expect. He is truly spontaneous in all ways of life."

Such methods may have given Dylan the freedom his art needed, but for those working with him it could be a nightmare. Anybody who couldn't keep up with his "spontaneity"

Within ten days, they had recorded, mixed, sequenced and cut a test pressing of the record and Columbia began preparing the record for release. But that wasn't quite the end of the story. Three months later, with the album about to go into the shops, Dylan went up to his farm in Minnesota for Christmas. While there, he played the album to his brother David, who suggested the album could be improved. Straight after Christmas, Dylan spent two days at **Sound 80 Studios** in Minneapolis, re-recording six songs with a bunch of local musicians and revising some of the lyrics. In particular, he toned down the hurt and anger on **Idiot Wind** and **If You See Her Say Hello,** two songs in which he had painted himself as the wronged party in his fractured relationship. Bizarrely, Dylan's children attended the sessions to hear him singing these extraordinary songs about their parents' broken marriage.

The relationship with Bernstein had by this time begun to cool. She was not there over Christmas and was appalled when she learned that Dylan had gone and re-cut half of the album without consulting Columbia. Yet somehow, the label still managed to get the drastically revised album into stores for January 17.

What's immediately notable about the album is the intensely personal nature of the songs. With the exception of some of the numbers about the break-up with Suze Rotolo on *Another Side*, Dylan's songwriting had always possessed a deeply enigmatic quality. Yet on *Blood On The Tracks* he exposes his feelings honestly, painfully and with raw emotion. We're never left in any doubt that he's dealing directly with the pain of the break-up of his marriage – "a corkscrew to my heart", as he sang on **You're A Big Girl Now**. Even Jakob Dylan, the couple's youngest son who was five when the album was released, admits that to this day he hears "my parents talking" in the songs.

The influence of **Norman Raeben** on the record is fascinating. "When you look at a painting, you can see any part of it or see it all together", Dylan said. That, he explained, was the effect he had been attempting to achieve in the songs on *Blood On The Tracks*. But whether it's the influence of Raeben or not, the record certainly contains some of Dylan's finest writing. "There is no wilful obscurity, nothing is thrown away, every line is made to count, yet they are thick with colourful imagery so tightly hewn together it dazzles the mind," Neil McCormick wrote in a brilliant reassessment of *Blood On The Tracks* in 2003. "The most intricate, eloquent and savagely remorseless examination of the downside of love ever committed to record."

Blood On The Tracks became Dylan's second consecutive studio album to top the American charts and made number four in Britain. Today it is regarded as one of the great Dylan records. Yet surprisingly, on its release, the reviews were mixed. In *Crawdaddy*, Jim Cusimano criticised the "instrumental incompetence". Nick Kent in *New Musical Express* called the playing "trashy" and declared, "I don't honestly know what good Dylan is any more." Jon Landau in *Rolling Stone* thought the record had been made "with typical shoddiness" and mocked the idea that it would be "treasured as deeply and for as long" as *Blonde On Blonde*.

Only a couple of critics got it right. **Paul Williams** hailed "the best album of the last five years by anybody". **Michael Gray**, one of the most perceptive of all writers on Dylan, wrote in *Let It Rock* of "the most strikingly intelligent album of the 70s". He also astutely noted that, in one quantum leap, *Blood On The Tracks* had reinvented Dylan as an artist whose creative prowess would not, after all, be forever bounded by the parameters of the 1960s, the decade he had done so much to define. Bizarrely, many years later in his autobiography, Dylan attempted to claim the songs on *Blood On The Tracks* were not autobiographical at all but "based on Chekhov short stories". Another of his little jokes, we must assume.

1975: "Doing what it is that I do"

"He must've been ready for another great surge of unafraid prophetic feeling." Allen Ginsberg, liner note to *Desire*

Dylan's affair with Ellen Bernstein might have suggested that he had given up on his marriage. In reality, it wasn't so. The songs on *Blood On The Tracks* were clearly some kind of catharsis for him and, after the album's release, it seemed that reconciliation was on the cards, particularly when Sara accompanied him to a benefit concert in Golden Gate Park, San Francisco, in March 1975. The couple posed for the paparazzi and the following night they were very visibly a couple again when they attended a party given by Paul and Linda McCartney on the *Queen Mary*, at its permanent mooring in Long Beach.

Yet their differences proved to be irreconcilable. In May Dylan flew to France to stay with **David Oppenheim**, who had been responsible for the painting on the back cover of *Blood On The Tracks*. Sara was meant to join him there to celebrate his 34th birthday. In the end she never did, leaving him "completely despairing, isolated, lost," according to Oppenheim.

Dylan stayed in France for six weeks, "drinking and screwing around" and visiting the annual Gypsy festival in the seaside town of Les Saintes Maries de la Mer in the Camargue, which inspired the song **One More Cup Of Coffee**. He also started writing **Abandoned Love**, with its telling opening line, "My heart is telling me I love you still." The song was

recorded for his next album, **Desire**, but then omitted, and eventually appeared on 1985's *Biograph*. However, one night watching the sun going down over some vineyards, Dylan decided it was time "to go back to America and get serious and do what it is that I do."

By June 1975 he was back in Greenwich Village, living in a loft borrowed from friends on Houston Street, visiting Rubin "Hurricane" Carter in prison (see box overleaf) and turning up at clubs such as the Bottom Line and the Other End (formerly the Bitter End), where on June 26 he saw Patti Smith. Recognising the voice of a fellow poet, Dylan was captivated by her unique mixture of rock'n'roll and free verse, which would shortly reach a wider audience on her debut album, *Horses*. "He started hanging out more," Smith recalls. "He was working out this Rolling Thunder thing – he was thinking about improvisation, about extending himself language-wise. In the talks we had, there was something that he admired about me that was difficult to comprehend."

Two days after meeting Smith, Dylan was driving around Greenwich Village when he spotted a Gypsy-looking woman – with long black hair that reached three feet down her back – carrying a violin case. It was **Scarlet Rivera**, who was at the time playing in a New York salsa band. Dylan immediately asked her

Rubin "Hurricane" Carter

The boxer **Rubin "Hurricane" Carter** was given a life sentence in 1967 for gunning down three people in a New Jersey bar. He went to jail protesting his innocence, claiming that he had been framed by the police and convicted by a racist court. The case was reopened in 1974, when the two main witnesses confessed to lying under oath. Carter wrote a short book called *The Sixteenth Round* and, when a copy was sent to Dylan, he was impressed enough to visit the boxer in prison. Dylan bought his story, and offered to write a song for him.

He turned to theatre director and lyricist Jacques Levy for help, apparently so emotionally involved in the campaign to "free Hurricane" that he was finding it hard to express his feelings objectively in song. "I wrote that song because it was tops in my mind, it had priority," Dylan said. "There's an injustice that's been done and the fact is that it can happen to anybody. We have to be confronted with that."

The dramatic song they came up with, **Hurricane**, opened with all the force of a tabloid news story, describing the pistol shots ringing out in the bar. It was a powerful return to the protest style of a decade earlier and, although it would be unfair to doubt Dylan's sincerity, it came at the perfect moment for him. He was about to go back on the road with

the Rolling Thunder revue and a bunch of his old Greenwich Village friends, and a cause was exactly what was needed.

The song itself, which was released as a single and prominently features **Scarlet Rivera** on violin, takes a certain poetic license with the facts. Carter's own violent and criminal past is conveniently ignored and the claim that he could have been "champion of the world" doesn't quite square with his very average record in the ring. Futhermore, not everyone on the Rolling Thunder Tour bought the story of the boxer's innocence: after talking to Carter on the phone, **Joni Mitchell** decided, "This is a bad person. He's faking it."

The 1975 leg of Rolling Thunder ended on December 8 at Madison Square Garden, New York, with a five-hour benefit show billed as "The Night Of The Hurricane", at which Muhammad Ali made an appearance. Carter was eventually granted a retrial and bailed in March 1976, only to be convicted for a second time in December. He was returned to prison where he remained until 1985, when his conviction was finally overturned on the grounds that it was based on "racism rather than reason". His story was later turned into a film called *The Hurricane,* starring Denzel Washington, with Dylan's song prominent on the soundtrack.

---

to his rehearsal studio. She remembers they played "One More Cup of Coffee", "Isis" and "Mozambique", all songs that would appear on *Desire*. That night Dylan took Rivera to a club to see Muddy Waters and Victoria Spivey and asked her to join his next band.

Over the next couple of weeks, Dylan hit clubs in Greenwich Village almost every night,

looking for fresh recruits. One regular haunt was **The Other End,** where he joined old friend **Ramblin' Jack Elliott** on stage one night. He also renewed his acquaintance with rockabilly bass player **Rob Stoner,** who he had known since 1971, and **Bobby Neuwirth,** an even older friend. Younger musicians such as **Steve Soles, David Mansfield,** David Bowie's former guitarist **Mick Ronson** and born-again Christian **T-Bone Burnett** were also accepted into the inner circle. As they hung out at The Other End, there was already talk of going on the road and playing unannounced in small clubs.

Another who came on board was the theatre director and writer **Jacques Levy**, who had helped Roger McGuinn write "Chestnut Mare" for The Byrds. After assisting Dylan finish a new song he was working on – **Isis** – the two moved out to Dylan's beach house in Long Island for ten days and worked on further material together. Levy helped Dylan to write fourteen more songs, including **Hurricane**, a campaign song for the boxer incarcerated on a murder rap; **Joey**, about the New York Mafia figure Joey Gallo; **Black Diamond Bay**, based on the work of Joseph Conrad; plus **Romance In Durango** and **Mozambique**. With the addition of **Sara**, another profound song to his wife – "sweet virgin angel, sweet love of my life" – Dylan found, by late July, he had a whole new album of songs waiting to be recorded, although it was only seven months since he had completed *Blood On The Tracks*.

He entered **Columbia Studios**, New York, on July 28 with a huge and unwieldy band of musicians. There were at least five guitarists including **Eric Clapton** (although he only stayed a day), the British soul band **Kokomo**, **Emmylou Harris** on backing vocals and Columbia in-house producer **Don Devito** behind the console. Over the next four days, *Desire* was recorded, although the big band was quickly slimmed down and Scarlet Rivera's

violin promoted to the dominant role. At the final session, Sara turned up, fresh from a holiday in Mexico. "She came to New York, I guess, to see if there would be some kind of a getting back together," Jacques Levy recalled. "I guess that was in her mind. I know it was in his mind."

Dylan recorded "Sara" with his wife on the other side of the glass. It must have been a hugely emotional occasion, as he asked for her forgiveness in song and pleaded, "Don't ever leave me, don't ever go." The dramatic version that ended up on the album was this take. "She was absolutely stunned by it. And I think it was a turning point," Levy remembers. "It did work." Two days later they flew off to the farm in Minnesota.

Is it rolling, Bob?

By the autumn of 1975 Dylan had decided to take the spirit he had enjoyed so much in the Village that summer on the road as a travelling revue. The core of the musicians was already in place. But Dylan wanted a grand-scale rolling circus. He asked Patti Smith to join them but, with her own career beginning to take off, she declined. He wanted to invite Phil Ochs, but sadly the singer-songwriter was not in any fit mental state. But there were plenty of other willing recruits. Ramblin' Jack Elliott signed on, as did Roger McGuinn. In a more surprising piece of bridge building, Dylan also persuaded **Joan Baez** to join them. **Allen Ginsberg** and movie star **Ronee Blakely** were also recruited and, in mid-October, Dylan and the entire party moved into the **Gramercy Park**

"He's always wanted to have that kind of gypsy caravan situation happening where it was loose and different people could get up and do different things." Robbie Robertson

Hotel and rehearsals began in earnest. Dylan decided to call the project **Rolling Thunder**. "I looked up at the sky and heard a boom. Then boom, boom, boom, rolling from west to east. I figured that should be the name," he explained.

With a film crew and playwright **Sam Shepard** in tow to prepare the on-the-road movie that would become ***Renaldo & Clara*** (see pp.271–273), the circus that rolled out of New York in late October 1975 was seventy-strong. The first stop was North Falmouth, Massachusetts,

Dylan with (to the left of him) Joan Baez, Richie Havens and Joni Mitchell at the fundraising concert for Rubin "Hurricane" Carter, December 8, 1975

where final rehearsals were held for the opening night on October 30 in the tiny War Memorial Auditorium in nearby Plymouth.

Fuelled by a genuine bonhomie and liberal quantities of drink and drugs, the revue was a remarkable spectacle. The staging by Jacques Levy was theatrical, creating an old-fashioned vaudeville feel, and Dylan came on stage without announcement, following warm-up songs by several of the other performers. Dressed in a fedora adorned with flowers, and often with his face painted white, the audience frequently failed to recognize him until he started to sing.

Inevitably, the segment with Baez, which swiftly grew from two to six songs, was a highlight; it was the first time they had appeared on stage together in a decade. And the campaign to free Rubin Carter, and the song that was part of it, became another centrepiece of the show,

Clara. As he declined to script anything, Shepard swiftly found his services were superfluous and instead set about writing the **Rolling Thunder Logbook**, a diary-style account of the enterprise.

A surprise presence on the tour was **Sara**, who had never enjoyed the on-the-road rock'n'roll lifestyle, but had been talked into playing the role of Clara in the film that Larry Sloman called a "mythocumentary". Looking thin and often strained, in one scene shot at Niagara Falls, Sara played a witch-goddess who sets Renaldo – Dylan – various tasks to prove his worth. It was not included in the final movie, although a scene in which Baez asked Dylan, "What would've happened if we had got married, Bob?" did make the cut. Looking slightly embarrassed, Dylan answered, "I married the woman I love."

The 1975 leg of the revue ended at Madison

> *"We were all very close. We had this fire going ten years ago and now we've got it burning again."* Bob Dylan, Plymouth, Massachusetts, October 1975

an important badge that said Dylan had not lost his old radicalism. On the opening night he was so carried away by the mood that he even made a rare political statement – one of his first of the decade. "I hear Massachusetts is the only state that didn't vote for Nixon? Is that true?" After the cheers had died down he responded, "Well, neither did we." Some nights the show ran for almost four hours, although Dylan was usually only on stage for about an hour of it.

On off-days musicians were cast as actors in the surreal scenes Dylan devised for *Renaldo &*

Square Garden, New York, on December 8, with a benefit performance for Rubin Carter. It was an emotional night at which an excited rumour went round that the boxer had been acquitted. In fact, it was another three months before he was granted bail pending a retrial. On its biggest outing, the band played sloppily and the cavernous MSG was a long way from the small and announced venues Dylan had originally intended. After 31 concerts in 40 days, the entire cast was exhausted and in need of a break.

The Life

1976: In the Eye of the Hurricane

"Dylan is now exploring his kingdom with a new majesty about him. He alone has the clear, clean authoritative strength to take his own monumental images, unbuild and rebuild them." Allen Ginsberg, *New Age Journal*, 1975

Although Dylan had finished recording *Desire* the previous July and at least seven of its nine songs had featured regularly on the **Rolling** **Thunder Revue**, the album did not reach stores until January 16, 1976. When it did, it became Dylan's third consecutive American number

Dylan performing at The Band's Last Waltz, November 1976

Bob and Neil

Dylan grew deeply suspicious and perhaps a little jealous of Neil Young in early 1972 when his album *Harvest* hit the top of the charts in both Britain and America. His main complaint was that the album's lead single, "Heart of Gold", sounded like him. "I used to hate it when it came on the radio. I always liked Neil Young but it bothered me every time I listened to Heart Of Gold," he complained. "I'd say, 'shit, that's me. If it sounds like me, it should as well be me'. I needed to lay back for a while, forget about things, myself included, and I'd get so far away and turn on the radio and there I am. But it's not me. It seemed to me somebody else had taken my thing and had run away with it and you know, I never got over it."

Given that so many people have copied him over the years, Young's main crime in Dylan's eyes seems to be selling more records than Bob. For, in truth, "Heart Of Gold" doesn't really sound that much like Dylan at all. Yet there's no doubt that Young was influenced over the years by him and he has readily acknowledged the debt. "There isn't a record that he's made that I haven't listened to," he told biographer Jimmy McDonough. "I liked Bob's music so much at one point I actually had to consciously not listen to it because it affected me so much. I realized at one point, if I listened too much, I'd become like him."

Inevitably, their orbits have crossed over the years since they first shared a stage together at the SNACK benefit in San Francisco in March 1975. In one odd story, Young's producer David Briggs found Dylan snooping around the house they had rented to record **Zuma** in 1975. Briggs grabbed him by the coat intending to throw the intruder forcibly off the property before he realized who it was. Dylan was invited in to the studio and played piano and guitar on a few numbers, before the session fell apart. The following year Dylan and Young were back on stage together at The Band's farewell, **The Last Waltz**.

Then, in 1985, Young rang Dylan and persuaded him to join Farm Aid, a charitable initiative in support of American farmers. Dylan also stayed for a while on Young's ranch in 1988. Shortly afterwards, Young joined Dylan's backing band for three dates in California, playing electric guitar on **Like A Rolling Stone**, "Gates Of Eden" and "Maggie's Farm", among other songs. The concerts launched what was to become known as the Never Ending Tour.

Into the 1990s, Young appeared at Dylan's thirtieth anniversary concert at Madison Square Garden in 1992, singing "Just Like Tom Thumb's Blues" and "All Along The Watchtower". Five years later, Dylan namechecked Young in "Highlands", the closing track on his **Time Out Of Mind** album.

one album and, surprisingly, his first platinum album for selling one million units. In Britain, the album peaked at number three.

The second leg of Rolling Thunder did not resume until April, although in the meantime there had been a second, poorly attended "Night Of The Hurricane" benefit in Houston in January with **Stevie Wonder** and **Stephen**

Stills guesting. The tour featured much the same cast as before, with Ronee Blakely the only significant absentee, and ran until late May without ever quite reaching the spontaneous heights of the autumn 1975 shows.

Several shows were cancelled due to poor ticket sales. The fact that Rubin Carter was now out on bail had dissipated the campaigning zeal, and "Hurricane" was not performed again after the Houston benefit. That his marriage was on the rocks once more did not help Dylan's mood either. He took up with a young actress called Sally Kirkland, although she was far from the only one. "He tried a lot of chicks," Rob Stoner said. "And he tried every kind of chick." In his set, many of the songs from *Desire* were replaced by bitter-sounding versions of songs from **Blood On The Tracks**.

Needless to say, with this new turn of events, Sara did not rejoin the tour and Dylan did not sing the song named after her. When she turned up towards the end in mid-May for his 35th birthday, he was less than happy. That she had Dylan's mother and his children in tow appeared to be an attempt to remind him of his family duties and obligations. According to Joan Baez, Sara looked "like a mad woman, her hair wild and dark rings around her eyes".

Dylan's latest on-the-road companion Stephanie Buffington had to make a hasty exit. Baez's own contribution to the unhappy party that ensued was to lead the throng in a communal chorus of "Happy birthday, dear Shithead".

Sara stayed on for a couple of days for the filming of a television special, at Colorado State University, Fort Collins, in late May, during which she had to endure listening to her husband spit out a demonic version of "Idiot Wind". When the show was broadcast in September under the title *Hard Rain*, it was accompanied by a live album of the same name. Two months later Dylan appeared at The Band's farewell concert, **The Last Waltz**, in San Francisco. His five-song set with his old partners in crime was to be his last live appearance for 15 months. By the time he took the stage again in Japan in February 1978, it would be as a divorced man.

1977: Everything is Broken

"Definition destroys. There's nothing definite in this world." Bob Dylan, 1976

The ending of Dylan's marriage was messy. But there was to be no *Blood On The Tracks*–style confessional: the world never got to hear the compositions he wrote in 1977, inspired by the final round of this emotional drama as he and Sara fought over custody of their children.

Steven Soles from the Rolling Thunder Revue recalls Dylan playing him and T-Bone Burnett between ten and a dozen new songs in the spring

of 1977, which were "very dark, very intense". One, he recalls, was called "**I'm Cold**" and was "scathing, tough and venomous".

Dylan has also confirmed the existence of the songs. "They dealt with the period as I was going through it," according to Dylan. "For relief I wrote the tunes. I thought they were great. Some people around town heard them. But I had no interest in recording them." They constitute another of the several lost albums of Dylan's career.

Sara formally filed for divorce on March 1, employing the most famous divorce lawyer in California, Marvin M. Mitchelson, who was recommended to her by **David Geffen**, still sore at having lost Dylan to his previous label, Columbia. In a statement to the court on her behalf, Mitchelson claimed she had come downstairs in their Malibu home on February 13 to find Dylan and their children at the breakfast table with "a woman called Malika". According to her deposition, Dylan struck her on the face and ordered her to leave. Sara moved into a hotel and alleged, "I can't go home without fear for my safety. I was in such fear of him that I locked the doors in the home to protect myself from his violent outbursts and temper tantrums."

New Age art therapist who had been employed to help the children cope with their parents' divorce by expressing their feelings through painting. By the time Sara returned from Hawaii with the children, McFree had moved in with Dylan and they had become lovers.

That summer, Dylan, McFree and the children all headed to the farm in Minnesota. According to McFree, Dylan was in a bad way. "I brought him back to life. He was practically dead," she said. "This guy was shot emotionally. The farm was really where he got back up on his feet again." She even claimed Dylan told her he had contemplated suicide. His bleak mood was not helped when he heard in August, during their stay on the farm, that **Elvis Presley** had died.

Inevitably, part of Dylan's recovery process was to write more songs, and it was on the

"My five children are greatly disturbed by my husband's behavior and his bizarre lifestyle." Sara Dylan, during divorce proceedings, March 1977

The allegations were uncontested and the divorce became final in June. Sara took custody of the children with the court commissioner retaining jurisdiction of their communal property "for future determination". Sara eventually received a settlement of 36 million dollars. It was unpleasant but less acrimonious than many divorces. Yet all that was to change when, to Dylan's fury, Sara took the children to **Hawaii** with the intention of finding a house there for them to make a new home.

While in Hawaii, Sara left her LA house in the care of a friend called **Faridi McFree**, a

farm that he wrote much of the next album, *Street-Legal*, just as he had written *Blood On The Tracks* there three summers earlier.

But when, on September 2, Sara's lawyer asked the court for permission for her to move the children to Hawaii, Dylan decided to fight. His attorney responded by asking the Santa Monica Superior Court to grant him sole custody on the grounds that Sara had violated a court order by previously taking the children to Hawaii without his permission.

He took the children while she returned to Hawaii to finalize arrangements to move there.

The Life

When Sara returned, she submitted a deposition to the court accusing Dylan and McFree of attempting to "brainwash" the children and to "deprive them of the natural love and companionship" of their mother. The children were ordered to be returned to their mother, but when the papers were served on Dylan at the Point Dume home where the children were staying, security guards refused entry to the court officials.

In an even more bizarre twist, Sara then decided to take custody of the children by force. She turned up at the children's school and demanded they leave with her, chasing them through the building with three private detectives. She was subsequently charged with battery after reportedly "punching and choking a teacher" who asked to see the court order and was eventually fined $125.

Fortunately, this incident appears to have brought everyone to their senses, for the sake of the children. In adulthood, **Jakob Dylan** recalled it as the worst day of his life and declined to talk further about it on the grounds that he'd probably "end up with a therapist". The Dylans were both caring parents and recognized that the situation could not go on. As Dylan later said, "Marriage was a failure. Husband and wife was a failure. Mother and father wasn't a failure."

By the end of December, they had agreed to what had been the only logical settlement all along. The children would remain in California with Sara, and Dylan would have open access to them. One of the conditions was that Dylan signed an agreement not to continue seeing McFree, who, unsurprisingly, Sara regarded as guilty of an act of gross and irresponsible betrayal.

Away from such traumas, Dylan spent most of his creative energy in 1977 editing *Renaldo & Clara* (see p.271) with the assistance of Howard Alk. And with the film finally due to premiere in January 1978 after eighteen months of painstaking editing, Dylan was finally ready to think about playing live again.

1978: "Alimony's killing me"

"I almost didn't have a friend in the world. I was under a lot of pressure, so I figured I better get busy working." Bob Dylan

"A telegram arrived from the Japanese promoter of the songs he expected Bob to do on tour. In other words he was a jukebox. He was playing requests." Rob Stoner

Dylan's reason for undertaking his 1978 world tour – his first world tour in twelve years – was simple enough. He needed the cash. Under Californian divorce law, Sara had been entitled to half his estate and had received a total of 36 million dollars. He retained a similar sum, but much of this was tied up in real estate. In addition, *Renaldo & Clara* had been a costly venture and Dylan had poured a lot of his own money into the film. The poor reviews that greeted its opening suggested he had little chance of recouping any of his investment. "I've had a bad year or two," he candidly admitted to the *LA Times*. "I've got a few debts to pay off."

In December 1977 he set about assembling a band, for the first time since the Rolling Thunder Revue, and turned to some of the same personnel, including Rob Stoner, David Mansfield and Steven Soles. They found Dylan irritable and distracted. He was always bummed out. He was chain-smoking and he was in a really bad mood," Stoner recalls.

Several of his other first-choice musicians, including Al Kooper, were unavailable and various other musicians were tried and rejected. Eventually, Ian Wallace, once of **King Crimson**, was recruited on drums along with Billy Cross on guitar, Alan Pasqua on keyboards, Bobbye Hall on percussion, Steve Douglas on horns and backing vocalists Helena Springs, Jo Ann Harris and Debbie Dye.

Throughout January they rehearsed at **Rundown Studios**, a rehearsal space Dylan had recently purchased in Santa Monica and which would be the centre of his activities for the next five years. They flew out for his first tour of Japan in mid-February, with a setlist mostly of greatest hits. The promoter had sent a list of songs he expected Dylan to perform, possibly the first time in his career anybody had told him what to sing.

The old Dylan would undoubtedly have treated such a demand as an insult and come up with a rival set that included everything but the requested songs. But with his bank balance diminished by the divorce and his ego bruised by the scathing reviews for *Renaldo & Clara* ("They weren't about the movie, they were just an excuse to get at me," he complained), he decided he had no choice but to comply.

The first night at Budokan, Tokyo, featured a marathon 28 songs, which at least gave him scope for a few less predictable selections, such as **The Man In Me** and "Going Going Gone". As a way of maintaining his interest while being expected to perform as a human jukebox, he delivered many of the songs with almost unrecognizable new arrangements, so that it would sometimes take audiences a minute or more to work out what they were hearing. The tour booklet described him as an "entertainer", and he had the band and singers wear stage costumes designed by **"Spoony" Bill Whitten**, which they hated and complained made them look like "hookers and pimps". This was Dylan as a Las Vegas–style showbiz turn.

After the first week, he added the only new song unveiled on the tour, **Is Your Love In Vain?**, which would appear on his next studio album, *Street-Legal*.

Now a divorced man, Dylan began to look for female company among his backing singers. He grew particularly close to **Helena Springs**, a young black woman fresh out of college, who had never toured before. Behind Dylan's back, her colleagues bitched that she was incapable of singing in tune and had been chosen for her looks rather than her voice.

Backstage at Earl's Court, June 1978

"There's an amazing presence or power here. But it is blocked, denied, kept out of reach…"

"Simply impossible to pay attention to for more than a couple of minutes at a time"

"His best since John Wesley Harding"

Paul Williams, Greil Marcus and Michael Watts review three apparently completely different albums called *Street-Legal*

More unusually, Dylan began writing songs with her, several of which, including "If I Don't Be There By Morning", "Stop Now", "Coming From The Heart" and "Walk Out In the Rain", he recorded but never released. He subsequently gave them to **Eric Clapton**, who included three of them on his album, *Backless*.

Soon another girlfriend, Mary Alice Artes, had joined the backing chorus. Then when they got to Australia in March, Dylan summoned **Carolyn Dennis**, who at the time had a gig singing backing vocals for Burt Bacharach. She claims she had never heard of Bob Dylan when she got the call. But both Artes and Dennis were soon to play significant roles in his life, well beyond the stage.

Changing of the Guards

With the world tour next due to touch down in Europe in June 1978, Dylan had a brief window to record a new album on his return from Australia and the Far East. *Street-Legal* was cut in five days in April at his Rundown Studios in Santa Monica, with a mobile recording truck.

The problem with the album was not the songs – most of which had been written while he was with Faridi McFree the previous summer, and several of which were extremely strong both melodically and lyrically. Nor was there anything wrong with the playing, although the horns and girlie choruses were not to everyone's taste.

But technically the recording was a disaster, sounding, as **Howard Sounes** put it, "like it had been recorded under wet cardboard". Dylan knew it, too. "I couldn't find the right producer," he complained. "So we just brought in the remote truck and cut it, went for a live sound." When he listened to the album on playback, he was so disheartened that he responded by sacking the entire band – only to rehire them again when he realized he had insufficient time to find replacements for the fast-approaching European tour dates.

Yet, according to the musicians, the problems with the sound were entirely of Dylan's own making. Violinist **David Mansfield** reported that the engineers attempted to record the album professionally, only to be told by Dylan, "Get rid of this crap, pull your stuff around in

The Life

a circle and let's just play." The live feel failed woefully to translate onto tape and it was not until the album was remastered for release on SACD in 2003, using the most sophisticated digital techniques, that it was restored to anything like how Dylan had originally meant the record to sound.

Although he was acutely aware of its failings, Dylan was bitterly disappointed when the album only reached number eleven in the American charts, a desperately poor showing considering the previous three studio albums

tion and while in London Dylan took the time to check out such punk/new wave acts as The Clash, Elvis Costello and Graham Parker. At one point during his stay, he encountered **Sid Vicious**, who threatened him with a knife for reasons he was too out of it to explain, before the doomed Sex Pistols' bassist was hustled away.

Dylan's Earl's Court shows were greeted with something approaching hysteria. *Melody Maker* ran an eight-page pull-out supplement and a review in the **Daily Mail** carried

> *"For every dollar I make there's a pool of sweat on the floor.*
> *It's a question of how much of it you can stand.*
> *How much can you stick it out?"* Bob Dylan, 1978

had all gone to number one. **Greil Marcus**, who had famously opened his *Rolling Stone* review of *Self Portrait* with the words "What is this shit?" attacked *Street-Legal* with similar ferocity as "utterly fake". In Britain, it fared better and made number three and received better reviews, particularly in **Melody Maker** which had failed to join in the praise for *Blood On The Tracks* and perversely declared *Street-Legal* to be Dylan's "best album since John Wesley Harding."

The favourable British reaction appears to have been swayed by the fact that *Street-Legal*'s release coincided with the hype surrounding a week of sell-out gigs at London's Earl's Court at the start of his first European tour since 1966, that had fans queuing for 48 hours before tickets went on sale.

Britain was in the throes of its punk revolu-

the headline: "The Greatest Concert I Have Ever Seen". After dates in Sweden, Holland, Germany and France, Dylan returned to Britain for an equally triumphant appearance before 200,000 people at the Blackbushe festival, at which Eric Clapton joined him for an encore of "Changing Of The Guards".

The "Vegas Tour"

Something went horribly wrong when Dylan returned to America after the triumphs of his European tour. After spending his customary summer on the farm in Minnesota, he began rehearsing for the American leg of his world tour at Rundown Studios, Santa Monica, in early September.

Opening in Augusta on September 15, he played 64 three-hour shows over the following 92 days – and the critics savaged him. He might have expected such a reaction in Britain, where the punk ethic was mercilessly demolishing all the old icons. Yet, instead, he had been treated as a conquering hero. In America, where being rich and famous is usually enough to guarantee a certain degree of sycophancy, he surely could have expected an easy ride. But it was as if the usually supine American media had scented blood over *Renaldo & Clara*, and were now moving in for the kill. Having initially dubbed it the **"alimony tour"**, they then began calling it "the Vegas tour", accusing Dylan of churning out the old hits in cabaret style.

He was genuinely hurt and even baffled by the reaction. "The writers complain the shows are disco or Las Vegas," he complained. "I don't know how they come up with those theories. We never heard them when we played Australia or Japan or Europe."

By the time the tour finished, the week before Christmas, Dylan had played an exhausting 115 live dates in ten months and replenished his diminished coffers. But towards the end he was patently not enjoying himself, playing the songs at an ever faster tempo and slurring the words. At band meetings, he angrily berated his musicians for being "too formulaic". Yet, despite all this, at the end-of-tour party in Miami he told them he wanted to keep the show on the road into 1979.

Over the Christmas break, however, he changed his mind and sacked them to head off in a very different direction. Bob was about to find God.

1979: With God on Our Side

*"Jesus put his hand on me. It was a physical thing.
I felt it over me, my whole body trembled. The glory of the Lord
knocked me down and picked me up."* Bob Dylan

The news that Dylan had undergone a "born-again" conversion in 1978 was for many fans the ultimate betrayal. At almost precisely the same moment, the Reaganite "moral majority" of Christian conservatives and fundamentalist reactionaries was planning its takeover of American politics. Didn't organized religion represent everything Dylan had always stood against? How could the most eloquent and articulate opponent of dogma now suddenly embrace it? In any case, wasn't he meant to be Jewish? (see p.112).

It happened in San Diego on November 17. But it could have been any other station of the cross as he was winding up the hectic world tour that had seen him play 115 live dates in 1978. He wasn't feeling too good. The set he was playing was perfunctory. He was going through the motions and he knew it. And then someone threw a small silver cross on stage.

The first surprise was that Dylan even noticed. The second was that he bent down to pick it up. The next night, in Tucson, he took the cross out and examined it in his hotel room, undergoing a full-blown religious experience in which he claimed "the King of Kings and Lord of Lords" appeared to him.

Less than a week later, Dylan was wearing the cross (or another like it) when he appeared at a concert in Fort Worth, Texas. On December 2, during the soundcheck for a gig in Nashville, he unveiled a new song called **Slow Train**, which spoke of his new faith. On the last date of the tour in Miami on December 16, he performed another new song that spoke of his religious conversion, **Do Right To Me Baby (Do Unto Others)**.

In January 1979, one of Dylan's girlfriends, Mary Alice Artes, approached Pastor Ken Gulliksen of an evangelical church called the

Jewish roots

Prior to his Christian conversion, Dylan had shown some interest in getting back in touch with his Jewish roots. After his father's funeral in June 1968, he confessed to Harold Leventhal, Woody Guthrie's former manager, that he had never really known the man who was Abe Zimmerman. Leventhal's response was to urge Dylan to get back in touch with his Jewish faith. Over the next few years he read widely around the subject and held talks with Rabbi Meir Kahane, a founder of the **Jewish Defense League**.

He visited the Wailing Wall in Jerusalem on his birthday in May 1971. *Time* magazine reported that he was considering changing his name back to Zimmerman. Dylan dismissed such reports as "pure journalese". But he did consider the possibility of taking his family to live on a kibbutz. Bruce Dorfman, the painter who was his neighbour in Woodstock, reported that when he returned from Israel he was seriously considering becoming a Hasid. Instead, by the end of the decade he had become a born-again Christian.

His conversion caused offence to members of his family and his Jewish friends. "I think it was for publicity, that's what I think," said his aunt Ethel Crystal. "He is Jewish-minded, plenty Jewish-minded, he was

brought up that way. He was bar mitzvahed." And, despite his Christian conversion, his children all had bar mitzvahs and he attended the ceremonies on each occasion. When he encountered Leventhal at a party in Hollywood in 1980, his old friend confronted him and demanded, "What have you got that cross dangling around you for?"

In 1982, there were strong rumours that he was again exploring his Jewish heritage, sparked by a picture of him wearing a yarmulke at the bar mitzvah of his son Jesse in Jerusalem. The following year there were further stories that he had been spending time with an ultra-orthodox sect called the **Lubavitchers** and even that he had recorded an album of Hasidic songs. Dylan kept silent, which only encouraged the rumours.

By 1986, Allen Ginsberg was claiming that Dylan had reverted back to "his natural Judaism". Dylan appeared with his son-in-law Peter Himmelman (husband of his step-daughter Maria) at the annual Jewish Chabad telethon in Los Angeles in November 1989 wearing a yarmulke and singing "Hava Nagila". But ultimately, the importance of his Jewish roots appears to have been cultural rather than religious.

The Vineyard Fellowship

The Vineyard Fellowship, to which Dylan's girlfriend Mary Alice Artes introduced him in late 1978, was a small evangelical church that peddled a New Age, born-again version of Christianity. It had been founded in Los Angeles in 1974 by the Lutheran pastor Ken Gulliksen, who had previously been a singer on the Christian music circuit. The church's style was informal. Gulliksen took services dressed in his shorts and counted a number of LA musicians among his congregation, including **T-Bone Burnett**, Steven Soles and David Mansfield, all of whom had played on Dylan's Rolling Thunder Tour.

The Fellowship placed particular importance on the final book of New Testament allegories, St John's *The Divine Revelation*, claiming that a code enabled the book to be read as a true prophecy of the imminent "end times". Another key text was **The Late Great Planet Earth** by Hal Lindsey, who claimed to have cracked the code to the Book of Revelation. The book claimed that scripture had accurately described 20th-century history and predicted that the battle of Armageddon would soon be fought in the Middle East. Dylan absorbed such theories and recycled aspects of them in several songs.

Vineyard Fellowship in the San Fernando Valley and told him that she wanted someone to speak to her boyfriend. Gulliksen sent two colleagues, Paul Esmond and Larry Myers, to meet Dylan in the West LA suburb of Brentwood. Within days he had signed up with the Fellowship. Sometime in the coming weeks, he was baptized and he and Artes commenced a three-month series of bible classes at the School of Discipleship.

"At first I said there's no way I can devote three months to this. I've got to be back on the road soon," he subsequently said. "But I was sleeping one day and I just sat up in bed at seven in the morning and I was compelled to drive over to the Bible school."

Attending four days a week, he was soon not merely a disciple but a proselytizing evangelist for the cause. Inevitably, more and more of his new songs began to reflect his faith. Fired with the fervour of the convert, his latest com-

positions were full of praise and damnation, salvation and hellfire, many of them directly influenced by the book of Revelation, which the Vineyard Fellowship believed was a literal account of the "End Times" that were coming.

At first he was unsure about recording the new songs and considered producing an album of **Carolyn Dennis** singing them. The songs "frightened him", he admitted. He hadn't wanted or planned to write them. He desired the songs to be put out there. But he knew if he released them under his own name "it would just mean more pressure".

Yet Dylan swiftly came round to the view that the Vineyard's message would have more force if his name was directly attached to it. "When I get involved in something, I get totally involved. I don't just play around the fringes," he explained. By the end of March, even before he had finished his scripture course, he had asked Mark Knopfler and drummer

Pick Withers of the newly ascendant band **Dire Straits** to play on what would, in effect, be his first album of gospel songs.

They entered the studio at Muscle Shoals, Alabama, in early May with producer Jerry Wexler, who had worked with the likes of **Aretha Franklin** and **Ray Charles**. The band Dylan assembled also included Tim Drummond that from henceforth he would sing only songs "given to me by the Lord". The tone of his sermonizing was hectoring and bellicose. "I told you the times they are changin' and they did," he said. "I said the answer was blowin' in the wind and it was. I'm telling you now Jesus is coming back and he is. There is no other way of salvation."

"I didn't expect this. And I want to thank the Lord for it."

A born-again Bob receiving his first Grammy, for "Gotta Serve Somebody"

on bass, Barry Beckett on keyboards, and Helena Springs, Regina Havis and Carolyn Dennis on backing vocals. He was in full-on evangelizing mode, even attempting to convert Wexler to Christianity. The veteran gave him a dusty response: "I'm a 62-year-old confirmed Jewish atheist. Let's just make an album," he told his would-be saviour.

Slow Train Coming was recorded in just five days, and a little more than three months later it was in the shops. That Dylan should make a Christian rock album, particularly one full of such hardcore evangelizing, was greeted with shock and dismay by many of his old fans. Even though the record was tempered with flashes of compassion and humanity, to many his zealotry was nothing short of grotesque. **Greil Marcus** accused him of trying "to sell a pre-packaged doctrine he's received from someone else." Charles Shaar Murray, in *NME*, recognized the power of the music but found the message "unpleasant and hate-filled".

What particularly offended many was that he turned his back on his old material, insisting

Perhaps surprisingly, none of this affected his record sales. In its first year of release, *Slow Train Coming* outsold *Blood On The Tracks* and *Blonde On Blonde*. It made number three in America and number two in Britain, and the single, **Gotta Serve Somebody**, won him a Grammy for best male rock vocal.

To Dylan this was evidence that he was indeed engaged in God's work and he dedicated his award to the Lord. It also meant that those who hoped that Dylan, having made his gospel album, would now move on, were in for a major disappointment. Instead, he did what any self-respecting evangelist would do. He decided that in order to reach the greatest number of lost souls, he needed to put a band together and take his message out on the road. Dylan now believed he was a messenger of God, whose duty it was to lead his fans to the salvation only the Lord could offer. "I follow God so if my followers are following me, indirectly they're gonna be following God, too," he blathered.

*"I had never heard of anybody who'd recorded songs
for 20 years and then one day just didn't play
any of them again. Just played nothing but new songs …
I got a kick out of that."* Bob Dylan 1981

*"All my stuff at that time was influenced or written
right off the gospel. But that was no reason to say
it wasn't a musical show."* Bob Dylan 1984

When He Returns

On his 1978 "Las Vegas" tour, Dylan had played a setlist of greatest hits. Now, a year later, he decided upon a show in which he would play no old songs at all. His new faith had inspired his most prolific bout of songwriting since 1967 and the **Basement Tapes**. There were only nine songs on **Slow Train Coming**. But he already had plenty more where they came from, all cut from similarly devout cloth.

With a band that included Tim Drummond, drummer Jim Keltner, guitarist Fred Tackett, Spooner Oldham and Terry Young on keyboards, and a trio of female singers, the tour opened with a two-week residency in San Francisco beginning on November 1, 1979.

The Vineyard Fellowship seconded Larry Myers to the tour to minister to Dylan's spiritual needs before the shows. Dylan would gather his musicians in a circle and instruct them to hold hands in prayer. His publicist was banned from the backstage area because he wasn't a believer.

Dylan's 90-minute set included no songs more than a year old, comprising all of **Slow Train Coming** and seven unreleased compositions, all celebrating Jesus Christ. In white T-shirt and black leather jacket, Dylan looked like an archetypal rock'n'roller. But as fans yelled for the old songs, he ignored them. He had dealt with boos before and seemed oblivious to the reasons why his audiences were even more bothered by religion than they had been by electricity.

On the plus side, the shows were full of nerve, the band was fantastic and the new songs had undeniable power, whatever you thought of their message. But the critics predictably savaged him with headlines such as "Born-Again Dylan Bombs" and "Bob Dylan's Godawful Gospel". **Joel Selvin**, one of the most respected newspaper critics in America, wrote: "Dylan is no longer asking hard questions and raising an angry fist. Instead he has opted for the soothing soporific which the simple truths of his brand of Christianity provide." A furious Dylan rang him at home and told him he was banned from future shows.

On a lighter note, a banner appeared in the audience one night saying, "**Jesus loves your** old songs, too!" Dylan took no notice and carried on with his gospel songs, interspersed with five-minute sermons full of references to the "End Times". By the time the tour got to Tempe, Arizona, and the disgruntled shouts of "play some rock'n'roll!" were growing louder, he was positively goading the crowd. "The spirit of the Anti-Christ is loose right now," he harangued the hecklers. "There's only two kinds of people. There's saved people and there's lost people. Remember that I told you that. You may never see me again. You may not see me, but sometime down the line you remember you heard it here, that Jesus is the Lord. Every knee shall bow."

He also swallowed wholesale some of the more bizarre scriptural interpretations of the contemporary political scene favoured by the Vineyard Fellowship, telling the crowd in Tempe that it was written in the Bible that Russia and China were going to attack the **Middle East**, where the Battle of Armageddon was going to be fought out. And when the world had been destroyed, "Christ will set up his kingdom and he'll rule it from Jerusalem," he thundered. "I know as far out as this may seem, this is what the Bible says."

At this point, someone in the crowd rather wittily shouted, "Everybody must get stoned!" But Dylan was not amused and ploughed on with further admonishments and another grim description of the "End Times" that were coming. In late December 1979, the Soviet Union sent troops into **Afghanistan**. For Dylan, it was yet further vindication that he had found the one and only true path.

Lost & Found
1980–89

"He's very hung up on being Bob Dylan. He feels he's trapped in his past."

Bono, 1988

Lost & Found
1980–89

1980: **The Children of Disobedience**

"You want rock'n'roll? You can go and see Kiss and you can rock'n'roll all the way down to the pit." Bob Dylan, November 1979

For those who were appalled by Dylan's conversion – such as Keith Richards, who cynically dubbed him "the prophet of profit" – there was worse to come. There had always been a stubborn streak to Dylan and, just as the opposition to his electric music had only made him turn the volume up higher, the more he was criticized for his gospel music, the more dogmatic and self-righteous he became.

Taking up another phrase from the literature of the Vineyard Fellowship, Dylan began talking about those who did not share his faith as "the children of disobedience". Coming from the man who had told mothers and fathers throughout the land not to criticize what they couldn't understand in **The Times They Are A-Changin'**, this was rich indeed. And his audience was about to make him pay the price for it.

With Helena Springs replaced on backing vocals by **Carolyn Dennis** (see p.120), Dylan resumed his evangelical tour early in January 1980. In Denver, Allen Ginsberg came to see him backstage and tried to impress on him

that the Christian God is one of *forgiveness*; Dylan ominously told him that God also "comes to judge". There was certainly plenty of judging going on in the songs that Dylan and his band went into the studio in Muscle Shoals to record in February.

Howard Sounes is one of the few Dylan biographers without an axe to grind. But his assessment of **Saved**, Dylan's second "born-again" album, is damning. "Many of the songs floundered where they should have rocked and most of the lyrics amounted to little more than religious clichés," he wrote. The Christian compassion that had redeemed *Slow Train Coming* had been replaced by a relentless eschatological belief that the end was nigh and that nonbelievers would burn in hell. "An artist celebrated for his rigorous intelligence and nonconformity, Bob was now setting Christian dogma to music."

Columbia, too, hated the album. When they sent the record out to radio stations and reviewers, they suppressed the obnoxious "us and them" sleeve painted by Dylan himself and

The Second Mrs Dylan

The rumours that Dylan had remarried in the 1980s were not finally confirmed until Howard Sounes's 2001 biography, *Down The Highway*. After his separation from Sara, Dylan had relationships with many of his backing singers, sometimes called the "Queens of Rhythm". Often he was conducting affairs with several of them at the same time. **Helena Springs**, **Mary Alice Artes**, **Clydie King** and **Carolyn Dennis** were among those who shared both his stage and his bed.

In 1985, in an interview for *The Boston Review*, he claimed that he had remarried in 1980, the year he is reported to have bought Artes a $25,000 engagement ring. But this appears to have been a typical Dylan piece of misinformation for there is no evidence that they were ever married. There were also stories that he had married King and had a child with her. Yet, although he is understood to have bought her a house in Los Angeles, no documentary evidence of this, either, has ever come to light.

However, Sounes's research turned up the fact that Dylan did marry Carolyn Dennis on June 4, 1986, the certificate being filed with the LA County registrar as a "confidential marriage". The wedding came six months after Dennis had given birth to Dylan's child, **Desirée Gabrielle Dennis-Dylan**, on January 31. But, despite motherhood, Dennis was on stage with her new husband every night during the 1986 tour and he used her to recruit the singers to the "Queens

of Rhythm", whose membership changed constantly. At one time, Dennis hired her mother, **Madelyn Quebec**, to sing alongside her.

Sounes discovered the marriage by using his professional training as a biographer to track down witnesses and sources that the authors – mostly music critics – of most of the vast number of books written about Dylan had never thought of asking. He further discovered that, in 1989, Dylan had bought a marital home for the pair of them at 5430 Shirley Avenue in the anonymous LA suburb of **Tarzana**. The neighbours never even knew the Dylans were there – and indeed, as the **Never Ending Tour** was in full swing, Bob seldom was. By 1991 the property had been transferred to Dennis's name and the following year they were divorced. She received a multimillion-dollar settlement and, after an application by Dylan's lawyers, a judge passed an order to seal the file on the divorce.

A vow of silence also appears to have been part of the settlement, for not even the resourceful Sounes was able to get Dennis to talk. When contacted, she told him: "Mr Dylan is a very private person, which is why the world has such a hard time trying to find out about his life."

Dylan semi-acknowledged her existence in *Chronicles*, although he inscrutably refers only to "my wife," without ever mentioning her name.

inserted the disc into a plain white sleeve with a promotional photo depicting a pre-conversion Dylan playing an acoustic guitar. The disguise failed to fool anyone. *Saved* became the first Dylan album since 1964's *Another Side Of...* not to make the American top twenty. It would be another seventeen years before he returned to the American charts.

The Life

1980–81: Back from the Brink...

"Is he a regular guy? No. Why would you want him to be?" Chuck Plotkin on producing *Shot Of Love*

There were probably several reasons why, after *Saved*, Dylan finally began to soften his fire-and-brimstone approach. The writer Gavin Martin believes that "he had to make a decision – could he best serve his saviour while neglecting his muse?" Declining sales and falling audiences must also have been a factor. Even Dylan at his most stubborn must have realized his sermonizing wasn't going to save anyone if there was nobody left to listen.

Whatever his thinking, after the final leg of his evangelical tour ended in May 1980, Dylan would never again perform an entirely religious set. By the time he resumed in the autumn of that year, his old songs had reappeared in the setlist, alongside such unusual covers as **Abraham, Martin and John,** and a superb and unashamedly carnal version of the old Peggy Lee hit, **Fever.**

Dylan was also very shaken by the murder of **John Lennon** in December 1980. Convinced that he could be the next victim of a fanatical fan, he decided that he needed more than the protection of the Lord and hired additional security and bodyguards. He even gave Tim Drummond, his band leader, a bulletproof vest which, somewhat surreally, he had sumptuously gift-wrapped.

When he came to begin recording a new album in the spring of 1981 – which would be released in August that year as *Shot Of Love* – Dylan had a sheaf of new songs that were more thoughtful and interesting to audiences

than almost anything on *Saved*. Some of them, such as **Every Grain of Sand,** had first been recorded in the autumn of 1980. Other powerful songs – including **Caribbean Wind,** written while on vacation in St Vincent, **Angelina,** and **The Groom's Still Waiting At The Altar** – didn't even make the album, despite being superior to many of the songs that did. We only found this out later, of course, when the tracks appeared on the box-set editions *Biograph* and *The Bootleg Series.* In an unprecedented move, "The Groom's Still Waiting At The Altar" was later added to the CD issue of the album.

Despite the long gestation of some of the songs, the bulk of *Shot Of Love* was recorded inside two weeks in May. The disc was produced by **Chuck Plotkin,** who had worked with Springsteen and who had been recommended to Dylan by David Geffen, after Jimmy Iovine had been tried and rejected. As for musicians, to the core members of his touring band – Fred Tackett, Tim Drummond and Jim Keltner – Dylan added **Benmont Tench** and **Steve Ripley** from Tom Petty's Heartbreakers, and guitarist **Danny Kortchmar.** Then, when the album was finished, he went back into the studio to re-cut one song, "Heart Of Mine", with **Ringo Starr** and **Ron Wood.**

Dylan didn't evangelize at Plotkin as he had done with his last producer, Jerry Wexler, but he still gave him a mess of trouble. His insistence on recording live, his irregular hours and his refusal to do overdubs or play anything more than two or three times all gave Plotkin endless headaches. Typical was the sublime vocal on "Every Grain Of Sand", the album's best song. Without warning, Dylan simply began singing at the piano. There was no voice microphone set up and so, when Plotkin saw what was happening, he ran over and held a mic next to Dylan's mouth, fearing it could be the only take he might get.

In effect, Plotkin was asked to produce the album from a set of rough mixes – and, when he tried to clean them up, Dylan complained that he was trying to make him sound "like the Doobie Brothers". Neither could he persuade Dylan to include some of the quality songs he left off the album.

There were still religious references and one of the preachy songs that made the album was

Bob, not quite all at sea, 1981

called **Property Of Jesus**. But by and large the dogma that had marred *Saved* was mercifully absent. Yet that wasn't the way the critics saw it. Many of them appeared still to be writing about the shortcomings of *Saved*, rather than the vast improvement that was *Shot Of Love*. Nick Kent in *NME* even called it "Dylan's worst album to date". Bob later complained: "All they talked about was Jesus this and Jesus that, like it was some kind of Methodist record."

1981–82: Talkin' Midlife Crisis Blues

*"Death don't come knocking at the door.
It's there in the morning when you wake up."* Bob Dylan, Malibu, 1978

By the time *Shot Of Love* was released in August 1981, the now 40-year-old Dylan had completed an eventful European tour. Since it followed only weeks after a tour by **Bruce Springsteen**, who played many of the same venues, the critics inevitably compared the two – and most declared Dylan second-best. That his pride was wounded was obvious when he told *NME*'s Neil Spencer, "I feel very strongly about this show. I feel it has something to offer. No-one else does this show. Not Bruce Springsteen. Not anyone."

On the tour, he still made the band link arms while he recited the Lord's Prayer every night and gospel songs continued to take up a fair portion of the show. But several events conspired to shake the previous certitude of his faith. On the last night of the tour in Avignon, France, just as he began to sing "Saved", a young man in the crowd fell onto the electricity cables and was electrocuted. The power was cut and in the confusion that followed a second death occurred when a girl fell from the upper tier of the seating. The song was discreetly dropped from the set, only reappearing once on the 27-date tour of North America that followed that autumn.

Then, on January 1, 1982, filmmaker **Howard Alk** committed suicide at Dylan's Rundown Studios in Santa Monica. They had worked together on various film projects since 1965's *Don't Look Back* and at the time Alk was working on another Dylan film idea he had reportedly gone cold on. Dylan decided to shut down the studio there and then.

Despite the crutch of his faith, Dylan's confidence was shaken. His life and his career appeared to be going off the rails. His response was to sit out 1982, a year in which his life centred around such events as the bar mitzvah of his son Samuel, and taking his youngest son Jakob to see The Clash at the Hollywood Palladium.

1983: The Return of the Jokerman

"It's time for me to do something else. Sometimes those things appear quickly and disappear. Jesus himself only preached for three years." Bob Dylan, 1983

By the time Dylan returned to the public eye in 1983, he had changed and the world had moved on, too. There had been stories in the press that he had abandoned his Christian phase to re-embrace the Judaism of his parents. The **Vineyard Fellowship** counter-briefed by insisting he was still "one of them". But, in stark contrast to his earlier eagerness to share his theological concerns with his audience, Dylan kept his own counsel. It soon became evident that his zealotry had dimmed and that he had decided his faith and his career were best kept in separate boxes.

Meanwhile, the music industry to which he was thinking of returning had transformed itself. The CD format had been introduced the previous year. And there was a new arrival on the scene called **MTV**, which elevated the three-minute promo film to a ridiculously exaggerated importance that meant before long record labels were spending as much on making videos as on the albums they were intended to promote. Dylan, a man who had always derided and despised fashionability, decided it was finally incumbent upon him to move with these a-changin' times.

"I've made a lot of records but record making isn't my area of expertise. I always approach it with some discomfort," he had admitted to Chuck Plotkin while making *Shot Of Love*. What he really meant was that he was a studio Luddite who had made no attempt to keep up with developments in recording technology. "I figured I could always get away with just playing the songs live in the studio and leaving," he admitted. But for his next album, he was determined to "take my time, like other people do".

In early 1983, **Frank Zappa, David Bowie, Elvis Costello** – and, according to one hard-to-credit rumour, **Giorgio Moroder** – were all sounded out about producing Dylan's next album. In the end he turned to **Mark Knopfler**, whose Dire Straits were just about the biggest band in the world at that point, and who had played on *Slow Train Coming*. Together they set about assembling a crack studio band that included former Rolling Stone **Mick Taylor** and the Jamaican rhythm section of **Sly Dunbar and Robbie Shakespeare**.

Sessions for the follow-up to *Shot Of Love* began at New York's Power Station Studios in April. Dylan meant what he had said about taking his time, although he still insisted on recording live. The main difference was that he found that digital multi-tracking allowed him to rewrite and edit his lyrics while recording. Vocals would be redone not because he didn't like the take, but because he had changed the words.

Having finished the record, Dylan had a disagreement with Knopfler over the mixing, claiming that the tracks sounded too predictable, "like an Eagles record". With Knopfler off touring with Dire Straits, in June 1983 he went back into the studio and restructured the album, at the same time re-recording several vocals.

Infidels eventually appeared in November 1983 and did marginally better than *Shot Of Love*, making number twenty in the US charts and number nine in Britain. There was no tour and, instead, Dylan was persuaded to make a couple of videos for the singles **Sweetheart Like You** and **Jokerman**. He could barely conceal his contempt for the new medium and proved hopelessly inept at lip-synching. "I'd say, 'Bob you've got to work harder'," **George Lois** who directed the "Jokerman" film recalls. "You've got to dub the motherfucker. You gotta put your words to your own work. It's gotta match. If it doesn't match you look like a schmuck."

Infidels was a fine record and Dylan's most accessible release of the decade so far. But, once again, it could and should have been even better. For the second consecutive album, Dylan eccentrically left off several of his best songs. The most criminal omission was **Blind Willie McTell**, one of his touchstone songs of the decade. "Lord Protect My Child", "Foot Of Pride" (for which the studio log shows 14 completed takes) and "Someone's Got A Hold Of My Heart" also merited inclusion but were dropped. All four songs eventually appeared on 1991's *Bootleg Series Volumes I-III*, where they were confirmed to be far superior fare to such clumsy tracks as **Union Sundown** and **Neighbourhood Bully**.

Nevertheless, *Infidels* was "half a great album and all of a great-sounding one", in Clinton Heylin's words. The guitar interplay between Taylor and Knopfler was dynamic, despite reported friction between them. And in "Jokerman" and **I and I**, the album contained a brace of classic songs. Both were still full of religious references. But they were couched in typically elliptical Dylan imagery again, rather than the hard-line dogma of his overtly evangelical albums.

1984: The Heritage Tour

"For me none of the songs I've written has really dated. People say they're nostalgia. But I don't know what that means, really. A Tale Of Two Cities was written a hundred years ago. Is that nostalgic?" Bob Dylan, 1984

Having refused to play any of his old songs on the gospel tours of 1979–80, Dylan had done a

complete volte-face by the time he took to the road in 1984, and reverted again to a setlist almost exclusively made up of oldies.

The year had opened promisingly with a rare television performance on the *David Letterman Show* in March. Backed by a bunch of young LA post-punk refugees including **Charlie Quintana**, **J.J. Holiday** and **Tony Marisco**, Dylan had typically changed the three-song set between the soundcheck and the appearance. With dozens of well-rehearsed songs to choose from, at the last minute Dylan decided to play one they hadn't rehearsed at all, Sonny Boy Williamson's **Don't Start Me Talking**. They also played "License To Kill" and "Jokerman" from the recent *Infidels* album.

The performance was passionate and exhilarating and it would have made perfect sense to take the sound out on the road. Instead, Dylan decided to turn the clock back for the tour of European stadia due to start in May 1984 and recruited a bunch of veteran 1960s rockers, including **Ian McLagan** of The Small Faces on keyboards and former Stone **Mick Taylor**, who had played on *Shot Of Love*.

The gospel material from *Slow Train Coming*, *Saved* and *Shot Of Love* was dropped. But so too was anything from 1970s albums such as *Planet Waves*, *Desire* and *Street-Legal*. Several songs from the towering *Blood On The Tracks* remained and there were a handful of selections from current album *Infidels*. For the rest, it was an unadulterated 1960s nostalgia show.

Carlos Santana, whose band was also on the bill, joined Dylan on guitar most nights, after his own set, and promoter Bill Graham even added **Joan Baez** to the line-up. Backstage, Dylan flirted with her. One night he ran his hand up her skirt and told her, "Wow, you got great legs." But, as in 1965, it was increasingly clear that Dylan didn't want her onstage and, after they had duetted at gigs in Hamburg and Munich, she wasn't invited to join him again.

The early shows were undoubtedly sloppy, although the *Daily Express* critic who caught a show in Brussels was unduly harsh when the paper gave him the centre-page spread to castigate "the least inspired rock concert it has been my misfortune to attend". As the tour went on, Dylan and band began to sound increasingly inspired and concerts in Barcelona, Paris, Newcastle and Wembley were arguably his most memorable of the decade.

The European tour ended in early July, by which time two million fans had given Dylan an ecstatic welcome at some 29 shows in 41 days. But there was to be no North American leg, even though he had not toured his homeland since 1981. Stung by the hostile reaction to the "Las Vegas" tour in 1978 and the sometimes half-empty houses for the "Born Again" shows, Dylan was reluctant to lay himself open to further ridicule. "I don't think I'll be perceived properly until one hundred years after I'm gone," he gloomily told Robert Hilburn of the *LA Times*, when the veteran critic flew in to interview him in Berlin.

The Life

1985: **Charity Covering a Multitude of Sins**

"I just did something that's going to be a big hit.
It'll be number one!" Bob Dylan to Ted Perlman and Peggi Blu, 1985

Dylan's prediction to friends in early 1985 that he was about to become a chart-topper again was spot on – the single in question spent a month at number one in the American charts that spring. Sadly, it wasn't a Bob Dylan record and he sang just four lines on it. The track was the **USA for Africa** charity single "We Are The World", the response of the American music industry to the appalling famine in Ethiopia (already highlighted by Bob Geldof, who had corralled the cream of British rock music into Band Aid to make the number one "Do They Know It's Christmas?"). Dylan was a hesitant and nervous participant. But it was almost inconceivable that the man who had been synonymous with the protest song should not be part of pop music's most powerful collective humanitarian response to suffering and injustice.

Organized by **Harry Belafonte** and with **Quincy Jones** producing, the project's participants included Diana Ross, Tina Turner, Smokey Robinson, Bruce Springsteen, Ray Charles, Paul Simon, Michael Jackson, Waylon Jennings and Stevie Wonder. When Dylan arrived late in the evening of January 28 at the A&M studio on Hollywood's Sunset Boulevard, he appeared uneasy and strangely aloof from the air of mutual celebration. Jones had hung a sign outside the studio saying "check your ego at the door". Dylan appeared to have taken the instruction a little too literally. When he came to sing his part, he was so reticent it took **Stevie Wonder**'s coaching at the piano to get him to sing his lines, a scene captured for posterity in the video of the event.

"The money going to starving people in Africa is a worthwhile idea," he later said. "But I wasn't so convinced about the message of the song." On *Empire Burlesque*, released in June 1985, Dylan sang "Charity is supposed to cover up a multitude of sins." The following month, the **Live Aid** concert would become one of the biggest professional sins of his life (see box, p.129).

Lost in the 1980s
Dylan has made a habit of dividing the critics over the years, but the release of *Empire Burlesque* in June 1985 polarized opinions even more sharply than usual. In *Time* magazine an excited Jay Cocks gave the record one of the best reviews of Dylan's career and ranked it alongside *Blood On The Tracks*. Under the headline "Rock's major magus brings it all back home again," he claimed that a single play of the album was enough to banish any suggestion that Dylan was a marginal figure from the past. "Empire Burlesque is full of turmoil and anger and mystery, an oblique diary … a record

of survival and a tentative kind of triumph." But other reviewers dismissed it as a record of no relevance or consequence, with Michael Gray offering the most withering critique. He found the album a "shameful spectacle", which reduced Dylan to "mewling his thin vocal way through a thick murk of formulaic riffs, kicks and echo-laden AOR noises devised with a desperate eye on rock radio".

Keltner was at the time just about the best rock'n'roll drummer in the world, and the notion that a machine could produce a better sound was surely anathema to Dylan's entire music-making philosophy.

One of the reasons Baker was given such free reign was that, for the first time since *Self Portrait*, Dylan lost interest in the record. After his usual recasting, which involved the com-

"Don't trust me to show you the truth,
When the truth may only be ashes and dust" Bob Dylan, *Empire Burlesque*

Despite having totally recast *Infidels* because he feared it was sounding too much like **The Eagles**, Dylan certainly wanted a hit again, which was why, having produced the *Empire Burlesque* sessions himself, he then brought in the 28-year-old dance-music titan **Arthur Baker** to remix the album. Known as "the mixmeister of pop", the in-vogue Baker had worked with New Order and Afrika Bambaata and had turned songs by Springsteen and Cyndi Lauper into dance hits. Summoned to Dylan's New York hotel suite, Baker was not explicitly told that his employer wanted his album to sound like a dance record. But he felt he had been hired to make the album "a little bit more contemporary". Adding synthesizers and other electronic textures, Baker gave *Empire Burlesque* a unity of sound that was impressive. But much of what he did – such as removing Jim Keltner's backbeat from **Trust Yourself** and replacing it with a programmed drum machine – was ill-advised.

plete re-recording of two tracks (**When The Night Comes Falling From The Sky** and **Tight Connection To My Heart**), he simply handed over the tapes and left Baker to it. "I brought it all to him and he made it sound like a record," he said.

Dylan had told Baker he hoped to follow Madonna and Prince to the top of the charts. Yet despite making three videos for "Tight Connection", "When The Night Comes Falling" and "Emotionally Yours", with Dave Stewart of the Eurythmics as executive producer, he was disappointed again. *Empire Burlesque* struggled to number 33 in America and only made number 11 in Britain, his worst chart-placing since *Street-Legal*.

The year ended with the release of *Biograph*, a mammoth five-LP retrospective that included many rare and unreleased tracks. It was issued amid much fanfare with a party for Dylan – at New York's Whitney Museum – attended by Neil Young, David Bowie, Pete Townshend,

The Life

The Live Aid Debacle

When Dylan was asked to headline the American end of **Live Aid** – to a global television audience estimated to be in excess of one billion – it should have been an opportunity to remind the world why he had once been the most important voice in popular music. Instead, it turned into the worst gig of his career.

Organized by **Bob Geldof** to raise money for the humanitarian disaster in Ethiopia, the twin Live Aid shows were held simultaneously on July 13, 1985, at Wembley Stadium, London, and the JFK Stadium in Philadelphia. The original plan had been for Dylan to sing **Blowin' In The Wind** with Peter, Paul and Mary. It wasn't the sexiest idea and Dylan knew it. He hankered after something a little funkier, so he asked **Ron Wood** of The Rolling Stones to play with him. Wood rang his partner in crime Keith Richards and the trio spent two days rehearsing.

Jack Nicholson did the introduction. "Some artists' work speaks for itself. Some artists' work speaks for its generation. It's my deep personal pleasure to present to you one of America's great voices of freedom. It can only be one man. The transcendent BOB DYLAN!" The performance was anything but transcendent. All three musicians were the worse for wear, having spent the long, hot afternoon in a caravan backstage drinking. They couldn't hear themselves because the stage monitors had been switched off. Then the sound began feeding back into the gigantic PA system.

Dylan began with **The Ballad Of Hollis Brown** but, whether or not the song had been rehearsed, Keith and Ronnie certainly didn't appear very familiar with it. And he added controversy to catastrophe by suggesting that some of the money being raised for starving families in Ethiopia

should be siphoned off to help ailing American farmers. Watching the show backstage at Wembley, Geldof was appalled. It showed "a complete lack of understanding of the issues", he complained loudly.

Dylan somehow got through **When The Ship Comes In**, a song he hadn't played live in 22 years. Then he broke a string during **Blowin' In The Wind** and had to borrow Wood's guitar while Richards appeared to be off in a world all of his own, playing a Chuck Berry riff. It was an utter fiasco and there was relief all round when Lionel Richie and the all-star chorus came on stage to sing "We Are The World".

When Willie Nelson and Neil Young decided to organize a **Farm Aid** benefit that September, Dylan, as the instigator of the idea, could hardly refuse the invitation to appear. But he had learned his lesson. Taking **Tom Petty and the Heartbreakers** along as his backing band, they played six songs – this time rehearsed during a week of careful preparation – and the show was a triumph. Yet it was seen by only a tiny fraction of those who had witnessed the Live Aid debacle.

Looking as uneasy as he sounded: Dylan with Ron Wood and Keith Richards at Live Aid

The Crouch End Connection

At the invitation of Dave Stewart of the **Eurythmics**, Dylan arrived in London in mid-November 1985. They spent four days recording at Stewart's studio, a converted church in Crouch End, north London. The sessions – Dylan's first in London in twenty years – were unproductive and hardly progressed beyond the jamming stage. In the end, the backing track for **Under Your Spell** – the final song on 1986's *Knocked Out Loaded* – was the only material that was ever released. But the visit did produce a legendary Dylan story.

One day, Dylan was invited round to Stewart's house in Crouch End, and he eventually arrived in a flustered state about an hour late. Stewart recalled: "I asked what had happened and he said, 'Well I rang the doorbell of number seven and this woman came to the door and I said 'Is Dave in?' And she said, 'No, he's at work, do you want to wait?' So Dylan waits and thinks, 'That's strange, he told me to come round.' And the woman's thinking, 'This is weird, he looks like Bob Dylan.' So she rang up her husband and asked him, 'Did you invite Bob Dylan to come round to our house?' The husband doesn't know what she's talking about and it turns out that Dylan has got the right number but the wrong street."

Eight years later, in July 1993, Dylan visited a five-bedroom property in Crouch End, reportedly with an interest in purchasing it. The story was leaked to the press and Dylan withdrew from the prospective sale.

"I want to make a record like Madonna or Prince.
I want to sell a lot of records." Bob Dylan to producer Arthur Baker

Billy Joel and Dave Stewart, among others. Not that Dylan appeared very interested in the project. "Most of my stuff has already been bootlegged, so to anybody in the know there's nothing on it they haven't heard before," he said. "All it is really is repackaging." Despite his lack of enthusiasm, *Biograph* became only the second box-set (following the precedent of none other than Elvis Presley) to receive a gold disc.

1986: **True Confessions and Writer's Block**

"It always seems like I'm up there walking the plank.
I never felt like I was searching for anything.
I always felt that I've stumbled into things." Bob Dylan, 1985

Before his first American tour since 1981, Dylan decided to road-test his new show – backed by **Tom Petty and The Heartbreakers** – in New Zealand, Australia and Japan. After the "Heritage Tour" of Europe the previous year, the so-called **True Confessions** Tour found him doing another about-turn. At the opening night in Auckland in February, just nine of the 25 songs dated from his 1960s heyday. Dylan had fallen under the spell of a different kind of nostalgia, playing covers of 1950s songs by the likes of **Rick Nelson** and **Hank Snow** (and, later in the tour, even an **Ink Spots** number). The shows were loose but enjoyably so, Petty memorably describing Dylan's approach as taking "the rehearsals on stage".

In Sydney, Australia, one of the two concerts was filmed for TV broadcast in America by HBO and later issued on video under the title *Hard To Handle*. Dylan used the broadcast to let it be known that he was still a believer in Christ. "John Wayne, Clark Gable, Richard Nixon, Ronald Reagan, Michael Jackson, Bruce Springsteen – they're all heroes to some people. I don't care nothing about those people," he said before the last song. "I have my own hero. I'm going to sing about him right now." He then performed **In The Garden** from the mostly unloved *Saved* album.

By late March, Dylan was back in America, oddly rapping a verse on **Kurtis Blow**'s release **Street Rock**. "He raps, he really raps," an excited Blow was quoted as saying. Yet given that "Subterranean Homesick Blues" can lay claim to being the world's first prototype rap song, perhaps Dylan's involvement wasn't so surprising after all.

In June he was back on the road with Petty and The Heartbreakers, playing 40-plus dates on the American leg of the True Confessions Tour, beginning with a benefit for Amnesty International in LA. It was the first time America had properly seen him in five years and he was well received, despite the presence of plenty of covers such as Ray Charles's "Unchain My Heart", "I Forgot (More Than You'll Ever Know)", "Let The Good Times Roll" and "Red Cadillac And A Black Moustache". According to Clinton Heylin, one of the more astute professional Bob-watchers, the preponderance of such covers was a case of Dylan "working his way back to the sources of popular song" in an attempt to reconnect with his muse. In *Chronicles*, he reveals that he had hit the lowest point of his career and was planning to retire. "Tom was at the top of his game and I was at the bottom of mine... My own songs had become strangers to me," he writes. "I was no longer capable of doing anything creative with them. It was like carrying around a package of heavy rotting meat." The painful fact was that, for the first time in his career, the world's greatest songwriter was struggling to write songs. "He said the words stopped coming. Suddenly it just wasn't there any more, like the well ran dry," close friend Ted Perlman revealed to Dylan biographer Howard Sounes.

The drying-up was evident when *Knocked Out Loaded* appeared in the shops in August 1986, just as the True Confessions Tour was winding up. Taking its title from a line in the New Orleans standard "Junco Partner", the eight-song, 35-minute album opened with covers of songs by Junior Parker and Kris Kristofferson and included an arrangement of **Precious Memories**. This left just five Dylan originals, three of which were co-writes with Sam Shepard, Petty, and Carole Bayer Sager, the wife of Burt Bacharach. The album's best song, **Brownsville Girl**, was a reworking of an *Empire Burlesque* outtake.

The outcome was bitterly disappointing to Columbia Records, who had hoped that on the back of a well-received and highly lucrative US tour, Dylan would be restored to the upper echelons of the charts. Instead, *Knocked Out Loaded* failed even to make the American Top 50 – the first Dylan album to do so since his debut almost a quarter of a century earlier. In Britain, the album struggled to number 35.

Knocked Out Loaded was so widely ignored that few even noticed in the small print of the lengthy "thanks" on the inner sleeve that Dylan had slipped in the name of **Desirée Gabrielle Dennis-Dylan,** the daughter he had recently fathered with Carolyn Dennis (see box on p.120).

That Dylan's self-confidence was badly shaken was evident in an interview with David Hepworth, during which he insisted that the collaboration with Petty, *Biograph* and *Knocked Out Loaded* had all been "someone else's idea". He also complained that he felt on tour the audiences had come to see Petty, rather than him.

After playing almost 100 concerts in the first half of 1986 and still failing to chart, it perhaps seemed time for a career shift. Dylan spent the second half of the year making the film **Hearts of Fire** (see p.274–275).

1987: Down with The Dead

"He was difficult to work with in as much as he wouldn't want to rehearse a song more than two times, three at the most. And so we rehearsed maybe one hundred songs two or three times." Bob Weir of the Grateful Dead

The beginning of 1987 found Dylan with a mangled hand and arm – he hasn't told us which one – in plaster, after what he describes merely as a "freak accident". He was due to start touring again in the spring, but for a while didn't know if he'd ever be able to play guitar again. While he recuperated, he started writing songs, mostly lyrics rather than melodies, including "Political World", "What Good Am I", "Dignity" and "Disease Of Conceit".

Once his hand had mended, he seemed ready to play with just about anyone in the hope that somewhere the spark might somehow be reignited, and the early months of the year found him abseiling across the face of popular music. He played on **Warren Zevon's** album *Sentimental Hygiene*, jammed in a Hollywood club with **George Harrison, John Fogarty** and

Taj Mahal, sang with **Michael Jackson** at Elizabeth Taylor's birthday party, performed at a gala tribute for **George Gershwin**, got on stage with **U2** and contributed a co-composition with Bono called "Love Rescue Me" to the band's *Rattle & Hum* album, and tried out former members of the **Sex Pistols** and **The Clash** at sessions for his own next album.

Then there was his collaboration with the **Grateful Dead**. Formed in San Francisco in the mid-1960s, The Dead had become the hippy house band during 1967's "Summer of Love" and built a huge following of "Deadheads" from their endless touring, when they would often play for four or five hours. Although on stage they were noted for their open-ended acid jams, they had also made some superb studio albums, most notably *Workingman's Dead* and *American Beauty*. Both released in 1970 and full of tightly structured songs, these albums had helped to kickstart the entire country-rock phenomenon. By the time Dylan teamed up with The Dead, they were on the point of releasing *In The Dark*, their studio comeback, but had been almost exclusively a touring outfit for seven years.

Jerry Garcia, the band's charismatic leader, shared with Dylan a vast repertoire of traditional folk, country and blues songs. Both men were, in effect, walking repositories of American music and they were inevitably drawn to each other, first sharing a stage during one of Dylan's San Francisco shows in December 1980. There had been speculation ever since that they would work together, but it was a show in Ohio in July 1986 – at which Dylan jammed with the entire band for the first time – that eventually led to the tour they undertook together in July 1987. The idea came not from Dylan but from the group, who had been covering his songs for years and referred to him as "The Oracle". As Garcia somewhat inelegantly put it, "We hit on him." This gave Dylan the advantage in negotiations and he reportedly demanded – and received – a 70:30% split in the tour receipts in his favour, despite the fact that, by this stage, The Dead were able to fill far bigger venues than he could.

Dylan and his new collaborators rehearsed for a couple of weeks (with Dylan walking out at one stage thinking he couldn't hack it) and were still ramshackle when they hit the road in early July. There were only six dates but the setlist was radically different every night. Bob Weir's estimation that they had partially rehearsed 100 songs but fully worked out none of them was an exaggeration, but not by much. And, true to form, at the first gig, Dylan – who the band called "**Spike**" because they already had a Bob – came up with several numbers that hadn't figured even in the vast number of songs they had semi-rehearsed.

Most Dylan fans hated the tour, but the collaboration had its merits. The Dead persuaded him to perform **Chimes Of Freedom** for the first time in 24 years. **John Brown**, which he had never rehearsed, was dusted down from the early 1960s and worked so well that Dylan kept it in his set after the tour. Further well-chosen songs included **Queen Jane Approximately** and **Stuck Inside Of Mobile**, performed for the first time live since 1966.

Bob, revitalised by The

The resulting album did not appear until early 1989 and Garcia's account of its compilation is hilarious, with Dylan apparently selecting tracks on the basis of cassette recordings played back through a $39 ghetto blaster.

In February 1989, Dylan showed up again at a Dead concert in Inglewood, California, and joined them on stage. The next day he called the Grateful Dead office and said he wanted to join the band full time. According to Bob Weir, most of the band were up for it. But when they took a vote, there was one hand against (believed to be bassist Phil Lesh), which nixed the plan. Still, there was a lasting legacy to Dylan's experience with the group. The Dead's belief that music is fundamentally a live rather than a recorded experience and that its power can only be fully realized in communion with an audience was a profound influence on the philosophy behind what was to become Dylan's own "Never Ending Tour".

After the Dead shows, Dylan reunited with Tom Petty and The Heartbreakers for a tour that opened in Israel in September 1987 and wound its way through Europe before concluding with four nights in London at Wembley Arena in mid-October. His film *Hearts Of Fire* opened while he was in London, but Dylan was a conspicuous absentee from the premiere. He must have known that it was a tawdry piece of work. Within weeks it had closed in the UK and the film never even got a US theatre release.

1988: The Road Goes Ever On

Having released nothing the previous year apart from the soundtrack to the wretched *Hearts Of Fire*, 1988 began busily for Dylan. In January he was inducted into the **Rock And Roll Hall of Fame** by Bruce Springsteen, who in a powerful speech paid the usual obeisance to Dylan's 1960s canon. But then he bravely stood up for his more recent output, claiming it had gone "unjustly under-appreciated" because his earlier work had cast such a long shadow. "If there was a young guy out there writing the *Empire Burlesque* album and "Every Grain Of Sand", they'd be calling him the new Bob Dylan," he claimed, with some justification. Afterwards, Dylan sang "Like A Rolling Stone" with Springsteen, **Arlo Guthrie** and **Mick Jagger** on backing vocals.

But despite Springsteen's championing of Dylan's recent work, there was not a huge amount to appreciate about Dylan's next album, **Down In The Groove**. Recorded in desultory fashion over a period of twelve fitful months spread across 1987 and 1988, it was just 32 minutes long, five minutes shorter even than *Knocked Out Loaded*. This meagre offering of covers and uninspiring original songs (two of them co-written with the Grateful Dead's lyricist **Robert Hunter**) was evidence that Dylan's writer's block had reached crisis proportions.

Dylan acknowledged the problem. "There's no rule that anyone must write their own songs," he said defensively. "You can take another song somebody else has written and you can make it yours." Indeed, The Byrds and several others had fashioned entire careers out of doing just that with Dylan's songs. But now he was the one scavenging for material. "Writing is such an isolated thing," he complained. "You're in such an isolated frame of

years since, Dylan has averaged around 100 dates a year. At the time of writing, the "NET" – as it has come to be known by Dylan fans – has clocked up more than 1600 shows and featured more than 400 different songs. As a sustained and monumental act of creative expression, there has simply been nothing else like it: Neil Young, Bruce Springsteen, U2 and The Rolling Stones are hopeless slackers by comparison.

"If you just go out every three years or so, like I was doing for a while, that's when you lose your touch." Bob Dylan, 1991

mind. You have to get into or be in that place. In the old days, I could get to it real quick. I can't get to it like that no more."

Down In The Groove fared even worse than *Knocked Out Loaded*. It stalled in the American charts at a humiliating number 61 and remains the worst-selling of all his studio albums. The "End Days" he had prophesied in his born-again phase appeared finally to have arrived, at least in terms of his career. Then, a week after its release, Dylan played the first date in what came to be known as the Never Ending Tour. Just at the very moment he looked to be out for the count, resurrection was at hand.

How Bobby got his Groove back

June 7, 1988, was a key date in Bob Dylan's career. For although we didn't know it at the time, that night in the Pavilion in **Concord**, California, was the first date in what has came to be known as the **Never Ending Tour**. In the

Dylan pinpoints the moment when the notion of the Never Ending Tour took shape in his mind to a performance in Switzerland the previous October. In a blinding flash, he saw a new mission: "I knew I've got to go out and play these songs. That's just what I must do." The moment of enlightenment came in the nick of time, for it arrived as he was despondently contemplating retirement, convinced that the spirit of his songs was "getting further and further away" from him. The critics had been telling him for so long that he'd lost his touch that he had come to believe them. "I'd reached the end of the line. I was gong to pack it in," he told *Newsweek*.

Instead, Dylan turned back to the tradition of his earliest inspiration, **Woody Guthrie**, and the rawness of **Elvis Presley**. He was going to reinvent himself as a travelling troubadour, a hobo minstrel taking his songs out to the people in a rediscovery of rock's liberating spirit. Night after night. In the work ethic, he

Keeping the dream live: Dylan in 1988

The Traveling Wilburys

The Traveling Wilburys were a happy accident that occurred by a simple twist of fate in April 1988 when **George Harrison** asked if he could use Dylan's garage studio at his home at Point Dume, Malibu, to record a bonus track that his record label, Warners, was demanding for a 12" single.

Harrison didn't have a song or a studio in which to record it and turned to **Jeff Lynne**, who was also in LA, producing Roy Orbison's *Mystery Girl* album. Lynne suggested they should get together in Dylan's studio and write something. "We phoned up Bob. He said, 'Sure, come on over'," Harrison recalled. "Tom Petty had my guitar and I went to pick it up. He said 'Oh, I was wondering what I was going to do tomorrow'. And Roy Orbison said, 'Give us a call if you're going to do anything, I'd like to come along'."

With Dylan joining in on harmony vocals and wheezy harmonica, the five of them recorded the impromptu **Handle With Care**, the title taken from the wording on a cardboard box in Dylan's garage. When Warners declared the track was far too good to throw away as a B-side, the quartet were encouraged to explore their collaboration further. The results surpassed expectations. Seldom can a superstar grouping have operated with such ego-free and informal joie de vivre.

Dylan, for one, felt liberated and the spirit of the music they were making reminded him of the sessions that had produced *The Basement Tapes* some twenty years earlier. As Orbison recalled: "We'd go to Bob's house and we'd just sit outside and there'd be a barbecue and we'd all just bring guitars, and everyone would be throwing something in here and something in there. And then we'd just go to the garage studio and put it down."

Dylan had a tour scheduled to start in June, so if they were gong to make an album, time was of the essence. Dylan said he had a week and a half free at the beginning of May and, with **Jim Keltner** augmenting the line-up on drums, they assembled at Dave Stewart's LA studio. The album was recorded in nine days.

The entire experience was relaxed and tension-free, and Dylan sounded like he was having more fun than he had done in years. The name evolved from the "Trembling Wilburys", a joke description Harrison had coined for an imaginary aliment that afflicts musicians towards dawn after a long night in the studio. Dylan became Lucky Wilbury, Lynne was Otis, Harrison was Nelson, Orbison was Left and Petty was Charlie T. Jr.

Dylan departed for his tour in better spirits than for a long time and the great comeback was underway. As Harrison remarked: "If all the Wilburys did was help to get Bob enthusiastic again, then that's something." In fact it achieved considerably more. When it was released in October 1988, *Traveling Wilburys Volume One* gave Dylan the first double platinum album of his career, and it stayed on the American chart for almost a year.

In April 1990 the Wilburys gathered again in a rented Spanish-style ranch house in the hills above LA. Orbison had died the previous December and two months later Dylan had appeared at a tribute concert to him where he had performed **Mr Tambourine Man** with Roger McGuinn, David Crosby and Chris Hillman from The Byrds.

The second Wilburys album, teasingly titled *Volume Three*, was released in October 1990. But Orbison's absence, fewer quality songs and the obvious difficulty of replicating something that had started out so spontaneously meant that the album never quite achieved the verve and spirit of its predecessor.

found a way of recovering his lost dignity. "A man must support his family, no matter what," he said. "Most of the people who work nine to five have got to, and I've a tremendous regard for that."

Up until that point, Dylan had never maintained his own band. He had employed various musicians for specific tours and turned for support to established groups such as The Hawks, Tom Petty & The Heartbreakers, and the Grateful Dead at different times. Now for the first time in his career he needed his own, standing group of musicians available on a permanent basis. As such, The Heartbreakers, who had accompanied him on his autumn 1987 dates, were no longer any use to him. They had their own career to follow. To put his own band together he turned to the guitarist **G.E. Smith,** who led the house band for the television show *Saturday Night Live*. After trying various options, by May they had settled on a stripped-down line-up of Smith and **Cesar Diaz** on guitars, **Kenny Aaronson** on bass and **Christopher Parker** on drums. The girlie chorus had gone. There weren't even any keyboards.

The historic first date of the Never Ending Tour was in itself a disappointing show and a set of poor reviews reflected it. But by the third or fourth gig of his 1988 tour, even those who had come along to bury Dylan found themselves praising his rediscovered verve and sense of purpose. "I had a gut feeling that I had created a new genre, a style that didn't even exist as yet, and one that would be entirely my own," he wrote in *Chronicles*.

Booked into theatres rather than stadiums

(in truth he could no longer sell them out), he played 71 dates over the next four months with a setlist that changed every night. In Chuck Berry's hometown of St Louis he performed **Nadine**. In Leonard Cohen's Montreal, he performed the Canadian singer-songwriter's **Hallelujah**. Neither song was played again. They were special, one-off gifts for fans in those cities. In all, more than 90 songs appeared in those 1988 gigs – some feat, given that the shows were relatively short, averaging only fourteen songs per night.

It was Dylan himself who coined the "NET" phrase. "It's all the same tour – the Never Ending Tour," he said in 1989. "It works out better for me that way. You can pick and choose better when you're just out there all the time and your show is already set up. You know, you just don't have to start it up and end it. It's better just to keep it out there."

After the 1988 American dates, Dylan had a break to record *Oh Mercy*, before picking up again with 99 dates in the course of 1989, during which **Tony Garnier** took over from Aaronson on bass. He was still in the band fifteen years later, having played more gigs with Dylan than anyone else in history.

Dylan has kept up the punishing schedule into the new millennium and into his sixties. We can only hazard a guess at what drives him, for he cannot be doing it for the money and he certainly has nothing left to prove. Perhaps it is a kind of escapism, for living semi-permanently on the road is a guaranteed way of avoiding the day-to-day mundanity of real life. "Going on stage, seeing different people every night in a combustible way, that's a thrill. There's nothing in ordinary life that even comes close to that," he admitted. And, being Dylan, there's also a certain stubbornness to his attitude. "An easy way out would be to say, 'Yeah, it's all behind me, that's it and there's no more'," he said in 1989 when the Never Ending Tour was still young. "But you want to say there might be a small chance that something up there will surpass whatever you did. Everybody works in the shadow of what they've previously done. But you have to overcome that."

Dylan once famously said he was just "**a song and dance man**" and in later years, in the art of performance he has found a way of keeping in touch with his muse without the need for prolific songwriting. But more than anything, it seems that he doesn't know what else to do. Dylan's entire life has been a search for something he has never quite found. He tried mind-expanding drugs, domesticity, fervent Christianity and re-exploring his Jewish roots. When he found that none of them provided the answers he was looking for, he put his life up on stage. "It's the only place where I'm happy. The only place where you can be who you want to be."

1989: The Quality of Mercy

"Don't treat him like God. It wigs him out. Don't dive into his soul, he finds that insulting." Advice note given by Dylan's office in 1989 to prospective interviewers

After the failure of *Down In The Groove* and in the face of his own obvious writer's block, Dylan considered abandoning the recording studio altogether. "Some people quit making records," he said. "They just don't care about it anymore. As long as they have their live stage show together, they don't need records. It was getting to that point for me. It was either come up with a bunch of songs that were original and pay attention to them, or get some other real good songwriters to write me some songs."

That he decided to give it another try was down to two people. The first was **George Harrison**, who during The Traveling Wilburys sessions in early 1988, urged and coaxed Dylan back towards songwriting health (see p.138). The second was U2's Bono, who, when one night at Dylan's house was shown the lyrics he had written while recuperating from his busted hand, suggested that Daniel Lanois (see box, below) was the producer who could help him realize them into an album. Dylan first met Lanois in September 1988 in New Orleans, where the producer was working with the **Neville Brothers**. He was instantly impressed. "We hit it off, he had an understanding of what my music was all about. It's very hard to

Daniel Lanois

Born in Canada in 1951, Daniel Lanois has rescued Dylan's recording career not once but twice – first when he produced 1989's *Oh Mercy* and again eight years later when he helmed *Time Out Of Mind*. It is surely no coincidence that they are probably Dylan's best two albums in the last 25 years.

Before working on *Oh Mercy*, Lanois had co-produced **Peter Gabriel**'s 1986 album *So*, a **Robbie Robertson** solo album, and *The Unforgettable Fire* and *The Joshua Tree* with Brian Eno for **U2**. He also made the Neville Brothers' album *Yellow Moon*, which included a hit version of Dylan's "With God On Our Side".

A gifted multi-instrumentalist and a phenomenal pedal steel player, Lanois was a musician before he became a producer, and he released his first solo album *Acadie* in 1989. It was followed in 1993 by *For The Beauty Of Winona*, and *Shine* exactly a decade later in 2003.

"What tends to happen with production is that you accept a nice invitation and then it escalates into a couple of years' work. Then another nice invitation comes along and years drift by without you even noticing," he said, explaining the long gaps between his own records. In addition to Dylan's *Time Out Of Mind*, among the other "nice invitations" he received during the 1990s were **Emmylou Harris**'s *Wrecking Ball* and U2's *All That You Can't Leave Behind*.

Asked if he feels frustrated at being better known as a producer than for his own albums, Lanois takes a practical view. "I'm proud of all the work I've done. To sit next to Bob Dylan for three months and watch him scratch out his words is a hard lesson to come by. You could take a decade of literature in university and not get to that place. So I regard it all as food."

"For me, record making is not just a job or a series of techniques. I pour my soul into it. It's that searching that people get from me, whether they like it or not. If you've got the searcher in you, then you never get lazy and you never rest. You never really answer the questions. They just keep on coming."

find a producer that can play and knows how to record with modern facilities. For me, that was lacking in the past," he said.

In March 1989 Lanois set up a mobile studio in a five-storey, turn-of-the-century house in New Orleans and called in local Louisiana musicians to get what he called the "swamp sound". To create the right ambience, he even fitted out the control room with moss, stuffed animals and alligator heads. Dylan encouraged Lanois to take control. "The recording studio is very foreign to me. The controls, the tape itself, the machinery is something that never really interested me enough to gain any control over it one way or another," he said when *Oh Mercy*, the album they made together, was released. "It would seem to me you'd need somebody there who knew you, who could push you around a little bit. Daniel got me to do stuff that wouldn't have entered my mind."

Lanois' skill lay in allowing full reign to Dylan's spontaneity while insisting that fine attention was paid to the detail. Few other producers could have got the balance so perfectly right. When it was flowing, Lanois simply allowed it to happen. For example, one of the best songs on the album, **Man In The Long Black Coat,** was recorded in one take without rehearsal. But on other tracks he insisted vocals were meticulously reworked and overdubbed.

Dylan gave a long and detailed account of the recording process in *Chronicles*. It's a rare insight into how a great album comes together, for there is no doubt that *Oh Mercy* is a brilliant record, both musically and lyrically. Again, Dylan left some major songs off the album, including **Series Of Dreams** and **Dignity**. But this time it didn't matter. The material that did make the album was so strong that the record wasn't compromised by their absence. Dylan was back "on message", and reviews were more positive than in years, typified by Andy Gill, in *Q*, who called it "a stunning return".

Oh Mercy made number six in Britain and number 30 in America, but its reputation has steadily grown over the years and it's now widely regarded among Dylan mavens as not only his best album of the 1980s, but his best since *Blood On The Tracks*.

Dylan's own relatively modest assessment, expressed in *Chronicles*, was that he felt Lanois had helped him create "a haunting not stumbling or halting album" with "something magical" about it.

It's Not Dark Yet

1990–

"The reason I can stay so single-minded about my music is because it affected me at an early age in a powerful way and it's all that affected me. It's all that ever remained true. Everything else changed."

Bob Dylan

It's Not Dark Yet
1990–

1990: Red Sky at Night

Suitably encouraged by the success of *Oh Mercy*, Dylan determined on a swift follow-up. In January 1990, only four months after the release of *Oh Mercy*, he began recording **Under The Red Sky**, this time in LA with the brothers Don and David Was producing. Recorded with a surfeit of superstar guests – **Elton John**, **Slash** from Guns N' Roses, **George Harrison**, Jimmie and Stevie Ray Vaughan, Al Kooper, David Crosby – the songs were not as strong as the previous set and the Was brothers went to great lengths to sound as different from Lanois' broodingly rich and languid textures as possible.

Dylan appeared less than happy while recording. Al Kooper dubbed it the "hood album",

The most remarkable Dylan gig ever?

There have been many memorable nights on the Never Ending Tour. Probably the most remarkable of all, however, was the performance Dylan gave on January 12, 1990, at **Toad's Place**, in New Haven, Connecticut. His first club gig in more than 25 years, it was intended as a warm-up for a winter tour that would take in two stadium shows in Brazil and ten further dates in Paris and London. Before a capacity audience of 700, Dylan performed some 50 songs in four sets stretching over more than four and a half hours, beginning at 8.45 pm and not ending until 2.20 am.

Three songs were premiered from *Oh Mercy*, including **Political World**, which he played no less than three times. And a number of other songs were unveiled that had never before been played live, such as *Empire Burlesque*'s **Tight Connection To My**

Heart. There were also eighteen cover versions, kicking off with Joe South's **Walk A Mile In My Shoes** and including Kris Kristofferson's **Help Me Make It Through The Night** as well as Bruce Springsteen's **Dancing In The Dark**.

Dylan remained in a good mood throughout, responding to requests for **Joey** and the Traveling Wilburys song **Congratulations**, and talking good-naturedly between songs. **Man Of Peace** was introduced as coming from his "religious period" and **Lay Lady Lay** as a song from the days when romance still mattered.

His creative renaissance was complete. And, during the ten shows he played in Europe a month later, a total of no fewer than 78 different songs were performed.

for Bob wore a hooded sweatshirt every day and kept his head covered during sessions, barely speaking to anyone. Slash for one was not impressed: "I finally met this little guy who looked like an Eskimo. It was a summer day and he's wearing a heavy wool sweater with a hood and a baseball cap underneath. He had big leather gloves and he appeared to be stoned out of his mind. He was really impolite. I didn't really have a good time."

On its release in September 1990, it was clear that *Under The Red Sky* lacked the profundity of *Oh Mercy*. But the critics were far too hasty in rubbishing the record. Some could not disguise their glee in dismissing Dylan's *Oh Mercy* revival as having been miserably brief, and the perceptive Allan Jones in *Melody Maker* was a lone voice among reviewers in recognizing the record's simple and straightforward, if rough-edged, virtues.

Under The Red Sky made number 38 in America and number thirteen in Britain. The disappointing reception both critically and commercially left Dylan so discouraged that he put his hood back up and didn't release another album of his own songs for seven years.

1991: Out of Time

"Power and greed and corruptible seed
seem to be all that there is" Bob Dylan, "Blind Willie McTell"

Despite his artistic renaissance, both on record with *Oh Mercy* and on stage via the Never Ending Tour, Dylan greeted the onset of the 1990s with some perplexity. He was drinking heavily and he felt a man out of his time, at odds with a world he increasingly felt had gone mad – and which seemed to be applauding him simply for having had the ability to endure.

In February 1991, he received a Lifetime Achievement award at the **Grammys**. With US troops fighting the first Gulf War he bravely and provocatively chose to sing **Masters Of War**, although whatever was ailing him meant the words were all but indecipherable. Ill or drunk, or perhaps both, he mumbled his way

through a bizarre short speech. "My daddy once said to me, he said 'Son, it is possible for you to become so defiled in this world that your own Mother and Father will abandon you. If that happens, God will believe in your own ability to mend your own ways'." Later he claimed that the ceremony had been like attending his own funeral.

But, whether he liked it or not, Dylan's 50th birthday was inevitably a time for looking back. He acknowledged this by sanctioning the release in March 1991 of a triple-album box-set – *The Bootleg Series Volumes 1–3* – which contained 58 previously unreleased tracks. What was most fascinating about the set was not the great songs of the 1960s that he had never released and that we all knew about via bootlegs and cover versions. Rather, it was the astonishing quality of the songs he had omitted from his more recent albums – many of them superior to the material he had released.

But the Grammy awards and the *Bootlegs* were merely distractions from Dylan's new vocation of endless touring. In the course of 1991 he played 101 dates, ranging from the awful to the sublime. The low point was a week of shows at London's **Hammersmith Odeon** in February, rated by many as his worst ever British appearances. Yet the year ended in triumph with an autumn tour of America that is reckoned to have included some of his very finest shows.

Somewhere in between the two, he found a way of coming to terms with both his own myth and mortality, and in doing so rediscovered his sense of purpose. He told Robert Hilburn of the *LA Times*, "It was important for me to come to the bottom of this legend thing, which has no reality at all. What's important isn't the legend, but the art, the work. A person has to do whatever they are called on to do." And, in Dylan's case, what he had to do was perform. That was the only way redemption lay and his commitment to the Never Ending Tour was redoubled. "If you are going to be a performer, you've got to give it your all," he told Hilburn.

1992–94: "Music That's True"

"Maybe a person gets to a point where they have written enough songs. Let someone else write them." Bob Dylan, April 1991

On October 18, 1992, Bob Dylan appeared with a star-studded cast at **Madison Square Garden**, New York, to mark his 30th anniversary in the recording industry. Billed on the tickets – priced between $80 and $150 – as "Columbia Records Celebrates The Music Of Bob Dylan", the event's timing wasn't quite historically accurate, for Bob had recorded his first album in November 1961. But nobody really cared.

Dylan's own feelings about the event were probably mixed. The previous year, he had found receiving the Grammy Lifetime Achievement award like attending his own funeral. And he must have felt a touch of the same thing lurking backstage for two hours while the likes of **Tracy Chapman, Stevie Wonder, Johnny Cash, Willie Nelson, Eric Clapton, George Harrison, Neil Young, Tom Petty, Lou Reed, John Mellencamp** and **Roger McGuinn** sang his songs. Eventually Dylan shambled onto the stage and performed acoustic versions of **Song To Woody** and **It's Alright Ma**. He was then joined by the massed cast for **My Back Pages** and **Knockin' On Heaven's Door** before he closed the show with a tender **Girl From The**

The Life

North Country. For his efforts, he received the lion's share of the $10 million the event grossed from pay-per-view TV rights.

The irony was that, as some of the biggest stars in the world were paying tribute to his songs, Dylan's compositional skills had dried up once again and he was reduced to recording the songs of others. In June 1992, he had entered a Chicago studio with the guitarist **David Bromberg** as producer and had recorded an album of semi-electric covers of traditional folk and blues. By late July, following a short tour of Europe, he had decided to add a couple of acoustic tunes to lend the album a change of pace and mood. In the event, he recorded fourteen further songs in a handful of afternoon sessions at his garage studio in Malibu, attended only by producer **Debbie Gold** and an engineer. He was so pleased with the results that he scrapped the Bromberg sessions and released thirteen of the acoustic tracks as the album *Good As I Been To You* in November 1992. An outtake from the sessions, The Duprees' **You Belong To Me**, subsequently turned up somewhat bizarrely in Oliver Stone's controversial film, *Natural Born Killers*. The Bromberg tapes remain unreleased.

There appears to have been a dual motivation

Dylan with Roger McGuinn (left), Tom Petty (extreme right) and others for the all-hands-on-deck finale of his 30-years-in-music celebration at New York's Madison Square Garden

Woodstock II

Dylan had been furious when the original Woodstock festival landed on his doorstep in August 1969. He pointedly snubbed the event and went out of his way to insist that the so-called "Woodstock generation" had nothing to do with him and should on no account look to him as its figurehead. But, a quarter of a century later, he let the organizers of Woodstock II know that he would be happy to appear at the festival's 25th anniversary commemorative event. Did he subsequently come to regret having missed the original when he saw what a mythic place it had assumed in popular culture? Or was he merely swayed by hearing that **Neil Young** had been offered $600,000 to appear?

Whatever the reason, he was given a similar fee to follow the **Red Hot Chilli Peppers** on the bill on August 14, 1994, and, dressed in a black western suit with white piping, he played a storming 78-minute, twelve-song set with his regular Never Ending Tour band. Highlights of the set included blistering versions of **Highway 61 Revisited** and **All Along The Watchtower**, a powerful **Just Like A Woman** and acoustic takes of **Masters Of War**, **Don't Think Twice It's Alright**, **It's All Over Now Baby Blue** and **It Ain't Me Babe**. To Dylan's evident surprise, he went down exceedingly well with a crowd that had mostly not been born when he had made his great 1960s albums.

After the performance, the patronizing female presenter of the live TV broadcast gushed: "We were all kinda holding our collective breath to see how he'd be received tonight, but it was great. I feel very, very proud of Generation X tonight: showing the whole world they are full of patience, wisdom and tenderness, they are into Dylan big time tonight at Woodstock '94." Regrettably, though, **Highway 61 Revisited** was the only Dylan track to be featured on the official *Woodstock II* album release.

Dylan's view of the event? "It was just another show, really. We just blew in and blew out of there. You do wonder if you're coming across, because you feel so small on a stage like that."

for *Good As I Been to You* and its companion volume, **World Gone Wrong**, which followed in 1993. The first was that, despite the burst of inspiration that had produced *Oh Mercy*, Dylan was finding songwriting an increasingly elusive art. He talked about it in several interviews in the early 1990s. "There was a time when the songs would come three or four at the same time, but those days are long gone," he told Paul Zollo. "Once in a while the odd song will come to me like a bulldog at the garden gate and demand to be written. But most of them are rejected out of my mind right away. You get caught up in wondering if anyone really needs to hear it."

The other impetus was Dylan's genuine love for traditional music, which, via such collections as the *Harry Smith Anthology*, was the wellspring of his own art. "Those songs worked their way into my own songs, I guess, but never in a conscious way," he said. "It's like nobody really wrote those songs. They just got passed down." Several traditional songs had found their way into Dylan's constantly evolving setlists on the Never Ending Tour, and – at the height of the vitriolic explosion of grunge rock – it seemed like a good idea to realease an entire, all-acoustic album of them.

In the magnetic narratives of the old songs – which Dylan described as "the music that's true for me" – he found a moral strength that he believed contemporary culture had lost. "My influences have not changed and any time they have done, the music goes off to a wrong place," he later observed. If the move was born of desperation, it was also a bold one. In the words of Nick Hasted, he had chosen "to tear away the compromises that had choked him and to re-embrace the source of his art".

Previous albums dominated by covers such as *Self Portrait*, *Dylan* and *Down In The Groove* had been rubbished by the critics. But, to Dylan's pleasant surprise, *Good As I Been To You* was greeted enthusiastically and, in some quarters, even rapturously. "Simply breathtaking", concluded Dave Henderson, while *Rolling Stone* praised the album's "stripped-down intensity". *Q* eulogized Bob's cracked voice and its "wise conviction that simply wasn't there when he started out", and the BBC Radio One DJ **John Peel** played Dylan on his show for the first time in more than a decade.

There was some criticism that Dylan had "borrowed" arrangements from previous interpreters and not credited the sources. Indeed, his music publishers were later forced to recognize Australian folksinger **Mick Slocum** as the originator of Dylan's version of the traditional ballad **Jim Jones** when legal action was threatened. But then similar accusations of plagiarism had been levelled at several of the tunes on Dylan's early albums.

It was no surprise that *Good As I Been To You* stiffed commercially, for Dylan had made a wilfully uncommercial album. The record stalled at number 51 in the American charts, although it sold respectably in Britain, where it reached number eighteen. But Dylan claimed no longer to care, insisting that "No man gains immortality through public acclaim."

He was so pleased with *Good As I Been to You* that he swiftly repeated the exercise with **World Gone Wrong**, released less than a year later in October 1993. If anything, the second album was even more spontaneous, recorded in a matter of days, "without a single change of strings". This time he sensibly included a fascinating commentary in the liner notes which was titled "About The Songs (what they're about)" and which cited his sources, including Blind Willie McTell, the Mississippi Sheiks and Doc Watson.

Some critics didn't get it and instead of being won over by the album's authenticity, found its lack of contemporary whiz-bang production values irritating. An affronted David Sinclair thundered in *The Times* against Dylan's "wilful incompetence" and "duff guitar playing". Presumably, his advance reviewer's copy had not included Dylan's accompanying note in which he anticipated and attempted to answer such criticisms. The problem with modern recording was its capacity "to wipe out the truth", Dylan observed in his first self-penned sleeve note in almost twenty years. We had all better look out, he warned, because digital trickery would soon mean "there won't be songs like these any more".

Nearer the mark was an insightful review in *Rolling Stone* that declared that the record revealed Dylan as "a genius blues singer, oracular and timeless". An equally enthused Bill Flanagan announced in *Musician* that *World Gone Wrong* was "for anyone with ears to listen and a heart to feel". Among those who felt the record's power profoundly was **Patti Smith**, who had just lost her husband, the guitarist Fred "Sonic" Smith. In her grief she played the record almost constantly, finding solace in "all those great old blues and other songs from the trove of his knowledge".

That Dylan was genuine in his reverence for the old songs is beyond doubt. In the liner notes he wrote of an American music that came from a time "before the celestial grunge, before the insane world of entertainment exploded in our faces". He championed the notion of "learning to go forward by turning back the clock" and offered up the album as "a few random shots at the face of time".

In an interview around the album's release, he paid even more explicit homage to the old bluesmen whose legacy he was drawing upon. "There was a bunch of us, me included, who got to see all these people close up – people like Son House, Rev Gary Davis and Sleepy John Estes. Just to sit there and be up close and watch them play, you could study what they were doing. Plus a bit of their lives rubbed off on you," he said. "Those vibes will carry into you forever, really, so it's like those people, they're still here to me. They're not ghosts of the past or anything. They're continually here."

Once again, the album was a commercial failure and Dylan conceded that he was going "against cultural policy" in modern America. Despite mostly enthusiastic reviews, *World Gone Wrong* struggled to number 70, his worst chart position for any studio album. In Britain the record reached number 35, on a par with *Knocked Out Loaded* as his worst-charting studio release. But at least an element of justice was done when the album won a Grammy as "best traditional folk album".

When Dylan was invited to record a set for the **MTV Unplugged** series in 1994, he suggested a similar mix of traditional songs, but was told by both MTV and Sony that something more commercial was required. "I would have liked to do old folk songs with acoustic instruments. But the record company said, 'You can't do that, it's too obscure'," Dylan reported. "At one time I would have argued but there's no point. OK, so what's not obscure? They said 'Knockin' On Heaven's Door'."

Dressed in a polka-dot shirt and shades that conjured up his iconic image of Newport circa 1965, he duly delivered a greatest-hits set, although it still took two sessions to record. From the uncomfortable first night, only **With God On Our Side** was ultimately used in the broadcast. But Dylan returned the next day and recorded a second set that included more hits and which provided the bulk of both the TV show and the accompanying CD release.

The album became his biggest seller in America since *Infidels*, reaching number 23 in the charts. It also returned Dylan to the British top ten, despite some poor (and very unfair) reviews that appeared to put him on the defensive. "I felt like I delivered something that was preconceived for me," he grumbled in an interview in *USA Today*.

Long-standing Dylan fans, however, had a more serious grumble when, during the course of the year, he allowed the international accountancy firm Coopers & Lybrand to use **The Times They Are A-Changin'** in a TV advert. True, it wasn't the author himself but **Richie Havens** singing the protest anthem. But Dylan had always refused such requests in the past and the news provoked a spate of mock obituaries that claimed Dylan had finally signed the death warrant of 1960s idealism.

1995–96: "The only place where I'm happy"

"There's a certain part of you that becomes addicted to a live audience." Bob Dylan, 1997

As he advanced into his mid-50s, Dylan's appetite for the Never Ending Tour showed no signs of diminishing. Rather, his belief that his identity and purpose was now inextricably tied up with being on stage only seemed to increase. In 1994, he had played 104 live dates. In 1995 the figure increased to 118. There were some unforgettable moments to sustain him and maintain the energy levels, such as performing **Masters of War** in **Hiroshima**. But it was still an astonishingly gruelling schedule.

Dylan had set out the philosophy of the Never Ending Tour way back in 1985, long before he had embarked upon his marathon odyssey. "I started as a travelling guitar player and singer. It had nothing to do with writing songs, fortune and fame. I could always play and that was the important thing – singing the song, contributing something and paying my way," he said. "To draw a crowd with a guitar, that's about the most heroic thing I can do."

By the mid-1990s, he had stopped talking about his "art" and had begun to talk about his "trade". And, like cabinets assembled by a furniture-maker, some gigs were better crafted than others. Some nights lightning struck (to borrow a phrase Dylan has used several times to describe a good gig) and sometimes it didn't. But his conviction that there was something "heroic" in simply being up there every night was unshakeable.

As the NET went on, averaging close to 100 dates a year, Dylan found he had successfully deconstructed his old myth, and created a new, more human, fallible and believable one. "Dylan has made himself readily available to everyone," as Nick Hasted put it in a brilliant essay on the Never Ending Tour in 2003. "If you miss him or he's rubbish, he'll be back soon enough, like a medicine show minstrel or the milkman. Meanwhile you can have a drink, or ten, and see what the night brings, and he may too. The ritual of rock stars, the legend-watching frenzy that once dogged him, are gone. He is merely a musician, accompanying private memories in the millions, for as long as he can hold a guitar." Put

Dylan and Bruce Springsteen playing a Rock And Roll Hall of Fame show, September 1, 1995

Poets, PhDs and the Nobel Prize

In September 1996, Professor Gordon Ball of the **Virginia Military Institute** formally nominated Dylan for the **Nobel prize for literature**. His submission claimed that Dylan had "restored the oral tradition with his minstrelsy. His work qualifies as both poetry and music." The nomination built up a considerable head of steam, with support from the likes of **Andrew Motion**, Britain's Poet Laureate, who called Dylan "one of the great artists of the century" and cited **Visions Of Johanna** as the best song lyric ever written. Other academics, including Professor Christopher Ricks, also lent their support to the nomination. In the end Dylan did not win the prize, but his supporters in academia have not given up the campaign.

simply, the Never Ending Tour stopped Dylan dying of fame. Despite its physical rigours, he concluded that dragging himself around the world to play for his fans was a preferable fate to locking himself away in his own version of Graceland.

Dylan's keenness to play, however, didn't extend to the recording studio, and it seemed that his songwriting had dried up completely. Although his setlists changed constantly and he was forever throwing in covers of songs by everyone from the Grateful Dead to Van Morrison, no new compositions of his own were introduced. *Under The Red Sky*, his last, poorly received album of new songs, had been released way back in 1990 and fans began to wonder if he would ever make another. "I hate recording, man. It's so unreal," he said when pressed on the question.

It certainly wasn't a lack of energy that kept him out of the studio. In addition to his own record-breaking number of shows in 1995, he performed "Like A Rolling Stone" with **The Rolling Stones** in Montpelier, France, in July. He duetted on "Forever Young" with **Bruce Springsteen** at the opening of the Rock And Roll Hall of Fame Museum in Cleveland in September. And he sang "Restless Farewell", which he hadn't performed in 31 years, as a special request at an 80th birthday celebration in Los Angeles for **Frank Sinatra** in November. Less happily, in August that year he also attended the funeral of **Jerry Garcia**, who he described as "a big brother who taught and showed me more than he'll ever know".

If 1996 sounds less hectic with "just" 86 dates, it was only because the Never Ending Tour did not resume until April. Once it did, the pace was as relentless as before. Dylan seemed to be enjoying himself on stage, too, and among those who joined him in the course of the year were **Roger McGuinn, Jewel, Aimee Mann, Ron Wood, Dave Matthews, Nils Lofgren** and **Van Morrison**.

Then in autumn came the news that fans had been waiting for, but had begun to fear would never arrive. It was whispered that **Daniel Lanois** had been given a set of acoustic Dylan demos and invited to produce a new album. Not even the unwelcome news that Dylan had sanctioned the Bank of Montreal to use "The Times They Are A-Changin'" in a TV advert could detract from the excitement.

1997: It's Not Dark Yet

*"The first time I heard Bob Dylan I thought of him as
something of a civil war type, a kind of 19th-century troubadour,
a maverick American spirit. The reediness of his voice and the
spareness of his words go straight to the heart of America."* Gregory Peck, 1997

The year 1997 turned out to be one of the most remarkable in Bob Dylan's extraordinary career. It was also almost his last. On May 25, the day after he had turned 56, he was admitted to hospital in Los Angeles, complaining of severe chest plains and breathlessness (see p.156). He had just finished a three-month tour of Japan and North America and was completing the mixing of his first album of new compositions in seven years at **Teatro Studios** in Oxnard, California. The songs were preoccupied with mortality, heartbreak and solitude, and when his doctors diagnosed a potentially fatal inflammation of the sac around the heart called pericarditis, it appeared that life was about to imitate art.

When we finally got to hear the songs, with the release of *Time Out Of Mind* in September, it appeared that Dylan had been divining his own fate. Even though the songs were recorded prior to his hospitalization, they sounded as if he knew something terrible was about to happen to him. The album was widely hailed as an artistic triumph and rated by many as his best work since *Blood On The Tracks* more than twenty years earlier. Even more remarkably, by August he was back on the road, the Never Ending Tour continuing as if nothing had happened.

So how and when did Dylan's songwriting return? Although there were times when he had struggled to write before, particularly in the mid-1980s, the period 1990–96 was unprecedented in his entire career. Never had he gone so long without any new songs. It seems likely that he tried to write, but little, if anything, was ever finished. "Unless a song flows out naturally and doesn't have to be chaperoned, it just dissipates," he admitted in 1995. "I'll write a verse down and never complete it."

After Jerry Garcia's death in 1995, Dylan spent a few days with the Grateful Dead's lyricist **Robert Hunter** and attempted to write some lyrics. It may have helped to shift the blockage, for many of the songs on *Time Out Of Mind* were apparently conceived in the early months of 1996 when Dylan found himself snowed in at his farm in Minnesota. He carried them around during the 86 live dates he played during the year, although none of them were unveiled on stage. Later in the year he stayed with **Ronnie Wood** in Ireland and was apparently working on lyrics every day, "tearing up cigarette packets to scribble lyrics", according to Howard Sounes.

Sometime before Christmas, Dylan met with Lanois in a New York hotel and read him the

Almost meeting Elvis

Dylan spent his 56th birthday on Saturday May 24 with his stepdaughter **Maria Himmelman** (daughter of Sara), who threw a small party for him at her Santa Monica home. He looked unwell and when he complained of chest pains, she persuaded him to talk to a doctor on the phone. The following day, he was admitted to St John's Hospital, Santa Monica.

Tests revealed that he was suffering from **pericarditis**, an inflammation of the sac around the heart, which made breathing difficult and was potentially fatal if not arrested in time. The condition was caused by a fungal infection called **histoplasmosis**, itself caused by spores found in soil contaminated by droppings from bats and certain species of birds in parts of southern America and along the Mississippi and Ohio rivers. Dylan believed he had inhaled the spores either from a river bank near one of his homes or on a motorcycle ride through a swamp area while recently on tour.

Bob spent six nights in hospital, but claims that he "didn't have any philosophical, profound thoughts. The pain stopped me in my tracks and fried my mind.

I was so sick my mind just blanked out." The news that he was ill with a "potentially fatal infection" made the front pages of the world's newspapers on May 29, but by June 1, after having been successfully treated by intravenous antibiotics and anti-inflammatories, Dylan left hospital. "I'm glad to be feeling better. I really thought I'd be seeing Elvis soon," he told reporters.

He went home for a further six weeks' recuperation. "I could hardly walk around my yard," he said later. "I had to stay in bed and sleep all the time." Yet by August, with *Time Out Of Mind* about to be released, Dylan was back on the road. "I'm doing as good as I can under the circumstances," he told *USA Today*. "I'm still taking medication three times a day. Sometimes it makes me a little light-headed and dizzy. And I need to sleep a lot."

The episode appears to have had no long-term detrimental effect on Dylan's health. In the twelve months following his return to the road, he played 113 live dates.

new lyrics, as if they were poems. His inspiration had been the kind of old blues and folk songs he had recorded on *Good As I Been To You* and *World Gone Wrong*. Phrases from old songs by the likes of **Jimmie Rodgers** and **Fats Domino** cropped up in his new compositions, but were then developed in new and profound directions. "The words were hard, were deep, were desperate, were strong," Lanois later recalled.

Dylan and Lanois agreed to begin recording at Criterion Studios in Miami, Florida, in January 1997. They assembled a team of musicians drawn from Dylan's touring band, plus drummers **Brian Blade** and **Jim Keltner**, steel-guitar player **Cindy Cashdollar** from Asleep At The Wheel, guitarists **Duke Robillard** and **Bob Britt**, and keyboard players **Jim Dickinson** and **Augie Meyers** from 1960s band The Sir Douglas Quintet. It was the latter's stark Vox organ that contributed much to the atmosphere of the record.

In Lanois' favoured style, the musicians were assembled in the shape of a horseshoe and recorded live. Dylan tinkered with the songs as they were recording, reworking lyrics and even transplanting entire verses from one song to another. There were sometimes profound musical changes to the songs in the studio, too. "There's always going to be a sense of discovery with Bob because, at the last second, without warning and as the record button is pressed, he'll change the key and time signature," Lanois recalled later. "The musicians will just look at themselves and dribble in and often Bob will say 'That's it'."

By the end of the sessions, Dylan had thirteen new songs recorded, eleven of which would eventually make the album. He was still tinkering with the running order in May when he fell sick. "I was putting songs on, taking songs off. I didn't know what picture it was forming. When I got sick, I had to let it go," he said following the album's release and his full recovery.

Some feared that he had returned too soon. On medical advice, he refrained from wheezing into his harmonica, and he looked tired and a little shaky at his comeback show in **Lincoln**, New Hampshire, according to eyewitnesses. His face appeared puffy and he sweated profusely. "I'm still taking medication three times a day. Sometimes it makes me light-hearted and dizzy," he admitted. At times, Dylan sat down for a rest between songs and his vocal range seemed to have narrowed, his recent illness having added to the ravage on his vocal chords and lungs that years of nonstop touring had already inflicted. But, opening with **Absolutely Sweet Marie**, he delivered a daring show that included such surprises as **Tough Mama** (played for the first time since 1974) and **Cocaine Blues**.

In spite of his near-death experience, by the

> *"I'm used to my records being slagged off and my shows misrepresented. I'm no longer used to the acceptance of a record."* Bob Dylan, 1997

> *"It is a spooky record because I feel spooky. I don't feel in tune with anything."* Bob Dylan in *Newsweek*, October 1997

The Great Comeback

Despite his motorcycle crash and a lifestyle in which drug and alcohol abuse had played a large part at different times in his career, Dylan had never missed a show in his life until July 1993 (when, bedridden for three days with a bad back in Lisbon, he had reluctantly cancelled a show in Lyon, France). His illness in the early summer of 1997 forced him to cancel an entire tour of Europe with Van Morrison. But he was back on the road by August 3.

end of 1997, Dylan had still somehow managed to fit in 96 live shows (ten more than the previous year when he had been relatively fit and well). They included a triumphant British tour and a show for the pope in Bologna, Italy, on September 27 (see box, overleaf). Three days later, *Time Out Of Mind*, his first collection of new songs in seven years, was released. Under the circumstances, it couldn't help but sound like "the final instalment of the tombstone blues", as Stuart Bailie put it. But the record garnered

Knockin' On Heaven's Door: Bob and the Pope

There was something surreal about Bob Dylan, a wandering Jewish minstrel, singing for Pope John Paul II at the **World Eucharist Congress** in Bologna on September 27, 1997. Broadcast live on Italian TV and before an audience of 300,000, which included the pontiff seated to one side of the stage on a raised dais, Dylan took to the stage in an embroidered suit that made him look like a riverboat gambler. Backed by his full Never Ending Tour band, he opened with "Knockin' On Heaven's Door". But by the time the song had ended, a much-reproduced camera shot caught the 77-year-old spiritual leader looking as if he had fallen asleep.

A Hard Rain's A-Gonna Fall followed, before Dylan mounted the dais and removed his Stetson hat as God's vicar-on-earth rose from his seat to shake hands. He then delivered a sermon, based in part on Dylan's lyrics: "You say the answer is blowing in the wind my friend. And so it is. But it is not the wind that blows things away. It is the wind that is the breath of and the life of the Holy Spirit … how many roads must a man walk down? One. There is only one road for man and it is the road of Jesus Christ." Dylan then returned to the stage and concluded by singing **Forever Young**.

Why did he do it? "You don't say no to the Vatican," Dylan insisted. But the cheque he was reportedly paid for $350,000 by the Papal promoter also helped.

his best reviews in years. "The original is back," *NME* enthused. "At his creative peak", *The Guardian* declared. Elvis Costello even reckoned it was the best album Dylan had ever made, and *Newsweek* put him on the cover for the first time in 23 years with the triumphant headline, "Dylan Lives". Dylan appears to have been genuinely astonished by the critical acclaim.

It can be argued that the critics were swayed into an unusual generosity by his illness. While he lay in hospital, the media had been full of favourable reassessments that had sought to restore Dylan to his rightful place as the most important songwriter of his generation. Bryan Appleyard in the *Sunday Times* had even insisted that in any list of the greatest rock albums ever made, nobody else could rank higher than 42nd, behind Dylan's entire oeuvre. However, several years on, it still sounds like one of the great Bob Dylan albums and the most profound expression popular music has yet managed of the process of ageing and confronting one's own mortality. "I have no great need to appeal to people who are still in high school," Dylan pointed out.

Time Out Of Mind made the top ten in both Britain and America and headed most critics' polls as the best album of 1997. It also secured Dylan three **Grammy** nominations, including album of the year. He went on to win all three – one more than his son Jakob's band, The Wallflowers. One of the greatest comebacks of all time was complete. "From the 18 years that separate his conversion from his illness, it seemed Dylan could do no right," Clinton Heylin wrote. "Now it seemed he could do no wrong."

1998–99: The Elder Statesman

"I don't want to put on the mask of celebrity.
I'd rather just do my work and see it as a trade." Bob Dylan

With his profile higher than it had been for a long time and *Time Out Of Mind* his best-selling album in twenty years, Dylan might have taken advantage of the chance to fill arenas again. Instead, he remained true to the spirit of the Never Ending Tour by playing smaller shows – 110 of them in the course of the year. So while The Rolling Stones played

Jakob Dylan

The only one of Dylan's children to become a professional musician, **Jakob Dylan** dropped out of art school in New York to form **The Wallflowers** in 1990. His concerned father was not keen on the idea. But he did not attempt to dissuade him and Jakob and band were swiftly signed to Virgin. When their 1992 debut album failed to sell and they were dropped, Dylan's fears for his son appeared to be justified.

One of the reasons Jakob fell out with Virgin was because he refused to exploit the family connection. He persisted with his songwriting and the band eventually signed to Interscope Records, who teamed him with his father's old sideman, **T-Bone Burnett**. Released in 1996, the band's second album, the Burnett-produced *Bringing Down The Horse*, went on to sell in excess of four million copies – more, according to official industry figures, than any Bob Dylan album and twice as many as *Blood On The Tracks*.

Dylan was every bit the proud father. "He made it on his own," he told the *LA Times* in 1997, when asked about his son's success. "If anything his name held him back. I think that held him back on his first record, to

tell you the truth. I think that record would have been accepted if he wasn't who he was."

In November 1997, father and son appeared together at a corporate show in San Jose, California, at which The Wallflowers opened and Bob Dylan took top billing. The pecking order was repeated at the 1998 Grammys, when Dylan won three awards and The Wallflowers two.

In public, Jakob has persistently refused to talk about his father and in his early days walked out on several interviews when pressed on the subject.."

By 2002, he was a little more relaxed on the subject. "I knew all of *Nashville Skyline* by the time I was four. So was I influenced? Why has anyone even got to ask the question?" But he went on to complain that his father's fans had made his early gigs hard by turning up and yelling for him to sing "All Along The Watchtower". "I thought if I ignored it, they'd figured out that I wasn't going to do it and they'd stop. And they did. But the sad thing is they are tragically disappointed in me. I really let them down. They honestly thought I was supposed to come to town and sing his songs."

the huge Madison Square Garden in January 1998, Dylan and **Van Morrison** earned themselves artistic Brownie points in the same week by playing the much more intimate Madison Square Garden Theatre.

In February, however, Dylan toured South America as support to the Stones, appearing with them to sing **Like A Rolling Stone** each night. By the middle of the year he was touring the US on a triple bill of classic singer-songwriters with **Joni Mitchell** and **Van Morrison**. He also fitted in his first appearance at the Glastonbury festival before heading off to Australia with **Patti Smith** in support. The autumn and winter brought further American jaunts, first with **Lucinda Williams** and then with Joni Mitchell again.

The renewed interest generated in his entire career by his illness and *Time Out Of Mind* was further sustained by the belated release of *Live 1966*, the fourth volume in Columbia's official *Bootleg Series* (though only the second instalment, since the series was launched with a triple box-set in 1991). Most reviewers hailed it as the greatest live album of all time.

There was no let-up in the touring schedule in 1999, either. In fact, the year produced 121 shows – the most in Dylan's entire career. They included 48 shows with **Paul Simon**, featuring nightly duets on songs such as **The Sound Of Silence** and **Knockin' On Heaven's Door**. And the unevenness of previous years seemed to have been ironed out of the concerts. Most nights "lightning struck" and poor shows were few and far between.

2000–06: Things Have Changed

"Doesn't it ever get tiring singing the same song over and over again?
No, it doesn't. That's the thing about music. It's not on the page.
It's got a life of its own." Bob Dylan

The new millennium could hardly have started worse for Dylan, with the death of his mother from cancer in January 2000. She was 84, and Bob and his brother David buried her in the Jewish cemetery in Duluth next to the grave where their father had lain since 1968. Dylan's grief, however, caused hardly a blip in the Never Ending Tour: the year found him playing another 112 shows, almost all of them of a uniformly high standard.

The year also saw the release of his first new material since *Time Out Of Mind* with the inclusion of **Things Have Changed** on the soundtrack of the Curtis Hanson–directed film, **Wonder Boys**, starring Michael Douglas. A delicious exercise in misanthropy, the song boasted a lyric that claimed "people are crazy and times are strange" but had a wry wit, with Dylan declaring that he "used to care but things have changed". To his evident delight, the song won an **Oscar**. "A lot of performers have won Grammies," he told Alan Jackson of *The Times*. "But very few have won Academy Awards. So that puts me on a different plateau."

Dylan turned 60 in May 2001 but there was still no relaxation in his touring schedule, with 106 concerts at which he played 121 different songs. As a tribute to his indefatigable energy as a live performer, Sony released **Bob Dylan Live 1961–2000**, a 16-track collection of mostly rare and unreleased recordings from different phases of his career. And his birthday provoked a spate of media tributes, including a *Rolling Stone* cover story in which U2's Bono was asked his thoughts on Bob. "It's like trying to talk about the pyramids. What do you do?" he replied. "You just stand back and gape."

Dylan himself spent his birthday in a studio in New York recording **Love And Theft**, the follow-up to *Time Out Of Mind*. Featuring his regular touring band plus **Augie Meyers** once again on organ, the album was released on a day when most minds were elsewhere – September 11, 2001. With the artist stepping into the producer's shoes (under the alias "Jack Frost"), the album contained a dozen new songs, one of which, **Mississippi**, was an outtake from *Time Out Of Mind* and which **Sheryl Crow** had already covered on her *Globe*

Bob at Newport Folk Festival, 2002 – 37 years after the electric debacle

Sessions album. Overall, it was a less important album than its predecessor. But it was fabulous nevertheless and found Dylan to be the "song and dance man" he had long professed he wanted to be, portraying the broad

Never Ending Stats

Since the Never Ending Tour is deemed to have "officially" opened in Concord on June 7, 1988, it had by the end of 2005 clocked up 1856 gigs in eighteen years. These break down as follows:

1988	—	71
1989	—	99
1990	—	93
1991	—	101
1992	—	92
1993	—	80
1994	—	104
1995	—	116
1996	—	86
1997	—	96
1998	—	110
1999	—	119
2000	—	112
2001	—	106
2002	—	107
2003	—	88
2004	—	113
2005	—	113

The volume of songs the NET has netted is similarly impressive. By the end of 2005, Bob had performed around 450 different compositions. According to the log kept by Olof Bjorner, the twenty most performed songs between 1988 and 2000 were:

1. **All Along The Watchtower (878)**
2. **Highway 61 Revisited (745)**
3. **Tangled Up In Blue (733)**
4. **Like A Rolling Stone (653)**
5. **Maggie's Farm (593)**
6. **Silvio (582)**
7. **Mr Tambourine Man (554)**
8. **Rainy Day Women # 12 & 35 (541)**
9. **It Ain't Me Babe (503)**
10. **Don't Think Twice It's Alright (466)**
11. **Masters Of War (431)**
12. **Blowin' In The Wind (407)**
13. **Stuck Inside Of Mobile With The Memphis Blues Again (390)**
14. **Ballad Of A Thin Man (313)**
15. **Just Like A Woman (303)**
16. **I Shall Be Released (280)**
17. **Everything Is Broken (270)**
18. **The Times They Are A-Changin' (269)**
19. **Love Sick (257)**
20. **It's All Over Now Baby Blue (245)**

spectrum of twentieth-century American music in a patchwork of genres that ranged from Appalachian folk picking through scratchy blues and rockabilly to vaudeville and show tunes via rock'n'roll and jazz. If *Time Out Of Mind* was about mortality, **Love And Theft**, as *Uncut* magazine's Nick Johnstone put it, found Dylan "recast as vaudeville entertainer putting on an escapist show while death lurks in the shadows". A spate of five-star reviews propelled the album to number five in America and number three in Britain. It was a matter of routine that it won Dylan another **Grammy**.

The following year, 2002, found him playing 107 dates in 14 different countries. On the recording front, there was a new song, **Waiting For You**, that appeared on the soundtrack of the movie *Divine Secrets Of The Ya-Ya Sisterhood*. The *Bootleg Series Volume 5* also appeared, featuring recordings from 1975's Rolling Thunder Tour.

In 2003, Dylan appeared in the film *Masked & Anonymous*, the soundtrack of which included new versions of "Cold Irons Bound" and "Down In The Flood" as well as takes of the traditional songs "Diamond Joe" and "Dixie".

The year 2003 also saw the reissue of fifteen of his best albums remastered for SACD 5:1 surround sound, often with spectacular results. In between all this activity, there was still space for 88 live shows, in many of which he played keyboards rather than guitar.

The year 2004 found Dylan playing 113 dates, the third highest total in the NET's history. *The Bootleg Series Volume 6* appeared in March, featuring an acoustic concert recorded in New York in October 1964. And it was also reported that Paramount Pictures was working, with Dylan's cooperation, on a biopic with the working title of *I'm Not There: Suppositions On A Film Concerning Dylan*, to be directed by Todd Haynes.

More controversially, Dylan appeared in a TV commercial promoting the lingerie brand **Victoria's Secret**. In the ad, his face – sporting a pencil moustache and eyeliner – was intercut with shots of scantily clad models cavorting in Venice to a soundtrack of **Love Sick** from *Time Out Of Mind*. It was the first time in his career that he had appeared in a TV advertisement, and it prompted a host of protests on Dylan Internet message boards. That he was still able to provoke such controversy into his sixties was at least evidence that it wasn't dark yet – even if at times the view had got a little murky.

Unlike record companies, publishers customarily announce their forthcoming titles a year or more in advance. Not Dylan, of course. After much rumour and speculation, Simon & Schuster finally revealed in late August 2004 that *Chronicles Volume One*, the first part of a supposed three-part autobiography, would be published in October. At the same time came the publication of *Lyrics 1962–2001*, the first such update since the 1985 edition.

When *Chronicles* arrived, it proved to be a remarkable read and was enthusiastically reviewed by heavyweight literary critics. Refusing to follow a linear narrative, Dylan switched intriguingly from his early days in Greenwich Village to his post-crash retreat in Woodstock and on to the late 1980s when he was considering retirement, before switching back again to evoke his first faltering steps in music. Beautifully written, it revealed little about his private life and indeed, some of the best passages weren't directly about Dylan himself at all, but lyrically described how he felt when he first heard the likes of Woody Guthrie and Robert Johnson. He was also excessively warm and generous about many of those such as Dave Van Ronk and Joan Baez who had helped him in his early career, but to whom he had perhaps behaved with less than total chivalry. In doing so, of course, he told us much about the development of his artistic genius, while at the same time keeping the enigma of his genius intact. *Chronicles* was also made available on both cassette and CD as a six-hour talking book, read by Sean Penn.

In May 2005 Dylan entered his 65th year, but there was no sign of him slowing up. In the course of the year, he played another 113 live dates and sounded in better voice than he had for a couple of years, largely eradicating an irritating tendency to end every line on an up-note that had nothing to do with the melody line and which had marred recent tours. When he got to London in November, he played a total of 50 different songs in the course of a five-night stint at the Brixton Academy.

The year was also notable for the TC screening of Martin Scorsese's documentary, *No Direction Home*, which garnered rave reviews when shown on British and American TV in September 2005. The film was also released as a two-disc DVD while the soundtrack, consisting almost entirely of previously unreleased material from 1959–66, appeared as *Volume Seven* of the *Official Bootleg Series*. Simultaneously, the ten-track album *Live At The Gaslight 1962* was released in a controversial move that saw the record only available in the US via Starbuck's outlets.

As for a new album, Dylan revealed in interviews around the publication of *Chronicles* that he had "five or six" new songs recorded for a follow-up to 2001's *Love & Theft* and was planning to go back into the studio before the end of 2004 to see if he could complete the record. A year later there was still no sign of it.

Bob FM: DJ Dylan takes to the airwaves

In May 2006 Dylan began a new sideline – as a radio disc jockey – and received some of the best reviews of his career. On his **Theme Time Radio Hour**, on XM Satellite Radio, he would play records linked by a specific topic – a different one each week. His first show concerned the weather, and had a playlist featuring **Muddy Waters**, Fats Domino, Frank Sinatra, Jimi Hendrix, Judy Garland, the Staple Singers and the **Carter Family**. Subsequent themes covered drinking, motherhood and baseball.

Most of the music he selected predated his career and many of the songs looked back to his own formative sources. "I think it's more akin to the way radio sounded in 1952 than it does in 2006," admitted XM Satellite Radio's Lee Abrams, who commissioned Dylan to present the shows. Dylan was given freedom to play what he liked, and he recorded the programmes independently of the station. "They deliver the show to us every week," Abrams revealed. "It's a big surprise when we open the package and listen."

What most impressed, and surprised, critics accustomed to Dylan's terse on-stage mumblings was his sense of humour, which ranged from corny jokes ("I just came back from a pleasure trip – took my mother-in-law to the airport") to deadpan. During the show featuring songs about the weather, he introduced **Slim Harpo**'s "Raining In My Heart" by saying: "Slim wrote a bunch of songs with his wife, Lovelle. Boy, I wish I had a wife like that, help me write songs!"

Part 2:
The Music

The Albums

Bob Dylan

YOU'RE NO GOOD | TALKIN' NEW YORK BLUES | IN MY TIME OF DYIN' | MAN OF CONSTANT SORROW | FIXIN' TO DIE | PRETTY PEGGY-O | HIGHWAY 51 | GOSPEL PLOW | BABY LET ME FOLLOW YOU DOWN | HOUSE OF THE RISING SUN | FREIGHT TRAIN BLUES | SONG TO WOODY | SEE THAT MY GRAVE IS KEPT CLEAN
Columbia; recorded November 20–22, 1961; released March 19, 1962; available on CD

Just 20 years old, Dylan recorded his debut album over two afternoons in November 1961, with producer John Hammond. It's difficult to reconcile the maturity of the recording with the baby-faced ingénue on the cover. Despite the presence of two of his own compositions, this is essentially Dylan in pre-writing phase, so the focus is very much on the performer. He passes with flying colours, sounding disarmingly authentic and making the big names of the folk revival such as Peter, Paul and Mary, and The Kingston Trio sound bland and anaemic by comparison.

The album finds Dylan still very much in thrall to the spirit of Woody Guthrie. Yet despite the critic Paul Williams' assertion that all we hear is "an interesting but immature white blues singer", he's already exuding a potent charisma that is all his own. His delivery is unique and idiosyncratic, but his sense of timing and his self-awareness are near perfect. Two examples are the tongue-in-cheek intro to **Baby Let Me Follow You Down**, with its references to "the green pastures of Harvard University", and the haunting way he sings **In My Time Of Dyin'**, one of the many songs on the album in which the spectre of death obsessively lurks.

In **See That My Grave Is Kept Clean** and **Fixin' To Die Blues** Dylan never sounds like a mere stylist, trying to copy Blind Lemon Jefferson or Bukka White, from whose recordings he learned the songs. He's certainly a showman – he's going for effect and knows exactly what he's doing. But he's also digging deep into a manic emotional intensity that no 20-year-old really has any right to possess.

The version of "The House Of The Rising Sun" was "borrowed" from Dave Van Ronk, but Dylan turns in a performance that is utterly definitive. **Man Of Constant Sorrow** is angelically beautiful, while "Pretty Peggy-O" is a hoot – pure vaudeville, burlesque brilliance.

Then there are his own two first recorded compositions. **Talkin' New York** is appealing enough but probably more noteworthy for the performance than the song – the little laugh in

The Music

his voice, the way he uses the guitar and harmonica to sustain the narrative and the effectiveness of the way he communicates irony and elicits sympathy. But **Song To Woody** – an honest portrayal of a young man walking in Woody's footsteps and at the same time discovering the world through his own eyes – is superb. It's from the heart, full of a sense of wonder and blessed with a genuine, and rare, humility.

This is where the legend starts and the "ramshackle vision of pure genius" (in the late Ian MacDonald's words) begins to take shape.

Live At The Gaslight 1962

A HARD RAIN'S A-GONNA FALL | ROCKS AND GRAVEL | DON'T THINK TWICE, IT'S ALL RIGHT | THE CUCKOO | MOONSHINER | HANDSOME MOLLY/COCAINE | JOHN BROWN | BARBARA ALLEN | WEST TEXAS
Columbia/Starbuck's; recorded Oct 1962; released Aug 30, 1965; available on CD

Long a favoured live recording among collectors as a bootleg, ten tracks from the legendary tape recorded at the Gaslight café in Greenwich Village in October 1962 were finally made officially available in 2005 via a controversial tie-up with Starbuck's. Perhaps the notion of making the album available exclusively via a chain of coffee shops in America was meant to be a clever commentary on the role of coffeehouses as key venues in the early 1960s folk boom. If so, it was lost on a lot of Dylan fans who smelt not the alluring aroma of freshly-brewed coffee beans but the stench of corporate exploitation.

Recorded on a small, portable tape recorder, the tracks have been expertly cleaned up and mastered to provide clarity and balance, and the nuances of Dylan's vocals and guitar picking are conveyed with considerable subtlety, given the non-hi-fi nature of the original recording. Recorded when he was in the middle of the elongated process of making his second studio album *Freewheelin' Bob Dylan*, it's a wonderful portrait of pre-fame Dylan playing in the heart of Greenwich Village for his earliest audience and a perfect snapshot of his transition from talented folk-interpreter to staggeringly original songwriter. As such it sits perfectly between his first two studio albums. Of the original songs, it contains one of the earliest performances of "A Hard Rain's A-Gonna Fall", while "Don't Think Twice" was similarly newly minted and is heard in an earlier and quite different version from the one that eventually appeared on *Freewheelin'*. "John Brown" (which he was still playing regularly on his autumn 2005 tour) and "Rocks And Gravel" (based on Brownie McGhee's "Solid Road" and originally intended for inclusion on *Freewheelin'* until other songs came along) had been around a little longer. The other six tracks are all traditional folk/blues tunes and when played alongside 1961's Minneapolis tapes, which feature similar repertoire, illustrate at just what an astonishing speed Dylan's genius was developing. The eight-minute version of "Barbara Allen" is a particular delight, although the recording of "West Texas" is unfortunately incomplete.

The Freewheelin' Bob Dylan

BLOWIN' IN THE WIND | GIRL FROM THE NORTH COUNTRY | MASTERS OF WAR | DOWN THE HIGHWAY | BOB DYLAN'S BLUES | A HARD RAIN'S A-GONNA FALL | DON'T THINK TWICE, IT'S ALL RIGHT | BOB DYLAN'S DREAM | OXFORD TOWN | TALKING WORLD WAR III BLUES | CORRINA CORRINA | HONEY JUST ALLOW ME ONE MORE CHANCE | I SHALL BE FREE

Columbia; recorded April 1962–April 24,1963; released May 27,1963; available on CD and SACD

The "difficult" second album? Not in Dylan's case, although the writing and recording was spread out over an entire year. His debut album had included just two original compositions, but his development as a songwriter was so rapid that this effortless-sounding follow-up contains as high a concentration of enduringly classic songs as almost any record in history. Recording began in April 1962, just a month after the release of Dylan's debut. But the songs he laid down at that first session, such as **Ramblin' Gamblin' Willie**, "The Death of Emmett Till" (his first protest song) and "Talkin' John Birch Paranoid Blues", were soon overtaken and failed to make the album that was eventually released more than a year later. By then Dylan had a couple of dozen new songs to chose from. Side one of the original vinyl release contained **Blowin' In The Wind**, "Girl From The North Country", "Masters Of War" and "A Hard Rain's A-Gonna Fall", all of which remain mainstays of a Dylan live performance to this day.

Flipping over the original vinyl brought side two's opener, **Don't Think Twice It's All Right,** one of the tenderest songs of leaving and regret in the English language, combining love, confusion, resignation and dignity within its allotted three and a half minutes. Then there's further social commentary with **Oxford Town** and **Talking World War III Blues**. That Dylan, who was still only 21, could include such fierce and potent protest and such tender, personal love songs on the same album is little short of astonishing. The album slightly runs out of steam towards the end, with covers of "Corrina Corrina" and "Honey Just Allow Me One More Chance", but picks up again with **I Shall Be Free**. Dylan's sharpest, wittiest song to date, it is replete with references to JFK, Brigitte Bardot, Sophia Loren, Yul Brynner, Charles de Gaulle and "the great granddaughter of Mr Clean".

The Times They Are A-Changin'

THE TIMES THEY ARE A-CHANGIN' | BALLAD OF HOLLIS BROWN | WITH GOD ON OUR SIDE | ONE TOO MANY MORNINGS | NORTH COUNTRY BLUES | ONLY A PAWN IN THEIR GAME | BOOTS OF SPANISH LEATHER | WHEN THE SHIP COMES IN | THE LONESOME DEATH OF HATTIE CARROLL | RESTLESS FAREWELL

Columbia; recorded August 6–October 24, 1963; released January 13, 1964; available on CD and SACD

Dylan swiftly came to disavow the mantle of protest singer, but his third album surely constitutes the most potent expression of the

The Music

genre ever realised, both in its zeitgeist timing and the maturity with which Dylan tackled his targets. In the tumultuous six months leading up to its release in January 1964, Martin Luther King had made his "I have a dream" speech and Kennedy had been assassinated. Dylan responded to his world-changing times with the anthemic title-track, **Only A Pawn In Their Game**, "With God On Our Side", and "The Lonesome Death Of Hattie Carroll", four of the sharpest protest songs ever penned, while the block lettering and stark black-and-white picture on the cover made the sleeve look more like a campaign poster than a record album.

"The Times They Are A-Changin'" may have been the album that cemented the "voice of a generation" tag (another label he spent years trying to disown). But – as on *The Freewheelin'* album – amidst all the righteous anger were haunting love songs of unbelievable tenderness: in **One Too Many Mornings** and **Boots of Spanish Leather**, both written for Suze Rotolo.

Elsewhere, **The Ballad Of Hollis Brown** and **North Country Blues** movingly display his empathy with the ordinary working man, in one case a dirt-poor sharecropper on a South Dakota farm and in the other unemployed miners in the Minnesota of his youth, dispossessed and disenfranchised by forces beyond their control. The album ends with **Restless Farewell**, its claim that "my feet are now fast

and point away from the past", suggesting that Dylan is already preparing to move on to the next phase of his mercurial career.

Another Side Of Bob Dylan

ALL I REALLY WANT TO DO | BLACK CROW BLUES | SPANISH HARLEM INCIDENT | CHIMES OF FREEDOM | I SHALL BE FREE #10 | TO RAMONA | MOTORPSYCHO NIGHTMARE | MY BACK PAGES | I DON'T BELIEVE YOU | BALLAD IN PLAIN D | IT AIN'T ME BABE
Columbia; recorded June 9, 1964; released August 8, 1964; available on CD

Another Side Of Bob Dylan marks the transition between the protest anthems and the trilogy of electric-rock masterpieces that would follow. Its stark acoustic accompaniment gives no hint of the wild sound Dylan was about to embrace and the subject matter is more directly personal and even confessional than most of his work, either before or since. Astonishingly, the eleven songs were all recorded in one six-hour, red-wine-fuelled session, which began at 7.30pm and concluded at 1.30am.

Written over a period of several months, the songs display a diversity of emotions. **All I Really Want To Do** is an enjoyable, light-hearted doodle, while "I Don't Believe You" is broken-hearted but jaunty. "Ballad In Plain

D" is maudlin, vicious and self-pitying but as irresistible as rubbernecking a motorway crash, while "To Ramona" is impossibly lovely, one of the most tender songs Dylan has ever written. **It Ain't Me, Babe** is simultaneously a caustic put-down and an exercise in self-justification, while "Spanish Harlem Incident" crackles with an exhilaratingly erotic charge ("Your temperature's too hot for taming, Your flaming feet burn up the street"). "I Shall Be Free #10" and "Motorpsycho Nightmare" are both full of acerbic wit.

The only track that even remotely resembles a protest song is **Chimes Of Freedom**, but the song is laced with layers of personal meaning and dazzlingly surreal wordplay. Yet the album's keynote song in terms of Dylan's future direction is **My Back Pages**. Documenting his disillusion with formal politics, he sneers at his old self for believing that life is black and white and declares in celebratory fashion, "I was so much older then, I'm younger than that now."

The Bootleg Series Vol 6: Live 1964 – The Philharmonic Hall Concert

THE TIMES THEY ARE A-CHANGIN' | SPANISH HARLEM INCIDENT | TALKIN' JOHN BIRCH PARANOID BLUES | TO RAMONA | WHO KILLED DAVEY MOORE? | GATES OF EDEN | IF YOU GOTTA GO, GO NOW | IT'S ALRIGHT, MA (I'M ONLY BLEEDING) | I DONT BELIEVE YOU | MR TAMBOURINE MAN | A HARD RAIN'S A-GONNA FALL | TALKIN' WORLD WAR III BLUES | DONT THINK TWICE ITS ALL RIGHT | THE LONESOME DEATH OF HATTIE CARROLL | MAMA YOU BEEN ON MY MIND | SILVER DAGGER (JOAN BAEZ) | WITH GOD
ON OUR SIDE | IT AIN'T ME, BABE | ALL I REALLY WANT TO DO
Columbia; recorded October 31, 1964; released March 29, 2004; available on CD

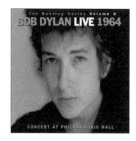

Dylan's acoustic concert at New York's Philharmonic Hall on October 31, 1964, was recorded by Columbia's engineers for a planned live album. A sleeve was produced and the catalogue number 2302 assigned. That it never appeared in the shops had nothing to do with any absence of quality. Rather, it was because by then Dylan was moving so fast that there was no time to schedule its release. Within nine months of the Philharmonic Hall appearance, he had delivered two new studio albums – *Bringing It All Back Home* and *Highway 61 Revisited* – and controversially gone electric in public for the first time at Newport. A live acoustic album would have been out of date almost as soon as it was pressed. Then a sequence of further tumultuous events, followed by Dylan's subsequent retirement from touring for seven years, meant that we had to wait until 1974's *Before The Flood* for his first official live album.

For years the illicit Philharmonic recording was one of the most highly-rated Dylan bootlegs among collectors, both for its content and for the exemplary sound quality. Forty years after the event, it finally got its official release, appearing as the sixth volume

The Music

of Columbia's *Bootleg Series* in March 2004.

The nineteen songs capture Dylan in headlong motion, snapped in a unique, brief and vital transitional moment in his development, as he stands trembling on the cusp between Woody Guthrie–influenced folk-protest singer and Rimbaud-inspired rock'n'roll poet. Early protest numbers that never made a studio album such as **Talkin' John Birch Paranoid Blues** and **Who Killed Davey Moore?** sit alongside five songs from his then-current album *Another Side Of Bob Dylan*. Three tracks apiece from *Freewheelin'* and *The Times They Are A-Changin'* jostle with the pure pop of the unreleased **If You Gotta Go, Go Now** (soon to be covered by Manfred Mann) and three then-unrecorded masterpieces that would imminently appear on the career-changing *Bringing It All Back Home*.

Dylan's rapport with his audience is extraordinary. He's kidding around and revelling in the adulation – funny, charming and self-confident. When it comes to the encore, the crowd calls out for favourite songs and one wag has them in peals of laughter by yelling for "Mary Had A Little Lamb". But nobody upstages Dylan in this mood. "Is that a protest song?" he deadpans. Then he sucks his harmonica and starts to sing, "I ain't looking to compete with you." As he continues the song, the falsetto on the first "all I really want to do" of the chorus is so outrageous that he cannot suppress an involuntary giggle.

Don't Think Twice finds him toying joyously with its familiar melody, taking it to the edge and beyond and exploring the familiar lyric with such wide-eyed wonder that it sounds as if he's singing it for the first time. "The Lonesome Death of Hattie Carroll" is delivered not only with a burning intensity but a heart-rending humanity. Joan Baez steps up to duet on a tender "Mama You Been On My Mind", an impassioned **It Ain't Me Babe** and a committed "With God On Our Side". On **Silver Dagger**, Dylan is even content to be her sideman, accompanying her on harmonica while her pure, soaring soprano flies solo. It is, perhaps, the apotheosis of their fleeting joint reign as the folk king and queen.

An intriguing insight into Dylan's state of mind at the time is provided by the prose poem **Advice For Geraldine On Her Miscellaneous Birthday**, which he wrote for the Philharmonic concert programme. In it, he warned against "going too far out in any direction", for people will feel "something's going on up there that they don't know about". As a prophecy of the turn his own career was to take, it's uncanny, and there are fascinating signposts to the brave but dangerous new world that awaited in early sketches of **Mr Tambourine Man**, "The Gates Of Eden" and "It's Alright, Ma (I'm Only Bleeding)".

Pretty soon he would be cranking up his amp and angrily telling The Band to "play fuckin' loud". But *Live 1964* proves Dylan's genius as a live performer crackled with electricity long before he ever plugged in.

Bringing It All Back Home

SUBTERRANEAN HOMESICK BLUES | SHE BELONGS TO ME | MAGGIE'S FARM | LOVE MINUS ZERO | NO LIMIT | OUTLAW BLUES | ON THE ROAD AGAIN | BOB DYLAN'S 115TH DREAM | MR TAMBOURINE MAN | GATES OF EDEN | IT'S ALRIGHT, MA (I'M ONLY BLEEDING) | IT'S ALL OVER NOW, BABY BLUE

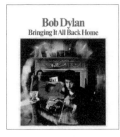

Columbia; recorded January 13–15, 1965; released March 22, 1965; available on CD and SACD

Together with The Byrds' recently released version of **Mr Tambourine Man**, *Bringing It All Back Home* marked the invention of the folk-rock revolution. On side one, the emphasis is primarily rock, as Dylan kicks off with the amphetamine-charged **Subterranean Homesick Blues**, rapping over a searing R&B groove on a lyric crammed with beat cynicism, drug paranoia and a streetwise nihilism that questioned the American Dream as potently as any of the earlier, more overt protest songs. "On The Road Again" offers a similar perspective, while "Maggie's Farm" is another raucous indictment of straight society, and the electrified talking blues **Bob Dylan's 115th Dream** is a hilarious dream-play pastiche of US history. In between, the tender **She Belongs To Me** and "Love Minus Zero/No Limit" bring fresh depths to the moon-in-June banalities that characterized pop romance at the time.

Apart from some subtle droplets of electric guitar on "Mr Tambourine Man", side two is all acoustic. Songs such as "Gates Of Eden" and **It's Alright, Ma (I'm Only Bleeding)** offer more considered critiques of society. But their "messages" are far removed from the cut-and-dried moralizing of the earlier protest songs, full of poetic influences drawn from the French symbolists such as Rimbaud and Baudelaire, the Beat writings of Ginsberg and Kerouac, the visions of William Blake, and the hipster slang of Beat comics such as Lenny Bruce and Lord Buckley, as well as the folk vernacular of Woody Guthrie. As a result, despite being acoustic, side two still possess all the attack and attitude of rock'n'roll. The lovely **It's All Over Now, Baby Blue** concludes the album with a suitable air of sad finality, the song's invocation to "Strike another match, go start anew" leaving no doubt as to Dylan's future intentions.

The woman on the front cover is Sally Grossman, the wife of Dylan's manager. Around her in the shot carefully staged by Dylan and photographer Daniel Kramer are records by Robert Johnson, Lotte Lenya, The Impressions and Eric Von Schmidt. Above the mantelpiece is a coloured-glass collage of a clown face Dylan had made for the owner of Bernard's Café, near the Grossmans' home. The grey kitten is Dylan's pet, Rolling Stone.

Highway 61 Revisited

LIKE A ROLLING STONE | TOMBSTONE BLUES | IT TAKES A LOT TO LAUGH, IT TAKES A TRAIN TO CRY | FROM A BUICK 6 | BALLAD OF A THIN MAN | QUEEN JANE APPROXIMATELY | HIGHWAY 61 REVISITED | JUST LIKE TOM THUMB'S BLUES | DESOLATION ROW

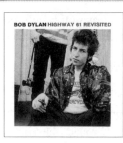

Columbia; recorded June 15–August 2, 1965; released August 30, 1965; available on CD and SACD

If side one of *Bringing It All Back Home* had shocked his old-guard fans, Dylan had at least tossed them a few crumbs of comfort on the acoustic second side. *Highway 61 Revisited* contained no such hedging of his rock'n'roll bets and its full-blown heresy left the folkies in no doubt that their erstwhile Messiah had abandoned them. One of the most revolutionary albums of all time, fusing raucous blues-based rock'n'roll with inspired and often surreal lyrics, it was a record that announced the folk revival was officially dead, and that the likes of Peter, Paul and Mary, and the Kingston Trio had probably better start looking for new jobs.

The band is uncompromising and explosive, creating swirling, multi-textured layers of sound that brilliantly reflect Dylan's stated desire to create "song paintings". Performance-wise, there's a nervous, amphetamine energy and a hipper-than-thou sneer – Dylan's words are delivered in a voice of savage cool that still pierces our complacency to this day. Adopting the position of the artist as an outsider looking in on an increasingly absurdist world, his weapons are no longer protest and righteousness but mockery and wit. **Tombstone Blues** is another savage indictment of the American Dream, the words spilling scornfully over a

suitably dirty-sounding riff. **Like A Rolling Stone** manages to sound cruel, celebratory, sneering and magisterial all at the same time, and, although very different in atmosphere, **Ballad Of A Thin Man** is like a companion piece – another of the withering put-downs that Dylan was now becoming famous for in his new guise as the king of the hipsters and the arbiter of cool.

Just Like Tom Thumb's Blues has a wonderfully wasted air and has been compared to T.S. Eliot's portrait of 20th-century alienation, *The Love Song Of J. Alfred Prufrock*, as Dylan paints a picture of intense sensory derangement, starting out on Burgundy but soon hitting the harder stuff. The comparison is not too fanciful, for Eliot himself gets a namecheck in the eleven-minute epic that is the Armageddon-as-staged-by-Fellini brilliance of **Desolation Row**.

If you had to sum up *Highway 61 Revisited* in a single sentence, suffice it to say that it is the album that invented attitude and raised it to an art form. Just take a look at the cover. Nobody from Johnny Rotten to Eminem has done it better to this day.

Blonde On Blonde

RAINY DAY WOMEN #12 & 35 | PLEDGING MY TIME | VISIONS OF JOHANNA | ONE OF US MUST KNOW (SOONER OR LATER) | I WANT YOU | STUCK INSIDE OF MOBILE | LEOPARD-SKIN PILL-BOX HAT | JUST LIKE A WOMAN | MOST LIKELY YOU GO YOUR WAY | TEMPORARY LIKE ACHILLES | ABSOLUTELY SWEET MARIE | FOURTH TIME AROUND | OBVIOUSLY FIVE BELIEVERS | SAD EYED LADY OF THE LOWLANDS

The Music

Columbia; recorded January 25–March 10, 1966; released May 16, 1966; available on CD and SACD

To the Nashville session men who played on *Blonde On Blonde*, Dylan appeared a creature from another world. And in a sense he was. The musicians assembled in Columbia's Music Row Studio had certainly never heard Jim Reeves singing lines like "the ghost of electricity howls in the bones of her face". What exactly was the epitome of New York bohemian druggie chic doing with a bunch of good ol' country boys and pickers from the backwoods of Tennessee?

In fact, Bob Johnston, the producer who suggested the improbable marriage, had come up with a stroke of genius. Unique as the onstage chemistry was between Dylan and The Band, it is doubtful whether in the studio they could have conjured an album anything like *Blonde On Blonde*, for so much of its potency came directly from the chemistry created by the culture clash. As Al Kooper, who plays organ on the album, put it, "You take those two elements, pour them into a test-tube and it just exploded." The result was not only the first but arguably the greatest double album ever made (the advent of new technology has meant that many single CDs now run at traditional double-album length of 70 minutes and more, but in the vinyl era only The Beatles' *White Album* and The Rolling Stones' *Exile On Main Street* came close to rivalling *Blonde On Blonde*). With Kooper and Robbie Robertson in the hipsters' corner and just about everybody else in the other, the playing from both sides is superb. You can hear musicians who are used to watching the clock and being paid by the hour being stretched beyond anything they've ever been asked to do on epics such as **Visions of Johanna** and **Sad Eyed Lady Of The Lowlands**, the album's two cornerstones. That such songs were cut in one perfect take is testament to the abilities of Johnston's Nashville players.

With the addition of Kooper's eerie organ and Robertson's guitar, they create what Dylan described as "that wild mercury sound". He had been feeling his way towards it on the previous two albums but the sound reaches its apotheosis on *Blonde On Blonde*. After "Visions of Johanna" and "Sad Eyed Lady Of The Lowlands", the album's third tour de force is **Stuck Inside Of Mobile With The Memphis Blues Again**, while tracks such as "Pledging My Time", "Temporary Like Achilles", "Obviously Five Believers" and "Leopard-Skin Pill-Box Hat" sound more Chicago than Nashville, with a tough-edged blues feel. Elsewhere, the album's diversity stretches from the "Norwegian Wood" pastiche **Fourth Time Around** (although the way Dylan tells the story, John Lennon took The

Beatles' tune from him) to the rambunctious, drunken marching-band arrangement of **Rainy Day Women #12 & 35** via the lovely **Just Like A Woman** and the exuberant **I Want You**, which marries typically complex Dylan imagery to a simple but engaging pop-song structure.

An astonished world wondered how Dylan could follow such an album. The simple answer was that he couldn't, except by falling off his motorcycle and, after eventually getting back on, riding off in a completely different direction.

The Bootleg Series Vol 4: Live 1966 – The "Royal Albert Hall" Concert

SHE BELONGS TO ME | FOURTH TIME AROUND | VISIONS OF JOHANNA | IT'S ALL OVER NOW, BABY BLUE | DESOLATION ROW | JUST LIKE A WOMAN | MR TAMBOURINE MAN | TELL ME, MOMMA | I DON'T BELIEVE YOU | BABY LET ME FOLLOW YOU DOWN | JUST LIKE TOM THUMB'S BLUES | LEOPARD-SKIN PILL-BOX HAT | ONE TOO MANY MORNINGS | BALLAD OF A THIN MAN | LIKE A ROLLING STONE
Columbia; recorded May 17,1966; released October 28, 1998; available on CD

By the time this legendary recording from Dylan's 1966 British tour was officially released 32 years after the event, it had been known for so long as the "Albert Hall concert" that Columbia stuck with this erroneous title, even though by now every Dylanologist knew it was actually recorded at Manchester Free Trade Hall. (They at least added quote marks to the title to indicate the location was not to be taken literally.)

Though most reviewers described it as the greatest live album of all time, many virtually ignored the first disc, which presents seven songs from the opening acoustic-half of the concert. These performances do not deserve to be overlooked. Dylan sounds stoned. But instead of destroying his concentration, whatever he's on gives him a self-absorbed intensity and confidence that is truly gripping. There are three tracks from the just-released *Blonde On Blonde* and the otherworldly acoustic version of **Visions Of Johanna** is mesmerizing. **Desolation Row** is another tour de force, the harmonica playing on **It's All Over Now, Baby Blue** is awesome and **Mr Tambourine Man**, which closes the acoustic set, is magical.

But it would be ludicrous to deny that it is the electric half of the concert that has deservedly given the recording its revered status. Recorded towards the end of a tumultuous world tour, Dylan and the band have been toughened and made stronger by the boos that had greeted them everywhere they went. **Tell Me, Momma**, the one song in the set never released on a studio album, tells you immediately how far he has pushed himself in the interest of his art. He sounds feral and half-crazed, yet resilient and fearless. The once-acoustic **I Don't Believe You** is introduced by Dylan saying, "It used to be like that, and now it goes like this." Is he trying to antagonize his audience? Certainly the atmosphere that makes the recording so memorable is created not just by Dylan and the musicians but also the audience, who make their presence felt at the beginning of the next track, **Baby Let Me Follow You Down,** as they slow handclap in unison, presumably in an attempt to disrupt him. If so, it doesn't work, for the performance that follows is blistering.

As the confrontation grows, the recording crackles with human static. Dylan takes on the audience by mumbling not-quite-audible non-sense words as if he's telling a story. Then as the audience hushes out of curiosity, he delivers the punchline, "… if you only just wouldn't clap so hard!" A magnificent version of **One Too Many Mornings** follows. Then comes the infamous "Judas!" shout, which fires Dylan up to produce the most electrifying, apocalyptic version of his greatest electric song, **Like A Rolling Stone.**

By the time of the album's eventual release, the recording had become so legendary that Radio 1 DJ Andy Kershaw was moved to declare, "I still can't believe they've finally put it out. I just keep staring at my copy."

The Basement Tapes

ODDS AND ENDS | MILLION DOLLAR BASH | GOIN' TO ACAPULCO | LO & BEHOLD | CLOTHES LINE SAGA | APPLE SUCKLING TREE | PLEASE MRS HENRY | TEARS OF RAGE | TOO MUCH OF NOTHING | YEA! HEAVY AND A BOTTLE OF BREAD | CRASH ON THE LEVEE | TINY MONTGOMERY | YOU AIN'T GOIN' NOWHERE | NOTHING WAS DELIVERED | OPEN THE DOOR HOMER | THIS WHEEL'S ON FIRE

Columbia; recorded March–October 1967; released June 26, 1975; available on CD

The heavily edited official version of *The Basement Tapes* was in many ways a disappointment when finally released eight years after the 1967 Woodstock sessions. The decision to make it available was largely taken as a response to the fact that, to Dylan's intense irritation, many of the songs were already in wide circulation on bootleg. Yet he left the preparation for their release to Robbie Robertson and serious question marks have to be raised about the judgement of The Band's guitarist, both in the selection of the material and over the unnecessary piano, guitar and percussion overdubs he added to several of the original tracks.

I Shall Be Released and "Quinn The Eskimo", both familiar from bootleg and cover versions, are notable omissions. So, too, are **Sign On The Cross, I'm Not There** and **Banks Of The Royal Canal,** three songs which are less well known but among the very finest of the 100-plus tracks that constitute the complete *Basement Tapes.* To Dylan fans their inclusion would certainly have been preferable to the five songs by The Band that Robertson added (**Orange Juice Blues, Yazoo Street Scandal, Katie's Been Gone, Bessie Smith** and **Ruben Remus**).

Yet at the time, most were grateful for the two dozen tracks they got. There's a wonderfully raw and rough-hewn roots quality to tracks such as **Yea! Heavy And A Bottle Of Bread**, "Please Mrs Henry", "Crash On The Levee (Down In The Flood)" and "Million Dollar Bash", while major compositions such as **This Wheel's On Fire**, "Tears Of Rage" and "Too Much Of Nothing" are evidence that, despite the fun and frolics and the off-the-cuff spontaneity of the sessions, Dylan had lost none of his masterful songcraft.

The cover, which features a strange cast of characters from the songs posing around a furnace, was shot in the basement of the YMCA in Los Angeles.

John Wesley Harding

JOHN WESLEY HARDING | AS I WENT OUT ONE MORNING | I DREAMED I SAW ST AUGUSTINE | ALL ALONG THE WATCHTOWER | THE BALLAD OF FRANKIE LEE AND JUDAS PRIEST | DRIFTERS ESCAPE | DEAR LANDLORD | I AM A LONESOME HOBO | I PITY THE POOR IMMIGRANT | THE WICKED MESSENGER | DOWN ALONG THE COVE | I'LL BE YOUR BABY TONIGHT
Columbia; recorded October 17–November 21, 1967; released December 27, 1967; available on CD and SACD

Dylan could not have made a record further removed from the psychedelic spirit of 1967 than *John Wesley Harding*. And this quantum shift was no accident, for he regarded the Summer of Love as hopelessly decadent. While the hippies declared love and peace and wore flowers in their hair, Dylan married the outlaw mythology of the Old West to Old Testament allegory and came up with a fearful portrait of human dread in the face of eternity. It was like the Bible meets the *Hank Williams Songbook* – two works that were reportedly among Dylan's main reading

matter at the time.

Recording once again in Nashville, Dylan had a sound in his head very different from either the swirling electricity of *Blonde On Blonde* or the jovial good humour of *The Basement Tapes*. In part, it was inspired by Gordon Lightfoot's second album, *The Way I Feel*, recorded in Nashville earlier in 1967 with Kenny Buttrey and Charlie McCoy (and Dylan would later cover Lightfoot's "Early Morning Rain" on *Self Portrait*). Working with the same musicians, plus Pete Drake on pedal steel, the sparse sound of *John Wesley Harding* is as stark as the parables that constitute the subject matter of its songs.

As I Went Out One Morning, "The Ballad Of Frankie Lee And Judas Priest" and "The Wicked Messenger" all possess an almost spooky quality. So, too, does the original version of **All Along The Watchtower**. Interestingly, Dylan virtually dispenses with choruses throughout the album. It's as if he's saying that singalongs are hardly suitable when the Four Horsemen of the Apocalypse are approaching. Then, at the album's end, he gives us a pointer to his next direction with the gentle country-blues of **Down Along The Cove** and the delightful country shuffle of **I'll Be Your Baby Tonight**, which simultaneously laughs at and celebrates the convention of the love song.

The starkness of the monochrome front-cover shot reflects the austerity of the music inside and depicts Dylan with Charlie Joy (an odd-job man who was working for the Grossmans, in whose back garden the picture was taken) and two musicians from the Indian group the Bauls of Bengal. They look exactly like extras from the cast of drifters, immigrants, hobos and outlaws whose stories are chronicled on the record. For long it was claimed that the upside-down faces of The Beatles were concealed in the tree in the background, and a number of erudite biographers have fallen for this story. There is a vague suggestion of faces in the tree bark; but that they were placed there deliberately by Dylan as some kind of message appears to be a myth. As the journalist Steve Lowe remarked, it is almost certainly "one of those things that happens by accident, like the face of Christ appearing in a kiwi fruit".

Nashville Skyline

GIRL FROM THE NORTH COUNTRY | NASHVILLE SKYLINE RAG | TO BE ALONE WITH YOU | I THREW IT ALL AWAY | PEGGY DAY | LAY, LADY, LAY | ONE MORE NIGHT | TELL ME THAT IT ISN'T TRUE | COUNTRY PIE | TONIGHT I'LL BE STAYING HERE WITH YOU
Columbia; recorded February 13–18,1969; released April 9, 1969; available on CD and SACD

"The new songs are easy to understand and there aren't too many words to remember," Dylan told *Rolling Stone* editor Jann Wenner in a masterpiece of understatement shortly before the release of *Nashville Skyline*. At just 27 minutes long, the brevity of the record seemed to confirm that the spokesman of his generation had little left to say. And many of his fans who had rather enjoyed puzzling over what he had

meant by such lines as "the ghost of electricity howls in the bones of her face" couldn't find too much depth in the handful of easy-to-remember words *Nashville Skyline* did contain. The liner note by Johnny Cash, which concluded "I'm proud to say that I know it, Here-in is a hell of a poet," may have been heartfelt. But he'd surely attached his tribute to the wrong album.

Bob's voice sounded different, too, having turned into a kind of syrupy croon. Dylan said it was down to having given up smoking, but whatever the reason, to many it encapsulated all that was anodyne and bourgeois about country music. And, alongside Johnny Cash's deep baritone on their duet, **Girl From The North Country**, Dylan wanders so absurdly off-key that you have to laugh, even though it's not meant to be funny.

In **Lay, Lady, Lay**, the album contained one unforgettable love song. The tender "I Threw It All Away" is also a classic, despite such clichés as "love is all there is, it makes the world go round", and the record closes on a high with the lovely **Tonight I'll Be Staying Here With You**. Elsewhere, there's the Cash duet, a harmless instrumental in "Nashville Skyline Rag", and five minor songs "without too many words to remember", the best of which is **Tell Me That It Isn't True**, which it's a shame Elvis Presley never recorded. But, from the gormless-looking country bumpkin on the cover to the banality of the

The Music

list of fillings in **Country Pie** ("blueberry, apple, cherry, pumpkin, plum"), it's hard to imagine how Dylan could have made a record more deliberately calculated to alienate his hardcore fans (though *Self Portrait* was still to come).

The critic Paul Williams observed, "Nashville Skyline is a very pretty album" and even a "magical" one. But he's equally correct when he went on to say that had Dylan's levels of originality and commitment as a performer stayed on a similar level, he would today be regarded not as a great artist but merely as a good entertainer. Put another way, had *Nashville Skyline* been a Gordon Lightfoot album or a Johnny Cash record, it would certainly have got decent reviews. But as the most literate songwriter in the history of popular music, Dylan's bar was raised far higher and there was no way he was going to receive critical acclaim for such inconsequential country hokum as **Peggy Day** and **One More Night**.

Self Portrait

ALL THE TIRED HORSES | ALBERTA #1 | I FORGOT MORE THAN YOU'LL EVER KNOW | DAYS OF 49 | EARLY MORNING RAIN | IN SEARCH OF LITTLE SADIE | LET IT BE ME | LITTLE SADIE | WOOGIEBOOGIE | BELLE ISLE | LIVING THE BLUES | LIKE A ROLLING STONE | COPPER KETTLE | GOTTA TRAVEL ON | BLUE MOON | THE BOXER | QUINN THE ESKIMO | TAKE ME AS I AM | TAKE A MESSAGE TO MARY | IT HURTS ME, TOO | MINSTREL BOY | SHE BELONGS TO ME | WIGWAM | ALBERTA #2
Columbia; recorded April 24,1969–March 5,1970; released June 8,1970; available on CD

"What is this shit?", wrote Greil Marcus in the opening words of his devastating four-page

demolition of Bob Dylan's *Self Portrait* in *Rolling Stone*. It remains one of the most savagely withering record reviews in the history of rock journalism and he spoke for most Dylan fans, who were left feeling perplexed, angry, betrayed and demoralized by the album.

Over the years the record has remained an object of ridicule. Then, in 2002, a modest rehabilitation began to take place. It started when Ryan Adams was asked if he didn't fear burning out and ending up making albums like *Self Portrait*. "I fucking hope so, man, because it's a great album", he replied. A few months later, *Uncut* magazine ran a reassessment of the record in its "Classic Albums Revisited" slot. The piece concluded that if the album was released now, many of the songs would be regarded as modern Americana classics and that the record's simple verities and absence of ego seem far more in tune with the spirit of our times today.

There is some "shit", particularly on the tracks that Dylan sent down to Nashville for syrupy overdubs of the kind that might have graced an Elvis Presley or an Everly Brothers record of the time. The opening track, **All The Tired Horses**, is like a joke, with its single repeated line, "All the tired horses in the sun, how'm I supposed to get any ridin' done?" Or could there be a suggestion of a pun there – "writin'" – to indicate that the greatest songwriter of the 20th century had hardly managed a decent new song on the record?

The likes of **Blue Moon** and **Let It Be Me** are ruined with slushy strings and trite pop arrangements. But there's genuine merit in **In Search Of Little Sadie, Living The Blues,** the sublime **Copper Kettle,** "Wigwam", "Alberta" and a ramshackle version of "Minstrel Boy", recorded at the Isle of Wight Festival with The Band. Two other live tracks from the festival, **Like A Rolling Stone** and **She Belongs To Me,** are less satisfactory performances and their presence is something of a mystery, for they only serve to add to the record's lack of internal coherence. But there is one interesting explanation, which Dylan himself offered in 1985 in the booklet of the *Biograph* career retrospective. To his immense irritation *Great White Wonder,* the world's first ever bootleg, had appeared in 1969, containing a ragbag of his unreleased live recordings and practice tapes assembled from different sources. Halfway through recording *Self Portrait,* it seems Dylan hit upon a similar concept: "I just figured I'd put all this stuff together and put it out, my own bootleg record, so to speak."

The notion that he was also deliberately making a record to subvert his own myth is almost certainly true up to a point. He wanted to be "just a singer making music". But, all these years on, *Self Portrait* can perhaps finally be seen for what it is – a personal scrapbook of the music that provided the backdrop to the evolution of Dylan's genius. As such it's a lot more witty and knowing than similar covers albums such as David Bowie's *Pin-Ups* or John Lennon's *Rock'n'Roll.*

New Morning

IF NOT FOR YOU | DAY OF THE LOCUSTS | TIME PASSES SLOWLY | WENT TO SEE THE GYPSY | WINTERLUDE | IF DOGS RUN FREE | NEW MORNING | SIGN ON THE WINDOW | ONE MORE WEEKEND | THE MAN IN ME | THREE ANGELS | FATHER OF NIGHT
Columbia; recorded June 2–5, 1970; released October 21, 1970; available on CD

After *Self Portrait,* Dylan needed an exercise in damage control and *New Morning* did the job more than adequately. With a dozen original compositions, the album showed that Dylan was still a creative force as a songwriter and the starting-over suggestion of the title was clearly deliberate. Many of the songs are deeply imbued with the Woodstock-inspired spirit of the contented family man. **If Not For You** is a joyously devotional love song that he also recorded as a duet with George Harrison. **The Man In Me,** "Winterlude" and "Sign On The Window" are paeans to married bliss that for the most part avoid sounding too self-satisfied but at times sail dangerously close. "Time Passes Slowly" is a hymn to the joys of fatherhood, and **One More Weekend** finds Dylan suggesting they "leave all the children home" and head off "some place unknown" to rekindle some romance and adventure.

And yet amid all the cosy domesticity (circumstances which Dylan never attempted to

The Music

repeat after his separation from Sara), there are signs that the old restlessness was stirring again – hints that, after four years in retreat, Dylan was finally tiring of peace and tranquility. On **Sign On The Window**, he sings "Marry me a wife, catch rainbow trout, Have a bunch of kids who call me Pa, That must be what it's all about", seeming almost as if he's trying to convince himself. And on **Time Passes Slowly**, though he contentedly sings "Ain't no reason to go anywhere", the song concludes with the line, "Time passes slowly and fades away" (which, incidentally, would later give Neil Young the title for his album *Time Fades Away*).

Elsewhere, **Went To See The Gypsy** is about Elvis Presley, **Dogs Run Free** is an enjoyable jazz vamp, and two songs – **Father Of Night** and **Three Angels** – appear to have a religious context. In fact, it subsequently transpired that the latter had a more literal explanation, referring to some Christmas decorations Dylan observed above a shop in New York. **Day of The Locusts**, one of the album's most interesting songs, is a typically Dylanesque account of his acceptance of an honorary doctorate in music at Princeton University in June 1970. The man standing next to him whose "head was exploding" was none other than a worse-for-wear David Crosby, who had accompanied Dylan to the ceremony.

Dylan later revealed that three of the songs, "Father Of Night", "Time Passes Slowly" and the jaunty title-track, were written for a Broadway play by Archibald MacLeish. When Dylan backed out of the production, the songs gave him the building blocks for a new record,

which partly explains *New Morning*'s rapid appearance after the disastrous *Self Portrait*.

Dylan

LILY OF THE WEST | CAN'T HELP FALLING IN LOVE | SARAH JANE | THE BALLAD OF IRA HAYES | MR BOJANGLES | MARY ANN | BIG YELLOW TAXI | A FOOL SUCH AS I | SPANISH IS THE LIVING TONGUE
Columbia; recorded April 24, 1969–June 5, 1970; released November 16, 1973; currently unavailable

"Guaranteed to net only horselaughs", said *Rolling Stone* on the release of this rag-bag of covers, shoddily thrown together against Dylan's wishes after he had left Columbia in 1973. "They were just not to be used. It was well understood. They were just to warm up for a tune," he complained. Then he hedged his bets by adding: "But I didn't think it was that bad, really."

The first statement at least has a grain of truth, for the songs were mostly recorded during the same sessions that produced the far superior *New Morning* album. But not all of the tracks were warm-ups, as Dylan claimed, for his original plan for *New Morning* had been another *Self Portrait*–style pick'n'mix of new songs of his own and covers old and new. It was only the critical slaughtering he suffered over *Self Portrait* that dissuaded him from repeating the exercise.

Reinterpreting traditional songs such as **Mary Ann, Sarah Jane** and **Spanish Is The Loving Tongue** is one thing. Dylan has done it throughout his career, from the 1962 debut album to *Good As I Been To You* and *World Gone Wrong* in the early 1990s. But why was the world's most covered songwriter crooning his way (badly) through covers of songs by less talented contemporaries such as Jerry Jeff Walker (**Mr Bojangles**) and Joni Mitchell (**Big Yellow Taxi**)? Given that the karaoke warm-up explanation does not quite pass scrutiny, it's a question that has never adequately been answered.

Columbia's motivation for releasing the sessions against Dylan's will, three years after the event, was more transparent. It was done in protest at losing their most prestigious signing to David Geffen's Asylum label. And calling it *Dylan*, as if the album represented some definitive statement, was merely adding insult to injury. When Bob returned to Columbia in the mid-1970s, he quietly demanded the offending item's deletion from the catalogue. Apart from 1988's *Down In The Groove*, it's the only Dylan studio album to suffer such an ignominious fate.

Pat Garrett & Billy The Kid

MAIN TITLE THEME (BILLY) | *CANTINA THEME (WORKIN' FOR THE LAW)* | *BILLY 1* | *BUNKHOUSE THEME* | *RIVER THEME* | *TURKEY CHASE* | *KNOCKIN' ON HEAVEN'S DOOR* | *FINAL THEME* | *BILLY 4* | *BILLY 7*
Columbia; recorded January–February 1973; released July 13, 1973; available on CD

It was touch and go for a while, but Dylan's first soundtrack commission turned out to be something of a triumph. Alternative versions to a couple of the songs in the film were included in the album. But in both formats, the music brilliantly evokes the sepia-tinted, elegy-for-a-lost-world mood of Peckinpah's movie.

Few films can ever have inspired an original composition as powerful as **Knockin' On Heaven's Door**. Composed late in the proceedings, it was written in direct response to watching the scene in the movie in which Sheriff Baker dies in his wife's arms. Ironically, Jerry Fielding, the professional Hollywood soundtrack composer brought in to assist Dylan, hated it. Never trust the experts.

It was typical of Dylan's spontaneous approach that the only song he had written in advance of arriving on the movie set in Durango was **Billy**, which is heard throughout both film and album in various instrumental and vocal incarnations. He fully expected to find all his inspiration on the set, but it was slow to come and the first recording session, in Mexico City, produced just one useable take, credited on the album as **Billy 4**. However, things soon picked up and the rest of the album was recorded during two days in Los Angeles with an acoustic band featuring Roger McGuinn and Bruce Langhorne on guitars, Byron Berline on fiddle, Russ Kunkel on percussion, Jim Keltner on drums and Terry Paul and Booker T. Jones on bass.

Despite the brilliant "Knockin' On Heaven's Door", in many ways it's Dylan's evocative, rough-hewn incidental music on tracks such as **Cantina Theme**, **Turkey Chase** and **River Theme** that makes the soundtrack work so well. Inevitably, these were ignored and dismissed as filler when the soundtrack album was released. But they do their job perfectly, despite Dylan's complaint, on seeing the movie's final cut, that "the music seemed to be scattered and used in every other place but the scenes which we did it for".

Planet Waves

ON A NIGHT LIKE THIS | GOING, GOING, GONE | TOUGH MAMA | HAZEL | SOMETHING THERE IS ABOUT YOU | FOREVER YOUNG | DIRGE | YOU ANGEL YOU | NEVER SAY GOODBYE | WEDDING SONG
Columbia; recorded November 2–10, 1974; released January 17, 1974; available on CD and SACD

For an album that was written to order, recorded hastily and thrown together because Dylan was instructed he needed some "new product" to promote on his first tour for eight years, *Planet Waves* is a highly satisfying and often absorbing piece of work. Titled *Ceremonies Of The Horsemen* until a last-minute title change, the album holds the distinction of being the only studio album Dylan ever cut with The Band, *The Basement Tapes* apart.

Lyrically, the family-oriented values that ran through *New Morning* infuse several of

the songs, including **Forever Young**, heard in two very different versions (and allegedly written for his youngest son Jakob) and **Wedding Song**. The latter is an unambiguous celebration of his marriage to Sara on which he goes out of his way to disavow his 1960s past: "It's never been my duty to remake the world at large, Nor is it my intention to sound a battle charge." It's as if he's reassuring his wife that although he's about to head out on the road for the first time in eight years, she has nothing to worry about. The song was added at the last minute when the album was being mixed, replacing **Nobody 'Cept You** (which later appeared on *The Bootleg Series Vols I–III*). It's the one song not to feature The Band and finds Dylan accompanied only by his acoustic guitar and harmonica.

Elsewhere, **On A Night Like This** is slight but appealingly jaunty and reminiscent of *John Wesley Harding*'s "Down Along The Cove". The arrangements on **Something There Is About You** and **You Angel You** contain the heavy imprint of Robbie Robertson and, apart from Dylan's vocal, would have sounded at home on one of The Band's albums. But scratch beneath the surface and there are hidden depths to the songwriting, particularly on **Going, Going, Gone** – a proud addition to the canon of great Dylan songs – and the stark catharsis of **Dirge**.

The front-cover art, by Dylan, contains the words "Cast-Iron Songs and Torch Ballads" in the lower right-hand corner, immediately above a carefully positioned CND symbol, intended to suggest he had not lost his old radicalism. In his handwritten sleeve notes, Dylan misspells Richard Manuel's name as "Manual", presumably a deliberate in-joke. Early versions of the album also included a handwritten Dylan poem on the back cover, torn from the first page of his tour diary and written three days before the opening date. It was later dropped from the CD reissue.

Before The Flood

MOST LIKELY YOU GO YOUR WAY (AND I'LL GO MINE) I *LAY, LADY, LAY* I *RAINY DAY WOMEN #12 & 35* I *KNOCKIN' ON HEAVEN'S DOOR* I *IT AIN'T ME, BABE* I *BALLAD OF A THIN MAN* I *UP ON CRIPPLE CREEK* I *I SHALL BE RELEASED* I *ENDLESS HIGHWAY* I *THE NIGHT THEY DROVE OLD DIXIE DOWN* I *STAGE FRIGHT* I *DON'T THINK TWICE IT'S ALL RIGHT* I *JUST LIKE A WOMAN* I *IT'S ALRIGHT, MA* I *THE SHAPE I'M IN* I *WHEN YOU AWAKE* I *THE WEIGHT* I *ALL ALONG THE WATCHTOWER* I *HIGHWAY 61 REVISITED* I *LIKE A ROLLING STONE* I *BLOWIN' IN THE WIND*
Columbia; recorded January–February, 1974; released June 20, 1974; available on CD

More than a dozen years into his career, and eight years after his 1966 "retirement", we finally get a live Dylan album, recorded during his return to the road with The Band. Of the 21 tracks, eight feature The Band alone, and under any other circumstances you'd be only too pleased to have live renditions of great songs such as **Up On Cripple Creek** and **The Weight**. But here it's a frustration for it means there's no room for Dylan singing "Hero Blues",

"Song To Woody", "The Lonesome Death Of Hattie Carroll", "Forever Young", "Just Like Tom Thumb's Blues", "Maggie's Farm", "Love Minus Zero/No Limit", "It's All Over Now, Baby Blue" or even "Mr Tambourine Man", all of which were given sterling performances during the 40-date tour.

Among the thirteen Dylan performances we do get, the highlights inevitably include **All Along The Watchtower** and **Like A Rolling Stone** (this time nobody shouts "Judas!"), and both performances offer further proof that the erstwhile Hawks really were the best backing band Dylan ever had. They're also in splendid form on a spirited **Most Likely You Go Your Way** and a terrific **Lay, Lady, Lay** with some particularly fine Robbie Robertson lead-guitar work. **It Ain't Me Babe** is given a strange new, bouncy tempo that doesn't quite work, but **Ballad Of A Thin Man** is mean, moody and quite magnificent.

The acoustic set comprises **Don't Think Twice, Just Like A Woman** and a spine-tingling **It's Alright Ma** that leaves you wanting more. But instead, The Band return with three more of their own compositions before Dylan rejoins them for a magnificent four-song finale, the least satisfying of which is the somewhat pedestrian **Blowin' In The Wind** that concludes the album.

The Music

Blood On The Tracks

TANGLED UP IN BLUE | SIMPLE TWIST OF FATE | YOU'RE A BIG GIRL NOW | IDIOT WIND | YOU'RE GONNA MAKE ME LONESOME WHEN YOU GO | MEET ME IN THE MORNING | LILY, ROSEMARY & THE JACK OF HEARTS | IF YOU SEE HER, SAY HELLO | SHELTER FROM THE STORM | BUCKETS OF RAIN
Columbia; recorded September 16–December 30, 1974; released January 17, 1975; available on CD and SACD

For many years it was Dylan's great trilogy of mid-1960s albums that dominated the upper reaches of polls listing "the best albums of all time", along with the likes of *Sgt. Pepper*, *Pet Sounds* and *Astral Weeks*. But in recent times, *Blood On The Tracks* has emerged in many surveys as the most revered of all Dylan releases. On it, he sounds vulnerable and all too human; seldom had he dipped his pen into his own veins so uncompromisingly. "I don't write confessional songs," he claimed, but there's no other way of describing *Blood On The Tracks*.

Tangled Up In Blue is an epic narrative in which Dylan shifts between the past and present and the first and third person "like a five and a half minute musical Proust". **Simple Twist Of Fate** is simply one of the saddest songs ever written, in a performance full of weary melancholy and regret. **Idiot Wind**, meanwhile, is all towering fury and edgy recrimination, possibly the nastiest of all

Dylan's venomously nasty songs, as he spits out the lines, "You're an idiot babe, It's a wonder that you still know how to breathe."

You're Gonna Make Me Lonesome When You Go, written about Ellen Bernstein, with whom Dylan was conducting an affair, finds him putting on a brave face but there's still a consuming sorrow at the song's core. **Meet Me In The Morning** is an atmospheric and sparse blues. Then comes the cinematic storytelling of the massive **Lily, Rosemary & The Jack of Hearts**, sustained throughout its sixteen verses by an incongruously bouncy arrangement.

There's more intense heartache on **If You See Her Say Hello**, which combines both acceptance of the end and longing for a fresh start. **Shelter From The Storm** renders the personal universal in the way only Dylan's greatest songs can. And the album ends with the black humour of **Buckets Of Rain**, a song Dylan would later re-record with Bette Midler.

Not even the fact that the half of the album recorded in September 1974 was then re-cut three months later in a different studio with different musicians can detract from the coherence of the work. Dylan may have been more dazzling, more inventive, more groundbreaking, mercurial and culturally significant in the 1960s. But, as Neil McCormick put it, he had never been "more true".

Desire

HURRICANE | ISIS | MOZAMBIQUE | ONE MORE CUP OF COFFEE | OH SISTER | JOEY | ROMANCE IN DURANGO |

BLACK DIAMOND BAY | SARA
Columbia; recorded July 28–31, 1975; released January 16, 1976; currently available on CD and SACD

There are two schools of thought about *Desire*. One holds that it is an overlooked masterpiece, unfairly eclipsed by following so hard on the heels of the dazzling *Blood On The Tracks*. The other is that it's an oddly unsatisfying follow-up, made too soon afterwards, which ultimately sounds overwrought and contrived.

All but two of the songs were co-written by Jacques Levy, a Byrds associate and musical theatre director. Levy's assistance on **Hurricane** was particularly invaluable, adding a theatrical touch to a lyric which Dylan was struggling with, trying to cram the complex cast of characters and conflicting testimonies of the subject matter (Rubin "Hurricane" Carter). Some of the other songs they wrote together, while staying at Dylan's beach house in Long Island, also possess an affecting theatrical flamboyance. "One of the things about those songs that's so wonderful is that they give Dylan a chance to do some acting," Levy said.

Black Diamond Bay opens with the line, "Up on the white veranda, She wears a necktie and a panama hat." It sounds more like a stage direction than a Dylan lyric. The eleven-minute **Joey**, about the Mafia boss Joey Gallo, is a morally ambiguous tribute to a thoroughly unsavoury and violent character who Dylan lauds as "king of the streets". With considerable naivety, Dylan claimed he had never considered Gallo a gangster. "I always thought of him as some kind of hero in some kind of way. An underdog fighting against the elements."

The best two songs are again about his marriage – the self-explanatory **Sara**, his "radiant jewel, mystical wife", and **Isis**, a long allegorical song about "a mystical child" from whom he is separated. At the song's end, the pair are reunited, although this happy ending is tempered by Dylan's confession that "what drives me to you is what drives me insane".

Dylan began recording the album with a big, chaotic studio band, which included five guitarists. When that patently wasn't working, he ruthlessly thinned down the ranks to a small core, heavily dominated by Scarlet Rivera's violin, which, along with Levy's input, makes *Desire* quite unlike any other Dylan album.

Emmylou Harris, who sings backing vocals on the record, was astonished at the way Dylan worked. "I'd never heard the songs before, and we did most of them in one or two takes," she recalled. "I just watched his mouth and watched what he was saying. That's where all that humming on the record comes from." Dissatisfied with her performance, she asked Dylan if she could "fix" her vocals. But in the end the album appeared as it was recorded. "I later realized that you just don't overdub a Dylan album," she observed.

The Music

The Bootleg Series Vol 5: Live 1975

TONIGHT I'LL BE STAYING HERE WITH YOU | IT AIN'T ME BABE | A HARD RAIN'S A-GONNA FALL | THE LONESOME DEATH OF HATTIE CARROLL | ROMANCE IN DURANGO | ISIS | MR TAMBOURINE MAN | SIMPLE TWIST OF FATE | BLOWIN' IN THE WIND | MAMA, YOU BEEN ON MY MIND | I SHALL BE RELEASED | IT'S ALL OVER NOW, BABY BLUE | LOVE MINUS ZERO/NO LIMIT | TANGLED UP IN BLUE | THE WATER IS WIDE | IT TAKES A LOT TO LAUGH, IT TAKES A TRAIN TO CRY | OH SISTER | HURRICANE | ONE MORE CUP OF COFFEE | SARA | JUST LIKE A WOMAN | KNOCKIN' ON HEAVEN'S DOOR

Columbia; recorded November 19–21 and December 4, 1975; released November 26, 2002; available on CD

Those lucky enough to have caught the Rolling Thunder Revue on almost any night between October and December 1975 all testify to a magical quality, quite different from the spirit of the second leg captured in the *Hard Rain* album and TV special the following year. Yet apart from bootlegs and versions of **Romance In Durango** and **Isis** included on 1985's *Biograph*, we had to wait until 2002 for the release of an official concert recording, when *Live 1975* became the fourth available live album dating from the period 1974–78.

Recorded over four nights in Boston, Cambridge, Worcester and Montreal, the 22 songs (spread over two CDs) find Dylan in magnificent form. Highlights are too many to list, although an acoustic **Mr Tambourine Man** (the only track from the show in Worcester on November 19) is pure genius. A solo **Simple Twist of Fate** which follows from Cambridge is another tour de force. Then Joan Baez joins him for **Blowin' In The Wind,** and you can feel the surge of excitement that runs through the crowd at seeing them on stage together again for the first time in ten years.

The sprawling band plays with surprising subtlety and hits a peak in Montreal, with fine new arrangements of **Tonight I'll Be Staying Here With You** and **A Hard Rain's A-Gonna Fall,** which even Robertson and The Band could hardly have bettered. It was widely regarded at the time as the finest of all the Rolling Thunder concerts and Dylan's solo spot from the show is represented by stunning versions of **It's All Over Now, Baby Blue** and **Love Minus Zero/No Limit.**

A number of the performances on *Live 1975* had previously been included in the film *Renaldo & Clara*, including **It Ain't Me Babe** and **Knockin' On Heaven's Door** from the Cambridge show, a magnificent solo **Tangled Up In Blue** and a fine band version of **It Takes A Lot To Laugh** from Boston, and aforementioned "A Hard Rain's A-Gonna Fall" from the mighty Montreal set. Versions of **Isis** and **Romance In Durango** from the same night were later included on the 1985 compilation *Biograph*. But the versions of the two songs included here were recorded at Cambridge and Boston, respectively.

The Last Waltz

BABY LET ME FOLLOW YOU DOWN | HAZEL | I DON'T BELIEVE YOU | FOREVER YOUNG | BABY LET ME FOLLOW YOU DOWN (REPRISE) | I SHALL BE RELEASED (FINALE)
Warners; recorded November 25, 1976; released April 29, 1978; available as a double-CD and a four-CD box set.

When The Band played their farewell concert at the Winterland, San Francisco, on Thanksgiving, 1976, the stage was rammed with special guests. Over the course of the evening Dr John, Muddy Waters, Eric Clapton, Neil Young, Joni Mitchell and Van Morrison all did their thing. But the climax of the show was, inevitably, the appearance of Dylan.

Sporting a white fedora with the brim rolled down, and accompanied by The Band, he played a blazing five-song, twenty-minute set that was perfectly judged. **Baby Let Me Follow You Down** and **I Don't Believe You** had both featured in the electric

set they had toured together in 1966. **Hazel** and **Forever Young** came from *Planet Waves*, the one studio album they had made together. Then Dylan led the massed throng on a grand finale of **I Shall Be Released**, the hymn he and The Band had concocted at Big Pink. The reprise of **Baby Let Me Follow You Down** which followed was an unrehearsed and spontaneous addition.

When the concert was released as a triple-LP in 1978, **Hazel** was missing from the recording. It was belatedly reinstated 24 years later when a deluxe four-CD box set of the concert was issued in 2002.

Hard Rain

MAGGIE'S FARM | ONE TOO MANY MORNINGS | STUCK INSIDE OF MOBILE | OH SISTER | LAY, LADY, LAY | SHELTER FROM THE STORM | YOU'RE A BIG GIRL NOW | I THREW IT ALL AWAY | IDIOT WIND
Columbia; recorded May 23, 1976; released September 10, 1976; currently available on CD

Tapes clearly suggest that the best of the Rolling Thunder shows took place in late 1975. By the time the revue reconvened in April 1976, a lot of its spontaneous energy had evaporated. This was immediately apparent at the first attempt at live recording for the *Hard Rain* documentary for NBC television in Florida. Disappointed with the results, Dylan aborted the project and at his own expense refilmed the penultimate show of the tour at Colorado State University on May 23, the day before his 35th birthday. Despite pouring rain in the open-air venue, this time both the film and accompanying album worked far better.

Of the nine tracks on the record, new arrangements of **Maggie's Farm** and **Stuck Inside Of Mobile** showcase the band in storming form. And **Lay, Lady, Lay** is rewritten: new words replace the song's original pledge

The Music

of devotion with a crude carnality – "Forget this dance, Let's go upstairs."

However, it's what was side two of the original vinyl release that is most remarkable: a "suite" of four of the key "marriage" songs from *Blood On The Tracks*, with **I Threw It All Away** pointedly thrown in the middle of them. Sara had turned up, unannounced, for the gig, sparking a highly charged performance of startling intensity, as Dylan found himself caught up all over again in the emotional maelstrom that had precipitated the writing of the songs in the first place. "It's like a punk record," Rob Stoner said. "It's got such energy and anger." You can hear best what he means on **Idiot Wind**. As Paul Williams wrote, "The man is not singing about some old maze he found his way out of years ago. He's singing about the web of confusion he sees around and inside him at this very moment."

The *Hard Rain* film features a radically different set of performances to the album, including duets with Baez, none of which made the record.

Bob Dylan At Budokan

MR TAMBOURINE MAN | SHELTER FROM THE STORM | LOVE MINUS ZERO/NO LIMIT | BALLAD OF A THIN MAN | DON'T THINK TWICE, IT'S ALL RIGHT | MAGGIE'S FARM | ONE MORE CUP OF COFFEE | LIKE A ROLLING STONE | I SHALL BE RELEASED | IS YOUR LOVE IN VAIN? | GOING, GOING, GONE | BLOWIN' IN THE WIND | JUST LIKE A WOMAN | OH SISTER | SIMPLE TWIST OF FATE | ALL ALONG THE WATCHTOWER | I WANT YOU | ALL I REALLY WANT TO DO | KNOCKIN' ON HEAVEN'S DOOR | IT'S ALRIGHT MA (I'M ONLY BLEEDING) | FOREVER YOUNG | THE TIMES THEY ARE A-CHANGIN'

Columbia; recorded February 28 and March 1, 1978;

released November 22, 1978; available on CD

Dylan had not planned to release a live album from 1978's 115-date world tour – and with good reason. He'd kept fans waiting twelve years for his first live album, *Before The Flood*, recorded on 1974's tour with The Band. Then he had swiftly followed it with 1976's *Hard Rain*. A third live album in four years might have been considered pushing his luck. "They twisted my arm to do a live album for Japan," Dylan explained in 1984. "It was the same band I used on Street Legal and we had just started finding our way into things on that tour when they recorded it. I never meant for it to be any type of representation of my stuff or my band or my live show."

It was Sony Japan who demanded the live recording, made over two nights at the Budokan auditorium in Tokyo, as a souvenir for those who had seen his ten shows – his first ever on Japanese soil. And when Dylan and new manager Jerry Weintraub (whose other clients included Sinatra and Neil Diamond) saw the sums the Japanese were offering for the record, they didn't protest too hard. Six months after its Japanese release, they also acquiesced to the set's international issue in response to "popular demand". In other words, the set was doing brisk business on import and there was more money to be made via an official release.

But Dylan's self-criticism of his own shows was accurate. Although many of the arrangements of the mostly familiar songs are radical, the band sounds like they haven't yet been broken in, and the doodlings of sax/flute player Steve Douglas are particularly irritating. Dylan's vocals lack his usual forceful presence and he sounds oddly detached – there's little sense of him feeding off the band, who are waiting for their employer to energize the proceedings.

More intriguing is the cryptic message Dylan penned to his Japanese fans on the sleeve: "The more I think about it, the more I realize what I left behind in Japan – my soul, my music and that sweet girl in the geisha house. I wonder does she remember me? If the people of Japan wish to know about me, they can hear this record. Also they can hear my heart still beating in Kyoto at the Zen Rock Garden. Someday I will be back to reclaim it."

Street Legal

CHANGING OF THE GUARDS | NEW PONY | NO TIME TO THINK | BABY STOP CRYING | IS YOUR LOVE IN VAIN? | SENOR (TALES OF YANKEE POWER) | TRUE LOVE TENDS TO FORGET | WE BETTER TALK THIS OVER | WHERE ARE YOU TONIGHT?
Columbia; recorded April 10–14, 1978; released June 13, 1978; available on CD and SACD

It was claimed at one time that *Street Legal* was the Dylan album most widely found clogging the bargain bins of the world's secondhand record stores. However, the remastering of the

album in 5:1 surround sound for its issue in enhanced Super Audio format in 2003 has recently helped to restore some of its battered reputation. Indeed, the SACD transformation of *Street Legal* is one of the strongest arguments yet that the new format is something more than just an "emperor's new clothes" trick on the part of grasping record companies to get us to buy a bunch of records we already own.

The album can be summed up in one simple phrase – fine songs ruined by poor recording, production and mixing. Backed by his touring band (but with Elvis Presley's bass player Jerry Scheff replacing the recently departed Rob Stoner), the songs are melodically strong and lyrically interesting – which makes it an even more tantalizing record given its sonic shortcomings.

Changing Of The Guards is a powerful opener, its first words "sixteen years" a reference to the length of time since Dylan started his public journey. Yet there's no narrative and you're left wondering what it is he's really trying to say. **Senor** is another almost great song, mixing potent lines ("Let's overturn these tables, Disconnect these cables, This place don't make sense to me no more") with mundane ones. **Baby Stop Crying** is a catchy rewrite of Robert Johnson's "Stop Breaking Down"; the deliciously lustful carnality of **New Pony** was inspired by Dylan's relationship with Helena Springs; and there's another fine song in **Is Your Love In Vain?**, which swiftly became one of the album's in-concert favourites. **Where Are You Tonight? (Journey Through Dark Heart)**

The Music

looks back on Dylan's marriage to Sara with regret and resignation rather than anger and bitterness, and is another tremendous piece of writing.

Slow Train Coming

GOTTA SERVE SOMEBODY | PRECIOUS ANGEL | I BELIEVE IN YOU | SLOW TRAIN | GONNA CHANGE MY WAY OF THINKING | DO RIGHT TO ME BABE (DO UNTO OTHERS) | WHEN YOU GONNA WAKE UP? | MAN GAVE NAMES TO ALL THE ANIMALS | WHEN HE RETURNS

Columbia; recorded April 30–May 4, 1979; released August 18, 1979; available on CD and SACD

There's no doubt that, technically, *Slow Train Coming* is one of the best-sounding Dylan albums of all. Recorded at Muscle Shoals with top session players and veteran producer Jerry Wexler, and superbly embellished by the stinging guitar breaks of Dire Straits' Mark Knopfler, the record sparkles where the previous studio album, *Street Legal*, had sounded like it was coming at you through a wall of mud. The improved fidelity did little to placate fans who were variously hurt, angered, bewildered or appalled by the born-again fervour of it all. But there are some undeniably wonderful songs on the album.

Precious Angel is one of Dylan's loveliest melodies, with a lyric that may be partly about Jesus Christ but almost certainly also refers to Mary Alice Artes, who introduced him to the Vineyard Fellowship. **Slow Train** and **Gotta Serve Somebody** are magnificent rock-gospel numbers. There's an evocation of dread to **Gonna Change My Way Of Thinking, When You Gonna Wake Up?** and **When He Returns,** the passion in Dylan's voice conveying the power and intensity of the change he has undergone.

There are also subtle changes of tone and pace. On **I Believe In You** the ferocity gives way to an appealing meekness. Then, just when it's needed most, a little light relief is provided by **Man Gave Names To All The Animals,** which is essentially a children's song, a reggae-tinged nursery rhyme included partly because the three-year-old son of Regina Havis, one of the backing singers, liked it.

But there still remains an uneasy feeling over Dylan's intention towards his audience. As Paul Williams put it, "Longtime listeners who are not evangelical Christians can't help but ask themselves, 'Is he trying to convert me? Is he calling me a fool? Is he sharing his feelings with me or mocking me?'" Yet not everybody was troubled by such questions; Sinead O'Connor cites it as the album that made her want to be a singer because it is "sexy and funky as well as being religious".

Dylan worked closely with the Columbia art department over the cover, coming up with a drawing in which the eye is drawn equally to the advancing train and to the pickaxe of the railroad worker/disciple whose axe is made to resemble a cross.

Saved

A SATISFIED MIND | SAVED | COVENANT WOMAN | WHAT CAN I DO FOR YOU? | SOLID ROCK | PRESSING ON | IN THE GARDEN | SAVING GRACE | ARE YOU READY?
Columbia; recorded February 11–15, 1980; released June 20, 1980; available on CD

Barely nine months after recording *Slow Train Coming*, Dylan was back at Muscle Shoals with Wexler and Barry Beckett producing again. This time he brought his touring band with him. But somehow *Saved* never quite recaptures the spark that made its predecessor a great album. The songs are not of the same high quality and many fans never even got beyond the repellent cover painting, which Dylan told friends had come to him in a dream.

Things open promisingly with a magnificent version of the standard **A Satisfied Mind**. **Covenant Woman** is an affectingly ambiguous song, communicating both love for a woman and love of God, mixing classic Dylanesque lines with hackneyed religious cliché. **Solid Rock** has the potential to be a great song and for a while became a concert favourite, when it was introduced as "Hanging On To A Solid Rock Made Before The Foundation Of The World".

Saving Grace and **What Can I Do For You?** are modern-day spirituals, while **In The Garden** is a melodramatic reworking of the Jesus story ("When they came for him in the Garden, did they know? Did they know he was the son of God?"). **Pressing On** is a stately song that just about avoids deteriorating into a dull thud. But **Are You Ready?**, on the other hand, is a wonderful, uplifting performance.

Overall, the album suffers from a hectoring "us and them" quality, as if Dylan is disparaging those who have not found what he has found – an attitude he had for the most part managed to avoid on the equally committed *Slow Train Coming*.

Shot Of Love

SHOT OF LOVE | HEART OF MINE | PROPERTY OF JESUS | LENNY BRUCE | WATERED-DOWN LOVE | THE GROOM'S STILL WAITING AT THE ALTAR | DEAD MAN DEAD MAN | IN THE SUMMERTIME | TROUBLE | EVERY GRAIN OF SAND
Columbia; recorded April–May, 1981; released August 12, 1981; available on CD

Looking at the sleeve of *Shot Of Love* you have to wonder whether, after *Saved*, someone said to Dylan, "Hey, Bob, you couldn't have come up with a worse cover if you'd tried," and that Dylan responded, "Wanna bet?"

Inside the unappealing pop-art pastiche lies a curate's egg of an album, hamstrung by two strange decisions on Dylan's part. The first was to instruct producer Charles Plotkin that he did not want to return to the polished sound that had worked so well on *Slow Train Coming*. The second was to omit three of the best songs recorded for the album

The Music

in "Caribbean Wind", "Angelina" and **Groom's Still Waiting At The Altar**. The latter was subsequently added to the album on its CD release and its presence greatly enhances the proceedings.

The title track, produced as a one-off by the R&B veteran "Bumps" Blackwell, has an edgy, insistent tension. The uptempo **Heart of Mine** boasts an appealing looseness, after being re-cut at the end of the sessions with Ringo Starr and Ronnie Wood. **Lenny Bruce**, written the night before it was recorded, is a moving homage to the late comedian, while **Dead Man Dead Man** and **Watered-Down Love** both have a powerful, white R&B groove.

The tender **In The Summertime**, which features some rich harmonica-playing, could equally be about Dylan's relationship with a woman as with his God. In fact, were it not for the preachy **Property Of Jesus**, allegedly written by Dylan in response to some snide remarks about his faith by Mick Jagger, the album could hardly be regarded as a born-again record at all.

The closing track, and one moment of true greatness, is **Every Grain of Sand**. The song is based upon Dylan's conversion experience. But, more than any of his other compositions from the period, it transcends his Christian fundamentalism in favour of a more inclusive and universal spirituality. If all the songs inspired by his Bible studies had been this compassionate and non-self-righteous, he would have escaped a great deal of criticism.

Dylan at the time regarded *Shot Of Love* as "a breakthrough" and the "most explosive" album he'd ever made. Few shared that view and *Rolling Stone* lambasted the record as "filled with hatred, confusion and egoism". But with a little more care in the sound and the song selection, *Shot Of Love* could have been Dylan's first great album of the 1980s instead of merely a very good one.

Infidels

JOKERMAN | SWEETHEART LIKE YOU | NEIGHBORHOOD BULLY | LICENSE TO KILL | MAN OF PEACE | UNION SUNDOWN | I AND I | DON'T FALL APART ON ME TONIGHT
Columbia; recorded April–June, 1983; released November 1, 1983; available on CD and SACD

Despite its title, the release of *Infidels*, with its absence of overtly religious material and message-free cover, seemed to mark a diminishing of the fervour of Dylan's born-again convictions. With just eight songs, it also seemed to suggest a parallel diminishing of his songwriting impetus. But it subsequently emerged that this was not the case, for a total of sixteen new compositions were recorded at the sessions. For the second consecutive album, Dylan chose to leave out some of the best tracks – in particular, the omission of **Blind Willie McTell**, one of the greatest songs in his entire canon, was inexplicable. What we are left with is another decent disc, but one that could have been much better. Nevertheless, it's one of those Dylan albums that today sounds far better than it did at the time (particularly in the SACD version).

The opener, **Jokerman,** is a major song, textually fascinating with a collage of images that lend themselves to almost endless interpretation. But **Neighborhood Bully,** which can be interpreted without too much imagination as a defence of the political stance of Israel, is, by Dylan's standards, a stinker. **Union Sundown** is a better song, full of drive and energy, despite some confusion in its message. Dylan may have conceived it as a diatribe against capitalism and corporate greed: what comes through is a potentially jingoistic message that buying goods not made in America is bad. **License To Kill** works, despite some similarly muddied thinking ("Man has invented his doom, first step was touching the moon" appears a particularly crass observation), and is graced with a magnificent chorus.

Man of Peace is an interesting idea, based around the old maxim that the road to hell can be paved with good intentions, and the notion that Satan can adopt a convincing disguise. But the original album version plodded and thudded where the band ought to be cooking, a victim of the disagreement between Dylan and producer Mark Knopfler over the mixing process. A vastly improved remix appeared on the upgraded SACD issue in 2003. In fact, the entire album is dramatically enhanced in the new format, which miraculously banishes the "loss of sureness, uncertainty and self-doubt" that the ever-perceptive Paul Williams detected in the original release. **I And I,** in particular, is among the songs that benefited most in the exercise that upgraded a total of fifteen Dylan albums to the clarity of 5:1 surround sound.

The album's second epic after "Jokerman",

it's a wonderful song about dignity and redemption, with the Jamaican rhythm section of Sly and Robbie superbly underpinning some tremendous guitar work from Knopfler and Mick Taylor. The rest of the album is made up of a brace of love songs in **Sweetheart Like You** and **Don't Fall Apart On Me Tonight.** Both are modest and graceful, although the former got Dylan into some trouble with feminists for its suggestion that "a woman like you should be at home, that's where you belong, taking care of somebody nice".

Real Live

HIGHWAY 61 REVISITED | MAGGIE'S FARM | I AND I | LICENSE TO KILL | IT AIN'T ME, BABE | TANGLED UP IN BLUE | MASTERS OF WAR | BALLAD OF A THIN MAN | GIRL FROM THE NORTH COUNTRY | TOMBSTONE BLUES
Columbia; recorded July 5, 7 and 8, 1984; released December 3, 1984; currently unavailable

Recorded at the end of his 1984 European stadium tour at shows in Newcastle's St James's Park, London's Wembley and Dublin's Slane Castle, Dylan's fourth live album in a decade has come in for more than its fair share of flak over the years.

One of the favourite parlour games of Dylanologists is to compile fictional live albums which allegedly represent a tour better than what has actually been released. *Real Live* has elicited many such lists, based on Michael Gray's claim that "You could hardly offer a worse live

The Music

album from Dylan's 1984 tour of Europe than this. The choice of songs is hopeless, the choice of performances injudicious, the production inexcusably murky."

Actually, it's not that bad at all, sounding very much as you would imagine Dylan would sound if he was backed by an early 1970s British rock group. This is unsurprising, given that his band included former Rolling Stone Mick Taylor and Faces keyboardist Ian McLagan. Carlos Santana also adds some burnished guitar to a version of **Tombstone Blues** recorded in Newcastle.

Tangled Up In Blue features a radical rewrite of the original lyric, although the performance (from Wembley) is slightly mannered. But **Highway 61 Revisited** and **Maggie's Farm** from the same show are barnstorming performances, with Taylor and Dylan exchanging great guitar licks over McLagan's driving keyboards. **Masters Of War** again proves its relevance in any day and age. And even without Sly & Robbie who played on the studio version, **I And I**, recorded in Dublin, gets a pleasing rock-reggae treatment.

One can argue there were better performances of the songs during the tour. Only those who have spent weeks listening to tapes of all 28 shows can really judge. But the criticisms of the choice of material are more confused. Concert-goers wanting a souvenir complained that many of the big hits were missing, including "Like A Rolling Stone", "Mr Tambourine Man", "Don't Think Twice", "Lay, Lady, Lay", "It's Alright, Ma", "Blowin' In The Wind", "All Along The Watchtower" and "Knockin' On Heaven's Door". In fact, they were omitted, for versions of all of them had already appeared on two previous live albums of relatively recent vintage. Then the serious Dylan-watchers griped that the selection was unadventurous because **Maggie's Farm** and **Ballad Of A Thin Man** were appearing on a live album for the third time. Sometimes you can't win. Especially if you're Bob Dylan.

Empire Burlesque

TIGHT CONNECTION TO MY HEART | SEEING THE REAL YOU AT LAST | I'LL REMEMBER YOU | CLEAN-CUT KID | NEVER GONNA BE THE SAME AGAIN | TRUST YOURSELF | EMOTIONALLY YOURS | WHEN THE NIGHT COMES FALLING FROM THE SKY | SOMETHING'S BURNING BABY | DARK EYES
Columbia; recorded February–March, 1985; released June 8, 1985; available on CD

From the jacket he's wearing on the cover to the synthesizers and programmed drums, *Empire Burlesque* seems the most dated of all Dylan's 1980s albums. For the fashion-victim look he has to shoulder full blame, but the dated sound owes more to dance producer Arthur Baker, who mixed the album. Having produced the original sessions himself, Dylan handed the album over to Baker, who couldn't resist adding the studio trickery that was in vogue at the time. Inevitably, it now sounds like a period piece – and is a rare example of Dylan following trends rather than making them. *Empire Burlesque* has been much derided as a result.

Despite all this, the album still sounds far better than just about any other mid-1980s record made with similarly modish technology. The reason, of course, is the quality of the songs – not his very best, perhaps, but still superior to those of any of his competitors. The Dylan wit of old is at work on the opener **Tight Connection To My Heart**, which borrows the lines "I'll go along with this charade until I can think my way out" from an exchange between Captain Kirk and Mr Spock in an early episode of *Star Trek*. Other lines in the song are playfully lifted from the Humphrey Bogart films *The Maltese Falcon*, *Sirocco* and *Key Largo*.

Much of the rest of the album consists of love songs. The gentle **I'll Remember You** could do without the echo Baker puts on the vocal, but it's still a beauty. **Emotionally Yours** finds Dylan reworking a bunch of simple romantic clichés, but the result is still affecting. **When The Night Comes Falling From The Sky** is full of anticipation and foreboding and would be a great Dylan song in just about any era. **Something Is Burning Baby** is another song of similar substance, made more effective by its martial pace and the soulful voice of Madelyn Quebec echoing Dylan's lines. **Trust Yourself** is a stirring blues-rocker with a touch of the gospel fervour of "Gotta Serve Somebody", but a very different message.

Never Gonna Be The Same Again is one of Dylan's most surprising melodies, with an unexpectedly quirky rhythm and a fade-out that sounds like classic mid-tempo Rolling Stones. It's a theme that is taken up on the horn-laden **Seeing The Real You At Last**, which finds members of Tom Petty's Heartbreakers helping out on a glorious Jagger/Richards-style rocker. By contrast, **Dark Eyes**, which closes the album, is performed solo and acoustic, its grace and mystery enhanced by the beauty of its lilting Irish melody.

Of the ten songs, only the trite **Clean-Cut Kid** misses the mark. If any Dylan album is ripe for favourable reassessment it is surely *Empire Burlesque*.

Biograph

LAY, LADY, LAY | BABY LET ME FOLLOW YOU DOWN | IF NOT FOR YOU | I'LL BE YOUR BABY TONIGHT | I'LL KEEP IT WITH MINE | THE TIMES THEY ARE A-CHANGIN' | BLOWIN' IN THE WIND | MASTERS OF WAR | LONESOME DEATH OF HATTIE CARROLL | PERCY'S SONG | MIXED-UP CONFUSION | TOMBSTONE BLUES | GROOM'S STILL WAITING AT THE ALTAR | MOST LIKELY YOU'LL GO YOUR WAY AND I'LL GO MINE | LIKE A ROLLING STONE | LAY DOWN YOUR WEARY TUNE | SUBTERRANEAN HOMESICK BLUES | I DON'T BELIEVE YOU | VISIONS OF JOHANNA | EVERY GRAIN OF SAND | QUINN THE ESKIMO | MR TAMBOURINE MAN | DEAR LANDLORD | IT AIN'T ME BABE | YOU ANGEL YOU | MILLION DOLLAR BASH | TO RAMONA | YOU'RE A BIG GIRL NOW | ABANDONED LOVE | TANGLED UP IN BLUE | IT'S ALL OVER NOW, BABY BLUE | CAN YOU PLEASE CRAWL OUT YOUR WINDOW? | POSITIVELY FOURTH STREET | ISIS | JET PILOT | CARIBBEAN WIND | UP TO ME | BABY I'M IN THE MOOD FOR YOU | I WANNA BE YOUR LOVER | I WANT YOU | HEART OF MINE | ON A NIGHT LIKE THIS | JUST LIKE A WOMAN | ROMANCE IN DURANGO | SENOR (TALES OF YANKEE POWER) | GOTTA SERVE SOMEBODY | I BELIEVE IN YOU | TIMES PASSES SLOWLY | I SHALL BE RELEASED | KNOCKIN' ON HEAVEN'S DOOR | ALL ALONG THE WATCHTOWER | SOLID ROCK | FOREVER YOUNG
Columbia; released October 28, 1985; available on CD

The Music

As the most bootlegged artist in history, Dylan finally decided to do the sensible thing and put out some of the unreleased gems fans had been privately collecting for years. Yet the triple-CD/ five-LP package *Biograph* was a hybrid affair that could have offered so much more. Of the 53 tracks, 31 songs were already available on other albums, leaving four non-album tracks previously available on singles, six unreleased live tracks and just a dozen previously unavailable studio recordings, a couple of which were merely alternate takes of songs from other albums.

Much of the "new" material was already familiar to collectors. The earliest of the previously unreleased tracks is 1962's **Baby I'm In The Mood For You**, an exuberant outtake from *Freewheelin'*, influenced by Jesse Fuller, whose "San Francisco Bay Blues" Dylan was also singing around the same time. **Percy's Song**, a powerful tale of the unfairness of the judicial system set to a tune borrowed from Paul Clayton (who had also provided the melody for "Don't Think Twice") was recorded in 1963 during the sessions for "The Times They Are A-Changin'". Much bootlegged, the song was memorably covered by Sandy Denny and Fairport Convention.

Lay Down Your Weary Tune came from the same sessions and was already familiar from a version by The Byrds. The lovely **I'll Keep It With Mine** was also covered by the Fairports, as well as Nico. Written in 1964 around the time of *Another Side Of Bob Dylan*, the version on *Biograph* is a wonderfully heartfelt performance at the piano recorded during the *Bringing It All Back Home* sessions.

Jet Pilot is the original, and radically different,

version of the song that would eventually become "Tombstone Blues" on *Highway 61 Revisited*. **I Wanna Be Your Lover** was recorded with The Hawks in October 1965 immediately after *Highway 61 Revisited*, and would not have sounded out of place on that album. **Quinn The Eskimo** was recorded with The Band in Woodstock in 1967 but not included on the official 1975 *Basement Tapes* release. Asked what it was about, Dylan replied it was merely "some kind of nursery rhyme".

Up To Me is a gem that was unaccountably left off *Blood On The Tracks*. It's almost like a companion piece to **Shelter From The Storm** and delivered in similarly spare style. **Abandoned Love** was written and recorded in 1975 for *Desire* but omitted from the album in favour of "Joey". It finds Dylan no nearer resolving the crisis in his marriage, written from the perspective of someone "despairing, isolate, lost". Finally, the jaunty "Caribbean Wind" with its dramatic narrative was written on vacation in St Vincent and is an outtake from 1981's *Shot Of Love*.

Only one track in the entire set, a demo of 1973's **Forever Young**, had never been bootlegged. But even avid collectors were impressed with the packaging and the impressive 32-page booklet, which included an insightful interview-cum-essay by Cameron Crowe and illuminating song-by-song commentaries from Dylan himself.

Knocked Out Loaded

YOU WANNA RAMBLE | THEY KILLED HIM | DRIFTIN' TOO FAR FROM THE SHORE | PRECIOUS MEMORIES | MAYBE SOMEDAY | BROWNSVILLE GIRL | GOT MY MIND MADE UP | UNDER YOUR SPELL
Columbia; recorded 1985–1986; released August 8, 1986; available on CD

In which the greatest songwriter of his generation gets writer's block. Just eight songs, three of them covers and three of them collaborations, are evidence enough that by the time of *Knocked Out Loaded*, Dylan was struggling to come up with sufficient material to fill even the shortest album.

Assembled from various sessions over a period of a year, three songs were left over from *Empire Burlesque*. One came from London sessions with Dave Stewart in 1985. Another came from sessions with Tom Petty and the Heartbreakers. Three more – all covers – were recorded with Al Kooper, T-Bone Burnett and others at Skyline studios in Topanga Canyon in April 1986. According to Kooper, "There were some really wonderful things cut at those sessions." If true, it's a shame Dylan didn't choose to use them. The best is an obscure rocking blues by Junior Parker called **You Wanna Ramble** that opens the album.

We will probably never know what on earth made him record a reggae version of the standard **Precious Memories**, complete with steel drums.

Or what possessed him to dub a children's choir all over Kris Kristofferson's **They Killed Him. Got My Mind Made Up** is a rock-flecked makeweight, co-written with Petty. The pop-lite of **Under Your Spell** was co-written with Burt Bacharach's wife, Carole Bayer Sager. **Maybe Someday**, written by Dylan alone, was an *Empire Burlesque* reject and is instantly forgettable. **Driftin' Too Far From The Shore**, his one other solo composition, is only marginally better.

That leaves just one major new composition in the epic **Brownsville Girl**, co-written with the playwright Sam Shepard. Originally recorded for his previous album as "Danville Girl", at eleven minutes long it takes up a third of the album. Lyrically and musically, its subtlety and intelligence makes it toweringly dominant on one of the weakest and least satisfying of all of Dylan's albums.

Down In The Groove

LET'S STICK TOGETHER | WHEN DID YOU LEAVE HEAVEN? | SALLY SUE BROWN | DEATH IS NOT THE END | HAD A DREAM ABOUT YOU BABY | UGLIEST GIRL IN THE WORLD | SILVIO | NINETY MILES AN HOUR | SHENANDOAH | RANK STRANGERS TO ME
Columbia; recorded April–May 1987; released May 31, 1988; currently unavailable

That two years elapsed between the weak *Knocked Out Loaded* and the frankly atrocious *Down In The Groove* is testament to just how completely Dylan's muse had deserted him.

There are more covers, including Hank Snow's **Ninety Miles An Hour (Down A Dead End Street)**, the Stanley Brothers' **Rank**

The Music

Strangers To Me, Wilbert Harrison's **Let's Stick Together**, **Shenandoah**, and even the old Guy Lombardo hit **When Did You Leave Heaven?** Two songs, **Silvio** (which became a live favourite) and the far less successful **Ugliest Girl In The World**, are collaborations with the Grateful Dead's lyricist, Robert Hunter. The lightweight **Had A Dream About You Baby** was recycled from the 1987 film, *Hearts Of Fire*. **Sally Sue Brown**, another cover, was recorded with Paul Simonon of The Clash and former Sex Pistol Steve Jones.

There's not a memorable new Dylan original on the album and most critics concur in finding no theme or purpose in the record. It doesn't even work in the way *Self Portrait* does, as a scrapbook of influences that redefines him through the songs of others. It merely sounds careless. Yet there are a brave few who have found some modest merit in *Down In The Groove*. Howard Sounes concedes that the material is slight, but detects "a cohesive and natural sound" and a prelude to Dylan's later career and his obsession with songs about "alienation, ageing and death".

Dylan & The Dead

SLOW TRAIN | I WANT YOU | GOTTA SERVE SOMEBODY | QUEEN JANE APPROXIMATELY | JOEY | ALL ALONG THE WATCHTOWER | KNOCKIN' ON HEAVEN'S DOOR

Columbia; recorded July 4, 19, 24 and 26, 1987; released February 6, 1989; available on CD

One of the purposes of this guide is to offer an objective reassessment of Dylan's oeuvre, free from the controversies and prejudices that inevitably coloured attitudes at the time. In some cases, hindsight suggests that hostile critics missed the point, as with *Self Portrait* and *Infidels*. In other instances, such as *Knocked Out Loaded* and *Down In The Groove*, even the distance of almost two decades has failed to ameliorate the original negative reactions. So what of *Dylan & The Dead*, not only one of the most derided albums in Dylan's canon but one of the most despised discs in rock history?

True, it is a flawed recording and among the justifiable criticisms is that Dylan's voice is in places mixed too low. But ultimately the harsh judgement is unfair. Dylan & The Dead actually sounds like a perfectly decent Grateful Dead covers album with the added bonus of the man who wrote the songs as guest vocalist. What those who dislike the record so much really hate is the very idea of Dylan working with a bunch of spaced-out, tie-dyed, acid heads. Fair enough. But that doesn't make the album that resulted from their union a bad record per se. As one reviewer put it when reappraising the album, "It's exactly what you would expect from putting Dylan out on tour with the Dead as his backing band."

The choice of material is intelligent,

Traveling Wilburys Volume One

HANDLE WITH CARE | DIRTY WORLD | RATTLED/LAST NIGHT | NOT ALONE ANYMORE | CONGRATULATIONS | HEADING FOR THE LIGHT | MARGARITA | TWEETER AND THE MONKEY MAN | END OF THE LINE
Warners; recorded April–May, 1988; released October 25, 1988; currently unavailable

After George Harrison and compadres Jeff Lynne, Tom Petty and Roy Orbison had recorded the track **Handle With Care** with Dylan in his Malibu garage studio in April 1988, their thoughts turned to an entire album. With drummer Jim Keltner drafted in as a "sidebury", they reconvened at Dave Stewart's Los Angeles studio the following month and Dylan started the ball rolling by suggesting they record something that sounded like Prince. The resulting track, **Dirty Mind**, was pieced together with lyrics found at random in pages of glossy magazines. Full of a playful wit, as Johnny Black has written, "The track sounds nothing like Prince, but it does sound like Dylan having more fun than he'd had since the 1960s."

Dylan's other two main songwriting contributions are **Congratulations**, an incisive song of bitter irony, and the epic **Tweeter And The Monkey Man**. Reputedly conceived by Dylan and Petty as a satire on Bruce Springsteen, it's a sharp vision of urban night-

mare that fuses blues nuances and Eagles-style backing vocals. According to Harrison, Dylan cut it live on the second take. He also sings one verse of **Margarita** and, needless to say, his contributions make the album. While the rest are content to concoct stylishly evocative 1950s pop pastiches, it is Dylan who provides the grit and the much-needed rough edges.

too. **Slow Train** had not featured on any of Dylan's previous four official live albums and cooks nicely with some clever use of dynamics that prove The Dead were far more sophisticated interpreters of Dylan's material than their detractors suggest. The same is true of **Gotta Serve Somebody,** and both songs remind us what a shame it is that a live recording from Dylan's early, incendiary born-again concerts

has not yet been issued as part of Columbia's "Official Bootleg" series.

Queen Jane Approximately is another song that had not previously appeared on a live album and it's a masterful performance to rank among the very best of Dylan's live recordings – the Dead play with impeccable sensitivity. **Joey** is less successful but is another new offering as a live album track.

All Along The Watchtower is a more familiar live staple and The Dead stick to the Hendrix arrangement that Dylan first adopted on tour with The Band in 1974. But Jerry Garcia's fluid lead-guitar playing unarguably adds something fresh. **Knockin' On Heaven's Door** concludes the album on a pedestrian note – but it's down to Dylan's oddly strangulated vocal, as much as it is the fault of The Dead.

Oh Mercy

POLITICAL WORLD | WHERE TEARDROPS FALL | EVERYTHING IS BROKEN | RING THEM BELLS | MAN IN THE LONG BLACK COAT | MOST OF THE TIME | WHAT GOOD AM I? | DISEASE OF CONCEIT | WHAT WAS IT YOU WANTED? | SHOOTING STAR
Columbia; recorded March–April, 1989; released September 22, 1989; available on CD and SACD

After two of the most unconvincing studio releases of his entire career, Dylan came storming back in 1989 with one of his strongest ever albums. The production on *Oh Mercy* by Daniel Lanois is superbly atmospheric, making it the best-produced Dylan album since Jerry Wexler's sophisticated sheen on *Slow Train Coming*. But a producer alone cannot make a great album. From somewhere a re-focused and inspired Dylan came up with a set of ten superior songs boasting a profound humanity, expressed with much of the poetic intuition of old and sung with a conviction that made the lacklustre, time-serving nature of his other late-1980s releases all the more baffling.

The unflinching theme of the album is life and love seen from the perspective of middle age, sad but reconciled to a world of fraying morality. The majestic resignation of the writing on **Most Of The Time** is matched by a heart-stopping performance. **What Was It You Wanted?** is a mature song about relationships that far transcends the usual banalities of a love song. The atmospheric **Man In The Long Black Coat** draws on the deep folk tradition of ballads such as "The Daemon Lover" and "The House Carpenter". **Political World** is almost like an update of **With God On Our Side**. **What Good Am I?** is an excoriating piece of self-analysis. **Ring Them Bells** and **Everything Is Broken** take on apocalyptic themes and **Shooting Star** is wistful but incisive.

Adding an ethereal, swamp-like sonority, Lanois makes Dylan's voice sound "like he's crouched next to you in the back seat of a broken down car", as Dave Henderson put it in his excellent book, *Touched By The Hand Of Bob*. All in all, more than a great comeback, *Oh Mercy* stands as arguably Dylan's best album since *Blood On The Tracks*.

Under The Red Sky

WIGGLE WIGGLE | UNDER THE RED SKY | UNBELIEVABLE | BORN IN TIME | TV TALKIN' SONG | 10,000 MEN | TWO BY TWO | GOD KNOWS | HANDY DANDY | CAT'S IN THE WELL
Columbia; recorded January–March, 1990; released September 11, 1990; available on CD

The artistic triumph of *Oh Mercy* made *Under The Red Sky* the most eagerly anticipated Dylan

album in a decade. Yet for some reason it failed to maintain the momentum, and critics were quick to claim that Dylan's revival had been a temporary flash-in-the-pan rather than the start of a genuine long-term renaissance. However, with the benefit of hindsight it's yet another album that sounds far better than many allowed at the time.

The replacement of Lanois in the producer's chair by the hip-at-the-time brothers Don and David Was wasn't an improvement. Nevertheless, they still manage to create a pleasing cohesion and unity of mood with a rough-edged, gutbucket R&B feel that is well complemented by a set of songs that find Dylan adopting a deliberately more direct, blues-based style of writing.

The title track (which features George Harrison on slide guitar) is a fable that evokes the Minnesota in which he grew up with almost nursery-rhyme imagery. **Born In Time**, which Dylan first attempted to record for *Oh Mercy*, is a lovely ballad with David Crosby on harmony vocals. The bluesy **TV Talkin' Song** describes a visit to Speakers' Corner in London's Hyde Park. And the magnificent **God Knows**, another song left over from the *Oh Mercy* sessions, trembles with the old fervour of his enduring belief in the imminence of "the End Times". **Unbelievable**, meanwhile, bristles with attitude and a splendid, suitably tough-edged riff to match.

Wiggle Wiggle (with Slash from Guns N' Roses on guitar) and **Two By Two** (with Elton John on piano) are enjoyable but lightweight songs that deliver no more than their unpromising titles would lead you to expect. But **Handy Dandy**, which finds Al Kooper re-creating the swirling Hammond-organ sound he invented on **Like A Rolling Stone**, is a corker and a lot smarter and more knowing than any song with such a silly name deserves to be. The album concludes on another high note with the uptempo **Cat's In The Well**, which has a rhythm borrowed from Junior Walker.

Perhaps the problem was that *Oh Mercy* had simply raised expectations too high. *Under The Red Sky* isn't as potent as a collection of songs. But it's a highly approachable and hugely enjoyable album, nevertheless.

The Bootleg Series Volumes 1–3

HARD TIMES IN NEW YORK TOWN | HE WAS A FRIEND OF MINE | MAN ON THE STREET | NO MORE AUCTION BLOCK | HOUSE CARPENTER | TALKIN' BEAR MOUNTAIN PICNIC MASSACRE BLUES | LET ME DIE IN MY FOOTSTEPS | RAMBLING GAMBLING WILLIE | TALKIN' HAVA NAGIELAH BLUES | QUIT YOUR LOW-DOWN WAYS | WORRIED BLUES | KINGSPORT TOWN | WALKIN' DOWN THE LINE | WALLS OF RED WING | PATHS OF VICTORY | TALKIN' JOHN BIRCH PARANOID BLUES | WHO KILLED DAVEY MOORE? | ONLY A HOBO | MOONSHINER | WHEN THE SHIP COMES IN | THE TIMES THEY ARE A-CHANGIN' | LAST THOUGHTS ON WOODY GUTHRIE | SEVEN CURSES | ETERNAL CIRCLE | SUZE (THE COUGHING SONG) | MAMA, YOU BEEN ON MY MIND | FAREWELL ANGELINA | SUBTERRANEAN HOMESICK BLUES | IF YOU GOTTA GO GO NOW | SITTING ON A BARBED WIRE FENCE | LAKE A ROLLING STONE | IT TAKES A LOT TO LAUGH, IT TAKES A TRAIN TO CRY |

The Music

I'LL KEEP IT WITH MINE | SHE'S YOUR LOVER NOW | I
SHALL BE RELEASED | SANTA FE | IF NOT FOR YOU |
WALLFLOWER | NOBODY 'CEPT YOU | TANGLED UP IN
BLUE | CALL LETTER BLUES | IDIOT WIND | IF YOU SEE
HER, SAY HELLO | GOLDEN LOOM | CATFISH | SEVEN
DAYS | YE SHALL BE CHANGED | EVERY GRAIN OF SAND |
YOU CHANGED MY LIFE | NEED A WOMAN | ANGELINA |
SOMEONE'S GOT A HOLD OF MY HEART | TELL ME | LORD
PROTECT MY CHILD | FOOT OF PRIDE | BLIND WILLIE
MCTELL | WHEN THE NIGHT COMES FALLING FROM THE
SKY | SERIES OF DREAMS
Columbia; released March 26, 1991; available on CD

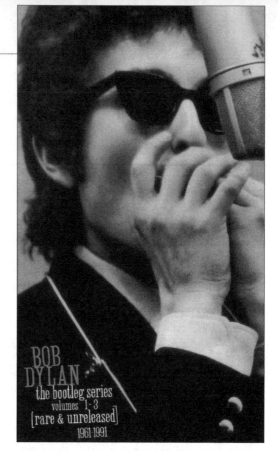

If 1985's *Biograph* had been something of a
wasted opportunity as far as serious collectors were concerned, with the rarities out-
numbered by familiar tracks, the triple CD
that launched *The Bootleg Series* was a cornu-
copia. None of the 58 tracks had previously
been commercially available and they were
drawn from every phase of Dylan's career,
with outtakes from his 1962 debut album
to 1989's 26th studio collection, *Oh Mercy*,
with stopovers at most points in between.

Almost half of the tracks date from his
prolific acoustic period from 1961 until early
1965. They include early talking blues such
as **Talkin' Bear Mountain Picnic Massacre**
and **Talkin' John Birch Paranoid**; protest
songs that never made official albums, such
as **Only A Hobo, Who Killed Davey Moore?**
and **Walls Of Red Wing**; and haunting love
songs such as **Mama, You Been On My Mind**
and **Farewell Angelina**.

There are fewer tracks from his white-hot
electric period in the mid-1960s, reflecting
how he tended to write and rewrite in the
studio with less fat left over. But **Sitting On
A Barbed Wire Fence** from the *Highway 61*

Revisited sessions and **She's Your Lover Now**
from an early abortive *Blonde On Blonde*
session are both magnificent, visceral performances.

Into the 1970s there are early and fascinating versions of several songs that appeared
in a radically altered state on *Blood On The
Tracks*. Then, into the 1980s, the inclusion
of ten high-quality outtakes enables one to
reconstruct the albums Dylan should have
released at the time but didn't. **You Changed
My Life, Need A Woman** and **Angelina** come

from the *Shot Of Love* sessions. **Tell Me, Lord Protect My Life, Foot Of Pride** and, best of all, **Blind Willie McTell**, were all recorded for but not included on *Infidels*. Finally, the splendid **Series of Dreams** is a song Daniel Lanois unsuccessfully attempted to persuade Dylan to include on *Oh Mercy*.

The package is completed by a splendid 60-page booklet with previously unpublished photos and superb track-by-track annotations by John Bauldie, the late editor and founder of the Dylan fanzine, *The Telegraph*.

Good As I Been To You

FRANKIE & ALBERT | JIM JONES | BLACKJACK DAVEY | CANADEE-I-O | SITTIN' ON TOP OF THE WORLD | LITTLE MAGGIE | HARD TIMES | STEP IT UP AND GO | TOMORROW NIGHT | ARTHUR MCBRIDE | YOU'RE GONNA QUIT ME | DIAMOND JOE | FROGGIE WENT A-COURTIN'
Columbia; Recorded July–August 1992; released November 3, 1992; available on CD

The cover of *Good As I Been To You* frames Dylan in unforgiving close-up, showing every crease and fold of his 51-year-old features. In an era of youth worship, he looks unbelievably ancient, the black-and-white photo

Traveling Wilburys Volume Three

SHE'S MY BABY | INSIDE OUT/IF YOU BELONGED TO ME | THE DEVIL'S BEEN BUSY | SEVEN DEADLY SINS/POOR HOUSE | WHERE WERE YOU LAST NIGHT? | COOL DRY PLACE | NEW BLUE MOON | YOU TOOK MY BREATH AWAY | WILBURY TWIST
Warners; recorded April, 1990; released October 23, 1990; currently unavailable

It was understandable that Dylan, Harrison, Petty and Lynne should attempt to repeat the success of the first Wilburys album. But it was perhaps not a good idea. Roy Orbison, whose operatic vocals had lifted the first record, had died in December 1989 at the age of 52. Without him, they never recapture the enthusiasm or spontaneity of *Volume One*.

Several of the songs are lightweight, although Dylan is again the most significant contributor, making the major vocal contribution on **Inside Out**, **If You Belonged To Me**, **Seven Deadly Sins** and **Where Were You Last Night?** He also sings a verse on four more songs: **The Devil's Been Busy**, **New Blue Moon**, **She's My Baby** and **The Wilbury Twist**.

And in case you were wondering – no, there never was a Volume Two. The deliberately confusing title was suggested as a prank by Harrison.

The Music

emphasizing the suggestion that he's from another time. In *Touched By The Hand Of Bob*, Dave Henderson complained that it looked "like one of those tacky reissues of legendary bluesmen, knocked out in 20 minutes flat". But that was surely the whole point for, as such, the image perfectly reflects the music inside – thirteen traditional folk and blues songs performed solo and acoustic, drawn from the deep well-spring of American music (though the ancestry of many can be traced back to Irish and English sources).

Frankie & Albert came from Mississippi John Hurt's version on Harry Smith's *Anthology Of American Folk Music*, although Dylan also knew the song from versions by Jerry Lee Lewis, Gene Vincent and countless others. **You're Gonna Quit Me** he had heard Rev Gary Davis sing in the early Greenwich Village days. **Tomorrow Night** was a traditional song he had probably learned from an early Elvis Presley recording on Sun, although he also knew the 1948 version by Lonnie Johnson. **Sittin' On Top Of The World** he had recorded in 1962 as a backing musician, adding harmonica to a version by Big Joe Williams. The song itself had first been recorded by the Mississippi Sheiks in 1930.

The brilliant **Hard Times** is based on Stephen Foster's 19th-century composition, "Hard Times Come Again No More". **Step It Up And Go** Dylan knew from several sources, including the Everly Brothers, as well as Blind Boy Fuller's original 1940 recording. The cowboy ballad **Diamond Joe** had been recorded by Cisco Houston, Tom Rush and Ramblin' Jack Elliott, all Dylan associates in the early 1960s. **Black Jack Davey** is another song Dylan had known at least as long, for there exists a 1961 tape of him singing it. The album concludes with the children's song **Froggie Went A-Courtin'** and if you don't break into the widest grin at the wondrous way Dylan sings it, then there's really no hope for you.

Several of the songs caused some controversy, for Dylan's arrangements closely followed contemporary recordings by other folk singers. The Irish ballad **Arthur McBride** was first collected in 1840, but Dylan's version owes much to that of the Irish singer-songwriter Paul Brady. **Canadee-I-O** bears a close resemblance to the version by the British folksinger Nic Jones, who recorded it on his classic *Penguin Eggs* album. The Australian folksinger Mick Slocum was the source of the arrangement of **Jim Jones**, a nineteenth-century Broadside ballad about a convict sent to Botany Bay. But, ultimately, borrowing and adaptation lies at the very heart of the folk tradition and songs in the "public domain".

What matters more is that Dylan's interpretations boast a superb, stripped-down intensity that is all his own. His voice has a unique tone and phrasing that is ragged and passionate and timeless. There's never any

The Music

The 30th Anniversary Concert

29 TRACKS BY 22 DIFFERENT ARTISTS, WITH DYLAN APPEARING ON: IT'S ALRIGHT, MA (I'M ONLY BLEEDING) | MY BACK PAGES | KNOCKIN' ON HEAVEN'S DOOR | GIRL FROM THE NORTH COUNTRY
Columbia; recorded live October 18, 1992; released September 1, 1993; available on CD

Tribute concerts can often be long on sentiment and short on content. But even before Dylan arrived on stage for the finale of what inevitably became known as "Bobfest", there's actually some rather good material on the double CD recorded on a star-studded stage at New York's Madison Square Garden on October 18, 1992. Under the musical directorship of guitarist G.E. Smith (returning for one night only after departing Dylan's backing band in 1990), and with Booker T and the MGs as the house band, highlights on the first disc include Stevie Wonder's **Blowin' In The Wind**; Lou Reed, who surprisingly chooses the obscure Infidels' outtake **Foot Of Pride**; and a fiery acoustic **Masters of War** from Pearl Jam's Eddie Vedder and Mike McCready.

Disc two opens with Neil Young offering a delightfully ramshackle **Just Like Tom Thumb's Blues** and a storming **All Along The Watchtower**. Eric Clapton contributes a rather good **Don't Think Twice**, done as an electric blues. The Band, with Smith on guitar in place of the absent Robbie Robertson, deliver **When I Paint My Masterpiece**. George Harrison breathes fresh life into **Absolutely Sweet Marie** and Roger McGuinn, backed by Tom Petty and the Heartbreakers, re-creates the jingle-jangle of the Byrds' version of **Mr Tambourine Man** and paves the way for Dylan's eventual appearance.

Sadly, the album does not include 1961's **Song To Woody**, with which he opened his set. But we do get a coruscating **It's Alright Ma (I'm Only Bleeding)** played solo before the great and the good join him for **My Back Pages**, with *eight* guitarists falling over each other and McGuinn, Petty, Young, Clapton, Harrison and Dylan all singing a verse each. **Knockin' On Heaven's Door** boasts an even larger cast. Then, after the TV satellite feed had been turned off, Dylan returned alone for a lovely acoustic **Girl From The North Country**.

sense that this is an exercise in nostalgia, for his connection with the music is clearly very much alive.

Good As I Been To You is a breathtaking record that offers what Michael Gray described as a telescope on a past that is "light years away from the world of Microsoft, McDonalds and MTV" and yet is still utterly real.

World Gone Wrong

WORLD GONE WRONG | LOVE HENRY | RAGGED & DIRTY | BLOOD IN MY EYES | BROKE DOWN ENGINE | DELIA | STACK A LEE | TWO SOLDIERS | JACK-A-ROE | LONE PILGRIM
Columbia; recorded May 1993; released October 26, 1993; available on CD

The artistic success of *Good As I Been To You* persuaded Dylan to do it all over again

The Music

with a second album of "public domain" traditional songs. Featuring a cover photo shot incongruously in Fluke's Cradle restaurant in Camden, north London, a fascinating liner note by Dylan explains the provenance of the songs and his reasons for choosing them. The traditional ballads **Love Henry** and **Jack-A-Roe** he had learned from Tom Paley of the New Lost City Ramblers in the early Greenwich Village days. **Blood In My Eyes** and **World Gone Wrong** were songs he had learned from pre–World War II recordings by the Mississippi Sheiks.

His arrangement of the popular **Stack A Lee** comes from the version by the coal miner Frank Hutchinson found on Harry Smith's *Anthology of American Folk Music*. The murder ballad **Delia**, which he had first performed on the Dinkytown folk circuit in Minneapolis around 1960, and **Broke Down Engine** had both been recorded by the peerless Blind Willie McTell. **Two Soldiers** he had learned from Jerry Garcia, who, in addition to his acid rock proclivities, was a major resource of traditional songs. **Lone Pilgrim** came from a Doc Watson recording. **Ragged And Dirty** he claimed to have learned from a record by Willie Brown, although his version also owes much to Sleepy John Estes' 1929 recording.

Like its predecessor, *World Gone Wrong* is another triumph. "All the friends I ever had

are gone," Dylan sings with almost unbearable poignancy on "Delia" so that, in a very real way, the album presages the songs about mortality and decay that would appear on his next studio album, 1997's *Time Out Of Mind*.

MTV Unplugged

TOMBSTONE BLUES | *SHOOTING STAR* | *ALL ALONG THE WATCHTOWER* | *THE TIMES THEY ARE A-CHANGIN'* | *JOHN BROWN* | *RAINY DAY WOMEN #10 & #35* | *DESOLATION ROW* | *DIGNITY* | *KNOCKIN' ON HEAVEN'S DOOR* | *LIKE A ROLLING STONE* | *WITH GOD ON OUR SIDE*
Columbia; recorded on November 17–18, 1994; released April 25, 1995; available on CD and DVD

The *MTV Unplugged* format could have been tailor-made for Dylan. What could be more perfect than the folksinger who had caused such consternation when he had first plugged in, reverting almost three decades later to a stripped-down acoustic style? In the event, MTV and Sony Music executives talked him out of his original intention of a solo country-blues set, à la *World Gone Wrong*, and he turned up with a five-piece band.

Quite why the MTV recording received such negative reviews at the time now seems inexplicable. On the CD release in 1995, Andy Gill wrote in Q, "No-one else, not even Guns N' Roses, would treat Dylan's songs in such a cavalier fashion." Michael Gray found it "contemptible, phony, tawdry". Yet viewing 2004's DVD release of the show, you have to wonder what on earth they were talking about, for it reveals a performance far more coherent and controlled than any of the critics were prepared to allow at the time.

Shooting Star is lovely and wistful. **All Along The Watchtower** is, for once, not done in the Hendrix arrangement and it's a pleasing change. **The Times They Are A-Changin'** sounds less defiant than the original – sad and reflective, and far more contemporary as a result. **John Brown** is a powerful antiwar song from 1963 never included on a studio album.

Desolation Row is given a wonderfully lyrical treatment. A gentle **Love Minus Zero/No Limit** is followed by an uptempo version of the **Oh Mercy** outtake **Dignity**. **Like A Rolling Stone** is a hybrid mix of acoustic guitars and swirling Hammond organ, and **With God On Our Side** brings proceedings to a splendid and stately close.

Time Out Of Mind

LOVE SICK | DIRT ROAD BLUES | STANDING IN THE DOORWAY | MILLION MILES | TRYIN' TO GET TO HEAVEN | 'TIL I FELL IN LOVE WITH YOU | NOT DARK YET | COLD IRONS BOUND | MAKE YOU FEEL MY LOVE | CAN'T WAIT | HIGHLANDS

Columbia; recorded January 1997; released September 29, 1997; available on CD

Even by Dylan's standards, coming seven years after his last collection of new songs, *Time Out Of Mind* was a spectacular comeback. The songs, with their themes of mor-

tality and solitude, were written and recorded before his close encounter with death. Yet somehow they seemed to describe, or, at least, foretell it.

His voice on the opening **Love Sick** sounds as if it is coming from another world, set against Augie Meyers' utterly spooky organ. **Dirt Road Blues** is a thrilling, half-crazed rockabilly tune with a lyric about endurance in the face of adversity. **Standing In The Doorway** is one of Dylan's loveliest ballads in years, full of a world-weary, end-of-the-line melancholia. **Million Miles** is a steamy blues shuffle.

Tryin' To Get To Heaven is a bittersweet, piano-led ballad with a clearly self-referential lyric. Once, he was knocking on heaven's door. Now he's merely trying to reach it before closing time. **'Til I Fell In Love With You** is a moody R&B workout. Then comes the album's centrepiece, **Not Dark Yet**. It's one of the finest songs in Dylan's entire canon and, according to Emmylou Harris, the greatest song ever written about growing old. "For those of us entering that door, it brings up things we didn't know we were capable of feeling," she explained, in 2003. "He put the poetry into that experience."

Cold Irons Bound is a snarling, bass-heavy blues that won Dylan a Grammy for best male rock vocal performance. **Make You Feel My Love** is the album's slightest composition, a standard love song lifted by a stately, almost hymn-like tune. **Can't Wait** is another atmospheric blues, slowed down almost to a heartbeat. The album concludes with the extraordinary sixteen-minute epic, **Highlands**, which finds Dylan as ghostly commentator, namechecking Erica Jong and Neil Young and resigned but unrepentant as he prepares for the end.

Lanois' production gives the album a widescreen but highly focused cinematic quality, looser and less ethereal than *Oh Mercy*, but every bit as effective in its ambience. Jim Dickinson, who is credited with keyboards on eight of the eleven tracks, claimed that by the time the producer had finished his alchemy, even the musicians couldn't tell "who's playing what".

Bob Dylan 1961–2000

SOMEBODY TOUCHED ME | WADE IN THE WATER | HANDSOME MOLLY | TO RAMONA | I DON'T BELIEVE YOU | GRAND COULEE DAM | KNOCKIN' ON HEAVEN'S DOOR | IT AIN'T ME BABE | SHELTER FROM THE STORM | DEAD MAN DEAD MAN | SLOW TRAIN | DIGNITY | COLD IRONS BOUND | BORN IN TIME | COUNTRY PIE | THINGS HAVE CHANGED
Columbia; released February 9, 2001; available on CD

Put together at the behest of Sony in Japan to coincide with tour dates there, an album of live tracks drawn from Dylan's first four decades as a performer was not a bad idea – particularly as eleven of sixteen performances were previously unreleased or of varying degrees of rarity.

The traditional **Wade In The Water** was recorded in Minneapolis in 1961, and **Handsome**

Molly in Greenwich Village a year later. Listening to them today, there's an astonishing consistency of mood with 1990s albums such as *Good As I Been To You* and *World Gone Wrong*, even though the technique is more rudimentary and the voice obviously younger. **Grand Coulee Dam** is one of the three songs Dylan performed with The Band at the Tribute To Woody Guthrie concert in 1968, the recording of which has long been out of the catalogue.

To Ramona and **It Ain't Me Babe** are outtakes from the films *Don't Look Back* and *Renaldo & Clara*, respectively. **Dead Man Dead Man** is a 1981 recording from one of the born-again tours. **Cold Irons Bound** was recorded on tour in America in 1997 and **Born In Time** (from *Under The Red Sky*) dates from 1998. The previously unrecorded traditional spiritual **Somebody Touched Me** was recorded at Portsmouth in 2000, as were **Country Pie** and **Things Have Changed**. The other five tracks are from widely available live albums.

Yet welcome as the rare material is, as a collection it's a ragbag that can't hope to represent forty years as a performing artist as anything more than a series of random snapshots. A more focused trawl through the last sixteen years of the Never Ending Tour would surely have made for a more coherent compilation.

The Music

Love and Theft

TWEEDLE DEE & TWEEDLE DUM | MISSISSIPPI | SUMMER DAYS | BYE AND BYE | LONESOME DAY BLUES | FLOATER (TOO MUCH TO ASK) | HIGH WATER (FOR CHARLEY PATTON) | MOONLIGHT | HONEST WITH ME | PO' BOY | CRY A WHILE | SUGAR BABY
Columbia; recorded May 9–26, 2001; released September 11, 2001; available on CD and SACD

Love And Theft is not as important an album as *Time Out Of Mind*. It's more immediate, the lyrics off-the-cuff and full of wit and spontaneity, and the spectre of death that haunted *Time Out Of Mind* has retreated to the shadows. But it's a marvellous, good-time album that is in effect a love letter to the roots of American music that have inspired and informed Dylan's entire career.

The energetic barroom boogie **Tweedle Dee & Tweedle Dum** captures the sound he was attempting on *Under The Red Sky* much more successfully than the Was brothers managed. **Mississippi**, meanwhile, is a powerful out-take from *Time Out Of Mind*, while **Summer Days** harks back to the early days of rockabilly. The roots of **Bye And Bye** and **Floater** are even older, lying in the days of vaudeville. As its title suggests, **Lonesome Day Blues** is tougher edged, a low-down-and-dirty twelve-bar workout.

High Water (For Charley Patton) is one of the album's highlights, a potent evocation of the Delta and the musical ghosts that live on in Dylan's head. **Moonlight** sounds almost like a Hoagy Carmichael song – but not quite, thanks to the fact that Dylan can only croak rather than croon.

The no-holds-barred rocker **Honest With Me** and the angular, moody blues of **Cry A While** hark back to the passion of his performances with The Hawks circa 1965–66. **Po' Boy** is one of the album's saddest songs, with an old-timey tune that, in the great folk tradition, makes you wonder where you've heard it before. The disc ends with the lovely, Appalachian strains of **Sugar Baby**.

An initial limited edition of the album came with a bonus CD featuring a 1961 recording of the traditional **I Was Young When I Left Home** and a 1963 alternate studio take of **Times They Are A-Changin'**, with a markedly slower tempo that quite changes the song's mood.

The Bootleg Series Volume Seven: No Direction Home – The Soundtrack

WHEN I GOT TROUBLES | RAMBLER, GAMBLER | THIS LAND IS YOUR LAND | SONG TO WOODY | DINK'S SONG | I WAS YOUNG WHEN I LEFT HOME | SALLY GAL | DON'T THINK TWICE, IT'S ALL RIGHT | MAN OF CONSTANT SORROW | BLOWIN' IN THE WIND | MASTERS OF WAR | A HARD RAIN'S A-GONNA FALL | WHEN THE SHIP COMES IN | MR TAMBOURINE MAN | CHIMES OF FREEDOM | IT'S ALL OVER NOW, BABY BLUE | SHE BELONGS TO ME | MAGGIE'S FARM | IT TAKES A LOT TO LAUGH, IT TAKES A TRAIN TO

CRY | TOMBSTONE BLUES | JUST LIKE TOM THUMB'S BLUES | DESOLATION ROW | HIGHWAY 61 REVISITED | LEOPARD-SKIN PILL-BOX HAT | STUCK INSIDE OF MOBILE WITH THE MEMPHIS BLUES AGAIN | VISIONS OF JOHANNA | BALLAD OF A THIN MAN | LIKE A ROLLING STONE
Columbia; recorded 1959–66; released Aug 29, 2005; available on CD

To accompany Martin Scorsese's film *No Direction Home* came the release of a two-disc, 28-song soundtrack album, of which only the Manchester 1966 recording of "Like A Rolling Stone" had previously been available on an official album. The full-length versions of performances that are mostly heard only in snippet form in the film are arranged chronologically, so they dramatically track the startling velocity at which Dylan was travelling in the 1960s and the rapidity of his development as a songwriter and performer. Disc one opens with his earliest known recording, "When I Got Troubles", taped by a school friend in 1959 when he was 17. It's hard to discern a special talent in development, although by the first professional studio recordings a couple of years later the seeds of genius are very obviously apparent. By the time we reach the five 1963 concert recordings – including jaw-dropping versions of "Blowin' In The Wind", "Masters Of War" and "A Hard Rain's A-Gonna Fall" – Dylan has morphed into a self-possessed young man with a command over both his material and his audience that is spellbinding.

However, it's disc two that contains most of the crown jewels – alternate versions of a dozen of the most coruscating songs from the 1965/66 white-hot trilogy of *Bringing It All Back Home/Highway 61 Revisited/Blonde On Blonde*. Three of them are seminal live performances, including a storming "Maggie's Farm" from the infamous 1965 Newport Folk Festival appearance with an electric band. The rest are studio outtakes that offer a compelling insight into his modus operandi and how the songs mutated while being recorded. "She Belongs To Me" is more tender than the familiar version, "Desolation Row" more sinister. "Visions Of Johanna" is faster and less ghostly; "It Takes A Lot To Laugh" has a tougher, bluesy edge and different words in its earlier incarnation as "Phantom Engineer". The discs come with an excellent 60-page booklet with detailed track information and essays by Andrew Loog Oldham and Al Kooper.

In addition, three download-only tracks that didn't make the album were made available from commercial download service providers by Sony Music in November 2005. They were "Baby Please Don't Go", recorded on April 25, 1962 during the *Freewheelin'* sessions; "Mr Tambourine Man", recorded live on July 26, 1964 at the Newport Folk Festival and an acoustic studio outtake of "Outlaw Blues", recorded on January 16, 1965.

50 Great Dylan Songs
and the stories behind them

The Music

> *"He changed language and he changed songwriting.
> I can't imagine what the world would be like
> without Dylan's songs."* Emmylou Harris, London, July 2003

1. Blowin' In The Wind

Recorded July 9, 1962; available on *The Freewheelin' Bob Dylan*

Composed in a matter of minutes in April 1962 at The Commons, a Greenwich Village coffeehouse opposite the Gaslight Club, **Blowin' In The Wind** was inspired by a long political discussion – which led Dylan to the conclusion that to see an injustice and not actively to oppose it is to condone it. "The idea came to me that you were betrayed by your silence, that all of us in America who didn't speak out were betrayed by it," he later said. Even worse, he added, was that people "don't even care".

With his friend **David S. Cohen** (who later recorded as David Blue) strumming the chords as he called them out, Dylan wrote the first and last verses on the spot. Oddly, he was not the first to perform the song in public. After writing it, he played the incomplete version to Gil Turner, who asked Dylan to teach him the song. Turner performed it on April 9, 1962, at Gerde's Folk City, where he was the MC, with the words taped to the microphone. A week later Dylan performed

it for the first time himself at the same venue, complete with an introduction in which he insisted it was "not a protest song". In a sense he was right for, unlike most protest songs, "Blowin' In The Wind" does not deal with a specific issue or incident. Instead, Dylan had come up with something far more valuable, a song that could be used as a universal anthem by almost anyone struggling for justice or freedom.

The melody was borrowed from an old spiritual, **No More Auction Block** (a song we know Dylan was familiar with for tapes exist of him singing it) and at first some of the Village veterans were not impressed. Dave Van Ronk pronounced it "dumb" and grumbled, "I mean, what the hell is blowin' in the wind?" A few weeks later, he was forced to change his mind when he heard some students singing a parody of the song in Washington Square Park, with the lyric altered to "The answer my friend, is blowin' out your end." Van Ronk admitted, "If the song is strong enough without ever having been recorded to start garnering parodies, the song is stronger than I realized."

Peter, Paul and Mary had a big hit with their 1963 cover version of the song, which went to number two in the US. But when Dylan's own version was released in August the same year, it failed to make any impression on the charts at all.

Early days: Dylan in the "Blowing In The Wind" era

2. A Hard Rain's A-Gonna Fall

Recorded December 6, 1962; available on *The Freewheelin' Bob Dylan*

One of Dylan's most powerfully poetic works, **A Hard Rain** started life as a long free-verse poem in the style of the French symbolists. Tom Paxton, one of the first to hear it, described it as "a wild and wacky thing, the likes of which I'd never heard before". Paxton claims he suggested to Dylan that he put a melody to the words. It's a nice story to tell his grandchildren, but Dylan surely planned to do so anyway – particularly as the first line of the poem was taken from the traditional folk ballad, **Lord Randall**.

The song must have been written in late September 1962, for the main inspiration for its apocalyptic imagery was the **Cuban missile crisis**, which brought America and the Soviet Union to the brink of nuclear war. "I wrote that song when I didn't figure I'd have enough time left in life, didn't know how many other songs I could write, during the Cuban thing," Dylan said. "I wanted to get the most down that I knew about into one song, the most that I possibly could, and I wrote it like that. Every line in that is actually a complete song, could be used as a whole song. It's worth a song, every single line."

Yet Dylan denied that the "hard rain" was nuclear fallout, as has often been supposed. "It's not the fallout rain, it isn't that at all," he said. "The hard rain that's gonna fall is in the last verse, where I say, 'the pellets of poison are flooding us all', I mean all the lies that are told on the radio and in the newspapers, trying to take people's brains away, all the lies I con-sider poison." Dylan worked on the lyrics at the Greenwich Village apartment of Hugh Romney, better known as Wavy Gravy, using a battered old Remington typewriter. Romney vividly recalls its composition: "That song kind of roared right out of the typewriter. It roared through him the way paint roared through Van Gogh."

By October, the Cuban missile crisis had reached its height – as Kennedy and Khrushchev went eyeball to eyeball and the world waited to see who would blink first – and the song was being sung all over Greenwich Village, not only by Dylan but by the likes of Pete Seeger, Richie Havens and Hamilton Camp. Astonishingly, when Dylan came to record it in December, he despatched the six-and-a-half-minute epic in a single take, during a session which also included single takes of **Oxford Town** and **I Shall be Free**.

3. Don't Think Twice, It's All Right

Recorded November 14, 1962; available on *The Freewheelin' Bob Dylan*

The first of Dylan's great love songs was inspired by **Suze Rotolo,** or rather her absence, after she had taken off for Italy in the summer of 1962. Dylan was distraught, ringing friends such as Dave Van Ronk in the middle of the night to

pour out his grief. The song finds Dylan attempting to come to terms with her absence. But being Dylan, of course, it's far more emotionally complex than that.

Some of his later compositions written for the women in his life were exercises in pure vindictiveness. This isn't one of them, but as he accuses Suze of wasting his "precious time", there's still a certain rancour mixed in with the undeniable tenderness.

The blunt-speaking Van Ronk thought the song was "self-pitying, but brilliant". Suze was ambivalent about it, describing herself as "torn", particularly when she heard a song written so directly to her performed by others, such as Peter, Paul and Mary. And she must have been mortified when, at the Newport Folk Festival in 1963, Joan Baez sang the song and pointedly introduced it as "about a love affair that has lasted too long". The rumours of the relationship between Dylan and Baez had reached Suze's ears and at this apparent confirmation, she left the festival in tears. Shortly after, she collected her things and moved out of Dylan's West 4th Street apartment.

In the time-honoured folk tradition, Dylan borrowed the melody from another tune – **Who's Gonna Buy Your Chickens When I'm Gone?** – which he probably learned from the singer Paul Clayton, who had adapted it for his own **Who's Gonna Buy Your Ribbon Saw?**. Dylan's publishers paid Clayton a "substantial sum" in settlement of any claim he may have had on the tune and the two singers remained close friends.

4. Girl From The North Country

Recorded April 24, 1963; available on *The Freewheelin' Bob Dylan*

Who was the **Girl From The North Country**? From the amount of ink the Dylanologists have

spilled on the subject over the years, you would imagine her identity was a matter at least as important as who killed Kennedy or whether Saddam Hussein had weapons of mass destruction. Some claim it was **Echo Helstrom**, Dylan's first serious girlfriend back in high school in Hibbing. Others believe it was **Bonnie Beecher**, the girl he met and fell in love with during his early excursions on the Dinkytown folk circuit in Minnesota. It's a shame to spoil a good argument, but the truth is that the song is probably an amalgam of the two women, with quite possibly hints of other old girlfriends in there, too.

Whatever the truth, it's a song full of an evocative nostalgia for a specific time in Dylan's early life and one of the most enduringly lovely compositions in his songbook. It was written in early January 1963 during his first trip to Europe when, in the middle of a four-week stay in London, he had flown to Italy to perform with Odetta, who was in Rome with Albert Grossman, the manager of both artists. It's possible that he had also entertained hopes of seeing Suze Rotolo there, for he was unaware that she had returned to New York just before Christmas.

Probably suffering a bout of homesickness, Dylan also wrote **Boots Of Spanish Leather** during his four-day stay in Italy. Yet "Girl From The North Country" betrays a British influence. The tune of the song owes something to **Scarborough Fair**, which Dylan had recently learned from Martin Carthy, while staying in his Hampstead flat. The song's nostalgic tone clearly remained potent for him. Six years later, he recorded "Girl From The North Country" again with Johnny Cash on 1969's *Nashville Skyline*.

5. Mixed Up Confusion

Recorded Oct–Nov 1962; available on the single *Mixed Up Confusion/Corrina, Corrina* and the box set *Biograph* (alternative take)

Had the world been more familiar with **Mixed Up Confusion**, there might have been less hue and cry three years later when Dylan "went electric". But although the song was released as Dylan's first single in December 1962, it was swiftly withdrawn and very few ever got to hear it. The critic Andy Gill makes a powerful case for "Mixed Up Confusion" as "the very first folk-rock recording", and when copies of the three-year-old track began to circulate in Britain in 1965, the sound convinced fans that it was from that year's *Bringing It All Back Home* sessions.

The lyric, allegedly written in the back of a taxi on the way to the studio, is slight by Dylan's standards. But the sound is extraordinary. Unusually, he cut the song no fewer than fourteen times in three frustrating sessions between October 26 and November 14. Two of them have now been released, and both make it abundantly obvious that "Mixed Up Confusion" is Dylan's attempt at making his very own Sun single. Backed by **Dick Wellstood** playing Jerry Lee Lewis–style piano, **Gene Ramey** on bass, **Herbie Lovelle** on drums and **Bruce Langhorne** and **George Barnes** on guitars, Dylan further made his intention clear by cutting a version of **That's All Right, Mama**, Elvis Presley's first single, at the same time.

Among the multiple takes of "Mixed Up Confusion" is allegedly a Dixieland version that has never seen the light of day.

6. The Times They Are A-Changin'

Recorded October 24,1963; available on *The Times They Are A-Changin'*

With **The Times They Are A-Changin'**, Dylan wrote a battle hymn for his generation. To understand fully the song's impact, you need to recall the context. At the time, The Beatles were top of the charts with "She Loves You", the Rolling Stones were still doing R&B cover versions, and Elvis Presley had just finished filming *Fun In Acapulco*. "The Times They Are A-Changin'" was quite simply like nothing else around at the time and the song ensured that popular music, if not the world, would never be the same again.

By the time it was released on Dylan's third album in January 1964, the assassination of President Kennedy had given the song an even greater resonance and Dylan opened his set with it the night after Kennedy's death. "I had to sing it, my whole concert takes off from there," he later told biographer Anthony Scaduto. "Something had just gone haywire in the country and they were applauding that song."

As vital as the words are, they cannot be separated from Dylan's masterful performance on record. As the critic Paul Williams has pointed out, his delivery shifts the emphasis from imagery to exhortative verbs in a quite deliberate way. The result is that the song hinges around such words as "gather", "admit", "accept" and "sink", and it's this that gives the song its anthemic quality. Dylan isn't merely observing or commentating and he's no longer just posing questions, as he had been content to do on "Blowin' In The Wind". He's urging each and every one of his listeners to take action – or to be swept aside by the flood.

Thirty years after the song's release, Dylan allowed **Coopers & Lybrand** to use it in a TV advert. It would be hard to think of anything more inappropriate. Perhaps it was just another example of Dylan attempting to debunk his own myth, but it was a sin some of his fans have found hard to forgive.

7. One Too Many Mornings

Recorded October 24, 1963; available on *The Times They Are A-Changin'*

There it sits in the middle of perhaps the most searing set of "finger-pointing" protest songs ever recorded – one of Dylan's most moving, reflective and lovely songs, again inspired by his rapidly deteriorating relationship with **Suze Rotolo**. When Dylan wrote **One Too Many Mornings**, Suze had just moved out of his apartment; he was hurt and angry, although his relationship with Joan Baez meant that he really had no right to feel he was the wronged party. He deals with the complexity of his feelings with astonishing maturity in a song that captures a moment of rare calm and insight in the middle of what must have been an emotional maelstrom.

He never quite gets around to admitting that he may have been in the wrong, but he's at least prepared to share the blame, conceding "you're right from my side, I'm right from mine".

The song was recorded back-to-back with **The Times They Are A-Changin'** at Columbia's Studio A in New York, further evidence of Dylan's dramatic ability to switch moods with utter conviction.

8. The Lonesome Death Of Hattie Carroll

Recorded October 23, 1963; available on *The Times They Are A-Changin'*

There's a powerfully journalistic quality to **The Lonesome Death Of Hattie Carroll**. But, although it's written as a piece of reportage that describes a real event, in Dylan's hands the song easily transcends the "who, what, when, where and why" role of the journalist, a description he once angrily used to put down another writer of protest songs, Phil Ochs.

The events described took place on February 8, 1963, at the Spinsters Ball at the **Emerson Hotel**, Baltimore. Hattie Carroll was a 51-year-old waitress and the mother of eleven children. When she was slow in serving a drink to **William Zantzinger**, the 24-year-old spoilt son of a wealthy farming family, he hit her around the head with his cane, allegedly shouting "When I order a drink I want it now, you black bitch!" Carroll died in hospital the following morning of a brain haemorrhage. Zantzinger was arrested and became the first white man in the state of Maryland ever to be charged with the murder of a black woman. But he was only found guilty of manslaughter and given a risible six-month prison sentence.

According to Baez, Dylan wrote the song in her house in California in the early autumn of 1963, although he later claimed he had written it in a café on 72nd Street in New York. The verse form he adopted borrows a pattern based on Bertolt Brecht's **The Black Freighter**, and he used it to pile the imagery of a poet on top of the economy of a news reporter. It's a brilliant technique that means he never has to mention that Carroll is black and Zantzinger is white, for the disparity he describes in their lives makes it perfectly obvious. Tom Waits remembers hearing the song for the first time and being staggered by the detail, unable to tell if the story was invented or from history.

Not everybody was so impressed. Many years later an unrepentant Zantzinger said of Dylan, "He's a no-account son of a bitch. He's just like the scum of a bag of the earth. I should've sued him and put him in jail." Needless to say, he never has and Dylan continues to perform the song in concert to this day.

9. Chimes Of Freedom

Recorded June 9, 1964; available on *Another Side Of Bob Dylan*

In February 1964, Dylan embarked upon a road trip with a bunch of friends that took him to Georgia, Mississippi, Louisiana, Colorado, Nevada and California. Five days into the trip, he visited civil-rights activists **Bernice Johnson** and **Cordell Reagon** in Atlanta and the following day he wrote **Chimes Of Freedom** in the back of a car. It's an extraordinary song, described by Andy Gill as "a compelling account of a visionary epiphany experienced during an electric storm, rendered in a hyper-vivid poetic style heavily influenced by the French symbolist poet Arthur Rimbaud". An equally moved Paul Williams has likened the song to Dylan's version of the Sermon on the Mount.

Is it a protest song? Any song from 1964 with the word "freedom" in the title must surely qualify. But, if so, it's a protest of an entirely new kind, as he generously imagines salvation for a universal army of "the countless confused, accused, misused" and "the luckless, the abandoned and forsaken". As the album's producer Tom Wilson said, "He's not so much a singer of protest as a singer of concern about people."

It's also one of the first Dylan songs in which he moves beyond conscious imagery and the confines of narrative and taps into some deeper truth. And the force of the song is further enhanced by a performance of shivering beauty which packs a powerful emotional punch long before the lyrics have begun to register. The song's universality was brought home thirty years later when the Senegalese singer **Youssou N'Dour** reinvented it as an anthem for the struggling masses of Africa.

10. To Ramona

Recorded June 9, 1964; available on *Another Side Of Bob Dylan*

To Ramona is one of Dylan's loveliest break-up songs. When asked about it some twenty years after its composition, he responded: "Well, that's pretty literal. That was just somebody I

The Music

knew." Like so many other songs on his fourth album, that somebody was almost certainly **Suze Rotolo**, with whom he had broken up for good in March 1964. Other songs on the album about Suze, such as "Ballad In Plain D" or "I Don't Believe You (She Acts Like We Never Have Met)" are essentially diatribes. "To Ramona" is more gracious ("Your magnetic movements still capture the minutes I'm in") and even leaves the door open to a possible future reunion ("Someday maybe, who knows baby, I'll come and be cryin' to you"). But the picture he paints of Suze's mother **Mary** and sister **Carla**, twisting her head "with worthless foam from the mouth" is distinctly less generous.

The song was written in **Vermilya**, Greece, where Dylan stayed in May 1964 immediately after his first major tour of England. In an intensive week's writing there he came up with most of *Another Side Of Bob Dylan*. From the handwritten manuscripts that have since emerged (on notepaper bearing the crest of the Mayfair Hotel where he had stayed in London), "To Ramona" appears to have originally started life as half a verse in another song on the album, **I Shall Be Free No. 10**, before developing an existence of its own. To the critic Sean Egan, it is "simply the finest thing ever to emanate from Dylan's pen, as he presents a whole romantic situation and an entire philosophical viewpoint in two immaculate stanzas". Dylan seems to have retained an affection for the song, too. It's the only track from *Another Side* that he saw fit to include on the career retrospective *Biograph* in 1985.

11. My Back Pages

Recorded June 9, 1964; available on *Another Side Of Bob Dylan*

Dylan hated the album title *Another Side Of Bob Dylan*, which was invented by producer Tom Wilson and which he felt lacked subtlety. Perhaps they should have followed the pattern of the third album and simply chosen one song as the title track. Had they done so, **My Back Pages** would have been the leading contender, for the song finds Dylan not only presenting his "other side" but surveying his past, waving goodbye to the wreckage and feeling rejuvenated as he prepares to embrace a bright, new, post-protest future – "I was so much older then, I'm younger than that now."

In one of his finest early lyrics, he admits that his youthful certainty was based on "half-wracked prejudice" and faces up to the realization that "I'd become my enemy in the instant that I preach." He's not merely turning his back on his more political songs but on his journalistic style, too. From now on, he will pursue a more allusive approach, rich in metaphor and symbolism and owing as much to the legacy of Allen Ginsberg and Jack Kerouac as to Elvis Presley and Woody Guthrie.

12. It Ain't Me Babe

Recorded June 9, 1964; available on *Another Side Of Bob Dylan*

As this chapter has already made clear, **Suze Rotolo** was the inspiration for many of Dylan's greatest early songs. During the summer of 1963, while she was away in Italy, he used her absence

Suze the muse: a happy Bob with the inspiration behind many of his greatest songs

The Music

as a creative spur. In an unusually heightened emotional state that ranged from jealousy, anger and hurt to tenderness, longing and pain, a batch of intensely personal songs poured forth, from **Don't Think Twice** to **One Too Many Mornings**. Then, in spring 1964 after their final break-up, Suze inspired a second raft of songs. One or two of them – the plainly undignified **Ballad In Plain D** in particular – should probably never have been recorded. But **To Ramona** and **It Ain't Me Babe** are exquisite masterpieces.

Although there's some suggestion that Dylan may have started writing **It Ain't Me Babe** on his first trip to Europe in January 1963, the song certainly wasn't completed then. Perhaps it was cast aside when, on his return to New York a week or two later, Dylan and Suze were happily reunited. The main part of the song appears to have been written on his British tour in May 1964, shortly after the final break-up. Most of the post-Suze songs on *Another Side* were written at the end of that tour when he took a vacation in Greece, but we can date "It Ain't Me Babe" a little earlier because, on his way there, Dylan stopped off in Paris and played the song to the German chanteuse, **Nico**.

The song is imbued with the bitterness of parting but there's also a universal humanity about its sentiments – that feeling of being in a relationship that has become too demanding or in which a partner's idealized expectations are too much to measure up to. Typically, Dylan piles most of the blame on Suze's unreasonable demands for someone who is "never weak but always strong". But there's some-

thing deeply moving and humble about his admission, "I will only let you down."

On another level, the song can be read as Dylan's divorce papers from the generation who wanted to make him their spokesman and even their martyr: "Someone who will die for you an' more." Regardless of your interpretation – and the two were surely equally intentional – the song's positioning as the closing track on Dylan's last all-acoustic album is hugely poignant.

The song was a top-twenty hit for **The Turtles** in 1966. It remains an in-concert favourite and during the Rolling Thunder tour in 1975, Dylan performed an updated version with additional lyrics.

13. Subterranean Homesick Blues
Recorded January 14, 1965; available on *Bringing It All Back Home*

Released as a single to trail *Bringing It All Back Home*, **Subterranean Homesick Blues** marks one of the seminal moments in rock'n'roll history. It was the world's first glimpse of Dylan's transformation from folk troubadour to electric messiah – and its impact was extraordinary.

Written in the apartment of John Court, an associate of Dylan's manager Albert Grossman, the song's metre owes something to a Woody Guthrie song called **Taking It Easy**, which contained lines such as "Mom was in the kitchen preparing to eat, she was in the pantry looking for some yeast." But Dylan grafts upon it a lyric of staccato, streetwise jive that offers a nihilistic critique of the American Dream that is arguably more devastating than any of the more overtly finger-pointing songs. To the lyrical pyro-

technics, he adds a souped-up R&B energy and a machine-gun delivery to create an extraordinary picture in sounds and words that was utterly revolutionary. How he makes the lines scan as the phrases tumble over each other defies logic – and, even more miraculously, it was recorded in one take. In its own way, "Subterranean Homesick Blues" is nothing less than the first rap song, some twenty years before rap came of age. And some of the lines, such as "You don't need a weatherman to know which way the wind blows", have since entered the language.

In another landmark associated with the song, Dylan and the filmmaker **D.A. Pennebaker** created a revolutionary promo film to accompany the revolutionary song. Filmed in an alley at the back of the Savoy Hotel in London in May 1965, the footage showed Dylan holding up cards containing key words from the lyric and formed the opening scene of the film *Don't Look Back*. It presaged the MTV era by almost two decades.

"Subterranean Homesick Blues" gave Dylan his first American top-forty single and his second British top-ten hit.

14. She Belongs To Me

Recorded January 14, 1965; available on *Bringing It All Back Home*

Despite its politically incorrect title, **She Belongs To Me** is one of Dylan's most moving,

if unconventional, love songs. That the lyric is partly about **Joan Baez** is made obvious in the line "She wears an Egyptian ring that sparkles before she speaks." Dylan had indeed given her just such a ring, so perhaps the song title was ironic, for the assertive Baez would never have submitted to belonging to any man.

Either way, the song pays tribute to her unswerving moral conviction ("She never stumbles, she's got no place to fall"). But Dylan objects to her desire to keep him as her pet protest singer ("a walking antique") and is wearied by her constant demands for flattery and attention ("bow down to her on Sunday"). Yet any sharpness in the lyric is juxtaposed against the unusual gentleness of Dylan's vocal and the sensitivity of the backing, which possesses a delicacy far removed from the raucous nature of "Subterranean Homesick Blues", recorded on the same night.

The opening line of the song provided the title of the film *Don't Look Back*, shot on the tour of Britain in 1965, when the relationship between Dylan and Baez fell apart.

15. Mr Tambourine Man

Recorded January 15, 1965; available on *Bringing It All Back Home* and *Biograph* (alternative take)

Dylan first attempted to record **Mr Tambourine Man** for *Another Side Of Bob Dylan*. He wasn't satisfied with the results and by the time he eventually released the song on *Bringing It All Back Home*, it had been in his live set for at least nine months. Written in February 1964 during the road trip across the southern United States that had also produced **Chimes Of Freedom**, Dylan started the song as they pulled out of **New Orleans**. They had spent the night carousing heavily and much of the swirling imagery reflects the fact that Dylan's head was full of the sights and sounds of the Mardi Gras they had just experienced. The song was finished some weeks later at the New Jersey home of his friend Al Aronowitz.

What else Dylan's head may have been full of is open to speculation. Despite such lines as "Take me on a trip upon your magic swirling ship" and "the smoke rings of my mind", he has always strenuously denied that "Mr Tambourine Man" is in any way a drug song. "That's not drugs. Drugs was never that big a thing with me, I could take 'em or leave 'em" he said when asked about "Mr Tambourine Man" in 1985. But there's no doubt a lot of marijuana was smoked and a lot of speed taken on that cross-country journey. It's also known that **Victor Maimudes**, one of his on-the-road companions, was responsible for introducing him to LSD, although the date is usually given as spring 1964, following a concert in Massachusetts.

Mind-changing substances probably were part of the writing of "Mr Tambourine Man". Yet the chemistry is largely irrelevant for it's clearly much more than a drug song – more a hymn to artistic transcendence as the author (the "ragged clown") joyously surrenders to the freedom offered by the "dancing spell" of his muse. Dylan has also cited Fellini's film *La Strada* as an influence.

The song was first recorded on June 9, 1964, during the marathon session at which he recorded the eleven songs of *Another Side*. Belatedly released on 1985's *Biograph*, it's a lovely performance with an extended harmonica solo prefacing the solo and Ramblin' Jack Elliott harmonizing on the choruses. Why Dylan was unhappy with it and omitted it from the album is hard to understand. "I felt too close to it to put it on" is the only explanation he has ever offered. The familiar hit version of the song was re-cut during the *Bringing It All Back Home* sessions in January 1965.

And who was the mysterious Tambourine Man, the figure leading Dylan onwards in pursuit of aesthetic perfection? The answer, if we are to believe the author himself, turns out to be somewhat prosaic: "Mr Tambourine Man, I think, was inspired by Bruce Langhorne," he has said. "Bruce was playing guitar with me on a bunch of the early records … and he had this gigantic tambourine. It was like really big. It was as big as a wagon wheel. He was playing and this vision of him playing this tambourine just stuck in my mind."

16. It's Alright, Ma (I'm Only Bleeding)

Recorded January 14, 1965; available on *Bringing It All Back Home*

One of the most remarkable aspects of Dylan's writing is its universality, and the ability of his songs to take on layers of fresh meaning – even years after they were written. Nowhere is this more evident than in **It's Alright, Ma**

(**I'm Only Bleeding**). Nine years after it was first recorded, the song became a highlight of Dylan's triumphant return to the road with The Band in 1974. The Watergate scandal and Richard Nixon's disgrace were gripping the nation and a palpable shiver went through the audience every night when the prophet Dylan declared "even the President of the United States sometimes must have to stand naked".

One of four acoustic songs recorded solo on *Bringing It All Back Home* (along with "The Gates of Eden", "It's All Over Now Baby Blue" and "Mr Tambourine Man"), in many ways it qualifies as a protest song, but of a highly sophisticated kind. If the earlier finger-pointing songs were the equivalent of news reports, "It's Alright, Ma" is a stinging editorial, with fifteen dizzying verses in which Dylan excoriates the shame of capitalism and consumerism.

The performance is masterful, too, as every syllable, every guitar strum and every breath has a mysterious clarity, so, as Paul Williams puts it, the listener has "to feel the words rather than receive them as ideas". Remarkably, "Mr Tambourine Man", "Gates Of Eden" and "It's Alright, Ma" were all recorded in the studio in a single uninterrupted take, one after another, without even a playback in between. It has often been said that Dylan has never made records as such. Rather he's a performing artist, some of whose best performances just happen to take place in a recording studio. The *Bringing It All Back Home* acoustic session was a case in point.

17. It's All Over Now, Baby Blue

Recorded January 14, 1965; available on *Bringing It All Back Home*

By the time of *Bringing It All Back Home*, it had become traditional for Dylan to close his albums with a song bidding adieu, whether to old friends, outgrown styles or disowned attitudes. **Restless Farewell** had closed *The Times They Are A-Changin'*. *Another Side Of Bob Dylan* had concluded with **It Ain't Me Babe**. On *Bringing It All Back Home*, proceedings were brought to a suitably poignant end with **It's All Over Now, Baby Blue**.

So who or what is getting the kiss-off this time? It was long rumoured the song was about **Paul Clayton**, an old friend who had been paid off for his part in inspiring **Don't Think Twice, It's All Right** and was one of Dylan's road companions in his February 1964 trip across the South. Dylan has since denied this and cited an old Gene Vincent song called **Baby Blue** that he used to sing back in high school. "Of course, I was singing about a different Baby Blue," he added without revealing a name. Many suspect that it was **Joan Baez**. Although they were still an item when the song was written and were about to embark upon a tour together, a restless Dylan was already planning to move on, in both personal and professional terms.

Yet by the last verse, the focus has changed and Dylan once again seems to be saying goodbye to his own old self, abandoning the "stepping stones" that brought him here and the vagabond camp-followers who now stand "in the clothes that you once wore". And, as with all of Dylan's declarations of closure, it's also the start of a fresh chapter, as he orders: "Strike another match, go start anew."

18. Like A Rolling Stone

Recorded June 15/16, 1965; available on *Highway 61 Revisited*

Just five months after recording *Bringing It All Back Home*, Dylan had so many new songs he was back in the studio again making *Highway 61 Revisited*, his first all-electric album. Central to the new LP was the visceral **Like A Rolling Stone**, surely his most famous composition of all, and a song with a strong claim as the greatest rock'n'roll record of all time.

Unusually, Dylan has given a detailed description of its writing. Tired and unwell when he returned home after his 1965 British tour, he claimed he had decided to "quit singing and playing" when he found himself writing "this song, this story, this long piece of vomit about twenty pages long, and out of it I took 'Like A Rolling Stone' and it made it as a single and I'd never written anything like that before and it suddenly came to me that that was what I should do." If he really had decided to quit, he proceeded to make the quickest comeback in history. He had flown back to America on June 2 and moved into a cabin in Woodstock with new girlfriend Sara Lowndes. Within little more than a week, he'd invited the guitarist **Mike Bloomfield** to stay to work on a bunch of new songs and by June 15 he was in Columbia's Studio A in New York cutting the first of several versions of "Like A Rolling Stone".

The song itself Dylan described as "just a rhythm thing on paper all about my steady hatred directed at some point that was honest. In the end it wasn't hatred. It was telling someone something they didn't know. Revenge. That's a better word, I had never thought of it as a song until one day I was at the piano and on the paper it was singing, 'how does it feel' in a slow motion pace. It was like swimming in lava." So who was the someone and what was the something Dylan was telling them? There have been many theories. The hapless Joan Baez again? Surely too easy a target. Baez herself believed the song was about **Bobby Neuwirth**, one of Dylan's closest allies on the 1965 tour. Or was it a cleverly disguised piece of critical self-analysis about Dylan himself? Andy Gill leans towards the latter theory, claiming that, under this interpretation, the climactic finale "You're invisible now, you've got no secrets to conceal" becomes not a triumphalist sneer but "a revelatory moment of self-awareness".

We shall probably never know the truth. But what we do know is that the song changed shape dramatically in the studio in the course of the different versions Dylan cut. Initially given a waltz-time, it only began to resemble the version we now know late in the day when session musician Al Kooper – who had been brought in by producer Tom Wilson and had not previously met Dylan – switched to organ. Astonishingly, Kooper was primarily a guitarist and had never even played the organ before, but his work on the final version,

The Music

laid down after several takes and false starts, inspired an entire school of organ playing.

Despite being six minutes long – unheard of for a single in those days – the song went to number two in America and number four in Britain. In the week of its release in July 1965, Dylan premiered the song live with an electric band at the Newport Folk Festival and was famously booed off the stage.

In January 1988, Bruce Springsteen described hearing the song for the first time when he inducted Dylan into the Rock And Roll Hall Of Fame: "I knew that I was listening to the toughest voice that I had ever heard. It was lean and it sounded somehow simultaneously young and adult. Dylan was a revolutionary. Bob freed your mind the way Elvis freed your body."

The *Highway 61* sessions, August 1965

The Music

19. Just Like Tom Thumb's Blues

Recorded August 2, 1965; available on *Highway 61 Revisited*

"This is about a painter down in Mexico City who travels from North Mexico up to Del Rio, Texas all the time. His name is Tom Thumb and right now, he's about 125 years old but he's still going. Everybody likes him a lot down there, he's got a lot of friends and this is when he was going through his blue period." So said a typically elliptical Dylan when introducing **Just Like Tom Thumb's Blues** on tour in Melbourne, Australia, in 1966. A more likely influence is Rimbaud's poem, *Ma Bohème*, which contains the lines, "I tore my shirt, I threw away my tie, Dreamy Tom Thumb, I made up rhymes as I ran."

Whatever its origins, it's a preternatural, south-of-the-border ballad that breaks the pop mould by eschewing both punchline and chorus. Instead, we get six verses of rich evocation of scene and situation, adding up to a vivid picture of alienation as Dylan switches back and forth between the first, second and third person until it's far from clear who's singing, who's being sung to and who's being sung about.

20. Desolation Row

Recorded August 4, 1965; available on *Highway 61 Revisited*

The poet Philip Larkin once reviewed **Desolation Row**, and wrote that he couldn't decide whether the words were "mysterious" or merely "half-baked". Over eleven epic minutes and ten complex stanzas, it sounds like great poetry, an impression only enhanced by the name-dropping of **T.S. Eliot** and **Ezra Pound**, who are held up to ridicule as "calypso singers laugh at them and fishermen throw flowers". But, as Larkin indicates, deciphering the song's layers of symbolism and absurdist imagery is not easy.

In broad terms, the song presents a Felliniesque carnival of human futility, dispassionately observed by Dylan gazing down from his vantage point high above Desolation Row. It's as powerfully subversive as any of his more direct protest songs, as most of the institutions of bourgeois western society are mocked. Philosophy, science and religion are put on trial and all found wanting as a bizarre cast of characters from Einstein and Robin Hood to Romeo and Casanova run through the song's cinematic scenes. Some have called the song Dylan's alternative State of the Union address, a suggestion that is not too fanciful, particularly in the light of his own tongue-in-cheek response when asked what he'd do if he was president. He answered that he'd get school children to memorize "Desolation Row" instead of "America The Beautiful".

Musically, it's quite different in tone from anything else on *Highway 61 Revisited*, replacing the predominant electric guitar and Hammond-organ sound with two simple guitars, played by Dylan and **Bruce Langhorne**. Logic says that it ought to grow repetitive as the pattern barely changes over eleven minutes. Yet somehow it never does.

21. Ballad Of A Thin Man

Recorded August 2, 1965; available on *Highway 61 Revisited*

When they'd finished recording **Ballad Of A Thin Man**, drummer Bobby Gregg laid down his sticks and told Dylan, "That's a nasty song, Bob." The songwriter took it as a compliment. At the core of this number (in which "thin" serves as a lateral version of shallow) is an encounter between the hipster world of Dylan and his entourage of freaks and the "straight" world of bourgeois society, represented by Mr Jones. Dylan's put-down of the hapless outsider is unrelenting; over a stern, doomy piano riff, he ends every verse by sneering "Something is happening here but you don't know what it is, do you Mr Jones?" Anybody who has seen the film *Don't Look Back* will recognize the similarity between this technique and the way he turns on the hapless student journalist who tries to ask him what his songs are about.

At the time of the song's release, Dylan was evasive about the identity of Mr Jones. "He's a real person. You know him but not by that name," he started promisingly – but continued in more characteristically cryptic fashion: "I saw him come into the room one night and he looked like a camel. He proceeded to put his eyes in his pocket. I asked this guy who he was and he said 'that's Mr Jones'. Then I asked this cat, 'Doesn't he do anything but put his eyes in his pocket?' And he told me, 'He puts his nose on the ground.' It's all there. It's a true story." Thanks, Bob.

A paranoid **Brian Jones** of The Rolling Stones was convinced that he was the subject of the song, although that probably tells us more about Jones's insecurity than it does about Dylan's intention. Some have reckoned that poor old **Joan Baez** was once again the target of Dylan's scorn ("Ms Joan?"). But the most credible candidate is a little-known journalist who had attempted to interview Dylan in the mid-1960s. Dylan himself admitted as much when he introduced the song at a 1978 concert by saying, "I wrote this for a reporter who was working for the Village Voice in 1963." In fact, the incident he was alluding to probably happened two years later at the Newport Folk Festival when student journalist Jeffrey Jones attempted to interview Dylan for *Time* magazine. He was apparently writing a piece about the proliferation of the harmonica in contemporary folk music. Later, Dylan bumped into Jones again in a hotel dining room and proceeded to mock him, yelling across the room, "Mr Jones! Getting it all down, Mr Jones?"

22. Positively Fourth Street

Recorded July 29, 1965; available as a single and on *Biograph*

If **Like A Rolling Stone** had established Dylan as the master of the hip put-down and **Ballad Of A Thin Man** was a thoroughly "nasty" song, with **Positively Fourth Street** he attempted to outdo both in sheer unpleasant brutality. Released as the follow-up single to "Like A Rolling Stone", the song, which took its title from Dylan's old address in Greenwich Village, closely follows the musical pattern of its

The Music

predecessor with **Al Kooper**'s Hammond organ again to the fore. Dylan's target is his old folkie friends from the Village – the same crowd he blamed for booing him at the Newport Folk Festival when he had turned up with a rock'n'roll band. He went into a New York studio to record "Positively Fourth Street" just four days later.

The vitriol steadily grows throughout the song's twelve verses, from the first line, "You gotta lot of nerve to say you are my friend," to the last: "I wish that for just one time you could stand inside my shoes, You'd know what a drag it is to see you." This is abuse elevated to an art form and entirely consistent with his behaviour at the time. Many have described his obvious enjoyment in his verbal demolition of those who stumbled into his orbit. "Dylan was very hostile, a mean cat, very cruel to people," said David Blue. And Blue was one of his closest friends at the time.

Released as a single in September 1965, the song made number seven in the American charts and number eight in Britain.

23. **Rainy Day Women #12 & 35**

Recorded March 10, 1966; available on *Blonde On Blonde*

Blonde On Blonde, the album many regard as Dylan's ultimate masterpiece, opened paradoxically with a throwaway romp that sounded as if it was played by a Salvation Army marching-band force-fed hallucinogenic drugs. Yet its refrain **"Everybody must get stoned"** was guaranteed to confer notoriety – a fact that Columbia was more than happy to exploit by releasing **Rainy**

Day Women #12 & 35 as a single in April 1966. Despite some predictable radio bans, the song went to number two in America and number seven in Britain.

Partly inspired by Ray Charles's **Let's Go Get Stoned** (which Dylan had allegedly heard in a Los Angeles coffee shop with Phil Spector), the writer of course denied any drug connotations. "I never have and never will write a drug song. I don't know how to. It's not a drug song. That's just vulgar," he insisted. Then you analyse Dylan's definition of a drug. "Opium, hash and pot – now those things aren't drugs," he told Nat Hentoff. "They just bend your mind a little. I think everybody's mind should be bent once in a while." And Dylan was bending his mind regularly at that time, and taking all kinds of uppers and downers just to keep going. "It takes a lot of medicine to keep up this pace," he told his biographer Robert Shelton during 1966.

"Rainy Day Women" was recorded on the last night of Dylan's Nashville sessions for *Blonde On Blonde*. He had considered getting in a genuine Salvation Army band and recording them in the parking lot. But the Nashville musicians he was using assured him they could play "pretty dumb" if they put their minds to it and were prepared to give it a shot. A trombonist was summoned and, fuelled by the cocktails and grass that Dylan insisted upon ("I'm not going to do

456893

this with a bunch of straight people," he told them), country's finest session men played extra "dumb" by swapping instruments. The entire track was cut by the time Robbie Robertson had returned from going out to buy a packet of cigarettes.

24. Visions Of Johanna

Recorded on February 14, 1966; available on *Blonde On Blonde*

On *Blonde On Blonde*, and its key track **Visions Of Johanna** in particular, Dylan attained a new pinnacle in the marriage of rock music and poetry. The imagery and symbolism of the song is often hard to unravel, but that hasn't prevented some of the brightest minds in the English departments of our best universities from trying. Professor Christopher Ricks described the album's lyrics as "variously extraordinary and insinuatingly true", and lines such as "the ghost of electricity howls in the bones of her face" are among the most potent in rock music. The argument that Dylan deserves the Nobel prize for literature really begins here.

Like much great poetry, literal interpretation of "Visions Of Johanna" is perhaps less important than mood and impression. One example will suffice. Somewhere in between the different versions of the song Dylan recorded during the period Novenber 1965–February 1966, the roles of the peddler and the fiddler in the final stanza were transposed. To puzzle over why it is the peddler rather than the fiddler who "speaks to the countess who's pretending to care for him" when the matter is of such little consequence

to the author himself suggests that the lit-crit approach to Dylan's lyrics is ultimately futile.

Originally titled **Seems Like A Freeze-Out**, the song predates most of the *Blonde On Blonde* material, and Dylan first attempted to record it with The Band in November 1965. **Joan Baez** believed parts of the song were about her after Allen Ginsberg asked her what she thought of the song. She later told Dylan biographer Anthony Scaduto that she believed the two of them were "in cahoots to make sure I never thought the song had anything to do with me". It's equally likely that there are strong elements of **Sara**, who Dylan had married on November 22, 1965, eight days before he went into the studio to record the song.

The two central female characters of the song represent the familiar dichotomy of womanhood found in much literature since the Bible – the available, carnal Louise and the Madonna-like Johanna. But the lyric also describes an artistic quest, a search for aesthetic perfection. A similar theme had also informed **Mr Tambourine Man**. "Visions Of Johanna" invariably comes out close to the top of the poll whenever Dylan fans are invited to vote on his greatest-ever song.

25. One Of Us Must Know (Sooner Or Later)

Recorded January 25, 1966; available on *Blonde On Blonde*

One Of Us Most Know was the breakthrough in the search for "that wild mercury sound" that Dylan had been searching for on *Blonde On Blonde*. It came after several months of false starts and frustration in the studio and once he'd cut it, he relocated to Nashville, Tennessee, and the rest of the album flowed swiftly, during sessions in February and March, 1966. So pleased was he with "One Of Us Must Know" that by then it had already been rush-released as a single, although surprisingly it failed to make the top thirty on either side of the Atlantic.

Recorded in Columbia's **Studio A** in New York, it features The Band (then still known as The Hawks) but augmented by the melodramatic interplay of **Paul Griffin** on piano and **Al Kooper** on organ. A close relative of another Dylan song called **She's Your Lover Now** (which eventually appeared on *The Bootleg Series Vols I–III*), the narrative is an inquest into a relationship that has recently ended. "I never really meant to do you any harm," Dylan sings, for once sounding almost contrite. If it was about **Joan Baez**, it's as close as he ever got either to a thank you or an apology for using her as a stepping stone in his own career.

26. Just Like A Woman

Recorded March 8,1966; available on *Blonde On Blonde*

Just Like A Woman has dramatically divided Dylan's critics over the years. Alan Rinzler in *Bob Dylan: The Illustrated Record* condemned it as "a devastating character assassination … the most sardonic, nastiest of all Dylan's put-downs of former lovers". Another critic dismissed it as a "complete catalogue of sexist slurs". Yet others, led by the song's gorgeous melody, regard "Just Like A Woman" as an affectionate portrait. Paul Williams, for exam-

ple, has written of the "love" in Dylan's delivery, which he believes overrides "any confusion aroused by the playful needling in the lyrics".

The song has long been believed to be about the mentally unstable **Edie Sedgwick**, and was later included on the soundtrack of Robert Margouleff's biopic of Edie, *Ciao Manhattan*. A New York scenemaker, model and acolyte of Andy Warhol (in whose films she appeared), Sedgwick met Dylan at the Kettle of Fish in Greenwich Village in December 1964 and swiftly become infatuated with him. There was talk of her making a record, a plan which foundered on the simple fact that she couldn't sing. There was also a suggestion that she and Dylan should co-star in a film, another project that came to nothing. Their relationship came to an end in January 1966 when Warhol told her that Dylan had secretly married Sara Lowndes.

However, Dylan makes clear the sexual attraction he felt towards Sedgwick in lines such as "I was dying here of thirst." And Sedgwick's presence can also be detected in another song on *Blonde On Blonde*, Leopard-Skin Pill-Box Hat. There have even been suggestions that she was the peroxide-blonde inspiration for the album title.

27. I Want You

Recorded March 10,1966; available on *Blonde On Blonde*

I Want You is something of an oddity as a mid-1960s Dylan song: an apparently straight pop number with a bouncy melody, a delightful guitar motif by Nashville sessioner **Wayne Moss**, a mischievous charm and perhaps the most direct and uncomplicated chorus he ever wrote. As such, it's no surprise that it was a top-twenty hit in Britain and America when released as a single in the summer of 1966.

Some who cannot accept that Dylan could write something so straightforward have speculated that it's actually a song about his alleged addiction to heroin. The notion is surely ludicrous and most will prefer to believe that the song is an honest expression of his desire for **Sara Lowndes**, whom he had recently married. Within the lyric there lurks a typical list of Dylanesque characters, from guilty undertakers to drunken politicians – but the object of his love provides a refuge from all of them.

The most easily identifiable character is **Brian Jones** as the "dancing child with his Chinese suit". Dylan had spent time showing him the clubs of Greenwich Village in November 1965, around the same period he was starting work on the songs for *Blonde On Blonde*, and Jones had just such a suit.

28. Sad Eyed Lady Of The Lowlands

Recorded February 15,1966; available on *Blonde On Blonde*

Although at eleven minutes and 23 seconds, the song is hardly any longer than "Desolation Row", "Sad Eyed Lady Of The Lowlands" was allotted the whole of side four of the original vinyl release that was *Blonde On Blonde* – a revolutionary act in itself. Some suspected that Dylan had overreached himself with a double album and simply run out of songs. But it seems to have been a conscious decision to allow a number that Dylan himself called "the best song I've ever written" to stand alone.

For once, there is no debate about the identity of the lady in question – and if there ever was, Dylan laid it to rest ten years after composing the song, when in **Sara**, one of the tracks on the 1976 album *Desire*, he recalled "Stayin' up for days in the Chelsea Hotel writin' Sad Eyed Lady Of The Lowlands for you". Sara, of course, was Sara Lowndes, the former model Dylan had secretly married in November 1965 in a ceremony attended only by his manager, Albert Grossman. "Sad Eyed Lady" contains plenty of clever word play and coded private imagery, but the devotion is obvious as he sings in a trance-like voice of Sara's "flesh like silk" and "saint-like face".

Dylan may have written most of "Sad Eyed Lady" in New York's **Chelsea Hotel**, where he kept an apartment for a long time after the wedding, hosting a famous party in early July 1966 for members of The Rolling Stones, and also entertaining Edie Sedgwick there. But by the time he came to record the song in Nashville on February 15, 1966, it was still not finished. He spent most of an extended day-and-night session at Columbia's **Music Row Studios** rewriting it while the cream of Nashville's session men – all being paid top union rates by the hour – sat around in the next room drinking beer and playing cards. According to one story, the musicians even got hold of a Ouija board and jokingly tried to divine exactly what Dylan was doing. Eventually he emerged in the small hours of the morning and declared the song was finished. It was recorded in a single take. Drummer Kenny Buttrey recalls: "I was playing one-handed, looking at my watch. And it kept on and kept on. We'd never heard anything like this before."

29. This Wheel's On Fire

Recorded July/Aug 1967; available on *The Basement Tapes*

The story of the recording of *The Basement Tapes* in the house rented by The Band in West Saugerties and known as **Big Pink** is told elsewhere (see pp.63–65). **This Wheel's On Fire** is one of the more substantial songs from the sessions and inevitably reminds us of Dylan's motorcycle crash in Woodstock the previous year. Not that there are any clues to what really happened on that fateful day in the cryptic lyric. The road down which Dylan's fiery wheel is rolling in the song represents the road of excess he was travelling prior to the crash; and when it "explodes", he's referring to far more than the locked wheel of his Triumph 500.

Dylan appeared one afternoon at Big Pink with the words to "This Wheel's On Fire" but no music. Hence the song is credited as a rare co-write with The Band's **Rick Danko**, who added a major part of the melody. Dylan delivers the lyric with great conviction, although,

as Paul Williams notes, you're never quite sure "what it is he's convinced of". With Levon Helm absent, guitarist **Robbie Robertson** played drums, and when the track was officially released for the first time in 1975, further drums and piano had been overdubbed.

By that point, however, the song was more than familiar from at least three cover versions. **Julie Driscoll**, backed by Brian Auger and The Trinity, had a British top-five hit with the song in April 1968, a version which was later used as the theme tune of the TV sitcom ***Absolutely Fabulous***. The Band also recorded the song on their debut album *Music From Big Pink* and The Byrds were responsible for yet another cover.

30. I Shall Be Released

Recorded Autumn 1967; available on *Official Bootleg Series Vols I–III* and *Greatest Hits Vol 2* (alternative version)

Along with "Down In The Flood" and "You Ain't Goin' Nowhere", **I Shall Be Released** was one of the first songs from *The Basement Tapes* to see the light of day, when a re-recorded version appeared on *Bob Dylan's Greatest Hits Vol 2* in 1971. Yet despite being one of the most powerful of his compositions from the period, it was oddly not among the two dozen tracks included on the cleaned-up official double album from the Big Pink sessions released in 1975. Perhaps Robertson, who compiled the official *Basement Tapes* release, felt the song was already over-familiar, for a version without Dylan had already appeared on The Band's debut 1968 album, *Music From Big Pink*, and a live version had been included on the 1974 tour album, *Before The Flood*. The original 1967 version was finally made officially available on 1991's *Bootleg Series Vols I–III*.

According to the liner notes of the 1985 Dylan-approved *Biograph*, the song was intended for *John Wesley Harding* but not finished in time. It would have fitted the mood of that album well, but the claim doesn't quite stack up, as the final *John Wesley Harding* sessions did not take place until mid-November, some time after the recording of *The Basement Tapes* version. But, whatever its origins, the song itself resembles a hymn, with a strongly spiritual message – the three verses deal with revenge, faith and acceptance – while the subtly shifting chorus first promises and then delivers salvation. Dylan's own humble vocal on *The Basement Tapes* version is perfectly complemented by the haunting falsetto harmony sung by the doomed Richard Manuel.

"I Shall Be Released" is one of the most covered of all Dylan songs, with versions by everyone from **The Hollies** and **Sting** to **The Heptones** and **Bette Midler**.

31. **All Along The Watchtower**

Recorded November 6, 1967; available on *John Wesley Harding*

It's an unusual compliment when a songwriter recognizes someone else's arrangement of their song as so definitive that the originator then copies the cover version. But that's exactly what Dylan has done with **All Along The Watchtower**, playing the song live for the last thirty years in a close approximation of the Jimi Hendrix version, rather than his own, starker original.

"I liked Jimi Hendrix's record and ever since he died I've been doing it that way", Dylan said in 1985. "Funny though, his way of doing it and my way of doing it weren't that dissimilar. I mean the meaning of the song doesn't change like when some artists do other artists' songs. When I sing it I always feel like it's a tribute to him in some kind of way." Dylan has even suggested that after the example of "All Along The Watchtower" he began to play **Masters Of War** the way he imagined Hendrix might have done it. He clearly felt a close affinity with the late guitarist and hinted that, in different circumstances, it might have been Hendrix who survived and Dylan who died: "He'd gone through like a fireball without knowing it. I'd done the same thing, like being shot out of a canon."

Dylan claimed the song came to him "during a thunder and lightning storm". Various commentators have also detected a biblical source – Isaiah's prediction of the **fall of Babylon** – and suggested that "the joker" and "the thief" represent different aspects of Dylan's own personality, caught between the honesty of his art and its commercial commodification.

32. **Lay, Lady, Lay**

Recorded February 14,1969; available on *Nashville Skyline*

When Dylan released **Lay, Lady, Lay** on *Nashville Skyline*, it was a case of third time lucky. In the summer of 1968, he had been asked to write some music for the film *Midnight Cowboy*. By the time he came up with a song that autumn, he had missed the deadline and the Harry Nilsson version of Fred Neil's **Everybody's Talkin'** was used instead of "Lay, Lady, Lay". Dylan next offered the song to the **Everly Brothers**, visiting them backstage at a New York concert and playing them the song. Although the duo hadn't had a big hit of their own in several years, an unimpressed **Phil Everly** turned it down.

Dylan finally recorded the song himself in Nashville in February 1969. Unusually, he had written the music before the words. "The song came out of those first four chords. I filled it up with lyrics, then the la la la type thing turned into the words Lay, Lady, Lay," he told Cameron Crowe. The lovely pedal-steel part was played by **Pete Drake** and the cowbells, which provide the highly effective staccato-like percussion, were added initially as a jest. When drummer **Kenny Buttrey** was dissatisfied with the drum part, producer **Bob Johnston** jokingly suggested he used bongos. Joining in the fun, Dylan suggested cowbells. Buttrey went along with the joke and got studio janitor **Kris Kristofferson** to hold them while he played. It fitted perfectly.

Clive Davis, president of Columbia, was convinced "Lay, Lady, Lay" was a hit single. Dylan was not so sure, and "begged and pleaded" with him not to release it. "I never felt too close to the song or thought it was representative of anything I do. Actually I was slightly embarrassed by it. I wasn't even sure I even liked the song," Dylan later recalled. Davis was proved right when "Lay, Lady, Lay" became the biggest single of Dylan's career.

Presumably the song was originally addressed to his wife, **Sara**. On the Rolling Thunder tour in 1976, with his marriage on the rocks, he added new lyrics, singing "Let's go upstairs, Who really cares", thus transforming an anthem of loving devotion into a crude invitation to casual sex.

33. If Not For You

Recorded August 12, 1970; available on *New Morning* and *Bootleg Series Vols I–III* (alternative version)

One of Dylan's most infectious love songs, **If Not For You** would have made a fine follow-up single to "Lay, Lady, Lay". Instead, it was left to **Olivia Newton John** to turn it into a hit, while **George Harrison** also released a version on *All Things Must Pass* before Dylan's own recording appeared as the opening track of *New Morning*. The song's appeal lies in its disarming warmth and simplicity – its straightforward depiction of a contented family man and loving husband. This seems to have been a genuine reflection of Dylan's state of mind at the time. Unusually, **Sara Dylan** visited the studio during the sessions and guitarist **Ron Cornelius** recalls being struck by the couple's obvious happiness, telling Dylan biographer Howard Sounes, "When you were around him and Sara and the kids, you envied what a great family feel this guy had."

"I wrote the song thinking about my wife," Dylan confirmed many years after their divorce.

"It seemed simple enough, sort of Tex-Mex. I would never explore all the possibilities of instrumentation in the studio, add parts and so forth, change the beat around, so it came out kind of folky." In fact, he made several attempts to record the song over the summer of 1970. The version that finally appeared on *New Morning* features **Al Kooper** on organ, **Charlie Daniels** on bass, **Billy Mundi** on drums and **Buzzy Feiten** on guitar. An earlier version recorded with George Harrison was eventually made available and Dylan – despite the divorce – remained fond enough of the song that he included different versions on both of his major box-set retrospectives, 1985's *Biograph* and 1991's *Bootleg Series Vols I–III*.

34. Knockin' On Heaven's Door

Recorded February 1973; available on *Pat Garrett & Billy The Kid*

Knockin' On Heaven's Door was not originally part of Dylan's music for Sam Peckinpah's film *Pat Garrett & Billy The Kid*. When he began to record the soundtrack in mid-January 1973, the song's place was taken by a slow, gospel-ish number called **Goodbye Holly**. Dylan had never scored a film before and an early recording session in Mexico City was disastrously unproductive. But experienced Hollywood arranger **Jerry Fielding** was brought in to assist and when he demanded a new song, a suitably galvanized Dylan came up with "Knockin' On Heaven's Door".

The song was inspired by the scene in which **Sheriff Baker** (played by Slim Pickens) dies in his wife's arms. "I wrote it for Slim Pickens and Katy Jurado. I just had to do it," Dylan later said. Like **I Shall be Released**, "Knockin' On Heaven's Door" has a hymn-like quality. "Just listening to the song, you know without being able to explain, that something somewhere has just broken through, has passed some kind of point of no return," according to Paul Williams.

It was recorded in Los Angeles, with **Roger McGuinn** on guitar, **Jim Keltner** on drums, **Terry Paul** on bass and **Carol Hunter, Donna Weiss** and **Brenda Patterson** on backing vocals, providing the song's heavenly choir. Performing the number in concert, Dylan usually adds an extra verse not in the version from the film, which begins "Wipe those tears offa my face, I can't see through them any more." Again, the words were a more or less exact description of the scene played out by Pickens and Jurado.

35. Forever Young

Recorded November 5 and 6 (two versions), 1973; available on *Planet Waves* and *Biograph* (original demo version)

Dylan wrote **Forever Young** in Tucson, Arizona, in early 1972, when his family spent much of the winter on a ranch he had bought north of Phoenix. He later described the circumstances in the liner notes to *Biograph*: "I wrote it thinking about one of my boys and not wanting to be too sentimental. The lines came to me, they were done in a minute. I don't know. Sometimes that's what you're given ... I certainly didn't intend to

The Music

write it. I was going for something else and the song wrote itself."

The boy he was thinking of was almost certainly **Jakob,** his youngest son, who had been born on December 9, 1969. He later went on to be the only of Dylan's children to become a musician and by the 1996 release of *Bringing Down The Horse*, the second album by his band The Wallflowers, Jakob's records were substantially outselling those of his father.

"Forever Young" was first recorded in an impromptu performance in June 1973 at the offices of Dylan's publishers in New York, when he sang it into an ageing reel-to-reel so that the words and music could be transcribed and copyrighted. Although the tape was later partially erased, the recording – a wonderfully moving and unselfconscious solo performance – was released in 1985 on *Biograph*. The first official release of the song came on *Planet Waves*, which featured two radically different versions recorded in November 1973 with The Band.

36. Tangled Up In Blue

Recorded December 30, 1974; available on *Blood On The Tracks* and *Bootleg Series Vols I–III* (alternative version)

There are those who will tell you that the opening track of *Blood On The Tracks* is the finest song Dylan has ever written: "A truly extraordinary epic of the personal, an unreliable narrative carved out of shifting memories like a five-and-a-half-minute musical Proust", Neil McCormick wrote in a critical reassessment of the album in 2003. Dylan himself claimed that **Tangled Up In Blue** took him "ten years to love and two years to write". Like much of the rest of the album, it was inspired by his estrangement from his wife **Sara,** the mother of his children and the healer of his soul, the dream woman he had idealized in **Sad Eyed Lady Of The Lowlands.**

Written while staying on his farm in Minnesota in July with his children, but without his wife, the song went through at least two "final" versions. The first was recorded in New York on September 16, 1974, and featured on test pressings of the album that were sent out that November. Over Christmas, Dylan asked his brother David's opinion of the album and, on his recommendation, cut fresh versions of several songs – with unknown local musicians in a Minneapolis studio on December 30. The re-takes included "Tangled Up In Blue", and this is the version that appeared on the album when it reached the shops less than three weeks later, on January 17.

The construction of the song is fascinating for the way that the meeting of the lovers, their relationship and the narrator's reflections are jumbled together during the seven verses, each of which captures a different fragment of the story. Dylan later revealed that he had attempted to capture the technique of a painter. "I was trying to do something that I didn't think had ever been done before. I wanted to defy time, so that the story took place in the present and the past at the same time. When you look at a painting you can see any part of it, or see it all together. I wanted that song to be like a painting." Later, during his "born again" phase, he changed some of the lyrics and introduced a biblical reference. A version of the song with revised words appeared on the 1984 album, *Real Live*.

What Sara Dylan made of it, we shall probably never know. With great dignity, in all the years since their divorce, she has never publicly spoken about their twelve-year marriage.

37. Idiot Wind

Recorded December 27, 1974; available on *Blood On The Tracks* and *Bootleg Series Vols I–III* (alternative version)

Even by the standards of *Blood On The Tracks*, **Idiot Wind** is one of the most painful songs Dylan ever wrote. His marriage to **Sara** is forensically examined and his heart laid painfully bare on lines such as "Peace and quiet's been avoiding me so long it seems like

living hell." Dylan clearly had some difficulty in coming to terms with the fact that out of this kind of torment and grief had come his most critically acclaimed set of songs in years: "A lot of people told me they enjoyed that album. It's hard for me to relate to that – I mean, people enjoying that type of pain," he complained when interviewed by his old friend Mary Travers (of Peter, Paul and Mary fame) on an Oakland radio station in March 1975, two months after the release of *Blood On The Tracks*.

The two versions of "Idiot Wind" that exist are quite different, both in attitude and lyrics. The first, recorded in **New York** on September 19, 1974, is more in sorrow than in anger, and full of a haunting despair. He re-recorded the song with altered lyrics in **Minneapolis** in December, ostensibly to make it less obviously autobiographical. Of course he didn't shoot a man called Gray, as the lyric claims. But the addition of such fictions only made the personal material all the more revealing, emphasized by the way the song is delivered as a howling, raging thing, spitting with bitterness and vengeance.

There has been speculation that the title of the song may have been inspired by Macbeth's meditation on the meaninglessness of life as "a tale told by an idiot, full of sound and fury, signifying nothing". A more probable source is the painter **Norman Raeben**, who taught Dylan in New York in 1975, and who had a saying about an "idiot wind blowing and blinding all human existence".

38. Simple Twist Of Fate

Recorded September 19, 1974; available on *Blood On The Tracks*

Any list of Dylan's fifty greatest songs could have included six or seven from *Blood On The Tracks*. But if we must restrict ourselves to just three, **Simple Twist of Fate** demands inclusion. Soft, mournful, hugely romantic and again painfully autobiographical, it boasts another powerful storytelling narrative and a strong claim to being one of the saddest songs ever written. As on "Tangled Up In Blue", past and present are merged as Dylan recounts the moment of parting between two lovers but attempts to preserve some emotional distance by projecting his own experience into the third person.

We're not deceived, of course. First, because of his total immersion in the moment, betrayed by a voice which no method actor could manage. And second, because he acknowledges the truth in the final verse when he declares "I still believe she was my twin": he's keeping the faith and hoping that another twist of fate will throw him and Sara together again. After the release of the album, husband and wife did attempt to reconcile their differences, but their reunion was ultimately disastrous and they divorced messily in 1977.

"A Simple Twist Of Fate" was not one of the *Blood On The Tracks* songs that Dylan felt compelled to re-record in Minneapolis after the album had been handed in to Columbia; the version heard on the record was cut in New York in September with Dylan's guitar and harmonica accompanied only by **Tony Brown's** bass.

39. Slow Train

Recorded May 3, 1979; available on *Slow Train Coming*

"I didn't want to write those songs at that period of time," Dylan admitted in conversation with Bono in 1984 about *Slow Train Coming*. "I wanted these songs out. But I didn't want to do it." In fact, he had toyed with the idea of giving them to girlfriend **Carolyn Dennis** to record. Many of his hard-core fans also didn't want him to record a born-again album, which appeared philosophically to countermand everything he had once represented. But whatever the arguments over his Christian conversion, they should not be allowed to obscure the fact that his newly-embraced religious fervour produced a great album, the white-hot core of which was **Slow Train**.

The song was first unveiled at a soundcheck for a gig at the end of Dylan's 1978 tour. This makes it the first fruit of his conversion, predating his enrolment in bible classes at the Vineyard Fellowship's "school of discipleship". Even opponents of Dylan's conversion have recognized the potency of the song. The production by **Jerry Wexler** and **Barry Beckett** sounds cleaner and friendlier on the ear than a lot of Dylan albums. The dramatic charge that comes from the energy of the apostate is striking, while the fire-and-brimstone prophecy of imminent apocalypse adds a potent spiritual terror. You can even argue, as Paul Williams does, that the song's "fierce bright penetrating howl of joy" finds Dylan regaining control of his sense of purpose.

For all of these reasons, "Slow Train" is not just a good Dylan song but a great one. And it was hardly the first time he had deployed biblical imagery. But many fans have a problem with the tone of the song, which in places sails dangerously close to the kind of language used by the jingoistically right-wing "born-again" fundamentalist lobby that was about to put Ronald Reagan in the White House. There's something unsettling about Dylan railing against "foreign oil controlling American soil" and "teaching pornography in schools" and he even lays himself open to accusations of racial prejudice with lines such as "sheikhs walking around like kings, wearing fancy jewels and nose rings". For many, "Slow Train" continues to leave a bad taste. But, despite such criticisms, it remains one of the best of his "born-again" songs.

40. The Groom's Still Waiting At The Altar

Recorded May 1981; available on *Shot Of Love* and *Biograph*

Anybody who bought *Shot Of Love* on its release in 1980 but failed to buy it again on its reissue on CD in 1986 missed the album's best song. For some inexplicable reason, Dylan omitted **The Groom's Still Waiting At The Altar** from his original running order for the album, instead throwing the song away as the B-side of the single **Heart Of Mine**. As soon as Dylan watchers heard it, they realised he had made a

serious mistake and the track even began to get radio play. The acclaim was such that Dylan eventually added the song to the reissue of *Shot Of Love* – the only time in his long career that an album has ever been changed after its release.

By the time of the reissue, Dylan had also responded to the demand of fans by including it on 1985's *Biograph* and unconvincingly attempted to explain his reasons for its original omission in the liner notes. "I listened back to the song and it felt too rushed," he said. "I felt we'd lost the original riff to the point where it was nonexistent. I listened back to it later and it sounded OK. But it wasn't really the way I wanted to play it." To the rest of the world, it sounded great and reminiscent of the fierce spirit of the *Highway 61 Revisited* material.

According to Dylan's account, the raw energy of the studio recording owed much to Ringo Starr and guitarist Danny Kootch. But there's also a magnificent live version with slightly different words circulating among collectors. Recorded in San Francisco on November 15, 1980, it features some devastating guitar playing from **Mike Bloomfield** (who had, of course, also played on *Highway 61 Revisited*). The other song he sat in on that night – his last stage appearance before his tragic death from a drug overdose – was "Like A Rolling Stone".

41. Every Grain Of Sand

Recorded May 1981; available on *Shot Of Love* and *Bootleg Series Vols I–III* (alternative version)

Before the belated addition of "The Groom's

The Music

Still Waiting At The Altar", the only song to achieve true greatness on Shot Of Love was the number that Dylan chose to close the album, **Every Grain Of Sand**. Besides the song's obvious religious nature, there's a self-portrait of isolation and despair at Dylan's failure to come to terms with what he calls "the reality of man", and this makes it one of the most moving lyrics he has ever written.

The admission that he's in a personal crisis ("the hour of my deepest need") means that the hectoring tone of many of Dylan's "born-again" songs is absent. He finds reassurance in God's presence all around – "In every leaf that trembles, in every grain of sand". But when he admits "other times it's only me", the song becomes a very human testament as well as a spiritual one. Written on his farm in **Minnesota** during the summer of 1980, and borrowing imagery from **William Blake**, it was "an inspired song that came to me", Dylan subsequently claimed. "I felt like I was just putting down words that were coming from somewhere else and I just stuck it out."

The album version of the song was recorded in an intense burst of activity in early May 1981, when Dylan recorded most of *Shot Of Love* in eight days. But the publishing demo he recorded in September 1980, with **Fred Tackett** on guitar and **Jennifer Warnes** on backing vocals, is equally sublime, and was released in 1991 on *The Bootleg Series Vols I–III*. **Nana Mouskouri** also recorded the song in 1981, after Dylan sent her a copy of the demo.

Bob in 1981, the year he recorded "The Groom's Still Waiting At The Altar" and "Every Grain Of Sand"

42. Jokerman

Recorded April/May 1983; available on *Infidels*

Many of Dylan's best songs have contained riddles and created their own sense of mystery. We still puzzle over the identity of Mr Jones, Queen Jane and the Sad Eyed Lady. And so it is with the song that opens the 1983 album *Infidels*. Is the Jokerman meant to be Dylan? Or Jesus Christ? Or Satan? Or perhaps all three? And is he related to the joker in "All Along The Watchtower"? Paul Williams has written brilliantly on the character, without coming up with any definite answers: "He's a clown, a hero, a fool, a devil, a saint, a joke, a mockery." Perhaps the nearest we can get to a conclusion is that the Jokerman is a projection of Dylan's own inner confusion and contradictions, expressed in a collage of images of the kind that only he knows how to create.

"Jokerman" may be a perplexing song. But it's also one of Dylan's most fascinating 1980s compositions, imbued with both grace and epic power. In the recording, **Mark Knopfler** and former Rolling Stone **Mick Taylor** provide the guitars, but the track is also given a subtle reggae feel by the Jamaican rhythm section of **Sly Dunbar** and **Robbie Shakespeare**. As Dunbar recalled, "Jokerman" was finished before they even realized they were recording: "He look at us and say, 'That's the take'. We couldn't believe how smooth it went."

When the song was released as a single, Dylan was persuaded – against his better judgement – to make a video to accompany it. MTV had been launched in 1981 and within two years was already claiming 16 million subscribers. But Dylan was unimpressed with the results. "All I saw was a shot of me from my mouth to my forehead on the screen," he told *Rolling Stone*. "I figure, 'Isn't that somethin'? I'm paying for that?'"

43. Blind Willie McTell

Recorded May 5,1983; available on *The Bootleg Series Vols I–III*

Willie McTell was born in 1901 and lived all of his life in Georgia. Blind from birth, his mother taught him to play guitar before he ran away from home in 1914 to play in medicine shows and on street corners. The acknowledged master of the twelve-string guitar, he sang in a warmer vocal style than many of the Delta bluesmen and made his first recordings in 1927. He was recorded by John Lomax in Atlanta in 1940 but had drifted into obscurity by the time of his death in 1959. That same year, **Sam Charters** kicked off the American folk-blues revival with an influential book and record called *The Country Blues*. It featured McTell's 1929 classic, **Statesboro Blues**, which is probably how an 18-year-old Bob Dylan first came to hear him.

Almost a quarter of a century after McTell's death, Dylan not only eulogized the great bluesman in the song that bears his name, but paid tribute to the entire heritage of African-American music, conjuring up a deep, dark and resonant dreamscape of the Old South populated by sweet magnolias blooming, plantations burning, chain gangs on the highway and ghostly slave ships.

The song was recorded for *Infidels* and its non-inclusion on that album is another of the perplexing decisions that characterized Dylan's career during the 1980s. He has since claimed he didn't think it was recorded "right" and "it never got developed in any way that it should have". Most fans beg to differ. When the track finally appeared on the official *Bootleg Series I–III* in 1991, one of his most vivid and heart-felt performances was revealed, with a soul-rending vocal that puts Dylan himself up there in the pantheon of the great blues singers.

44. Brownsville Girl

Recorded May 1986; available on *Knocked Out Loaded*

Less is often more. But seldom with Dylan, whose sustained epics from "Desolation Row" to "Sad Eyed Lady Of The Lowlands" have always counted among his most gripping compositions. The eleven-minute **Brownsville Girl** stands in that same great tradition and is by far the most outstanding track on the otherwise lacklustre *Knocked Out Loaded*.

The result of a collaboration with the playwright **Sam Shepard** (who Dylan had employed to write the script of the film *Renaldo & Clara*), the song was originally called **Danville Girl** or **New Danville Girl** and recorded for possible inclusion on 1985's *Empire Burlesque*. It didn't make the cut but was reworked in May 1986 with additional lyrics as "Brownsville Girl" in a gloriously half-sung, half-spoken version. Among the backing vocalists is **Carolyn Dennis**, who Dylan had recently married in secret after the birth of their daughter **Desirée Gabrielle**.

There's a remarkably penetrating analysis of both the song and the recorded performance in Michael Gray's magisterial *Song And Dance Man*. It's too long even to paraphrase here, but in his conclusion Gray detects genius in "every breath and pause, every unseen tilt of the head, every sung and every spoken syllable, every long line and every switch of mood … not a false moment, not a foot wrong". Yet according to Shepard, the song came about almost by accident. "We tossed around a bunch of ideas, none of which really got anywhere and then we just sort of started telling stories to each other," he recalled to Dylan-biographer Howard Sounes. "One of the stories that he began was actually the first line of that song. He says 'One day I was standing in line for this Gregory Peck film', and I said 'Why don't we just use that?'" From Dylan's recollection of watching **The Gunfighter**, they built an epic and absorbing seventeen-verse tale of the Old West, full of surprising, shifting images.

Shepard also offered an interesting insight into Dylan's modus operandi. The song is full of unusually long lines and the playwright was worried how all the words could be squeezed into the song's metre. "Don't worry about it. It'll work," Dylan told him. Inevitably it did. "The way he squashes phrasing and stretches it out is quite remarkable," Shepard noted afterwards.

Dylan once claimed the song was written partly in response to Lou Reed's **Doin' The Thing That We Want To,** which similarly starts with the writer going to the theatre to see a play. If so, it's a nice conceit, for the play in

Reed's song was Shepard's *Fool For Love*. As to the song's location – whether Danville or Brownsville – there are a dozen towns of both names spread across different states throughout the West. Similarly, the song appears suspended somewhere between history, fiction and myth.

45. Everything Is Broken

Recorded April 3,1989; available on *Oh Mercy*

In early 1989, on the recommendation of **Bono,** Dylan turned to **Daniel Lanois** to produce the follow-up to the previous year's *Down In The Groove,* which had received some of the worst reviews of his career. In a previously unpublished interview with this author in Los Angeles, February 2003, Lanois described the experience of watching Dylan at work. "I sat next to him for two months while he wrote the album and it was extraordinary," he recalled. "Bob overwrites. He keeps chipping away at his verses. He has a place for all his favourite couplets and those couplets can be interchangeable. I've seen the same lyrics show up in two or three different songs as he cuts and pastes them around, so it's not quite as sacred ground as you might think." **Everything Is Broken,** one of the most powerful songs on *Oh Mercy,* is a case in point. It was first cut in New Orleans in March 1989 as **Broken Days.** By April, Dylan had completely rewritten it and given it a new title.

The song reflects a familiar Dylan theme of the 1980s: a man who feels out of step with the prevailing ethos of his time. He once declared with all the moral certitude of a preacher that

the decade would be remembered by history as "the age of masturbation". The connection with everything he cared about was being broken. "It's all been neutralized, nothing threatening, nothing magical, nothing challenging. For me I hate to see it. It's like 'conscience' is a dirty word."

46. Most Of The Time

Recorded March 1989; available on *Oh Mercy*

Most Of The Time is the most atmospheric track on Dylan's best album of the 1980s. Part of that is due to the eerie dobro sound of producer **Daniel Lanois,** who also recruited a bunch of New Orleans musicians including **"Mean" Willie Green** on drums, **Brian Stoltz** on guitar and **Tony Hall** on bass to get what he called "that Louisiana swamp sound".

One day in March 1989, the band were waiting for Dylan in the house at 1305 Soniat Street where Lanois had set up his mobile studio. They passed the time by running through a new arrangement of one of his new songs. When he eventually walked in, Dylan listened and demanded, "So what's this supposed to be?" When they told him it was **Most Of The Time,** he picked up a guitar and said, "That's not how it goes. This is how it goes." The tape was rolling and the take that followed was the one that made the album. "I never did come up with any definite melody, only generic chords," Dylan confessed in *Chronicles.*

Lyrically it's a song about coping after the end of a love affair. The fact that the relationship is cast in the distant past has led some to infer

The Music

that, a dozen years after their divorce, Dylan was still thinking and writing about Sara.

47. Not Dark Yet

Recorded January 1997; available on *Time Out Of Mind*

Many of Dylan's fans have long regarded him as a prophet and so there was no real surprise when on 1997's **Not Dark Yet** he appeared to be describing his own end. Nothing particularly prescient about that, for we must all come to dust. But what gave Dylan's song a preternatural quality were the events that occurred between the recording of "Not Dark Yet" in January 1997 and its release in September that year.

In May he fell ill with **pericarditis**, a potentially fatal swelling of the sac around the heart. As Dylan himself later joked, for a time it seemed that he was about to meet Elvis. He recovered, but his close escape gave songs such as "Not Dark Yet" an almost spiritual resonance. As the writer Nick Johnstone has remarked, every time you hear him sing "It's not dark yet, but it's getting there," the world-weariness of his voice makes you feel "the ominous journey to that hospital bed already under way."

Assisted by the brooding quality of **Daniel Lanois'** impeccable production (the first time they had worked together since 1989's *Oh Mercy*), it's one of the finest performances not just of Dylan's later period but of his entire career. As Emmylou Harris told this writer in July 2003, "Not Dark Yet is the greatest song ever written about growing old. For those of us

who are entering that door, it brings up things we didn't even know we were capable of feeling. He put the poetry into that experience and it's one of my favourite records ever."

48. Love Sick

Recorded January 1997; available on *Time Out Of Mind*

October 1, 1997, on a blustery night in Bournemouth. It's the opening night of Bob Dylan's British tour and among the well-known classics – from "Like A Rolling Stone" to "Mr Tambourine Man" – he includes just one song from his new album, *Time Out Of Mind*. The song is **Love Sick** and, after the first three or four bars, an odd thing happens. The audience starts clapping. It spoke volumes for the obsessive dedication of Dylan's fanbase, for as *The Times* reported the following day, the song "was recognized instantly despite the fact that the new record has only been in the shops three days".

If he was only going to play one new song, it was a fine choice, too. "Love Sick" opens and sets the tone for the album with the stark stabs of **Augie Meyer**'s Farsifa organ offset against a spooky Dylan vocal. The latter, memorably described by Michael Gray as "choking phlegm", oozes the pain of betrayal from every syllable over a slow, claustrophobic beat that admits no daylight. "We treated the voice almost like a harmonica when you over-drive it through a small guitar amplifier", **Lanois** said in describing how he gave the vocal its melodramatic quality. On a less technical level, Dylan explained to *Newsweek*:

"It is a spooky record, because I feel spooky. I don't feel in tune with anything."

49. Things Have Changed

Recorded summer 1999; available on *Wonder Boys OST* and *The Best Of Bob Dylan Vol 2*

The track that finally won him an Academy Award, **Things Have Changed** was Dylan's first new song since 1997's *Time Out Of Mind*. It was also his first composition we heard that had been written since his close brush with death. The mortality crisis may have been over, but the lyrics are still preoccupied with impending doom: "I'm standing on the gallows with my head in a noose, Any minute now I'm expecting all hell to break loose," Dylan sings at one point. The chorus echoes one of his most familiar themes in later years, the notion of a man out of step with his times: "People are crazy and times are strange, I'm locked in tight but I'm out of range, I used to care but things have changed".

The first song he had written specifically for a film since "Knockin' On Heaven's Door" in 1973, "Things Have Changed" was used as both the main and end-title theme of *Wonder Boys*, staring Michael Douglas and directed by **Curtis Hanson** (whose other credits include *LA Confidential*). The rest of the soundtrack album on which the song appeared wasn't bad either, with offerings from a veritable who's who of 60s contemporaries, including Neil Young, Van Morrison, Leonard Cohen, John Lennon, Tim Hardin and Tom Rush.

50. High Water (For Charley Patton)

Recorded May 2001 in New York; available on *Love And Theft*

Like his song **Blind Willie McTell** almost two decades earlier, **High Water (For Charley Patton)** found Dylan once again paying homage to the Delta blues singers who had inspired him. The philosophy behind it was explained at length to Alan Jackson in the only interview he gave to a British journalist about the album. "When I survey the horizon, I don't see anyone who has the same influences as me and who has stuck to them. Realistically, my influences haven't changed and any time they have done, the music's gone off to a wrong place."

Asked in the same interview about how he responded to changing fashion, he dismissively waved his hand. "I just plough my own furrow regardless. The people I listen to were never fashionable, as far as I'm aware. Guthrie? Was he ever fashionable? I don't think so. Or Leadbelly? Or the great Robert Johnson? How many records did he sell in his lifetime? Very few. Whereas Al Jolson, he was fashionable. And what happens? In every era, the fashionable people go out of fashion as soon as the prevailing wind changes."

It's a brilliant exposition of what drives Dylan's own art and the name of Charley Patton belongs alongside Leadbelly and Johnson on the list he gave Jackson. Born in Mississippi in 1891, Patton was one of the originators of the blues. He taught Howlin' Wolf to play and was an influence on an entire generation of Delta bluesmen. He lived the life, too

– he was imprisoned, drunk heavily, had eight wives and was a consummate showman who played his guitar behind his back and above his head almost half a century before Jimi Hendrix performed the same trick. He made his first recordings in 1929 but died five years later of a chronic heart condition at the age of 43.

A longtime fan, Dylan claimed that the riff in "Highlands" on 1997's *Time Out Of Mind* was based on a Patton song (unidentified, although "Dry Well Blues" has been suggested). The same Dylan album also included "Dirt Road Blues", which in part derived from Patton's "Down The Dirt Road Blues". "High Water (For Charley Patton)" directly namechecks Patton's 1929 recording **High Water Everywhere**, written about the great Mississippi flood of two years earlier.

I Shan't Be Released
Dylan and the bootleggers

"The bootleg records, those are outrageous" Bob Dylan

The accolade of "most bootlegged artist in history" is a dubious honour, and a status Dylan has often railed against. He was the subject of the first-ever bootleg of the rock'n'roll era when *Great White Wonder* appeared in July 1969 – and, 35 years later, he was still keeping the illicit recording industry busy with his Never Ending Tour. Almost every one of the 100-plus shows a year he has played since 1988 has been taped and circulated among collectors.

Only **the Grateful Dead** rival him for the number of pirated recordings in circulation, although unlike the Dylan bootlegs, The Dead's "unofficial" CDs are hardly unauthorized: up until Jerry Garcia's death in 1995 the band made a point at their concerts of creating a special area by the mixing desk for the army of tapers. If they were going to be bootlegged, the band reasoned, they at least wanted to sound good.

Dylan, by contrast, has launched several lawsuits to stop the bootleggers and in 1985 he used the liner notes of the *Biograph* box set to launch a withering attack on the pirates: "The bootleg records, those are outrageous," he railed. "I mean they have stuff you do in a phone booth. Like nobody's around. If you're

The Music

just sitting and strumming in a motel, you don't think anybody's there, you know. It's like the phone is tapped and then it appears on a bootleg record. With a cover that's got a picture of you that was taken from underneath your bed and it's got a striptease type title and it costs 30 dollars. Amazing. Then you wonder why most artists feel so paranoid."

Just how paranoid was illustrated in a 1998 court case in which Dylan's right-hand man,

Jeff Rosen, described the security measures taken to keep demo tapes and other unreleased material from falling into the wrong hands: "The location of all such material is kept secret, doors and elevators require several key accesses, are fully alarmed and the most valuable material is maintained in vaults."

Today, with downloading and the instant technology to burn pirate CD-Rs at home in seconds, the bootlegging industry is estimated

Bob at Newport, inadvertently providing the 1964 sections of the *Folk Rogue* bootleg

The Music

to be worth five billion dollars a year. It's all a long way from the thick vinyl and plain white cardboard cover of *Great White Wonder*. This author's copy of the double LP, purchased in London in early 1970 from a dealer who continues to operate to this day, even goes to the subterfuge of a fake label that declares the record is by **Dupre and His Miracle Sound** and lists a bunch of fictitious track titles.

The bootlegging phenomenon was unwittingly launched by *Rolling Stone* editor Jann Wenner when, in June 1968, he reviewed a pirated tape under the headline "Dylan's Basement Tape Should Be Released". Within little more than a year, *Great White Wonder*, which included a selection of seven tracks from *The Basement Tapes*, was openly on sale in "underground" stores such as **The Psychedelic Supermarket** in Hollywood. Produced by two Californian hippies, the pirates were interviewed anonymously in *Rolling Stone* in 1969. "Dylan is a heavy talent and he's got all these songs nobody's ever heard," said one of the bootleggers, identified only as Patrick. "We thought we'd take it upon ourselves to make this music available." The record was soon circulating in Europe, too, originally in an edition pressed in Sweden.

In addition to the tracks from *The Basement Tapes*, *Great White Wonder* included a handful of outtakes and demos that Dylan had lodged with his publishers from 1963 to 1965, **Living The Blues** from a Johnny Cash TV show in 1969, and a plethora of tracks recorded in a Minnesota hotel room in December 1961.

On the album's release, the recordings were a complete revelation, filling in valuable gaps in Dylan's history. Early copies were of surprisingly decent sound quality, although the bootleg itself was soon being bootlegged with a reduction in sound quality each time it was copied. As there was no copyright protection in America until 1972, *Great White Wonder* was widely distributed and even got radio play on college and underground stations. It is claimed that the double LP eventually sold 350,000 copies, although by its very nature there is no way of checking this figure.

In the wake of its success, other Dylan bootlegs followed. **Little White Wonder** (known as *Waters Of Oblivion* in America) and *Troubled Troubadour* both unearthed more songs from *The Basement Tapes*. They were soon followed by the appropriately titled *Stealin'* and *GWW: Talkin' Bear Mountain Massacre Picnic Blues*, pressed in lurid green see-through vinyl. Live recordings, too, became a rich source of material, and early pirated concert releases included Dylan's most renowned bootleg of all, the electric half of the Royal Albert Hall/Manchester May 1966 show with The Hawks. It first appeared in Europe as early as 1970 under the title *In 1966 There Was* and, shortly after, as a double package called *Zimmerman Looking Back*, teamed with a December 1965 acoustic concert recorded at the Berkeley Community Theatre. The impact of bootlegging was such that the 1966 electric set became widely revered as one of the greatest live recordings ever made, even though it was not officially released by Columbia until 1998, as volume four of the official *Bootleg Series*.

"That Dylan boots outsell those by any other artist is hardly surprising, given that no other artist has stockpiled such a vast untapped archive in rock'n'roll history," according to Mick Houghton, who has been collecting Dylan recordings since his days writing for the British magazine *Let It Rock* in the early 1970s. "By comparison, The Beatles and Hendrix were stillborn, while even the other so-called singer/songwriter 'giants' like Bruce Springsteen or Van Morrison, don't come close to matching Dylan's prolific output. Even Neil Young, despite a reputation for discarding whole albums (Homegrown, Chrome Dreams, Times Square), is a relative minnow."

The ragbag that was *Self Portrait* (see p.180) was in part Dylan's "if you can't beat 'em, join 'em" response to the bootleggers, and a heavily truncated version of *The Basement Tapes* officially saw the light of day in 1975. But it wasn't until **Biograph** in 1985, which included seventeen previously unreleased tracks, that Dylan made a belated systematic response to the pirates. Then, in 1991, he released the official **Bootleg Series** with a three-CD package that included 58 rare or unreleased tracks. Yet the series, which at the time of writing had just reached volume six with the release of the 1964 New York Philharmonic Hall concert, has only exposed the merest tip of the iceberg. Even today, half of the tracks that appeared on the historic *Great White Wonder* a quarter of a century ago are still not officially available.

The nature of bootlegging in recent years has changed. With the demos and studio outtakes now either all out there or under the tight security that Jeff Rosen described, it is Dylan's ceaseless touring that has provided a bottomless well for the pirates. In contrast to the huge sales that *Great White Wonder* generated, the average run of a Dylan live bootleg today from the Never Ending Tour is probably no more than 500 to 1000. But while during the last 15 years, there have been only six Dylan studio albums, there have been in excess of 1600 gigs – and a high percentage of them are available, if you know where to look. In addition, Dylan has seldom recorded with his touring bands and so live tapes can often offer a radically different take or a new arrangement of a familiar composition. As Dylan said in 1989: "No two shows are the same. It might be the same song, but you find different things to do within that song which you don't think about the night before." This alone renders the live bootlegs an essential companion to the studio albums if we are to undertand Dylan's constantly evolving art.

Without entering into arguments about copyright and the ethics of bootlegging, on a musical level the pirates have undoubtedly done us a service. As Mick Houghton observes, "It's beyond question that some of his most famous bootlegs, like The Basement Tapes and Live At The Royal Albert Hall are of greater historical importance than many of the official records." In his more reflective moments, Dylan himself may also privately concede that the bootlegs have done him no real disservice, and that the efforts of the pirates have played an important part in the building of his legend.

I Shan't Be Released

Fifteen "must-own" Dylan bootlegs

There are literally hundreds of Dylan bootlegs, so it is impossible to catalogue them all here. The following is a selection of the most significant, chosen to represent different eras of his career. For more, take a stroll through **The Bob Dylan Bootleg Museum** at **www.bobsboots.com**

1. The Minnesota Tapes

A triple CD of the Minneapolis hotel-room recordings from May and December 1961. Some of the material was on the original *Great White Wonder* but it's fascinating to track the rapidity of Dylan's growth in the seven months that separate the two sessions.

2. The Gaslight Tapes

Recorded at the Gaslight Café in Greenwich Village in the autumn of 1962, this bootleg is still essential, for the official 2005 release *Live At The Gaslight* (via Starbuck's) is incomplete. The full bootleg adds seven more songs to the ten you get with your latte: "Hezekiah Jones", "No More Auction Block", "Motherless Children", "Ballad Of Hollis Brown", "Kindhearted Woman Blues", "See That My Grave Is Kept Clean" and "Ain't No More Cane".

3. The Witmark Years

After Dylan signed a publishing deal with Witmark Music, it became his practice to register new songs by recording demos of them in the publisher's New York office. Arranged chronologically, *The Witmark Years* includes 41 well-known and not so well-known songs, arranged chronologically from "Blowin' In The Wind" in summer 1962 to "Percy's Song" in 1964. Occasionally, the performances are a little stiff – they are only publisher's demos, after all. But it's a fascinating collection and the sound quality is mostly excellent.

4. The Freewheelin' Bob Dylan Outtakes

Includes the first electric sessions that produced the "Mixed Up Confusion" single, interpretations of Robert Johnson's "Milk Cow Blues", Woody Guthrie's "Sally Don't You Grieve" and Hank Williams' "(I Heard That) Lonesome Whistle", alongside unreleased originals including "Rambling Gambling Willie", "Talkin' John Birch Paranoid Blues" and "Let Me Die In My Footsteps", all originally slated for *Freewheelin'* but removed at the last minute. Further Dylan compositions not to have made the official album include "Hero Blues", "Talkin' Hava Nagielah Blues" and "The Death of Emmett Till". Another delight is an almost note-perfect copy of Elvis Presley's version of "That's Alright, Mama".

5. In Concert

Scheduled for release by CBS as a live album for Christmas 1963, featuring recordings from concerts at Carnegie Hall on October 26, and NYC Town Hall on April 12 that year, the bootleg even sports the original cover art, commissioned but never used. The album was scrapped because "The Times They Are A-Changin'" was already recorded and the songs for *Another Side Of Bob Dylan* followed so swiftly that there was simply no room in the release schedule.

The album opens with Dylan reciting an eight-minute poem, *Last Thoughts On Woody Guthrie* (also available on the official *Bootleg Series Vols I–III*) and of the other eight songs, only "When The Ship Comes In" ever appeared on an offical Dylan studio release. The protest songs "Who Killed Davy Moore?" and "Percy's Song" are among the highlights.

6. Folk Rogue

Spanning Dylan's contrasting appearances at the Newport Folk Festival in 1964 and 1965, the brief acoustic set from July 1964 includes "All I Really Want To Do", "To Ramona", "Chimes Of Freedom" and the as-yet-unreleased "Mr Tambourine Man", before Joan Baez joins him for an encore of "With God On Our Side". The infamous 1965 set, in which Dylan first turned up the volume, is discussed at length on p.48.

7. The Lonesome Sparrow Sings (aka Thin White Mercury Music)

The 1965/66 outtakes from Dylan's most exciting and innovative creative onslaught, arranged in chronological order: several of the tracks such as "Sittin' On A Barbed Wire Fence", "Phantom Engineer", "I Wanna Be Your Lover", "Tell Me, Momma" and "She's Your

Love Now" may be unfinished, but they still surge with visceral power. History in the making and a vital addendum to the *Bringing It All Back Home*, *Highway 61 Revisited* and *Blonde On Blonde* trinity.

8. A Tree With Roots

The most complete version of *The Basement Tapes* available contains 107 tracks, sumptuously packaged across four CDs. Listening to it makes one realize how Robbie Robertson not only remixed the life and energy out of the tracks on the official 1975 release, but that he also omitted some of Dylan's finest songs from the period, including "Sign Of The Cross", "All American Boy" and "All You Have To Do Is Dream". Equally essential are covers such as "The French Girl" and "Banks Of The Royal Canal", by the Irish playwright and occasional singer Brendan Behan.

9. Blood On The Tracks (New York Sessions)

Dylan dramatically altered *Blood On The Tracks* just three weeks before its January 1975 release, when he re-recorded five tracks in Minneapolis. This bootleg restores the album to the original format of the test pressing made at A&R Studios, New York, in September 1974. If anything. the radically different earlier takes of "Tangled Up In Blue", "Idiot Wind", "Lily Rosemary And The Jack Of Hearts", "You're A Big Girl Now" and "If You See Her, Say Hello" have even more intimacy and hurt than the versions that made the official release.

The Minneapolis Tapes

During 1960 and early 1961, Dylan's artistry was developing with astonishing rapidity. He still wasn't writing much of his own material, but he was mastering his craft, learning and performing literally dozens of new songs mined from the rich vein of traditional folk music, the blues and the Woody Guthrie songbook. By the time he recorded his first album in New York, in November 1961, he had refined this material into his own unique style. But it's fascinating to hear his search for his own musical identity taking shape during this period via a series of widely circulated tapes made by friends in Minneapolis.

The earliest was recorded by Bonnie Beecher, some time in the autumn of 1960, in a Minneapolis apartment. It contains versions of the traditional **Red Rosey Bush** and **Johnny We Hardly Knew You**, Woody Guthrie's **Jesus Christ** (to the tune of **Jesse James**), **I'm A Gambler**, Jimmie Rodgers' **Blue Yodel**, **Muleskinner Blues**, the Memphis Jug Band's **K.C. Moan**, and a sequence of four talking blues including Guthrie's **Talkin' Columbia** and **Talkin' Merchant Marine** plus **Talkin' Inflation Blues** and an improvised song for one of Dylan's roommates called **Talkin' Hugh Brown**.

The tape shows he's some way short of the finished article and his guitar work is crude. But several of the elements are already in place. The timing on "Red Rosey Bush" is idiosyncratic but brilliant, while on "Johnny We Hardly Knew You" he dramatically

affects an Irish accent. His self-absorption in his art is obvious, and yet the effect is charming and likeable.

In May 1961, when he had already been in New York for four months, he returned to Minneapolis, where Tony Glover recorded 25 songs at Bonnie Beecher's apartment. Subsequently circulated as *The Minneapolis Party Tape*, the mixture is similar to before – traditional folk and blues songs such as **Will The Circle Be Unbroken**, **Death Don't Have No Mercy** and **Wild Mountain Thyme**, and almost a dozen numbers associated with Guthrie, including **Pastures Of Plenty**. There's also a whimsical original called **Bonnie, Why'd You Cut My Hair**, apparently a reference to a scalping his girlfriend had given him the previous year. He's good and getting better, with one of the most appealing moments coming on "Pastures Of Plenty", which Dylan prefaces by declaring that Woody had told him "I sing it better than everybody". As he says it, he somehow manages to sound both boastful and humble at the same time.

The third Minneapolis tape is the best known. Recorded again by Glover at Bonnie Beecher's apartment, many of the 26 songs appeared on *Great White Wonder*, the world's first-ever bootleg album (which appeared in 1969). The quality of the performances is superb, but that's no surprise as it was recorded on December 22, 1961 – a month after the sessions with John Hammond that produced Dylan's first Columbia album (see p.167–168).

10. Rock Solid

Another live recording which was originally scheduled for official release but later dropped, reportedly because CBS was uncertain about how to promote Dylan's gospel songs. Recorded at Massey Hall, Toronto, on April 19, 1980,

some prefer the bootleg of the following night, released as *Solid Rock*, but both brim with the raw passion of his born-again fervour. Then again, there are those who will tell you that *Contract With The Lord Volumes 1 And 2* is even better, recorded during his two-week residency in San Francisco in November 1979. Whichever recording you go for, there are none of the old hits, only songs that serve the Lord, such as "Slow Train", "Precious Angel" and "In The Garden".

11. Stadiums Of The Damned (aka Child's Balloon)

A double CD recorded in New Orleans in November 1981. Once again, it was recorded by CBS for a possible live album, and the sound quality is immaculate. By now Dylan had relented from the uncompromising attitude of the first born-again tour and was playing blasts from the past alongside the gospel material. The set includes the only ever live performance of "Thief On The Cross".

12. Rough Cuts

Infidels was one of several albums in the 1980s that Dylan perversely altered between recording and release to produce an inferior collection that didn't reflect the best of what he had achieved in the studio. The double live-in-the-studio CD *Rough Cuts* contains the outtakes from the month-long *Infidels* sessions at the Power Station, New York, during April/May 1983. Several of the rejected tracks, including "Foot Of Pride" and "Blind Willie McTell", later turned up on the official *Bootleg Series* but there are still plenty of outtakes and unreleased songs here that capture a brilliant line-up that, sadly, never toured with Dylan.

13. The Genuine Bootleg Series

Columbia's official *Bootleg Series* has still only scratched the surface of the unreleased Dylan archive. Thus, some bright spark came up with the notion of an unofficial companion to the officially sanctioned *Bootleg Series*. Like the 1991 Columbia release, the *Genuine Bootleg Series* is a three-CD package that spans Dylan's entire career. The series has now gone on to encompass two further three-CD packages.

14. From The Vaults Vols I and II

That there hasn't been an official live release yet from the Never Ending Tour is perhaps surprising, although a large number of live tracks from the 1990s have been made available at different times as official downloads from www.bobdylan.com. The two volumes of *From The Vaults* compile these tracks and, as they are taken from official sources, the sound quality is fantastic. On the other hand, as there are almost as many bootlegs as there have been gigs in recent years, you may prefer to seek out the recording of the particular night on which you were lucky enough to catch the man.

15. Never Ending Covers

During the Never Ending Tour, Dylan has played an astonishing number of covers. Some of them have been one-off performances, never to be heard again. Others have become staples. The nine-CD box set *Never Ending Covers* compiles 130 of them, recorded between 1988 and 2000. From The Beatles' "Nowhere Man" to Charles Aznavour's "The Times We've Known", it's a mind-boggling collection that ranges from the convincing and inspired to the bewildering "why did he do that?" awfulness.

Curiosities & Covers
Dylan Top 10s

Ten comic Dylan songs

"He's an absolute fucking riot!"
Chrissie Hynde on Dylan, August 2003

1. Talkin' John Birch Paranoid Blues
Available on *The Bootleg Series Vols I–III* (1991)

The John Birch Society was a right-wing orga-nization, born in the McCarthyite era, obsessed with imagined communist infiltration. In Dylan's sharp satire, a member of the society looks under his bed for a Red, up his chimney, in the glove compartment of his car and down his toilet. Less amusingly, Dylan was banned from singing the song on *The Ed Sullivan Show* in May 1963. To his credit, he walked off the set and refused to appear on the programme.

2. I Shall Be Free
Available on *The Freewheelin' Bob Dylan* (1963)

Given the intensity of the protest and the poignancy of the love songs on *Freewheelin'*, Dylan decided he'd better leave 'em laughing. The hilarious "I Shall Be Free" namechecks Yul Brynner, Charles de Gaulle and President Kennedy, who calls up Dylan and asks him what will make the country grow. "Brigitte Bardot, Anita Ekberg, Sophia Loren … country'll grow" comes the answer. OK, it loses something on the page. But on the record his timing is master-ful and, on such form, an alternative career in stand-up could have awaited.

3. I Shall Be Free No. 10
Available on *Another Side Of Bob Dylan* (1964)

Sadly, Dylan never released "I Shall Be Free" numbers two to nine, if they ever existed. But when he found himself getting over-serious on *Another Side Of Bob Dylan*, as he picked at the scabs of his break-up with Suze Rotolo, he lightened proceedings with a comic talk-ing blues that sounds as if it was more or less delivered on the hoof, and which contains the self-mocking, "I'm a poet, and I know it, hope I don't blow it…"

4. Motorpsycho Nightmare

Available on *Another Side Of Bob Dylan* (1964)

The other lighter moment on *Another Side*, "Motorpsycho Nightmare" can "be read as a broad satire on the antagonism between bohemian urban cool and reactionary rural conservatism", as Andy Gill writes. "But why bother?" Much better simply to enjoy the joke, as Dylan yells "I like Fidel Castro and I like his beard" at a reactionary farmer who responds by throwing a copy of the *Reader's Digest* at his head.

5. Bob Dylan's 115th Dream

Available on *Bringing It All Back Home* (1965)

In which Dylan's comic wit turns epic. His "115th Dream" is a satirical vision of the great American Dream, in which the *Mayflower* is skippered by Captain Ahab from Melville's *Moby Dick*. Renamed "Arab" for the occasion, he waves good luck to Christopher Columbus on a surreal voyage to disinvent the New World.

6. Please Mrs Henry

Available on *The Basement Tapes* (1975)

Typical of the bonhomie of *The Basement Tapes*, "Please Mrs Henry" is a drinking song in which a penniless Dylan begs the barmaid for another drink, makes a clumsy pass at her and ends up practically pissing himself ("if I walk too much farther my crane's gonna leak") before collapsing in laughter in the final chorus.

7. You Ain't Goin' Nowhere

Available on *Greatest Hits Volume 2* (1971) and *The Essential Bob Dylan* (2002)

After Dylan had recorded the amiable "You Ain't Goin' Nowhere" with The Band in Woodstock in 1967, Roger McGuinn and The Byrds covered the song on their ground-breaking country-rock album *Sweetheart Of The Rodeo* the following year. In response, Dylan re-recorded the song in 1971 with new lyrics that took a gentle dig at The Byrds' leader. "Pack up your money, pull up your tent, McGuinn 'cos you ain't a-goin' nowhere."

8. Clothes Line Saga

Available on *The Basement Tapes* (1975)

"Clothes Line Saga" is Dylan's parody of "Ode To Billie Joe", a 1967 hit for Bobbie Gentry about a suicide. Nobody dies in Dylan's song. But imitating Gentry's narrative style, it is off-handedly reported that the previous night downtown, the vice president has gone mad. "Hmm, say, that's too bad," Dylan sings before folk go back to the far more important business of seeing whether the clothes are dry on the line.

9. Wiggle Wiggle

Available on *Under The Red Sky* (1990)

At least, you hope Dylan meant it as a joke. "Wiggle to the front, wiggle to the rear, wiggle til you wiggle right out of here," he sings, before bizarrely exhorting us to "wiggle like a bowl of soup." It's all most perplexing. But when he concludes by hissing, "Wiggle like a big fat snake," the erotic-comic effect produces such a broad smile that you forgive the song's utter banality.

10. Cry A While

Available on *Love And Theft* (2001)

Love And Theft must be the funniest album of Dylan's entire career. The humour is there in almost every song with throwaway lines such as "Jump into the wagon love, throw your panties overboard," "I'm sitting on my watch, so I can be on time," "I'm no pig without a wig," "Freddie or not, here I come" and, best of all, in "Cry A While": "Last night across the alley there was a pounding on the wall, it must have been Don Pasquale making a 2am booty call."

Ten must-own Dylan rarities

Despite the Biograph box set and the official *Bootleg Series*, Dylan's recorded work is still littered with rarities and obscure tracks not found on any regular album release. Here are ten collector's items that, with a little perseverance, you might be lucky enough to hunt down without resorting to bootlegs...

1. Ye Playboys and Playgirls (1963)

A duet with Pete Seeger, recorded at the 1963 Newport Folk Festival. It appeared later that same year on the Vanguard album *Newport Broadside (Topical Songs)* and in the UK on a seven-inch EP.

2. Talkin' Devil (1963)

Along with demo versions of "John Brown" and "Only A Hobo", recorded for the folk magazine *Broadside*, the brief talking blues "Talkin' Devil" was released for contractual reasons under the pseudonym Blind Boy Grunt on *Broadside Ballads Vol 1* in 1963.

3. House Of The Risin' Sun (1964)

In December 1964, producer Tom Wilson went into the studio with Dylan's 1962 acoustic recording of "House Of The Risin' Sun" and overdubbed electric instrumentation in imitation of The Animals' hit version of the song. He did so without Dylan's knowledge and the track was never released until it somewhat oddly appeared on a CD-ROM version of *Highway 61 Revisited* in 1995.

4. I Ain't Got No Home (1968)

In January 1968, Dylan emerged from his Woodstock retreat to appear with The Band at a Woody Guthrie tribute concert at New York's Carnegie Hall. Their performance of three Guthrie songs – "The Grand Coulee Dam", "Dear Mrs Roosevelt" and, best of all, a blistering "I Ain't Got No Home" – were included on the album *Tribute To Woody Guthrie Vol One*, now long deleted. "The Grand Coulee Dam" was later included on the album *Bob Dylan Live 1961–2000*.

5. New Morning (1971)

"Is it rolling, Bob?," Dylan famously asks producer Bob Johnson at the beginning of "To Be Alone With You" on 1969's *Nashville Skyline*. He repeated the trick two years later on *New Morning*, jauntily declaring "here we go" at the start of the title track. But you will need to find an early vinyl copy to hear it, for the line was later deleted.

6. George Jackson (1971)

A dramatic return to the protest format, recorded in November 1971, "George Jackson" was released as a single just a week after it had been cut, with a big-band version on the A-side and an acoustic take on the flip. The former appeared on the 1978 Japanese compilation **Masterpieces**. The B-side did not.

7. Wallflower (1972)

Dylan recorded the lovely, country-tinged "Wallflower" at the same sessions that produced "George Jackson". That verson of the song eventually appeared on *The Bootleg Series Vols I–III* some twenty years later. But an even better take of the song, prominently featuring Dylan, appeared on the late Texan rocker Doug Sahm's 1972 album **Doug Sahm And Band**. Dylan's heard on guest vocals on two other tracks on the album, too.

8. Rita May (1976)

A slight but appealing *Desire* outtake co-written with Jacques Levy and released as a single in 1976, coupled with a live version of "Stuck Inside Of Mobile With The Memphis Blues Again" from the *Hard Rain* album. Its only appearance on LP came two years later on the Japanese-released *Masterpieces* set.

9. Renaldo & Clara (1978)

A soundtrack album from the film *Renaldo & Clara* was never released. But Columbia did circulate a four-track promotional disc that included "People Get Ready", "Never Let Me Go", "Isis" and "It Ain't Me, Babe".

10. Trouble In Mind (1979)

This dark slice of blues was recorded for, but then omitted from, *Slow Train Coming*. The track was released instead as the B-side of the album's first single, "Gotta Serve Somebody".

Ten songs with Dylan in 'em

1. Way Back In The 1960s

Incredible String Band (1967)

Robin Williamson cast himself in the role of an old man looking back on his youth in the 1960s – from an imagined vantage point of somewhere in the middle of the 21st century – in this song from The Incredibles' second album *5000 Spirits Or The Layers Of The Onion*. "There was one fellow singing in those days and he was quite good," he nostalgically recalled. "I mean to say that his name was Bob Dylan…"

2. Hey Bobby
Country Joe and the Fish (1970)

To the likes of Country Joe MacDonald, Dylan's apparent abandonment of radical causes after 1966 was unforgivable. "Hey Bobby, where you been? Missed you out on the streets, Hear you got yourself another scene, it's called a retreat," MacDonald chided on this song from *CJ Fish*, his final album with the band. And his anger gets even more self-righteous: "Sick and tired of hearing your lies, Takes nothing less than truth to get me high."

3. Song For Bob Dylan
David Bowie (1971)

"That song laid out what I wanted to do in rock. It was at that period that I said 'OK, if you don't want to do it, I will'. I saw the leadership void," a coked-up Bowie told *Melody Maker* in 1976, explaining not only why he'd written Bob a song on *Hunky Dory* but also why we didn't need Dylan any more because we had the Thin White Duke instead.

4. Telegram Sam
T Rex (1972)

"Bobby's all right, Bobby's all right, he's a natural born poet, he's just outta sight," Marc Bolan philosophized on T Rex's chart-topping hit. John Peel once claimed he had seen Bolan write the entire lyric to a song in a BBC lift between reception and studio; you can't help thinking it was probably "Telegram Sam". Heaven knows who Sam was, but Bobby the "natural born poet" could surely only be one person.

5. Looking Into You
Jackson Browne (1972)

"The great song traveler passed through here and he opened my eyes to the view, And I was among those who called him a prophet and I asked him what was true," Browne crooned earnestly on his 1972 debut album as he gave voice to the debt every songwriter of the era owed to Dylan. Suitably inspired and with his dues paid, in the song Browne then goes off to search "for the truth that is my own".

6. Garden Party
Rick Nelson (1972)

"Over there in the corner much to my surprise was Mr Hughes, hid in Dylan's shoes, wearing his disguise," former teen star Ricky Nelson sang on his superb journey through rock'n'roll's past. As well as **Howard Hughes** and Bob, the likes of John and Yoko and Chuck Berry are also commemorated before Rick concludes in Dylanesque fashion, "If memories were all I sung, I'd rather drive a truck."

7. I'm So Restless
Roger McGuinn (1973)

Having built his Byrds career plundering Dylan's back catalogue, on "I'm So Restless" from his debut solo album, McGuinn looked critically in turn at the example set by rock's unholy trinity of Mr D (Dylan), Mr J (Jagger) and Mr L (Lennon), only to reject them all. Despite Mr M's remarkable lack of gratitude, Mr D was generous enough to play harmonica on the track.

8. Diamonds and Rust
Joan Baez (1975)

"Well I'll be damned, here comes your ghost again … the unwashed phenomenon, the original vagabond," Baez sang on "Diamonds and Rust". Dylan was clearly touched by the song and during the Rolling Thunder tour, he asked Baez to perform it in his dressing room for him. When he got the title wrong, Baez paid him back by teasing him she had really written the song for her husband, David. A gullible Dylan swallowed the story and, according to the account in Baez's book *And A Voice To Sing With*, he was crestfallen.

9. Talking New Bob Dylan Blues
Loudon Wainwright (1991)

"I didn't start writing until '68, It was too damn daunting, you were too great, I won a whole lot of Bob Dylan imitation contests though," Wainwright deadpanned in this hilarious tribute written for the great man's 50th birthday. Then he offered a rapid-fire appraisal of the Dylan canon ("Self Portrait? Well it was an interesting effort") and lined up Prine, Springsteen and himself as Big Bob's "dumb-ass kid brothers".

10. Mr Jones
Counting Crows (1993)

Even a fictional character in a Dylan song could inspire further songs. John Lennon was the first to namecheck the hapless Mr Jones from "Ballad Of A Thin Man" when he sang, "Feel so suicidal, just like Dylan's Mr Jones" in "Yer Blues" on The Beatles' *White Album*. Then came Counting Crows, whose Adam Duritz on their debut album sang, "I want to be Bob Dylan, Mr Jones wants to be someone just a little more funky…"

The twenty best cover versions

A purely subjective list of the obvious and not-so-obvious…

1. The Band: When I Paint My Masterpiece
Available on *Cahoots* (1971)

2. The Byrds: Mr Tambourine Man
Available on *Mr Tambourine Man* (1965)

3. Julie Driscoll, Brian Auger and The Trinity: This Wheel's On Fire
1968 single, available on *A Kind Of Love In* (1967–71)

4. Fairport Convention: Percy's Song
Available on *Unhalfbricking* (1969)

5. Thea Gilmore: I Dreamed I Saw St Augustine
Available on *Songs From The Gutter* (2002)

6. Emmylou Harris: Every Grain of Sand
Available on *Wrecking Ball* (1995)

7. Jimi Hendrix: All Along The Watchtower
Available on *Electric Ladyland* (1968)

8. Tracy Nelson: It Takes A Lot To Laugh, It Takes A Train To Cry
Available on *Tracy Nelson* (1974)

9. Spirit: Like A Rolling Stone
Available on *Spirit Of 76* (1976)

10. Youssou N'Dour: Chimes Of Freedom

Available on *Wommat (The Guide)* (1994)

11. Sinead Lohan: To Ramona

Available as a single (2001)

12. Johnny Cash: It Ain't Me Babe

Available on *The Essential Johnny Cash* (2002)

13. K.T. Tunstall: Tangled Up in Blue

Available as a single (2006)

14. Cowboy Junkies: If You Gotta Go, Go Now

Available on *Rarities, B-Sides and Slow, Sad Waltzes* (1999)

15. The Specials: Maggie's Farm

Available on *Best Of The Specials* (2000)

16. Nina Simone: Just Like Tom Thumb's Blues

Available on *The Very Best Of Nina Simone* (1998)

17. Christy Moore: The Lonesome Death Of Hattie Carroll

Available on *Burning Times* (2005)

18. Johnny Rivers: Positively Fourth Street

Available on *Realization* (1967) – nominated by Dylan as his own favourite cover of any of his songs

19. Richie Havens: Just Like A Woman

Available on *Mixed Bag* (1966)

20. The Handsome Family: Just Like Tom Thumb's Blues

Available on *Uncut Presents Highway 61 Revisited Revisited* (2005)

Ten improbable covers

What on earth were they thinking?

1. **The Chipmunks:** Mr Tambourine Man

2. **Burl Ives:** The Times They Are A-Changin'

3. **Jonathan King:** Million Dollar Bash

4. **James Last:** Like A Rolling Stone

5. **Cliff Richard:** Blowin' In The Wind

6. **William Shatner:** Mr Tambourine Man

7. **Nancy Sinatra:** It Ain't Me Babe

8. **The US Navy Steel Band:** Blowin' In The Wind

9. **Lawrence Welk:** Don't Think Twice, It's All Right

10. **Mae West:** If You Gotta Go, Go Now

Part 3:
The Movies

> *"I'm not a movie star. But I've got a vision to put up on the screen."*

Bob Dylan, January 1974

Dylan in the Movies

Don't Look Back

D.A. Pennebaker, 1965

"One of the most influential rock films ever made." – TIME OUT NEW YORK

The first, and arguably still the greatest, rock documentary of them all got off to an initially unpromising start. According to the story long told by director D.A. Pennebaker, **Albert Grossman**, Dylan's manager, walked into the filmmaker's New York office one day and announced, "I represent Bob Dylan. Is anybody here interested in making a film about him?" But Pennebaker was out at the time, and his business partner, **Richard Leacock**, allegedly asked Grossman, "Who's Bob Dylan?" Fortunately, Grossman was undeterred and returned later, when Pennebaker was in, to ask if he would like to accompany Dylan and film him on his forthcoming 1965 British tour. "Sure," he answered.

Born in Illinois in the 1930s, Pennebaker had begun making documentary films in the early 1950s, and by the 1960s he was making programmes for the TV networks ABC and NBC. Agreeing to fund the making of the film himself, Pennebaker came to a handshake deal with Dylan in a New York restaurant. Using handheld 16mm cameras, and working to a tight budget, he and his crew arrived in Britain with Dylan and his entourage on April 26, 1965. They began work immediately, filming Bob disembarking the plane, and at the press conference held immediately after in **Heathrow Airport**'s VIP lounge – at which Dylan promptly set the tone for the entire tour and film, holding a giant light-bulb and offering surreal answers to the questions.

Thirteen days later, on May 8, Pennebaker filmed what was to become *Don't Look Back*'s iconic opening scene in an alley at the back of London's Savoy Hotel. In effect, what they shot that day was the world's first music video, as Dylan held up a series of placards containing the words to **Subterranean Homesick Blues**. The concept was Dylan's own and the footage was later shown on British TV as a stand-alone promo film when the song was released as a single.

Dylan allowed Pennebaker – who he nicknamed **The Eye** – almost unrestricted access, with the result that some highly candid footage appears in the film. At one point, Dylan throws a tantrum during a party in his hotel room at the Savoy, yelling, "Who threw the fucking glass? If somebody doesn't tell me who did it, you're all gonna get outta here and never come back." Other scenes show him freezing out **Joan Baez,** and turning savagely on a would-be interviewer from a student newspaper.

Some, including **The Beatles**, who were in attendance while Dylan held court, astutely managed to stay out of camera shot. But, for the most part, Pennebaker could hardly believe his luck. Dylan attracted a coterie of fascinating characters drawn from London's bohemian hinterland and beyond. It was like the circus had come to town. All that Pennebaker, the fly on the wall, had to do was point and shoot.

The result is an extraordinary portrait of a chameleon-like Dylan, that on the surface appears remarkably raw and honest. "He is at times disengagingly charming, at others blisteringly acerbic. Hip one second, petulant the next," C.P. Lee wrote in *Like A Bullet Of Light – The Films Of Bob Dylan*. "Dylan can be shown snarling, swearing, singing, smiling, shining and sulking and still be the genius he is," Ralph Gleason enthused.

Yet although it is *cinéma vérité*, at the same time there's no doubt that Dylan is in one sense very much "acting" for the camera. "It's not so much 'about' Dylan", Pennebaker said of his film. "Because Dylan is sort of acting throughout the film. And that's his right. He needs some protection in a sense against that process. But I think that what you do find out

a little bit is the extraordinary pressure of having to go out and be absolutely perfect. He had to be extraordinary where most of us settle for just being adequate."

Needless to say, the music is magnificent. Although we never get full-length versions of the songs, at least as interesting as the in-concert footage are the snippets of Dylan playing backstage and in hotel rooms, in which we get to see the process of songwriting at work.

Back in **New York** by the end of May 1965, Pennebaker took his time assembling the footage into a movie. It wasn't until April 1966 that he had a finished cut to show Dylan who, to his credit, ultimately made no alterations. "When Bob first saw the film, he was shocked and said we needed a lot of changes," Pennebaker recalled. "The second time he saw it with a writing pad in his hand, he came out saying 'no changes'." Dylan did suggest that the glass-throwing scene in the hotel room should be excised. But when Pennebaker told him, "I think it matters to the story and I can't cut it out," he raised no further objection.

Don't Look Back finally premiered in **San Francisco** on May 17, 1967. Today it is widely acknowledged as the groundbreaking template for all future "rockumentaries". Yet at the time the reviews were distinctly mixed. "A relentlessly honest, brilliantly edited documentary permeated with the troubadour-poet's music", *Variety* enthused, and the *LA Times* found it a "continuously engrossing and revealing portrait of Dylan and his milieu. The camera has become an X-Ray." But middle America failed to comprehend the portrayal of Dylan's hipster world at all. "The worst film I've ever seen," wrote one reviewer in the *Kansas City Star*. "A sort of boring off-color home movie of the neighborhood's biggest brat blowing his nose for 90 minutes," the *Atlanta Journal* complained. The bad reviews were reprinted like badges of honour at the back of the Ballantine paperback edition of the film's transcript.

Dylan himself later complained that the film "showed only one side" and "made it seem like I wasn't doing anything but living in hotel rooms, playing the typewriter and holding press conferences." He has a point. The entire film was shot in a brief two-week period, while he was living in a tour bubble. But, as a portrait of the unreal world in which he was existing at the time, it's as real as it gets.

Eat The Document

D.A. Pennebaker/Bob Dylan, 1966

One of the characteristics of Dylan's career has been a fear of repeating himself. Which is perhaps why he turned against *Eat The Document*. The film was essentially conceived as a second *Don't Look Back* – another European tour, this time with The Hawks, filmed by D.A. Pennebaker with his hand-held camera once again in *cinéma vérité* style.

Yet there were differences. This time, ABC Television came up with a $100,000 advance for a 60-minute documentary, to be part of a series called *Stage 66*. Dylan vetoed the original title of *Dylan By Pennebaker*, insisting that it was going to be his movie. "He wanted

to direct it, and he asked me if I would help him film it," Pennebaker says. Shot on the infamous May 1966 tour, during which Dylan was heckled for the electric half of his concerts, another big difference is that, unlike the previous year's movie, the film is in colour.

Eat The Document opens with Dylan taking a snort of something while seated at the piano. According to Pennebaker, Dylan told him "Rick Danko and I are going to snort some methedrine. This is what it's like. This is life on the road. Film it, let truth be our judge." How he thought ABC Television was ever going to screen that particular scene, heaven only knows. Later on, the film includes a notorious scene in which Dylan and John Lennon sprawl in the back of a limousine, clearly whacked to the gills on something or other.

Some of the cast are familiar from *Don't Look Back*, including **Albert Grossman**, road manager **Bobby Neuwirth**, and **Howard Alk** and his wife **Jones**, who again assisted Pennebaker with the filming. But the presence of **The Hawks** adds a new dimension, while the cast of celebrities traipsing through Dylan's court this time around includes **Johnny Cash**, **Steve Winwood** and **Cathy McGowan**, presenter of the TV show *Ready Steady Go!*.

The end result is far more confused and fragmentary than *Don't Look Back* – and this has to be put down to the fact that Pennebaker had much less control. "Dylan was a very peculiar director," Pennebaker says. "He didn't know what he wanted and people wandered around, so you ended up filming things for no particular reason."

The music, which should perhaps have been central as Dylan and The Hawks were hitting astonishing peaks of intensity and controversy during their electric sets, takes a back seat to the surreal tableaux of disorientating off-stage scenes, some of which were clearly set up. But extracts from **Tell Me Mama, Baby Let Me Follow You Down, I Don't Believe You, Like A Rolling Stone** and **Ballad Of A Thin Man** give a flavour of the music's excitement. **Mr Tambourine Man** is the only song from the acoustic set to make it into the film.

Pennebaker reportedly has his own out-takes from the film, which include more of the music. His own, tantalizing recollections of watching Dylan and The Hawks during the tour makes you all the more hungry to see them. "It was the first time I had ever seen Dylan really happy in the middle of the music," he said. "He was jumping around like a cricket and the music was incredible. The sound of that band was the best sound I ever heard."

Back in New York after the tour was over, Pennebaker began to put together a rough edit for Dylan, who spent two or three days looking at the rushes in late July 1966. Then came the **motorcycle accident**. Pennebaker visited Dylan shortly afterwards in Woodstock. But, notwithstanding any injuries he had suffered, Dylan then took over the editing, with assistance from Howard Alk. When they missed the deadline to make that autumn's TV schedules, Dylan was forced to pay back ABC's advance. That gave him total control over the footage, and much of it he destroyed, cutting the original film with scissors and throwing the unused footage in the garbage.

Dylan and Alk finished editing sometime in early 1967, although the film was not premiered until February 1971 at the **Academy of Music** in New York. Screenings of *Eat The Document* have been very rare since, although it was shown in 1998 in Los Angeles, when it was accompanied by a panel discussion featuring Pennebaker and **Mickey Jones**, Dylan's drummer on the tour.

As a postscript, in early 2004 Jones released a DVD of his home movies shot on the tour (available as *World Tour 1966 – The Home Movies: Through The Camera Of Bob Dylan's Drummer Mickey Jones*). The footage is frankly disappointing. There's little sign of Dylan and none of the music but plenty of shots of hotels and tourist sights. But the commentary in which Jones recalls the historic tour is interesting enough. Bootleg DVDs of *Eat The Document* itself are surprisingly easy to find, if you know where to look.

Pat Garrett And Billy The Kid

Sam Peckinpah, 1973

When Dylan received the screenplay for **Pat Garrett And Billy The Kid** from the young screenwriter **Rudy Wurlitzer** in October 1972, the initial invitation was to write a couple of songs for the movie. But, as Dylan read the script, he became intrigued enough to wonder if there could be a part for him.

The following month he flew to **Durango** in Mexico to meet the director, **"Bloody Sam" Peckinpah** – who had apparently never heard of Bob Dylan. According to Wurlitzer, the night Dylan arrived he was greeted by the sight of a monumentally drunk Peckinpah standing naked in front of a mirror shooting at his reflection with a gun.

The director was won over when Dylan played him the song **Billy**, which he had already written, and he offered him the part of **Alias**, a member of Billy's outlaw gang. According to C.P. Lee, "The visual storyteller could sense a link with Dylan the oral storyteller – both artists blended a centuries-old tradition with something new."

With **James Coburn** cast as Sheriff Pat Garrett and the singer **Kris Krisotofferson** as Billy, Dylan moved his family to Durango to begin shooting and scoring the film in late November. Things went wrong almost from the start. A serious influenza epidemic was sweeping Durango and dozens died, including Peckinpah's special-effects man, **Bud Hulburd**. The director himself fell ill, and clouds of dust swirled around the town, causing respiratory problems.

At the first screening of the daily rushes, Dylan was in for a shock. A faulty camera meant that part of the screen was blurred.

Peckinpah leapt up, howling obscenities, and proceeded to urinate all over the screen. Coburn turned to Dylan and said, "Now you know what you've gotten yourself into."

Peckinpah, fighting some internal demons of his own, as well as the MGM studio bosses, who were concerned that he was out of control and over-budget, spent much of his time drinking himself into oblivion and throwing knives. At one point he hurled a blade, which landed just inches from the head of actor **Harry Dean Stanton**. Dylan's confidence as an actor began to wilt visibly. He had originally been given a decent part in Wurlitzer's script. But as shooting continued his role was pushed further and further to the margins. "What Dylan was left doing was very much like what the character was doing," Kristofferson recalled. "Floating without any direction from Sam."

One of Dylan's children fell ill, and he was getting an understandable earful from his wife Sara. "She got fed up almost immediately. She'd say to me 'What the hell are we doing here?'" Dylan later confessed. But it was a good question and he soon shipped the family out – first to Los Angeles and then to London for a Christmas break – before returning in January to finish shooting his scenes and record the soundtrack.

Yet, although he's always peripheral to the main action, Dylan's shuffling performance is undoubtedly charismatic. "He's got a presence like **Charlie Chaplin**. You see him on screen and all eyes are on him. There's something about him that's magnetic. He doesn't even have to move," Kristofferson reckoned.

The Movies

One reviewer described his performance as little more than "an assortment of tics, smirks, winks, shrugs and smiles". But that's exactly what makes him so watchable. And he delivers some wonderful lines. In his first big scene, when he presents himself to Billy's gang, he is asked his name...

"Alias."

"Alias what?"

"Alias anything you please."

In another scene, Coburn asks him, "Who are you?" Dylan replies, "That's a good question." Whether Peckinpah quite knew what he was getting or not, it is an utterly Dylanesque moment. Equally brilliant is the scene in the cantina, where Garrett has caught up with the gang, and despatches the outlaws one by one – as an oblivious Dylan puts on his wire-framed glasses and incongruously reads the labels on the cans stacked on the shelves on

Alias entertains the kids

the other side of the room. While death and mayhem are going on all around him, Dylan's voice intones, "Beans, beans, beans and spinach, beef stew, salmon, tinned spinach…" It's surreal and bizarre, and ought to be ludicrous. Yet somehow Dylan steals the entire scene.

Dylan later recalled the making of the film with mixed feelings. "There I was, trapped deep in the heart of Mexico. With some madman. It was crazy, all these generals making you jump into hot ants, setting up turkey shoots and whatever and drinking tequila till they passed out. Sam was a wonderful guy though. He was an outlaw. A real hombre."

Too much of an outlaw for MGM, evidently. When the film was finished, the studio took Peckinpah's film from him and butchered it. On its release in the summer of 1973, critics and public alike were left bewildered by the result, although the more perceptive realized that there was probably a great film lurking in there somewhere and wondered what had happened to it. "Did the studio ruin an interesting film, or did it merely try to salvage a hopelessly muddled one?", Paul D. Zimmerman wondered in *Newsweek*.

Eventually, in 1989, some four years after Peckinpah's death, we had our answer when the director's original cut was released. It was a revelation, and this time the critics raved about a film that has now taken its place alongside Peckinpah's own *The Wild Bunch* in the pantheon of great westerns. "Gone was the incoherent tale of cowboy revenge," *Uncut* magazine's Damien Love wrote. "And in its place, an elegiac meditation on betrayal and the passing of age, through which Dylan's music flowed like a river catching twilight."

Dylan's performance did not kick-start the movie career he might have hoped for, and the experience left him disillusioned with Hollywood. "I learned working in Pat Garrett that there is no way you can make a really creative movie in Hollywood," he later complained. "You have to have your own crew and your own people to make a movie your own way." It was in the moment of that realizaton that Dylan's next movie venture, *Renaldo & Clara*, was born.

Renaldo & Clara

Bob Dylan, 1977

At one point it looked as if Dylan might have spent 1975 playing his hero **Woody Guthrie** in the biopic *Bound For Glory*. Instead, the part went to David Carradine, and Dylan ended up shooting his own film, *Renaldo & Clara*, on the road during his Rolling Thunder Tour. Co-directed by **Howard Alk**, who had worked on *Don't Look Back* and *Eat The Document*, it's a film that defies logic and convention. Part tour documentary, part narrative-free improvised drama and part obscure myth-making, it was a unique cinematic vision that was savaged upon its release and has remained seldom seen since.

Once Dylan had taken the decision to have the tour filmed, the movie he fashioned from it took on a life of its own. Other than his desire for something more interesting than a straightforward documentary, initially Dylan had little idea what kind of film he wanted to make (and there are those who argue that he was no clearer at the end of it). He wanted the spontaneity of *Don't Look Back* and *Eat The Document*. But he wanted something more than *cinéma vérité*, too, so he rang the young playwright **Sam Shepard** and invited him along to provide "dialogue". Shepard probably guessed it wasn't going to work from their first meeting, when Dylan told him, "We don't have to make any connections. None of this has to connect. In fact it's better if it doesn't connect."

Once on the road, any notion of a script was abandoned, along with structure, narrative, chronology and even fixed characters. Dylan decided he wanted to improvise and "see what happened". In addition to the concerts that were filmed, the musicians, who included **Joan Baez, Ramblin' Jack Elliott, Roger McGuinn** and the poet **Allen Ginsberg**, were dragged into a series of bizarre improvised scenes in which they were asked to play a cast of ill-defined characters. Dylan was Renaldo, and his wife **Sara** played Clara. Baez played various characters, including the Woman In White (who is confusingly also played in some scenes by Sara). **Ronee Blakley** also plays Sara, while veteran rocker **Ronnie Hawkins** appears as Bob Dylan. Allen Ginsberg appears reading his poem *Kaddish* and there's a visit to the grave of **Jack Kerouac**.

When the second leg of the Rolling Thunder Tour ended in May 1976, Dylan and Alk were left with the perplexing problem of how to turn more than 100 hours of haphazard foot-age into something resembling a marketable film. It took them the rest of 1976 and most of 1977 and they eventually came up with a film that sprawled over almost four hours.

With commendable avant-garde bravado, Dylan began the editing process by sorting the scenes into themes: God, rock'n'roll, poetry, women, sex, marriage, death, and so on. Instead of a plot, he was thinking more along the lines of the composition of a painting. As Clinton Heylin has observed, Dylan's role models were not Ford, Huston or Hitchcock but Cézanne, Modigliani and Salvador Dalí. It was the same impressionistic "painterly" approach that had worked so well on *Blood On The Tracks*. But it translated less well to the screen.

The music is triumphant and many of the scenes are fascinating. The Dylan–Baez–Sara triangle was rich with possibilities and there's a strange, non-linear logic to the film. But the lack of anything resembling a narrative thread is disarming and its wilful obscurity infuriated the critics who, when the film premiered in early 1978, turned on Dylan with a ferocity greater than anything they had ever directed at his music.

Alk and Dylan undertook a round of interviews to defend, if not explain, their creation. Yet their words only served to add to the general bafflement. Alk called it "the movie you haven't dreamed yet". Dylan told *Playboy* magazine, "It's about the essence of man being alienated from himself and how in order to free himself, to be reborn, he has to go outside himself." To *Rolling Stone*, he insisted the film's integrity lay in "being faithful to the subconscious". But, clearly hurt by the terrible reviews, he immediately contradicted himself by claiming it was meant to have been "a more structured film" and, with a cavalier disregard for the truth, blamed Shepard for the abandonment of a script.

Renaldo & Clara is a failure, but a heroic one, flawed by Dylan's apparent inability to fully appreciate the differences between songwriting and filmmaking. As C.P. Lee put it, "The lessons that he had learned over long years in the studio, fast improvisational changes, completing lyrics on the spot, couldn't be applied in front of cash-devouring cameras." Instinct, his greatest asset as a musician, proved in the world of filmmaking to be an expensive blind alley.

The Last Waltz

Martin Scorsese, 1978

With **Muddy Waters, Dr John, Van Morrison, Joni Mitchell** and a wild-eyed **Neil Young** among the guest stars paying tribute, **The Band**'s cocaine-dusted farewell concert in San Francisco's palatial Winterland Ballroom on Thanksgiving Day, 1976, was brilliantly filmed by **Martin Scorsese**. The climax of the evening, of course, was Dylan, and it produced typical drama. Even as the show was starting, he had apparently not decided whether he would allow his short set to be filmed. Howard Alk had advised him to instruct the cameras to be turned off, on the

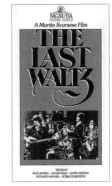

grounds that his appearance in Scorsese's movie might detract from the release of his own imminent *Renaldo & Clara*.

Eventually, five minutes before he went onstage, Dylan gave word that he would allow just two numbers to be shot. The cameras duly began to roll at the start of the fourth number, as he led The Band into a regal version of **Forever Young**. Then Dylan spontaneously reprised **Baby Let Me Follow You Down**, a song he had already played. Thinking he didn't want it filmed, Dylan's aides frantically tried to stop the cameras and it was only threats of physical violence by promoter Bill Graham that ensured the cameras kept shooting. Finally, Dylan led the all-star cast in a stately version of **I Shall Be Released**.

His appearance is brief but it is the crowning glory of what remains one of the best concert movies ever made. "While ostensibly about The Band, Scorsese's editing makes no bones about how much a Dylan event it became. Everything else disappears behind his presence. Scorsese does nothing to hide or minimize this effect," the *Village Voice* noted. The Band's Robbie Robertson also readily conceded that Dylan had practically stolen their show: "He looked amazing in the film. Almost like a Christ figure. A Christ in a white hat. I mean, what more could you ask for?"

The Movies

Sadly, the cameras did not capture a famous moment backstage between Dylan and Neil Diamond. Feeling smugly pleased with himself after his appearance, Diamond asked Dylan how he could possibly follow him. "Waddaya want me to do?" Dylan responded. "Go on stage and fall asleep?"

Hearts Of Fire

Richard Marquand, 1987

Some fourteen years after *Pat Garrett And Billy The Kid*, Dylan made his second Hollywood movie. How he must wish he hadn't bothered. *Hearts Of Fire* is not only the worst film Dylan has ever appeared in, it's probably one of the worst movies ever made about rock music. Or almost anything else, come to that.

The plot was banal enough, with Dylan playing cynical, retired rock star turned chicken farmer Billy Parker. His teenage lover, Molly Maguire (played by **Fiona Flanagan**), dreams of her own pop career, and leaves Dylan for jaded English synth-pop sensation James Colt, played by **Rupert Everett**. The latter sings "Tainted Love" and is stalked by a suicidal blind girl with a gun, which she eventually turns on herself. Towards the end, Molly turns up at Parker's place and tells him he was right all along, and that the music business is shit. How Dylan must have smiled at that one. But as a love triangle, it possesses none of the nuances of the real-life drama of Dylan, Sara and Joan Baez.

The dialogue was trite, and Everett and Flanagan turned in performances of such staggering ineptitude that Dylan – the only non-professional actor in the movie – demonstrably showed up their woodenness. In fact, Dylan is the only reason to sit through the grisly spectacle, although he must have wished he'd been as smart as **David Bowie** and **Sting**, who both turned down Everett's role of Colt. He was the last character cast for the film and, according to Marquand, he actively lobbied for the part. The director was then invited to meet Dylan at his Malibu home, where they spent a day getting drunk on red wine and deciding that they could work together.

Perhaps Dylan was impressed by Marquand's CV, which included **Return Of The Jedi** and the classy Glenn Close/Jeff Bridges thriller, **Jagged Edge**. Perhaps, given that Dylan was suffering from writer's block at the time, making a movie seemed like a welcome relief from the burden of songwriting. If so, he was mistaken, for part of the motivation of Marquand and the film's backers in casting Dylan was that they hoped to get a high-profile soundtrack album out of his involvement. Asked about his songs for the film at a press conference at London's National Film Theatre in August 1986, Dylan was forced to admit that they weren't written yet, but that he hoped to come up with something on the set – as he had done with "Knockin' On Heaven's Door" when making *Pat Garrett And Billy The Kid*. In the event, Dylan contributed two mediocre new songs in **Had A Dream About You, Baby** and **Night After Night**, and delivered cover versions of John Hiatt's **The Usual** and Shel Silverstein's **Couple More Years**. It was left to veteran James Bond composer **John Barry** to provide the incidental music.

Dylan is the only one of the film's lead actors to display any charisma. Quirky and unconventional, he has none of the professional panache that is taught in drama school. But he's oddly compelling and is the only one who doesn't appear to be acting – except, strangely enough, when he's playing the part of a musician on stage, where his naturalness evaporates and he becomes stiff, displaying a total inability to lip-synch.

There are some nice self-referential touches. At one point, Molly is watching a video of Parker in his glory days, which turns out to be Dylan's 1971 performance in **The Concert For Bangladesh**. In another scene, Parker and Molly drive past a cinema that is showing *Pat Garrett And Billy The Kid*. But really, such moments are clutching at straws.

Marquand died the week before the film opened, aged just 49, and Dylan failed to show at the London premiere, even though he was in town. Presumably he stayed away in the knowledge that the film was an embarrassment, although he could hardly have expected that it would be so badly received that it was withdrawn after a week, and that plans for an American theatre release were unceremoniously dropped altogether.

Catchfire

Alan Smithee/Dennis Hopper, 1989

Catchfire hardly qualifies as a Dylan movie, for he's barely on screen for half a minute. But it merits inclusion here, if only for its intriguing parallel with *Easy Rider*. In 1969, Dylan asked for his name to be taken off the theme song he'd written for Hopper's film, because he dis-

How Dylan tried to change the ending of *Easy Rider*

When **Dennis Hopper** asked if he could use **It's Alright, Ma (I'm Only Bleeding)** in his 1969 film, ***Easy Rider***, Dylan demurred. The problem was he hated the end of the movie, in which Hopper gets shot by a hippie-hating redneck while freewheeling down the road on a chopper with his long-haired drug buddy, played by **Peter Fonda**. "You can't end it like that," Dylan told Hopper. "Peter should go back and blow those guys away." Eventually, Dylan agreed to let his song be used, so long as it wasn't played, as Hopper wanted, over the closing credits. "Man, it's depressing enough as it is", he complained.

Then, according to Hopper, Dylan did a remarkable thing. He took out a pen and paper and wrote, "The river flows, it flows to the sea, wherever that river flows, that's where I want to be, flow river flow." He handed the verse to Hopper and said, "Give this to McGuinn, he'll know what to do with it." The Byrds' leader then duly added the line, "All they wanted was to be free" and the film's title song, **The Ballad Of Easy Rider**, was born. Despite his key role in writing the song, Dylan refused to allow his name to appear on the credits, because he still couldn't stomach the film's ending.

approved of the ending (see box). Two decades later, Dylan played a cameo in the Hopper-directed *Catchfire*, a movie from which Hopper subsequently removed his name following a dispute with his studio over the final cut.

Hopper stars as a saxophone-playing Mafia hit-man on the trail of an artist and murder witness, played by **Jodie Foster**. While hunting her down, he quizzes another artist – who wields a chainsaw while cutting up chunks of brightly coloured wood. When he flips up his visor, it is none other than Dylan, who says he hasn't seen Foster's character for a while. "Our forms aren't exactly simpatico," he explains.

Masked And Anonymous

Larry Charles, 2003

Dylan's first serious return to cinema since the ill-fated *Hearts Of Fire* was greeted with the usual negative reviews when *Masked And Anonymous* premiered at the Sundance Film Festival in 2003 (attended by Dylan himself, suitably masked and anonymous in a blonde wig and a blue woolly hat). Veteran critic Roger Ebert set the tone when he dismissed the film as "a vanity production beyond reason". The poor reviews helped to ensure that the film did not even get a cinema release in Britain. And yet, when it eventually appeared on DVD in May 2004, it proved to be a fascinating piece of work: "bewildering, beautiful, incisive, incoherent, intriguing and infuriating", as journalist Damien Love described it in *Uncut* magazine.

Dylan co-wrote the screenplay, under the alias **Sergei Petrov**, apparently coming up with the idea as a byproduct of his writing for the *Love And Theft* album. In the film he basically plays himself, although his character masquerades as **Jack Fate**. The autobiographical content is reinforced by the fact that his real-life touring band of **Charlie Sexton, Larry Campbell, Tony Garnier** and **George Receli** appear as Simple Twist Of Fate, a Jack Fate tribute band. But, although the movie is both by and about Dylan, Ebert's criticisms were nevertheless misguided because it is also about so much more. As Damien Love wrote, the film raises "hard questions about America, about political mayhem, about race, about business, government and the media; about the co-opting of the counter-culture; about corruption and greed; about image and reality and how they get mistaken for each other; about the artists' responsibility".

Shot for just seven million dollars – and inside three weeks, during a rare gap in Dylan's touring schedule – *Masked And Anonymous* is set in an alternative universe in which America has degenerated into a banana republic ravaged by civil war and ruled by a dying dictator. Jack Fate is a burned-out cult rock-star rotting in jail, who is bailed to play a TV benefit concert for war victims. During the concert he delivers lacerating versions of such "Jack Fate" classics as **Blowin' in the Wind, Dirt Road Blues, Down in the Flood, Dixieland, Drifter's Escape, Not Dark Yet** and **A Hard Rain's A-Gonna Fall**. Other familiar Dylan songs are rendered by Japanese punk bands and Italian rappers.

Former Seinfeld writer Larry Charles co-

The man behind the *Masked*: Dylan with Jessica Lange at the 2003 Sundance festival

to give us money feel comfortable they're going to get their money back". Yet it is Dylan in a cowboy suit, sporting a Clark Gable pencil moustache, who dominates the screen. And, despite the panning of the film by the Sundance critics, Charles refuses to be cowed in his admiration of his leading man. "People were very cold, ruthless," he says. "They'd say, 'Well Bob Dylan's never sold a movie ticket.' I mean, we're talking the only American artist who will survive the collapse of civilization."

As for Dylan – or rather Jack Fate – he concludes in the film, "I was always a singer, maybe no more than that. I stopped trying to figure everything out a long time ago."

wrote the script. "Bob dumped all this paper on the table and said, 'I don't know what to do with these'," Charles recalls. "I looked through and said, 'Well you could take this and put it together with this and that could be a character who says this.' It was almost like a William Burroughs cut-up technique. There was no plan. The film began to emerge naturally."

Masked And Anonymous marked **Larry Charles**'s debut as a director and its spectacular cast includes **John Goodman, Jessica Lange, Jeff Bridges, Penelope Cruz, Mickey Rourke** and **Val Kilmer**. According to Charles this was "because we thought we had to surround Bob with enough stars to make the people who are going

No Direction Home

Martin Scorsese, 2005

Shown over two parts on American and British TV in October 2005 and then immediately made available as a double DVD, Scorsese's magisterial, three-and-a-half-hour biopic covers Dylan's early years and career until the end of the tumultuous 1966 world tour. The use of previously unseen footage from the time is magnificent and rich with memorable musical performances, including such legendary moments as the 1965 Newport Folk Festival and the infamous 'Judas' exchange in Manchester on the 1966 world tour. Dylan himself provides a long and revealing interview, broken up into short segments so that he's effectively offering his own running commentary on his life and times throughout the film. Oddly, however, the interview was not conducted by Scorsese but by Dylan's manager, Jeff Rosen, sometime in 2003, which has caused some to question the film's status as a genuinely independent portrait. Among those lending their own illuminating memories are Joan Baez, Suze Rotolo, Maria Muldaur, Liam Clancy, Allen Ginsberg, Al Kooper, Dave Van Ronk and various other survivors of the early 1960s Greenwich Village folk scene.

Divided into two parts, the first traces Dylan's Minnesota roots and his early musical education, covering such influences as Hank Williams, John Jacob Niles and, of course, Woody Guthrie, all of whom are seen in archive footage. "He was like a sponge," says Tony Glover, "picking up people's mannerisms, accents." Film of the young Dylan is then cleverly used to illustrate the point, before part one ends with his triumphant 1963 Newport Folk Festival appearance.

The second part deals with Dylan's struggle to handle his fame and his transition from folk hero to electric messiah. Using previously unseen footage from a variety of sources, including both of D.A. Pennebaker's tour films, the speed at which he is travelling is dramatically conveyed, as is the pressure he is under, although there is also considerable humour, particularly in the clips from various press conferences in which he tries to avoid answering inane questions and resists the 'spokesman/conscience of his generation' tag with surreal wit. It's clear that the stress eventually gets to him ("I just want to go home," he says towards the end of the 1966 tour, by which time he looks like a man who is about to die), yet his defiance is positively heroic. But perhaps Scorsese's ultimate triumph is that although the film reveals so much, by the end the enigma and mystery of the source of Dylan's genius somehow still remains inviolate – as it should be.

In addition to the live footage featured in the film (the full performances of which are captured on the soundtrack CDs), DVD extras include complete performances of "Blowin' In The Wind" from a 1963 TV show, "Girl Of The North Country" and "Man Of Constant Sorrow" from 1964 TV appearances, "Mr Tambourine" Man from the 1964 Newport Folk Festival, "Love Minus Zero/No Limit" filmed live on the 1965 tour, and "Like A Rolling Stone" and "One Too Many Mornings" from the 1966 tour.

Part 4:
Dylanology

Dylanology

Dylanology

The Strange Case of A.J. Weberman

Stalkers and obsessive fans are part and parcel of the fame game. They go with the territory when you're a celebrity. But there has surely never been a stranger case than that of **Alan Jules Weberman**, whose bizarre pursuit of Bob Dylan included raiding his dustbins and analysing his garbage in an attempt to decipher his enigmatic songs and uncover his secrets.

Today, any self-protective celebrity would have his security staff rough up the offender or get his lawyer to seek a cease-and-desist order. Yet in 1971, when Weberman's harassment was at its height, Dylan did an extraordinary thing: he offered to meet his tormentor for a chat. Then he followed up the encounter with two lengthy and candid phone calls lasting almost an hour in total and which Weberman taped and promptly circulated to fellow Dylan collectors.

Born in 1945, Weberman became obsessed with Dylan in the mid-1960s while studying at Michigan State University, where he invented

Dylanology, studying the song lyrics with the kind of detailed textual analysis usually reserved for the work of Shakespeare, Spenser or Milton. "I realized it was poetry and required interpretation," he says. "So I developed the Dylanological Method which is looking at each word in the context in which it appears and looking for words that have a similar theme that cluster around it."

One of his theories was that Dylan had left clues about his **alleged heroin addiction** scattered throughout his songs. In an attempt to prove his theory, he even placed an advert in *The Village Voice*, seeking a specimen of Dylan's urine. Quite who he thought might come forward or how he would authenticate the pee is uncertain.

When this didn't work, he hit upon the idea of going through the dustbins outside Dylan's house at 94 MacDougal Street in New York's Greenwich Village. He didn't find any syringes or evidence of heroin addiction. But among the soiled diapers, empty cans and coffee grounds, he found plenty of interesting material: a discarded

Dylanology

letter to Johnny Cash, a tracklist of outtakes from a recent album, a postcard from Dylan's mother, and a royalty statement for $149,000.

An excited Weberman decided he had invented a new science – **garbology** – and, pronouncing himself the world's greatest authority on Dylan, he started writing newspaper articles analysing what could be deduced about the singer's art from what was to be found in his trash can. Infuriated that the object of his fascination had stopped singing protest songs, he formed the **Dylan Liberation Front** and had badges made up saying "Free Bob Dylan From Himself" and "Dylan's Brain Belongs To The People".

At first, Dylan treated it all as a humorous prank. Entering into the spirit of the joke, he filled his dustbins with every noxious substance he could find and even set booby traps. "It's the price of fame, I guess," Dylan told journalist Robert Shelton. "We loaded up the garbage with as much dog shit as we could – mousetraps, everything – but he still kept on anyhow."

Weberman's response was to buy a stronger pair of industrial protective gloves. So Dylan offered to meet him, even rolling up his shirt sleeves to show there were no track marks when Weberman accused him of being a junkie. Over the next few days, Dylan made two phone calls to him to discuss the article he was writing about their meeting.

Unaware that he was being bugged, Dylan tried reason, bullying, mockery and appealing to Weberman's better nature. At one point, he even tells Weberman he is going to write a song about him called "Pig" and threatens to have badges made up with the word superimposed on

Weberman's face. "You go through garbage like a pig. You're a pig mentality," Dylan taunted.

Weberman responded that he could do with the publicity. "Yeah, well that's the one reason why I wouldn't do it, but I got a good song if ever I want to do one," Dylan replied petulantly. The exchanges continued for 50 astonishing minutes. Yet the meeting and phone calls resolved nothing. On May 23, 1971 – Dylan's 30th birthday – Weberman was back outside Dylan's home leading a demonstration. "Dylan's sold out!", he chanted through a megaphone. "Pig!", his fellow demonstrators shouted. He then unveiled a birthday cake he had baked for Dylan – decorated with 30 hypodermic needles instead of candles.

Fortunately, the Dylans were not at home, having left that morning for a vacation in Israel, although some of Dylan's children and their nanny were forced to endure the demonstration. **John Lennon and Yoko Ono** were moved to write an open letter to *The Village Voice* demanding that Weberman publicly apologize for his campaign of "lies and malicious slander".

Several months later when Sara Dylan caught Weberman with a reporter from the Associated Press going through the garbage again, she confronted him. When Dylan learnt what had happened, he chased Weberman through Greenwich Village on a bicycle. When he caught up with him, he knocked him to the ground and the two wrestled in the gutter until they were separated by passers-by. "I wouldn't fight back because I knew I was wrong," Weberman says today. But at the time he treated the attack as a badge of honour. "Not too many people have that opportunity

– to have Dylan on top of them," he told *Rolling Stone*. "Maybe his wife."

Yet, oddly, Dylan appears to have taken some notice of the criticisms of his obsessive fan. One of the most interesting exchanges on the tapes involves Weberman asking him to play charity concerts. "I'm talking about a benefit concert in Madison Square Garden, you could play to 20,000 people for free," he urged. Six months later Dylan appeared at the Garden with George Harrison to raise funds for Bangladesh and Weberman claimed vindication. "I often ask myself, if I got a chance to record another telephone conversation with Dylan, what would I try to convince him of this time?", he says today. "I would try to persuade him to write songs protesting September 11."

In 1980 – the year that another obsessive rock fan called Mark Chapman murdered John Lennon – Weberman published a book called *My Life In Garbology*, which also detailed his exploits trawling through the trash of Jackie Kennedy, Gloria Vanderbilt and David Rockefeller. Compared to Chapman, Weberman's obsession was intrusive but relatively harmless. But garbology eventually caught up with him. In the late 1990s, he was sent to prison for running a door-to-door marijuana delivery service, convicted on the evidence of discarded pot wrappers – found in his dustbin.

The tapes of the Dylan–Weberman phone calls were finally released on CD as *Bob Dylan – The Classic Interviews Volume 2*, by Chrome Dreams in 2004.

Dylan Country

There is no official shrine, such as Elvis Presley's Graceland, or an equivalent to the guided coach tours of The Beatles' Liverpool to mark the sites associated with Bob Dylan's life and career. This is partly because, unlike Elvis and The Beatles, Dylan is still an active performer. We need no monument to him because we can still see the man himself on stage on something like 100 nights every year. Furthermore, Dylan has spent much of his restless life as a rolling stone, seldom putting down roots in any one place for too long. Howard Sounes, in his biography *Down The*

Highway, identified an extensive property portfolio that Bob has amassed. Yet Dylan probably spends more nights in hotels and on tour buses than in any one of the several places he may occasionally call home.

Nevertheless, there is a Dylan trail that crisscrosses America, from Hibbing, Minnesota, to Greenwich Village and Woodstock in the east and to Los Angeles in the west. He will also be forever associated with certain sites in London – places that provided the background for the iconic footage of *Don't Look Back*, for example.

Minnesota

Dylan's primary childhood home still stands at 2425 Seventh Avenue, in **Hibbing**, Minnesota. The family moved into the nine-room, two-storey detached house in 1948. Entering by the front door, you walked straight into the living room. Dylan and his brother David shared a bedroom with two windows at the back of the house, one looking down Seventh Avenue and the other down 25th Street. Dylan's father Abe converted the basement into a recreation room and panelled the walls in pine cladding, into which Dylan carved his initials, "B.Z.", next to the wall-mounted telephone.

Two blocks away was **Hibbing High School**, where Dylan and his brother both enrolled. In Howard Street, one of the town's two main thoroughfares, it is still possible to see the sites of such landmarks as the **Androy Hotel**, where Dylan's bar mitzvah was held. The **L&B Café**, where Dylan hung out with Echo Helstrom, was on the opposite side of the road and next to the café was the **Moose Lodge**, where he first played her the piano after she had jimmied the lock on the lid with her penknife.

Dylan moved to the twin cities of **Minneapolis and St Paul**, 190 miles south of Hibbing, in the autumn of 1959, when he enrolled at the **University of Minnesota**, on the east bank of the Mississippi. The Jewish fraternity house where he initially lived was on University Avenue SE. Yet he spent far more time in the bohemian district known as **Dinkytown** than on campus. The centre of Dinkytown was the junction of 4th Street SE and 14th Avenue SE in downtown Minneapolis.

The **Ten O'Clock Scholar**, Dylan's favourite hangout, was situated on 14th Avenue between 4th and 5th streets. Within a block were also **Melvin McCosh's bookshop** where he purchased volumes of poetry (including books by such Beat poets as Ginsberg and Ferlinghetti and possibly the works of Dylan Thomas), the **Varsity Cinema**, which he frequented, and **Gray's drug store**, above which he rented a room for a while. It was at the Ten O'Clock Scholar that Dylan met girlfriend Bonnie Beecher, and heard the likes of musicians such as Spider John Koerner and Dave Glover. He also got to play there, until he was sacked after asking for a pay rise, whereupon he relocated to a pizza restaurant called the **Purple Onion** in St Paul. The apartment of his friend Jon Pankake was at 1401 6th Street SE, and it was here that Dylan broke in and infamously "borrowed" some of Pankake's records when he was out of town for a couple of weeks.

Dylan's trips back to Hibbing during the 1960s were few and far between. But in the early 1970s, he bought an 80-acre farm just northeast of Minneapolis on the **Crow River**, presumably to be near his family and his roots. He converted an old farmhouse on the property into a family home and a nearby barn was turned into an art studio. During the 1970s, he spent most summers there with his children and wrote *Blood On The Tracks* while staying there in July 1974. In December that year, while spending Christmas and New Year on the farm, he re-cut several tracks for the album at **Sound 80 Studios** in Minneapolis. The *Street-Legal* album was also largely written on the farm.

New York City

When Dylan arrived in New York on January 24, 1961, he headed straight for **Greenwich Village**, which was already well established as the heart of the booming folk revival. His first stop was the **Café Wha**, a basement club at 115 **MacDougal Street** run by Manny Roth. According to legend, after his brief performance, Roth asked the audience to find Dylan a place to stay for the night.

In another version told by Robert Shelton, who at the time was the folk critic of *The New York Times*, Dylan's first New York appearance was at **The Commons**, another basement coffeehouse on the west side of MacDougal Street, near Minetta Lane, later renamed the **Fat Black Pussycat**. Whatever the exact chronology, Dylan was a regular at both venues. In a postcard to friends in Minneapolis in February 1961, he singled out The Commons as a place "where people clap for me" and it is claimed to be where "Blowin' In The Wind" was written.

Gerde's Folk City was another early venue Dylan played within a fortnight of his arrival in New York. Located at 11 West Fourth Street, the club had space on the ground floor of a dingy six-storey building, situated between the West and East villages. It had been run since 1958 by Mike Porco, who was sufficiently impressed by Dylan when he turned up at the Monday hootenannies, or open-mic nights, to offer him his first formal booking in New York. Porco demanded proof of his age, but was so utterly won over that he paid Dylan's musicians-union fees when he booked him for a week-long residency supporting John Lee Hooker in April 1961. It was at Gerde's that Dylan first met other folk singers such as Dave Van Ronk and Tom Paxton. The first major review of a Dylan performance was of a residency at Gerde's, written by Shelton and published in *The New York Times* on September 29, 1961.

The Gaslight was another coffeehouse, at 116 MacDougal Street, where Dylan played a week's residency with Dave Van Ronk in July 1961 and where he was first introduced to his future manager, Albert Grossman. A Gaslight performance from October 1962 featuring early versions of "A Hard Rain's A-Gonna Fall" and "Don't Think Twice, It's All Right" went on to become one of his most famous bootlegs. "Masters Of War" also had its premiere there. When the Gaslight got too crowded, Dylan often repaired next door to the Kettle Of Fish Tavern, frequented by the Beats and with a jukebox stacked with jazz records. **The Bitter End** was yet another regular hangout, located in Bleeker Street, and converted into a folk club from a former bistro called the Cock'n'Bull by Fred Weintraub. A second Bleeker Street club at 160 was **The Village Gate**. Chip Monck had an apartment in the same building, which is said to be where Dylan wrote at least part of "A Hard Rain's A-Gonna Fall".

A haunt of a slightly different nature from the clubs and coffeehouses was Izzy Young's **Folklore Center**, at 110 MacDougal Street. This was the tiny location that was the "music shop, meeting place and gossip mill" in Shelton's description. Dylan performed there, wrote songs on a typewriter in the back room (including one called "Talkin' Folklore Center") and also gave two interviews to Young that were published in the magazine *Sing Out!* and which were instrumental in disseminating Dylan's early self-mythologizing.

Dylan spent his first months in the Village sleeping on friends' couches and by the summer of 1961 he was staying regularly in the fourth-floor apartment of Miki Isaacson at **1 Sheridan Square**. Isaacson ran what amounted virtually to a home for stray folkniks and Dylan often jammed there with other musicians, including Ramblin' Jack Elliott. At the same time, Dylan's girlfriend Suze Rotolo lived in a third-floor apartment in the same building with her mother Mary and sister Carla.

Dylan strikes another match in the Kettle Of Fish, Greenwich Village, NYC

In December 1961, Dylan took a cramped two-room first-floor rear apartment at **161 West Fourth Street**, for which he paid $60 a month. Suze moved in shortly after, even though, according to Robert Shelton, there was barely room for one person, let alone two. "It was a very small place to have someone constantly playing chords over and over again," Suze recalled. "But I never minded." The cover shot of *The Freewheelin' Bob Dylan* was taken one afternoon in February 1963, depicting Dylan and Suze walking down the middle of a snow-laden Fourth Street by Columbia photographer Don Hunstein. In the 1965 song "Positively Fourth Street", Dylan used his old address as a symbol of his scorn for his former folk-music acquaintances. By then he had new places to rest his head in New York. By late 1964, after the final break-up with Suze, and when he was starting to tour heavily, he tended to stay at the **Earle Hotel**, right on Washington Square, the symbolic centre of the Village. Joan Baez often stayed there with him.

A little later, in 1965, he took an apartment at the **Chelsea Hotel**, a bohemian New York landmark on 23rd Street between Seventh and Eighth avenues. When it was built in 1884 it was for a brief time the tallest building in New York. It became a hotel in 1905 and famous guests and residents included Thomas Wolfe, Virgil Thomson and O. Henry. Dylan moved in with Sara when he returned from his British tour, although around the same time he also bought a house in Woodstock. In the song "Sara" on the 1976 album *Desire*, he recalled staying up all night and writing "Sad Eyed Lady Of The Lowlands" for her in the Chelsea.

In late 1969 when he had tired of seclusion in Woodstock, Dylan moved back to New York, buying a townhouse at **94 MacDougal Street**, below Bleeker Street, right in the heart of his old stomping ground. It was outside this address that A.J. Weberman organized his various protests against what he saw as Dylan's "selling out", and rifled through Dylan's dustbins. This harassment was partly responsible for Dylan relocating to the West Coast.

Dylan's third Greenwich Village phase occurred after his separation from Sara when he began hanging out again in the folk clubs and coffeehouses in the early summer of 1975, while living in a borrowed loft on **Houston Street**. It was over drunken evenings in clubs such as **The Other End** on Bleeker Street (formerly The Bitter End) that he met the likes of Patti Smith and planned the Rolling Thunder Revue tour.

One of the few significant Dylan locations outside the Village was Columbia's **Studio A**, a short distance uptown on Seventh Avenue. It was here that Dylan recorded his first five albums. In the 1970s, the studio was renamed **A&R Studios** and Dylan continued to use it, making much of *Blood On The Tracks* there.

Woodstock

Dylan's introduction to the pastoral attractions of **Woodstock**, about 90 miles upstate from New York City, came first via Peter Yarrow (of Peter, Paul and Mary fame), who had a wooden cabin there, and then via his manager

Albert Grossman, who had a home in Striebel Road in nearby **Bearsville**. From the summer of 1963, Dylan was often to be found at Grossman's house, where he had a room set aside for him, sometimes staying there with Joan Baez. It was to the Grossmans' home that Sara Dylan brought her husband minutes after his motorcycle accident on July 29, 1966.

When the accident occurred, Dylan was riding from the Grossmans' property back to his own recently purchased mansion known as **Hi Lo Ha** on Camelot Road, **Byrdcliffe**, about a mile out of Woodstock. The Byrdcliffe colony had been founded in 1902 when the heir to a Yorkshire textile fortune, Ralph Radcliffe Whitehead, bought up seven farms below Mead's Mountain, and constructed thirty buildings on the land.

The sprawling eleven-bedroom Byrdcliffe house in the Arts and Crafts style that Dylan bought in the summer of 1965 was once owned by the architect and theatre director Ben Webster. Bob purchased it after being impressed by a visit to John Lennon's mansion in Weybridge, Surrey, during his 1965 British tour, but it was the height of Dylan's "white hot heat" period and he was unable to spend much time at the house until after the motorcycle crash, when it became his retreat. For a while, he relished the quiet domesticity it offered and most mornings during 1967–68 he was to be seen walking daughter **Maria** along Upper Byrdcliffe Road from the house to the school bus stop.

Dylan was eventually hounded out of the property by intrusive fans and in May 1969 moved his family to another Arts and Crafts mansion on **Ohayo Mountain Road** on the other side of Woodstock. Once owned by Walter Weyl, founder of *The New Republic*, the house was set in 39 acres, but Dylan bought an additional 83 acres of surrounding woodland to enhance his privacy further. Within a few months, however, the Dylans had returned to New York, and Bob eventually sold the house in 1973.

Another site associated with Dylan in Woodstock was the **Café Espresso** at 59 Tinker Street. Owned by Frenchman Bernard Paturel and his wife Mary Lou, Dylan often played chess there. At one point he stayed in a room above the café, finding it a quiet spot where he could write songs undisturbed when Grossman's house got overcrowded. Paturel later became Dylan's chauffeur.

However, the most famous "Woodstock site" has to be **Big Pink**. The house, which still stands, was not actually in Woodstock but located in the tiny nearby hamlet of **West Saugerties**. Set in the middle of a 100-acre estate, it was rented to The Hawks (as The Band were then still known) in early 1967 for $275 a month by a local restaurant-owner. The rent was effectively paid for by Dylan, for at the time he was employing the group on a retainer. The split-level house was dubbed "Big Pink" by the musicians because it was painted the colour of a strawberry milkshake. For around eight months during 1967, Dylan drove over to the house most days around noon in either a Ford station wagon or a baby blue Mustang, and would either clatter away at a typewriter in an upstairs room or record downstairs in the basement.

Los Angeles

By 1971, Dylan owned a mansion in Woodstock, a townhouse in Greenwich Village, a beach house on Long Island and a ranch house in Arizona. He then rented a home in **Malibu**, an upmarket beach community just outside Los Angeles and, from that point on, the West Coast became the family's main home.

Buying a property on the **Point Dume** peninsula ten miles north of Malibu and a short walk from **Zuma Beach**, Dylan and Sara employed the architect David C. Towbin to refashion the house in an extravagant and fantastical style. Just one wall of the existing structure was retained as, over three years, the house was transformed into a wood-framed, fairy-tale palace with some twenty rooms. Dylan instructed Towbin to make the so-called **Great Room** big enough to "ride a horse through". At one point, 56 hippy artisans were said to be living on the site in tepees, adding hand-painted tiles, elaborate glasswork and wooden carvings to the interior decor. A kiln was even built so that tiles could be manufactured on site.

A visually striking onion-dome offering views all the way down to Santa Monica pier was planted on top of the house. Often described as "Sara's folly", the construction of the Point Dume house also coincided with the Dylans' marriage falling apart. Some even said it contributed to their estrangement, and by summer 1974 Sara had moved out. The couple later reunited but when they eventually separated for good, it was Dylan who kept the house. It was in the garage studio here that the

first Traveling Wilburys single, "Handle With Care", was recorded in 1988.

Much of Dylan's recording in Los Angeles, however, was done not at his home studio but at **Rundown Studios**, a three-storey building at 2501 Main Street in **Santa Monica**, on which he took a five-year lease in September 1977. Used heavily as both a rehearsal and recording space over the next few years, Dylan had a bedroom constructed upstairs and often stayed there after a long session rather than driving back to Point Dume. He abandoned Rundown after the filmmaker Howard Alk committed suicide there on January 1, 1982. Dylan's Music Touring Company Inc was also located in Santa Monica, at **2219 Main Street**.

It was in California that Dylan joined the Vineyard Fellowship during his "born-again" years. Based in the **San Fernando Valley**, the church itself did not have a dedicated building, and held services in different locations, sometimes even on the beach. But during early 1979, Dylan daily attended the church's bible classes in a nondescript room above a real-estate office in **Reseda**, on the northwest outskirts of LA.

London

Dylan's favourite London hideaway for most of his career has been the **Mayfair Hotel** in Berkeley Square. The BBC put him up there in December 1962 on his first trip outside the United States, to appear in the TV drama *Madhouse On Castle Street*. He stayed there again during his 1964 visit and, when he took a holiday after the tour in Greece to compose

Dylanology

the songs for *Another Side Of Bob Dylan*, many of the lyrics were written on notepaper bearing the hotel's insignia.

On his 1965 visit, manager Albert Grossman switched his star turn to the higher-profile **Savoy Hotel** on the Strand. It was here that some of the best scenes in *Don't Look Back* were shot, including the *Subterranean Homesick Blues* sequence, which was filmed in an alley at the back of the hotel.

By the 1966 tour, however, Dylan was back at the Mayfair, receiving members of The Beatles in his hotel suite. In later years, Dylan continued to use the hotel – he has never owned a London property, although he was in the early 1990s reported to be house-hunting in Crouch End (see p.130) in north London, near where he had recorded parts of *Empire Burlesque* at Dave Stewart's **Church Studios**.

Other London haunts associated with Dylan before he graduated to grander venues such as the **Royal Albert Hall, Earl's Court** and **Wembley** include **The Pindar of Wakefield** pub at the King's Cross end of Gray's Inn Road, **Les Cousins** folk club at 49 Greek Street in Soho, **The Troubadour** in Earl's Court, and **Bunjies** at 27 Litchfield Street. He made appearances at all of them during his first visit to London in December 1962.

The Wisdom of Bob...

"A song is like a dream and you try to make it come true."

Chronicles

"I can see God in a daisy. It must be wonderful to be God. There's so much going on out there that you can't get to it all. It would take longer than forever."

Malibu, 1976

"Keep a good head and always carry a light bulb."

London, 1965

What made you decide to go the rock'n'roll route?

"Carelessness. I lost my one true love. I start drinking. The first thing I know I'm in a card game. Then I'm in a crap game. I wake up in a pool hall..."

Playboy magazine, 1966

"They certainly booed, I'll tell you that ... they've done it a lot of other places. I mean they must be pretty rich to be able to go some place and boo. I couldn't afford it if I was in their shoes."

San Francisco, 1965

"Music filters out to me in the crack of dawn. Sometimes you get a little spacey when you've been up all night."

Malibu, 1978

"I don't play folk rock ... I like to think of it more in terms of vision music. It's mathematical music."

Los Angeles, 1965

"Everybody has their own idea of what's a poet. Robert Frost, President Johnson, Allen Ginsberg, Rudolf Valentino – they're all poets. I like to think of myself as the one who carries the light bulb."

London, 1965

"I've done more for Dylan Thomas than he's ever done for me."

New York City, 1966

"If I thought Dylan Thomas was that great, I would have sung his poems and could just as easily have changed my name to Thomas."

Playboy magazine, 1978

"My haystacks weren't tied down."

Chronicles

"Pain sure brings the best out in people, doesn't it?"

New York City, 1971

"I think women rule the world and that no man has ever done anything that a woman either hasn't allowed him to do or encouraged him to do."

1984

"I'm just a song and dance man."

San Francisco, 1965

"Shit man, I'm only me. You know that's who I am. We are all the same. No one is on any higher level than anybody else."

Creem magazine, 1975

"I'd gotten a cosmic kick in the pants. I probably should have been wearing steel underwear."

Chronicles

"If I told you what our music is really about, we'd probably all get arrested."

1965

"I always needed a song to get by. There's a lot of singers who don't need songs to get by. A lot of 'em are tall and good looking, you know? They don't need to say anything in order to grab people. Me, I had to make it on something other than my looks or my voice."

1987

"I have weak eyes. Try them for yourself. See the world as Bob Dylan sees it."

London, 1965

Dylanology

"My songs are just me talking to myself. Maybe that's an egotistical thing to say, but that's what it is. I have no responsibility to anybody except myself."

London, 1965

"I do know what my songs are about."

And what's that?

"Oh, some are about four minutes. Some are about five. And some, believe it or not, are about eleven or twelve."

New York, 1966

"Songs aren't going to save the world."

Los Angeles, 1965

"I found myself writing this song, this story, this long piece of vomit, about 20 pages long, and out of it I took 'Like A Rolling Stone'."

Canada, 1966

"I had been anointed as the Big Bubba of Rebellion, High Priest of Protest, the Czar of Dissent, the Duke of Disobedience, Leader of the Freeloaders, Kaiser of Apostasy, Archbishop of Anarchy, the Big Cheese. What the hell are we talking about? Horrible titles any way you want to look at it."

Chronicles

"Almost anything else is easy, except writing songs."

Malibu, 1976

"Sometimes you get people rushing to the stage but you just, you know ... turn 'em off very fast. Kick 'em in the head or something like that. They get the picture."

San Francisco, 1965

"To me it's not a business. It's never been a business and never will be a business. It's just a way of surviving."

July 1984

Do you take drugs or something?

"I don't know. I don't know I've ever seen a drug. I wouldn't know..."

Los Angeles, 1965

"The criminal drug situation takes place in suburban housewives' kitchens, the ones who get wiped out on alcohol every afternoon and then make supper. You can't blame them and you can't blame their husbands."

New York, 1965

"There are so many lies that have been told, so many things that are kept back. Kids have a feeling like me, but they ain't hearing it no place. They're scared to step out. But I ain't scared to do it, man."

New York, 1962

"When your environment changes, you change. You've got to go on and you find new friends. Turn around one day and you're

on a different stage, with a new set of characters."

Malibu, 1978

"Sometimes you feel like a club fighter, who
gets off the bus in the middle of nowhere,
no cheers, no admiration, punches his way
through ten rounds or whatever, always making someone else look good, vomits up the
pain in the back room, picks up his check
and gets back on the bus heading out for
another nowhere."

Biograph, 1985

"You can get sex anywhere. If you're looking
for someone to love you, now that's different.
I guess you have to stay in college for that."

New York, 1966

"The real magic of women is that
throughout the ages, they've had to do all
the work and yet they can have a sense of
humor."

Playboy magazine, 1978

"I really was never any more than what
I was – a folk musician who gazed into
the grey mist with tear-blinded eyes and
made up songs that floated in a luminous
haze."

Chronicles

"On some of my earlier records, I sounded
cross because I was poor. Lived on less than

Man of many words: Bob a-ponderin', 1963

Dylanology

ten cents a day in those times. Now I'm cross because I'm rich."

London, 1965

"I sometimes dream of running the country and putting all my friends in office. That's the way it works now, anyway. I'd like to see Thomas Jefferson, Benjamin Franklin and a few of those other guys come back. If they did, I'd go out and vote."

Malibu, 1976

"In your eyesight, you see your victim swimming in lava. Hanging by their arms from a birch tree."

On writing "Like A Rolling Stone", 1965

"An article would hit the streets with the headline, 'Spokesman Denies That He's A Spokesman.' I felt like a piece of meat that someone had thrown to the dogs."

Chronicles

"You don't have to starve to be a good artist. You just have to have love, insight and a strong point of view. And you have to fight off depravity."

Malibu, 1978

"I don't care one bit about the '60s. I didn't grow up in the '60s, so Bob Dylan the '60s protest singer isn't me at all."

London, 1997

"Politics and social trends don't really concern me. Left, right or middle – it's all just the same to me. I'm not sufficiently schooled in politics to have a real view."

London, 1997

"Music attracts the angels in the universe. A group of angels sitting at a table are going to be attracted by that…"

Rolling Stone magazine, 1978

"We'd have more in common if we went out fishing and said nothing. It would be a more valuable experience than sitting around and talking."

Playboy magazine, 1978

"I felt done for, an empty burned-out wreck. Too much static in my head and I couldn't dump the stuff."

Chronicles

"I'm a firm believer in the longer you live, the better you get."

New York, 1968

"Folk music is a word I can't use. Folk music is a bunch of fat people."

New York, 1966

"Sometimes I can make myself feel better with music, but other times it's still hard to get to sleep at night."

1978

"These so-called connoisseurs of Bob Dylan music, I don't feel they know a thing or have any inkling of who I am or what I'm about. It's ludicrous, humorous and sad that such people have spent so much of their time thinking about who? Me? Get a life, please. You're wasting your own."

London, 2001

"My fame was immense, could fill a football stadium, but it was like having some weird diploma that won't get you into any college."

Chronicles

"God, I'm glad I'm not me."

Reading a newspaper article about himself, 1965

The "New Bobs"
Bruce and ten other contenders

The search has been on since around 1965 for the "new Dylan". But the tag has generally proved to be more of a curse than a blessing. Unless your name happens to be Bruce Springsteen, of course…

1. Bruce Springsteen

The biggest and most successful "New Bob" of them all – and the one who transcended the tag the most effortlessly. Signed to Columbia by John Hammond, who had signed Dylan more than a decade earlier, Springsteen's debut album appeared in 1973. At the time Dylan hadn't toured in seven years and the throne appeared to be vacant. Bruce was enthusiastically awarded the crown by critics, although it took another two years before he achieved real commercial success and became known as **"The Boss"**. He then went on to best Dylan by a considerable margin chart-wise, with 1975's *Born To Run* selling six million copies, while *Blood On The Tracks*, released in the same year, sold two million.

"New Bob" rating: 4/5

2. Phil Ochs

A committed Greenwich Village folkie, Phil Ochs wanted to be the new Dylan from the moment the original arrived on the block. Joan Baez took his "There But For Fortune" into the charts, and his *I Ain't Marching Any More* became a civil rights anthem. But although they were friends for a while, Dylan was eventually to sneer at Ochs that he wasn't really a songwriter but a mere journalist. They fell out big time one day in 1965 when Ochs told Dylan that he didn't think "Won't You Please Crawl Out Your Window" would be a hit single. Dylan stopped his limo and threw Ochs out of the car. Ochs had the last laugh when he was proved right and the song only scraped the American charts at number 58. After suffering serious bouts of schizophrenia, Ochs hung himself in 1976, while Dylan was on the Rolling Thunder tour, which he had been too ill to join.

"New Bob" rating: 3/5

3. Donovan

Known in the mid-1960s as Britain's answer to Dylan, Donovan Leitch can be seen in *Don't Look Back* singing worshipfully for the great man, who responds with a somewhat caustic "It's All Over Now, Baby Blue" in return. Earlier in the film Dylan asks, "Who's this Donovan?" and Alan Price mischievously replies "He's a better guitar player than you." Donovan's earliest protest songs such as "**Universal Soldier**" were sung in a nasal whine that was clearly derivative of Dylan. He copied his hero's early look and also followed him by "going electric" on songs such as "Sunshine Superman". But by 1967, the two singers had veered off in vastly different directions: Dylan towards roots and

country music, Donovan into fey hippy mysticism as a Beatles camp follower, joining them in India with the Maharishi.

"New Bob" rating: 3/5

4. Barry McGuire

Immortalized by the flattering namecheck – "McGuinn and McGuire couldn't get no higher" in **The Mamas and the Papas'** "Creque Alley", the former New Christy Minstrel's claim to Dylan's mantle rested on one song, "Eve Of Destruction". The song made the top five in 1965, sharing the charts with Donovan's "Universal Solider" and Baez's version of "It's All Over Now Baby Blue" – in commercial terms, the high-water mark of the 1960s folk revival. McGuire's claims to rub shoulders with Dylan collapsed somewhat when people realized he hadn't actually written the song, which was a P.F. Sloan composition originally rejected by The Byrds. He ended up becoming an evangelist and making gospel albums.

"New Bob" rating: 1/5

5. Steve Goodman

Dylan released nothing under his own name in 1972. But in mid-September that year he turned up at Atlantic's studio in New York and played piano and contributed backing vocals to the title track and "Election Year Rag" on Goodman's 1973 album *Somebody Else's Trouble* under the pseudonym Robert Milkwood Thomas. A close friend of John Prine, Goodman was discovered by Kris

Donovan, with unconvincing guitar sticker, 1965

Kristofferson in 1971 when the search for the new Dylan was at its height. His most enduring song, "City Of New Orleans", was an American hit for Arlo Guthrie, but despite the personal stamp of approval of Robert Milkwood Thomas, his career sadly never really took off. He suffered from leukaemia and died from liver and kidney failure following a bone-marrow transplant operation in 1984.

"New Bob" rating: 2/5

6. John Prine

"There's a hole in daddy's arm where all the money goes, and Jesus Christ died for nothing I suppose," sang John Prine on his strung-out Vietnam vet song, "Sam Stone". Taken from Prine's eponymous 1972 debut album, it's one of the best Dylan lines that Dylan never wrote – which is perhaps why Dylan turned up at the **Bottom Line** in Greenwich Village one night shortly after its release to back Prine on harmonica on the song. It was enough to catapult Prine up there alongside Loudon Wainwright among the more convincing pre-Springsteen pretenders to Bob's crown during the man's "abdication" at the turn of the decade. Prine went on to forge a career as a distinctive individual talent and a master craftsman capable of both poignancy and wit. His songs have been covered by everyone from Bonnie Raitt to John Denver.

"New Bob" rating: 3/5

7. Loudon Wainwright III

"I'm not the new anyone. Media people call you the new something because it's the only way they know," Wainwright once complained, and his early career suffered more than most from the "new Dylan" tag. His first album appeared in 1969 and his nasal delivery and sardonic songs, several of them in the talking blues style once favoured by Dylan, made the comparisons inevitable. But Wainwright recovered well, and in 1973 had a surprise hit with **"Dead Skunk"**, a humorous song which set him on a new path as one of the funniest songwriters of our times. Years later he even wrote a hilarious song called "Talking New Bob Dylan Blues", in which all of those dubbed with the label over the years get together for a weekly self-help support group at Bruce Springsteen's house.

"New Bob" rating: 3/5

8. Jesse Winchester

When Jesse Winchester fled to Canada on receiving his Vietnam call-up papers, his credentials as a draft dodger marked him out as an obvious potential heir to Dylan's protester-in-chief role. His claims were further enhanced when his 1970 debut was produced by Robbie Robertson, and he was signed by Dylan's manager Albert Grossman. His best compositions included "The Brand New Tennessee Waltz", "Yankee Lady", "Biloxi" and the Vietnam protest song **Pharoah's Army**. He went on to make a low-key but satisfying career in the country-rock market after he was eventually pardoned by President Carter. Elvis Costello, Joan Baez, Emmylou Harris and Tim Hardin have all covered his songs.

"New Bob" rating: 2/5

9. Arlo Guthrie

There was a nice symmetry to Arlo Guthrie being hailed as a new Dylan for, of course, it was Arlo's father Woody who was Bob's first and greatest inspiration. Arlo first came to prominence in 1967 with the hilarious draft-avoiding epic **Alice's Restaurant** and the Dylan comparisons were unavoidable, given that both men had either inherited or copied so many of Woody's phrases and mannerisms. He has continued to write effective protest songs, and his "Presidential Rag" was the best song written about Nixon and the Watergate scandal. He also enjoyed a hit with "City of New Orleans", written by fellow folkie and rival "new Dylan" Steve Goodman.

"New Bob" rating: 2/5

10. Steve Forbert

Forbert didn't arrive in New York, from his Mississippi roots, until 1976, but he set about making up for lost time by busking at Grand Central Station and playing the same Greenwich Village coffeehouses that Dylan had done 15 years earlier. He made his first album **Alive On Arrival** in 1978 and his acoustic guitar, harmonica playing and distinctively scratchy vocals, allied to his tough, streetwise poetry inevitably drew Dylan comparisons. He enjoyed a minor hit with "Romeo's Tune" in 1979 and then made four albums for Epic. Forbert has continued to record for a variety of labels and his 1988 album *Streets Of This Town* was produced by Garry Tallent from Springsteen's E Street Band.

"New Bob" rating: 1/5

11. Jakob Dylan

After all the years of searching, was the new Dylan closer to home than anyone realized? The only one of Bob's offspring to follow in the old man's footsteps (he refers to his brothers and sisters as "civilians"), *Bring Down The Horse* by Jakob Dylan's band **The Wallflowers** has become the best-selling album in America to bear the Dylan name in the last 25 years. Initially Jakob (who was the subject of Dylan's 1973 song "Forever Young") denied any influence from his father. But once he'd established himself, his attitude relaxed. "Every other songwriter in the world has been influenced by my dad. So why should I be any different?" he admitted. Dylanologists can have a lot of fun interpreting his songs as part of a father–son dialogue. One of them is called "Letters From The Wasteland" (mailed from "Desolation Row", presumably). Another, called "I've Been Delivered", offers an obvious echo to Dylan's anthemic "I Shall Be Released", from *The Basement Tapes*.

"New Bob" rating: 4/5

Books, Fanzines & Websites

"the dust of rumour covers me..."

Books About Dylan

You can't accurately measure Bob Dylan's importance in record sales, for according to the statistics The Carpenters and even Ozzy Osbourne have sold more albums. But you might calculate the man's contribution to our times by the amount of literature devoted to him.

Nearly four decades ago, he wrote a song called **My Back Pages**. The world's music journalists appeared to take it as an invitation, for since then there have been literally millions of pages, thousands of chapters and hundreds of volumes analysing his every song lyric and poking into every nook and cranny of his singular life.

So much has been written about rock's greatest living poet that Patrick Humphries and John Bauldie once apologetically titled their contribution to the literature *Oh No! Not Another Bob Dylan Book*. And you are now holding in your hand yet another. In 2004, Dylan finally had his own say with the first volume of his own autobiography.

Yet somehow, at the end of all Dylan's back pages, he remains an enigma. We can know more about his life than is decent, and recite the song lyrics backwards – and yet his body of work retains the veil of mystery that is essential to all great art. Which is exactly as even his most exhaustive biographer would surely wish it to be.

Bob Dylan: **Chronicles Volume One**
Simon & Schuster

Well you didn't expect a conventional autobiography did you? Instead of offering a chronological account of his life and times, the first volume of *Chronicles* is book-ended with chapters about Dylan's early years, while in the middle he fast-forwards to Woodstock in the late 1960s and then the late 1980s, when he toured with the Grateful Dead and recorded "Oh Mercy" with Daniel Lanois. Anyone looking for lurid kiss-and-tell celebrity memoirs would have been disappointed. He refers several times to a wife, but they're different wives and he fails to note his divorces and never mentions either of his spouses' names.

There are no confessions about his drug consumption or explanation of his religious conversion. Yet as an account of the development of an artist, how he trained himself to become the greatest songwriter the world has ever known and his subsequent struggles to live up to his own legend, *Chronicles* allows us inside Dylan's head in a way we've never experienced before – and needless to say, it's one of the most fascinating places you've ever been.

Robert Santelli: **The Bob Dylan Scrapbook 1956–66**

Simon & Schuster

Published exactly a year after *Chronicles*, *The Bob Dylan Scrapbook* is essentially a companion volume to his official autobiography. The text by Robert Santelli is almost incidental and although collectors will cherish the previously unpublished photos, the real meat lies in the facsimile items of memorabilia tucked inside almost every page, from handwritten lyrics to ticket stubs and concert flyers via newspaper articles and even a cardboard cut-out Bob from a 1965 promo campaign.

Robert Shelton: **No Direction Home – The Life And Music Of Bob Dylan**

Da Capo Press

Shelton's early reviews in *The New York Times* helped to launch Dylan's career and the two men became close friends. This biography should have been the first one out but, as Shelton later said, every time he thought the book was finished, Dylan went and did something newly remarkable and so he did not eventually add the final full stop until 1986. His account of the early years is as definitive as you would expect. After all, Shelton was there, and an interview conducted on a private plane high above Nebraska in March 1966 is one of the most insightful Dylan ever gave. If Shelton is less assured on the post-1966 story, his accuracy on any of the key events has never seriously been doubted. At one time the book was intended to appear in two volumes, and there have been persistent rumours since his death in 1995 of a "director's cut", reinstating the unused material.

Anthony Scaduto: **Bob Dylan**

Helter Skelter

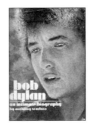

Former crime reporter Anthony Scaduto beat Shelton by fourteen years as the author of not only the first Dylan biography, but one of the first serious rock biographies of them all. As such, it was a landmark book and many Dylan fans retain an enormous affection for it, although it was obvious on re-reading the 1996 reprint that it has become very much a period piece. Scaduto had direct access to most of the key players in Greenwich Village, and some direct contact with Dylan, who surprisingly confessed to liking the book on its publication in 1972.

Dylanology

Howard Sounes: **Down The Highway – The Life Of Bob Dylan**

Doubleday

It's a measure of Dylan's cultural significance that these days his biographers are drawn from far beyond the ranks of specialist rock writers. Howard Sounes's subjects prior to Dylan included the mass murderers Fred and Rosemary West and the writer Charles Bukowski. His research for *Down The Highway* included some 250 original interviews and he came up with much that is new, including revelations about Dylan's complex and tangled personal relationships and previously unknown details about Dylan's business and property empire (he apparently has seventeen homes, but spends more time in his tour bus than in any single one of them).

Sounes's investigation of the mysterious 1966 motorbike accident has to be the most thorough yet, with Sarah Grossman, widow of Dylan's manager, speaking on the record for the first time. But his assessments of the recorded legacy are also unerringly sharp. Only someone who knows and understands Dylan's work could have picked out the obscure but magnificent version of "I Ain't Got No Home" with The Band at the 1968 Woody Guthrie tribute concert as a key moment.

Clinton Heylin: **Bob Dylan – Behind The Shades**

Viking

The second edition of *Behind The Shades* appeared in 2000, a fully revised and updated version of a biography first published in 1990 to mark Dylan's then-imminent half century. As a music specialist and Dylanologist of long standing, Heylin is more interested than Sounes in muso-speak, the intricacies of the stories behind the songs, and the making of the albums. But he's a skilled biographer as well as an incisive music critic, and his attempt to explore the ongoing conflict between Dylan the private human being and Dylan the artist whose audience regards him as public property is fascinating. He has strong personal opinions which he's never afraid to express, and his account of the "born-again" years is a tour de force.

David Hajdu: **Positively 4th Street**

Bloomsbury

Concentrating on the story from Dylan's arrival in Greenwich Village in 1961 to the drug-induced burnout five years later and the retreat to Woodstock, David Hajdu's elegant book is conceived as a four-hander, with the other corners of the ring held by Joan Baez, her sister Mimi and her husband, the bohemian singer and writer Richard Farina. It's a beautifully written account but it never completely works, simply because Dylan towers above the other three in our interest and swiftly leaves them trailing in his wake. Hajdu might have written a more cohesive book by broadening his scope to a history of the 1960s Greenwich Village folk scene rather than concentrating on the oddly matched quartet he chose. Nevertheless, he powerfully evokes the spirit of the times and there are some fascinating insights into the complexities of Dylan's relationship with Baez.

Greil Marcus: Invisible Republic – Bob Dylan's Basement Tapes

Picador; Owl Books

Marcus conceived and planned his marathon study of Dylan's seminal work from the Woodstock years while driving across North America listening to bootleg versions of the *Basement Tapes*. When it dawned upon him that within the songs lay what virtually amounts to an alternative history of Americana, he devised a similarly broad commentary. At times his prose is dense and difficult to read. But the erudition is enormous as he ranges over civil rights, mining disasters and Appalachian folklore, and occasionally even talks about the songs.

Greil Marcus: Like A Rolling Stone – Bob Dylan At The Crossroads

Faber & Faber

Published to coincide with the 40th anniversary of a song he claims as one of the seminal and most dramatic moments in the history of popular culture, Marcus gives us far more than a mere account of the writing and recording of "Like A Rolling Stone". Of course, he does that with clinical attention to detail via new interviews with the likes of Al Kooper and producer Bob Johnston. But in typically erudite fashion, he also dissects the pop vortex of 1965 into which Dylan leapt and offers a series of fascinating and stimulating digressions on the cultural significance of other tangential subjects ranging from Petula Clark to Sam Cooke.

Carl Benson (ed): The Bob Dylan Companion

Schirmer

An anthology that traces Dylan's career over forty years through contemporary articles, reviews, opinions, interviews and all manner of other Bob-induced rantings and ravings. More than lives up to its title as an essential companion that offers access to much of the raw material and primary sources which the major biographies only have space to refer to in footnotes.

C.P. Lee: **Like The Night**

Helter Skelter

Was it the most explosive moment in the history of rock'n'roll? C.P. Lee certainly thinks so, and went to impressive lengths to track down the man who shouted "Judas!" at Dylan at the Manchester Free Trade Hall in May 1966. Around this pivotal moment, he constructs a brilliant narrative of an incendiary tour that is far more revealing in its way than anything the cameras captured for the documentary film *Eat The Document*.

Andy Gill: **My Back Pages – Classic Bob Dylan 1962–69**

Carlton

The "stories behind the songs" series is a tried and tested format. Here, Andy Gill offers an insightful guide album-by-album and song-by-song through the early canon from the first album up to and including *Nashville Skyline*. Gill is a fan with a true anorak's attention to detail. But he pulls it off and avoids impenetrability by combining his obsessive interest with a lively writing style and the sheer force of his enthusiasm for his subject.

Larry Sloman: **On The Road With Bob Dylan**

Helter Skelter

Engrossing first-hand account of life on the road

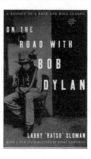

with the Rolling Thunder Revue by Sloman, who earned the nickname "Ratso" on the tour. His battles to gain access to Dylan are wittily retold but when he does penetrate the inner sanctum the zestful encounters are more than worth it. Sara Dylan, Joan Baez, Ginsberg et al are a fascinating enough supporting cast to warrant a book in themselves. But it's "the little genius downing tequila after tequila" who remains the charismatic centre of attention, even when Sloman can't get anywhere near him.

Michael Gray: **Song And Dance Man**

Cassell

Of all the academics who have spent their lives obsessively picking over the metaphors and similes of Dylan's lyrics when they could have been watching football or playing pool, Gray remains by far the sharpest and most insightful. The third revised and updated version of *Song And Dance Man* appeared in 2000 some 28 years after the first edition was published, by which time it had grown to three times its original length. Scholarly without being suffocating, and intellectual but not intimidatingly so, the new chapters include a magisterial account of Dylan's debt to the blues and an almost equally impressive discussion of his use of nursery rhyme. Gray's preface, in which he reviews 44 Dylan albums in curt précis, presents some hilarious light relief to the heft of the rest of his heavyweight analysis. "The dreariest, most contemptible, phony, tawdry piece of product ever issued by a great artist," he writes of 1995's "MTV Unplugged". Ouch.

Mike Marqusee: Chimes Of Freedom – The Politics Of Bob Dylan's Art

New Press

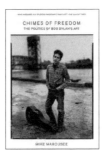

Longtime committed left-wing activist Marqusee examines the protest songs and Dylan's role as a political leader, and concludes he passes muster as a revolutionary. It is basically a Marxist analysis yet, like Paul Foot's similarly motivated study of the poet "Red Shelley", there's something undeniably warm and romantic about Marqusee's belief that Dylan "exudes the spirit and the pain of human liberation".

Andrew Muir: Razor's Edge: Bob Dylan And The Never Ending Tour

Helter Skelter

Obsessively detailed road-test reports of Dylan's magnificent touring addiction. Informative and far more readable than you might imagine with plenty of personal anecdote to counterbalance the set-list mentality. The book comes complete with tables of every song played and other fascinating NET statistics.

Bob Dylan: Lyrics 1962–2001

Simon & Schuster

The third edition of Dylan's collected lyrics appeared in 2004 and was long overdue, as the previous volume took us only as far as *Empire Burlesque* in 1985. In truth he's hardly been prolific in recent decades, for the new edition adds just 54 original compositions he has recorded over the last 20 years – exactly ten fewer songs than are included from the first two years of his recording career, 1962–63. Also worth tracking down is *Drawn Blank*, a collection of his on-the-road drawings sketched between 1989 and 1992, and published by Random House.

Clinton Heylin: A Life In Stolen Moments – Bob Dylan Day By Day 1941–95

Music Sales

A monumental and meticulously researched account of every significant concert, guest appearance, recording session and pause to blow his nose, chronicled in a day-by-day diary spanning Dylan's entire career. You want to argue over the date Dylan recorded "Like A Rolling Stone" or "Mr Tambourine Man"? Take it up with Clinton Heylin. But be warned. He's almost certain to be right.

Neil Corcoran (ed): Do You Mr Jones? With Bob Dylan And The Professors

Chatto & Windus

Arguably this is the sort of thing that gives Dylanologists a bad name – a bunch of academics discussing Bob's lyrics and bandying such portentous sentences as "syntactically, these accumulations work by subtly expressive use of what rhetoric calls polysyndeton." But, on the other hand, if Dylan really is a serious contender for the Nobel prize for literature, why shouldn't he be subjected to the same sort of lit-crit scrutiny afforded a Shakespeare or a Milton?

Dave Henderson: Touched By The Hand Of Bob

Black Book Company

An appealing year-by-year hike through Dylan's career, with plenty of fans' reminiscences and brief but cogent assessments of all the albums. Readable, well presented and refreshingly devoid of the worthiness of much Dylan literature, if somewhat on the slight side.

John Bauldie: Wanted Man

Penguin

John Bauldie was the editor of the quarterly Dylan magazine *The Telegraph*, and a dedicated Dylanologist who won the respect of the great man himself – he was invited to write the booklet that accompanied the offical *Bootleg Series Volumes I–III*. *Wanted Man* is a collection taken from the magazine's regular column of that name in which friends and associates of Dylan were invited to recount their experiences. Patti Smith, Paul McCartney and a hilarious Ron Wood are among those sharing their favourite Bob moments.

C.P. Lee: Like A Bullet Of Light – The Films Of Bob Dylan

Helter Skelter

The section in this *Rough Guide* on Dylan's cinematic exploits can only scratch the surface when compared to C.P. Lee's excellent and exhaustive 220-page study. Published in 2000, it therefore doesn't include *Masked And Anonymous*. But it does assess not only the major films but also the minutiae of music videos, TV specials and sundry other guest appearances on camera.

Paul Williams: Bob Dylan Performing Artist (Vols I, II and III)

Omnibus

The founder of seminal American rock magazine *Crawdaddy!*, Paul Williams was one of the most astute early Dylan-watchers. Long before Dylan himself came to the conclusion that his art could only live through performance, Williams had also come to the same conclusion. His masterful two-volume study of Dylan's genius as a performer – both on record and in concert – first appeared in the early 1990s. It's full of critical bull's-eyes that have made it a set text with Dylanologists. The third volume, subtitled *1986–90 and Beyond: Mind Out Of Time*, appeared in 2004, and covered the origins of the Never Ending Tour, the Traveling Wilburys and the studio albums *Oh Mercy* and 1997's *Time Out Of Mind*.

Tracy Johnson: **Encounters With Bob Dylan – If You See Him, Say Hello**

Humble Press

Presumably inspired by John Bauldie's *Wanted Man*, this is a charming book based upon the simple premise of 50 people giving first-hand accounts of their experiences with the world's most reclusive and enigmatic rock star. They range from musicians who have worked with Dylan to surprised fans who bumped into him in back alleys. Some of the best accounts are even about encounters that never quite happened and near misses. Could anyone else in rock music inspire such a book? Almost certainly not.

Wilfrid Mellers: **A Darker Shade Of Pale – A Backdrop To Bob Dylan**

Faber

Wilfrid Mellers wrote his first book about music in 1946, when Dylan was just five years old. Then, after almost thirty years of writing about classical music, in 1973 he published *Twilight Of The Gods,* a book about The Beatles that turned into a classic. Dylan was an obvious next choice of subject matter, although Mellers published books about Bach and Beethoven before *A Darker Shade Of Pale* finally came out in 1984. The result is a musicological equivalent of the academic lit-crit Dylan studies.

John Gibbens: **The Nightingale's Code – A Poetic Study Of Bob Dylan**

Touched Press

John Gibbens is himself a poet who, as a young man, fell heavily under Dylan's lyrical spell. He started *The Nightingale's Code* as a labour of love in the early 1980s, but it took him until 2001 to complete it – even though his study deals almost exclusively with Bob's

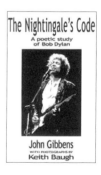

1960s and 1970s work. At times it reads like a university dissertation. But in between the metrical analysis of the anapaests and iambics, he's actually got some rather interesting things to say, and the chapter which analyses

Dylanology

"Desolation Row", likening it to a street-talking transliteration of T.S. Eliot's poem *The Wasteland*, is a real humdinger.

Derek Barker (ed): ISIS – A Bob Dylan Anthology and Bob Dylan Anthology Volume Two – 20 Years Of Isis

Helter Skelter/Chrome Dreams

Two volumes of the best essays and interviews from the pages of *Isis*, the longest-running and best of the Dylan fanzines, purveyors of splendid erudition, insane obsession and searching insight since its inception in 1985.

Benjamin Hedin (ed): Studio A – The Bob Dylan Reader

Norton

A rather good anthology published in 2004, that includes extracts from classic texts by the likes of Shelton, Marcus, Heylin, Hadju and Gray, reprints of seminal articles by the likes of Lester Bangs, Clive James, Christopher Ricks and Ralph Gleason, and such clever selections as Johnny Cash's famous 1964 "Shut up! and let him sing!" letter to *Broadside*, two poems in Dylan's honour by Allen Ginsberg, and Bruce Springsteen's speech at his Rock and Roll Hall Of Fame induction.

Fanzines

Isis/Wicked Messenger

The longest-running Dylan magazine still in print, *Isis* was established in 1985 and ever since has provided an information service that puts the official Sony Music channels to shame. It also includes a diary-style newsletter called *Wicked Messenger*, produced for the past twenty years by Ian Woodward. Other regular columns include Henry Porter's unofficial CD round-up and a compendium of worldwide press coverage. Subscription information is available from Isis, PO Box 1182, Bedworth, Warwickshire CV12 0ZA, England.

On The Tracks/Series Of Dreams

Articles, critiques, commentary, album and book reviews, but with an emphasis on oral history, via in-depth interviews with musicians who've worked with Bob Dylan, friends and acquaintances – plus a classic Dylan interview reprinted in every issue. *On The Tracks* also produces an annual Collector's Issue catalogue, offering hundreds of collectible items for sale. The main magazine appears three times a year but it's supplemented by the monthly newsletter *Series of Dreams*. For subscriptions check the *On The Tracks* website at www.b-dylan.com

The Bridge

Another excellent British-based magazine that has been appearing three times a year since 1998. Subscriptions are available from PO Box 198, Gateshead, Tyne and Weir NE10 8WE,

England, or e-mail the.bridge@virgin.net

Freewheelin'

Launched in September 1985 and now with more than 200 issues under its belt, in 2002 *Freewheelin'* was relaunched as the first Bob Dylan magazine on the Internet. The 'Freewheelers, as they call themselves, also get together for an annual Dylan convention. Check out the magazine online at www.freewheelin-on-line.info

Websites

Bob Dylan Official Site

www.bobdylan.com

The official site, with all the news, discographies, links to the Sony shop and so on that you would expect. But there are two features that make it a cut above most official websites. The first is a lyric search-engine. Type in a word or two of a half-remembered line, from even the most obscure Dylan song, and chances are that the entire lyric will come up. Then there are the downloadable performances, from early songs recorded in Minneapolis in 1961, to live tracks from the most recent tour.

The latest additions at the time of writing were six performances from dates in Boston and New York in spring 2005.

Expecting Rain

www.expectingrain.com

A pioneering site, with a superb news service, which provides new links every day to newspaper and magazine articles containing references to

Dylan from all over the world. Other features include a discography, essays on Dylan's influences, a who's who of all those who have ever come within his orbit, a picture gallery of Hibbing and even a section compiling the jokes he took to telling from the stage in the late 1990s.

Bringing It All Back Homepage

www.punkhart.com/dylan

Established in 1994, this is a good source of articles and reviews, although it doesn't seem to be updated as often as it could be.

Bob Dates

www.execpc.com/~billp61/dates.html

The best source for tour dates, with ticket info and links to relevant box offices and ticket agents. There are also reviews and set-lists supplied by a huge network of fans – they are often up on the site almost before Dylan has left the stage.

About Bob Dylan

www.bjorner.com/bob.htm

Created by Swedish fan Olof Björner, this site is a treasure-trove of information about the Never Ending Tour. The yearly chronicles allow you to click on a date and call up set-lists from every gig since the NET started. Other useful features include lists of cover versions and a lyric archive.

The Bob Dylan Bootleg Museum

www.bobsboots.com

Claiming a million hits a month, and billing itself as "The Bob Dylan Bootleg Museum", this site contains the definitive guide to all of the unofficial recordings, complete with reviews of both content and sound quality. You can't buy them from the site, but bobsboots does maintain a list of traders.

Roots Of Bob Dylan
www.bobdylanroots.com

A site created by Manfred Helfert in Germany dedicated to the folk revival of the late 1950s/ early 1960s and Dylan's pivotal role in it. Lots about Woody Guthrie and Greenwich Village, too.

Bob Dylan Picture Galleries
www.angelfire.com/de/dylanite

An impressive series of picture galleries, covering every era and aspect of Dylan's career. There are literally thousands of images, as well as a shop selling rare posters.

Dylan Daily
www.dylandaily.com

Edited by Gerry Smith, a fine service offering daily news updates that are particularly good on set-lists and concert reviews and a monthly newsletter, emailed by free subscription.

Index

Index

Index

Index

Index

Index

Rough Guides To A World Of Music

'stick to the reliable Rough Guide series' **The Guardian** (UK)

'Over the past few years the Rough Guide CDs, with their stylish covers, have distinguished themselves as approachable and well-chosen introductions to the music of the countries concerned. They have been consistently well-reviewed and, like the guidebooks themselves, stand out as an obvious first choice for journeys in world music' **Simon Broughton, Editor Songlines**

Hear sound samples at WWW.WORLDMUSIC.NET

Now you can visit www.worldmusic.net/radio to tune into the exciting Rough Guide Radio Show, with a new show each month presenting new releases, interviews, features and competitions.

Available from book and record shops worldwide or order direct from World Music Network, 6 Abbeville Mews, 88 Clapham Park Road, London SW4 7BX, UK T. 020 7498 5252 F. 020 7498 5353 E. post@worldmusic.net

THE ROUGH GUIDE TO
chick flicks
Samantha Cook

BROADEN YOUR HORIZONS

COMPUTERS Blogging • The Internet
iPods, iTunes & music online • Macs & OSX
PCs & Windows • Playstation Portable
Website Directory: Shopping Online
& Surfing the Net
FILM & TV American Independent Film
British Cult Comedy • Chick Flicks
Comedy Movies • Cult Movies • Gangster
Movies • Horror Movies • Kids' Movies
Sci-Fi Movies • Westerns
LIFESTYLE Babies • eBay • Ethical
Shopping • Pregnancy & Birth
MUSIC Classical Music • Heavy Metal
Hip-Hop • Jazz • Opera • Punk • Reggae
Rock • Soul and R&B • World Music Vol 1 & 2
Book of Playlists • The Beatles • Bob Dylan
Elvis • Frank Sinatra • Pink Floyd
The Rolling Stones
POPULAR CULTURE Books for Teenagers
Children's Books 0-5 & 5-11 • Cult Fiction
The Da Vinci Code • Lord of the Rings
Poker • Shakespeare • Superheroes
Conspiracy Theories • Unexplained
Phenomena
SCIENCE Climate Change • The Universe
Weather

www.roughguides.com

L MUSIC GUIDE FOR MAC & PC

12 Editions • 3 Million Copies Sold • PC & M

iPod

Music
otos
deos
ras
ttings
uffle Songs

GH GUIDE to
Pods
iTunes & music online

ITION:
RS IPOD NANO, VIDEO IPOD & IPOD SHUFFLE

THE ROUGH GUIDE to
The
Internet
Peter Buckley & Duncan

the filth • the fury • the fashion

The songs • the singers • the stories • the sou

GH GUIDE to
unk

THE ROUGH GUIDE to
Soul and R&B

THE ROUGH GUIDE to
The ## Rolling Stones
Sean Egan

THE ROUGH GUIDE to
Blogging

Rough Guides presents...

"Achieves the perfect balance between learned recommendation and needless trivia"
Uncut Magazine reviewing Cult Movies

Other Rough Guide Film & TV titles include:

American Independent Film • British Cult Comedy • Chick Flicks • Comedy Movies
Cult Movies • Gangster Movies • Horror Movies • Kids' Movies • Sci-Fi Movies • Westerns

BROADEN YOUR HORIZONS

ROUGH
GUIDES

D: Rough Guide
DIRECTIONS for
short breaks

For more information go to www.roughguides.com

ROUGH GUIDES